CENTRAL SOCIETY OF

EDUCATION

Third Publication
of 1839

AUGUSTUS M. KELLEY PUBLISHERS

New York 1969

Published by
WOBURN BOOKS LIMITED
9 RUSSELL CHAMBERS, BURY PLACE, LONDON WC1

Published in the United States by
Augustus M. Kelley, Publishers
New York, New York 10010

First edition   1839
New impression   1969

Printed in Holland by
N.V. Grafische Industrie Haarlem

THE SOCIAL HISTORY OF EDUCATION

GENERAL EDITOR : VICTOR E. NEUBURG

First Series — No. 3

CENTRAL SOCIETY OF EDUCATION

THE SOCIAL HISTORY OF EDUCATION
GENERAL EDITOR: VICTOR E. NEUBURG
First Series of Eight Titles

CENTRAL

SOCIETY OF EDUCATION.

Third Publication.

PAPERS

BY

C. Baker, Esq.
B. F. Duppa, Esq.
F. Liardet, Esq.
W. S. O'Brien, Esq. M.P.

George Long, Esq.
Rev. S. Wood.
William Smith, Esq.
G. R. Porter, Esq. F.R.S.

Thomas Wyse, Esq. M.P.

LONDON:

PRINTED FOR TAYLOR AND WALTON,

BOOKSELLERS AND PUBLISHERS TO THE SOCIETY,

UPPER GOWER STREET.

1839.

NOTICE.

The Committee of the Central Society of Education hold themselves responsible only for the general tendency of the work; as the name of the author appears at the end of each paper.

CENTRAL

SOCIETY OF EDUCATION.

PROSPECTUS.

IT is the object of this Society to collect, to classify, and to diffuse information concerning the Education of all classes, in every department, in order to learn by what means individuals may be best fitted in health, in mind, and in morals, to fill the stations which they are destined to occupy in Society.

For the attainment of this object, the Society proposes to obtain, and from time to time (probably periodically) to publish, 1st, Accounts of Systems of Education already established, whether in this country or abroad; 2nd, Discussions of the Value of Various Branches and Means of Education; 3rd, Accounts of Books, Maps, Models, and other aids of Education.

Notwithstanding the importance which is now generally attached to Education, and the opinion which many entertain that in this country it is in many parts imperfect, and does not tend to fit men for the fulfilment of their peculiar duties; there is not in the metropolis a single Association and scarcely a work devoted to recording and suggesting improvements in this the most essential of all Sciences and Arts.

The labours of the Committee will divide themselves under five principal heads :

1. Primary or Elementary Education.
2. Secondary Education.
3. Superior or University Education.
4. Special or Professional Education.
5. Supplementary Education.

If their materials are as extensive as they hope, the Committee will issue periodically separate publications in each of these departments.

It is a question of great interest, whether the expense attending residence at our Universities can be curtailed, or is inseparable from the circumstances of the pupils who resort there; and whether in them, as well as in our Public Schools, the system of Education is the best that can be pursued; whether, for instance, some acquaintance with the Modern European Languages, and with Natural History, and a more intimate knowledge of Modern History, and the Moral, Political, and Physical Sciences, would interfere disadvantageously with the main studies of those Seminaries. The discipline of our Public Schools is also an important subject of discussion; by some it is strongly censured, by others it is spoken of with unmixed approval: one class requiring that the moral character of the Pupil should be an object of direct culture, the other alleging that this is sufficiently formed by the general tone of the School and the matters studied there; the one demanding that care should be taken of the health and bodily developement of the Pupil by prescribed athletic exercises, the other affirming that the ordinary games of English schoolboys sufficiently provide for that want. Perhaps the truth lies between the two parties, and the object of the Society will be to elicit the truth.

The Society being necessarily composed of members of various religious denominations, it is obvious that they can have no sectarian objects in view, whenever they may admit (as they intend to do) into their Publications articles which shall discuss the best modes of uniting Intellectual and Religious Education without offending the opinions of any class of Christians.

The Society cannot doubt that it will obtain the co-operation of those who are occupied in conducting Establish-

ments of Education in this country, (a profession among
the most important that can be confided to man, and the
just appreciation of which it will be the natural tendency
of these inquiries to produce,) when it is known that the
publications of the Society are not intended to be the partial advocates of certain methods, or the blind assailants
of established systems, but that their pages will be open
to the temperate reasonings of able and conscientious
men, whichever side of the questions controverted, touch-
ing Education, they may advocate.

It is the opinion of many persons in this kingdom, that
professional Education is best left to the conduct of the
individual, and that the compulsory interference of the
State, or of Academies, is, at least, needless. It surely
concerns Professional Men, as well as the Public, to inquire by what means professional knowledge may be best
acquired, and professional competence best certified ; and
this discussion will find place in the publications of the
Society.

Few men who have investigated the facts, will deny
that large classes of the poor in this country are without
any instruction, and that the instruction given to the remainder is insufficient, and little fitted to render them
better labourers or better men. A Society, therefore,
devoted (as this will be) to searching out the means of
affording to the poor an Education suited to their wants
and their duties, may claim the support of all who have at
heart the happiness and virtue of the People, and the security of the State.

Besides the Education which is obtained at Schools, at
the Universities, in the offices of Professional men, or in
the workshop of the Tradesman, there is a *supplementary*
Education obtained, principally in mature age, by means
of museums, libraries, and literary and scientific institutions ; this Education is of great value, and is increasing.

The Society propose to pay much attention to those objects, and to consider how supplementary Education may be extended and directed.

In any publication which the Society may issue, care will be taken to announce that the Body is not responsible for all which that Publication may contain; but that the statements, whether of fact or of opinion, are those of the Writer, and not of the Society: for whilst, on the one hand, the Society considers that it would not be consistent with the discovery of truth, or with the respect which it entertains for its correspondents and contributors, to prescribe any set of opinions to which the Writers must conform themselves; on the other hand, it cannot make itself answerable as a body for sentiments in which, possibly, a portion of its Members may not concur.

It has been determined that no expenses shall at any time be incurred beyond the funds actually in hand.

The Society will consist of Members who are qualified by the annual payment of one pound and upwards, or one payment of ten pounds, and upwards, to the funds of the Society.

The government of the Society will be vested in a Committee of Fifty, ten of whom will go out of office annually, when their places will be supplied by the Members of the Society at their Annual Meeting; the Members of the Committee who go out of office being re-eligible.

CENTRAL SOCIETY OF EDUCATION.

HONORARY MEMBERS.

Prince Lubomerski.
Mons. De Fellenberg, Hofwyl, Switzerland.
John Duer, Esq. New York, United States.
The Rev. G. W. Woodbridge, Boston, United States.
Signor Mario Arpino, Naples.
Mons. Ducpetiaux, Brussels.
Enrico Mayer, Florence.

LIFE MEMBERS.

Ablett, Jos. Esq.
Bedford, the Duke of.
Beamish, Richard, Esq.
Benyon, Miss.
Byron, the Lady Noel.
Cranstoun, Lord.
Denman, Lord.
Dilke, Wentworth, Esq.
Dunfermline, Lord.
Fitzherbert, E. H. Esq.
Fripp, C. Bowles, Esq.
Gilbart, J. W. Esq.
Gray, J. E., Esq. F.R.S.
Grosvenor, Lord Robert, M.P.
Gurney, Jos. John, Esq.
Hewitt, Capt. W. V.
Heywood, Sir B. Bart.
Heywood, James, Esq.
Hume, J. B. Esq.

Lansdowne, the Marquess of.
Macartney, Dr.
Mackenzie, Sir G. S.
Marshall, L. Esq.
Morgan, J. M. Esq.
Porter, Mrs. G. R.
Preaulx, Osmond, Esq.
Radnor, the Earl of.
Rice, Right Hon. T. S. M.P.
Ricardo, Ralph, Esq.
Ricardo, Samson, Esq.
Russell, Lord John, M.P.
Slaney, Robert A. Esq. M.P.
Steuart, Robert, Esq. M.P.
Thornton, Lieut.-General.
Vardon, Thomas, Esq.
Warburton, Henry, Esq. M.P.
Wilkinson, Wm. Arthur, Esq.

ANNUAL SUBSCRIBERS.

Aldam, William, Esq.
Algar, O. T. Esq.
Allen, Alexander, Esq.
Amory, W. Esq.
Atkinson, Charles C. Esq.

Baker, Charles, Esq.
Barwell, John, Esq.
Bastard, T. H. Esq.
Bangley, George, Esq.
Beckford, William, Esq.

Beckford, Francis, Esq.
Becter, Andrew, Esq.
Bellew, R. Montesq. Esq.
Bermingham, Thomas, Esq.
Bourke, Lieut.-General Sir Rd.
Brotherton, Joseph, Esq. M.P.
Bowles, Miss E. H.
Browne, Henry, Esq.
Bulwer, Sir E. L. Bart. M.P.
Burke, St. George, Esq.
Burrell, Rev. H. M.
Burt, C. T. T. Esq.

Carpenter, Rev. Dr.
Cathay, G. Esq.
Chaloner, Miss.
Chapman, Sir M. L. Bart. M.P.
Chance, Robert Lucas, Esq.
Chance, William, Esq.
Christie, —, Esq.
Clark, Mathew, Esq.
Clendining, John, Esq. M.D.
Coates, Thomas, Esq.
Coode, George, Esq.
Crawfurd, Sharman, Esq.
Cropper, James, Esq.
Currie, Raikes, Esq.

De Morgan, Augustus, Esq.
Dennistoun, S. A. Esq.
Dennistoun, Lieut. R. E.
Dillon, John, Esq.
Dowling, A. S. Esq.
Doyle, Lieut.-Col.
Duckworth, William, Esq.
Duppa, B. F. Esq.

Ebrington, Lord Viscount.
Edgeworth, Miss Maria.
Edwards, Edward, Esq.
Ellis, Sir W.
Ellis, Carteret J. W. Esq.
Ellis, William Stone, Esq.
Elphinstone, Howard, Esq.
Emerton, Rev. J. H.
Evans, George, Esq. M.P.
Evans, William Bertram, Esq.
Ewart, William, Esq. M.P.

Ferguson, Robert, Esq. M.P.
Ferguson, Sir R. A. Bart. M.P.
Ferguson, Capt. R.N. M.P.
Field, E. W. Esq.
Field, Meyrick, Esq.

Ffrench, Fitzstephen, Esq. M. P.
Fletcher, Joseph, Esq.
Fry, Alfred, Esq.

Gem, Harvey, Esq.
Gibson, Rev. R. jun.
Glasse, W. B. Esq.
Goadby, William, Esq.
Gordon, W. Esq.
Grant, Horace, Esq.
Grattan, James, Esq.
Greig, Woronzo, Esq.
Grey, W. T. Esq.
Grote, George, Esq. M.P.
Grubbe, Rev. J. A. Hunt.

Hambleton, Rev. Josh.
Hamilton, Sir Wm. Bart.
Harris, A. C. Esq.
Hawes, Benj. jun. Esq. M.P.
Heathfield, Richard, Esq.
Heathcoat, John, Esq. M.P.
Heldenmaier, B. Esq.
Hennell, Charles, Esq.
Hickson, W. E. Esq.
Hill, M. D. Esq.
Hill, Arthur, Esq.
Hill, Frederick, Esq.
Hincks, Rev. Dr.
Hodges, T. L. Esq. M.P.
Holland, Edward, Esq.
Hone, Joshua, Esq.
Horner, Leonard, Esq.
Hume, Joseph, Esq. M.P.
Hunt, George, Esq.

Innes, John, Esq.

Jephson, C. D. O. Esq.
Jerrard, Dr.
Jervis, John, Esq. M.P.
Jervis, Swynfen, Esq. M.P.
Johnstone, Ebenezer, Esq.
Jamieson, Mrs.
J'Anson, Edward, jun. Esq.

Kelley, Thomas F. Esq.
Kempson, George S. Esq.
Key, T. H. Esq.
Kenrick, Rev. George.
Knight, Charles, Esq.

Lalor, John, Esq.
Lambert, Mrs.

Lambert, D. Esq.
Lambert, Monsieur.
Law, Edward, Esq.
Lawrence, John T. Esq.
Leader, J. T. Esq. M.P.
Leahy, D. Esq.
Le Marchant, Dennis, Esq.
Lemon, Sir Charles, Bart. M.P.
Liardet, Frederick, Esq.
Lilford, Lord.
Lindley, W. Esq.
Lovelace, the Earl of.
Long, George, Esq.
Lynch, A. H. Esq. M.P.

Mackenzie, Sir F. A.
Macready, W. C. Esq.
Mahony, Pierce, Esq.
Malleson, Rev. J. P.
Martin, Sir Roger, Bart.
Martineau, Miss Harriet.
Martin, William, Esq.
Mayne, S. Esq.
Mayo, —, Esq. M.D.
Menteath, C. G. Stuart, Esq.
Molesworth, Sir Wm. Bart. M.P.
Maubert, J. F. Esq.
Morse, Arthur, Esq.
Murray, Rt. Hon. Sir J. A.
Murch, Rev. Jerome.

Naylor, Samuel, jun. Esq.

O'Brien, W. Smith, Esq. M.P.
O'Connor Don, The, M.P.
O'Loughlin, Rt. Hon. M.

Paget, John, Esq.
Parrinton, J. Esq.
Pashley, Robert, Esq.
Pillans, Professor.
Potter, Richard, Esq. M.P.
Porter, G. R. Esq.
Porter, Miss E.
Porter, Miss F.
Pocock, C. Esq.

Rathbone, William, Esq.
Reddington, T. N. Esq. M.P.
Reid, Dr.
Ricardo, Moses, Esq.
Ricardo, Francis, Esq.
Rider, Thomas, Esq.

Rothman, R. W. Esq.
Ryland, Arthur, Esq.

Salmon, Edward, Esq.
Scrope, Poulett, Esq. M.P.
Simpson, James, Esq.
Smith, Benjamin, Esq. M.P.
Smith, —, Esq.
Smyth, Lewis, Esq.
Southey, George, Esq.
St. George, C. M. Esq.
Stothert, George, Esq.
Strangeway, J. H. Esq.
Strutt, Edward, Esq. M.P.

Talfourd, Mr. Serjeant, M.P.
Taylor, John, Esq.
Taylor, James, Esq.
Taylor, R. Esq.
Thompson, A. T. Esq. M.D.
Thorneley, Thomas, Esq. M.P.
Torrens, Col.
Tremenheere, Seymour, Esq.
Tufnell, E. Carlton, Esq.
Tucker, Henry, Esq.
Tulk, C. A. Esq.

Urquhart, David, Esq.

Villiers, Hon. C. Pelham, M.P.
Vermingston, Thomas, Esq.
Vivian, Sir Hussey, Bart. M.P.

Wallis, E. T. Esq.
Wainewright, J. Esq.
Ward, H. G. Esq. M.P.
Walton, Mr.
White, John Meadows, Esq.
Wittich, W. Esq.
Wilderspin, W. Esq.
Wilks, John, Esq.
Willett, Edward, Esq.
Williams, William, Esq. M.P.
Williams, Charles Wye, Esq.
Wilson, Thomas, Esq.
Wise, J. A. Esq.
Wood, Miss.
Wordsworth, C. Esq.
Wyse, Thomas, Esq. M.P.

Yates, J. A. Esq. M.P.
Yates, Richard, Esq.
Yates, Rev. James.

CONTENTS.

CENTRAL SOCIETY OF EDUCATION.

INFANTS' SCHOOLS.

INSTITUTIONS for extending the benefits of education among the people have too often been looked upon with discouragement and dismay where they ought to have been hailed as the precursors of that virtuous and highly-cultivated state of popular society which is the greatest of blessings to a nation.

Sunday Schools had to contend with many difficulties; Lancasterian Schools and National Schools made a very slow progress in their earlier days, and were even viewed with jealousy and fear. It was prognosticated of Mechanics' Institutions that they would spread the baneful effects of debating societies throughout the land, and that knowledge would render our artisans too independent of their employers. The experience of nearly half a century has been sufficient to show, not only that no evils can result from the enlightenment of the popular mind, but that, in just the same proportion as the mass of the people become educated, will be their love of order, industry, and sobriety; and that refinement of the intellect tends to set men free from immoral and debasing pursuits and animal gratifications.

Infants' Schools, on their first institution, had many of those discouragements to contend with which prevented the success of the earlier attempts for the improvement of the many; but they have outlived the day of their adversity, and even these, the latest of primary establishments for education, are almost universally acknowledged to be very powerful moral aids to popular regeneration, and to possess most decided claims for support.

The superior training which a well-directed Infants' School is enabled to accomplish, the settled habits of order induced by such training from a very early age, and the high degree of moral power which is called into active exercise, have been found to be a most valuable preparation for the more advanced schools. We are disposed to set a somewhat lower value on the intellectual benefits of such schools than on their physical and moral effects, because we know that when the educational machinery of the country is perfect, and when every child can have a fair proportion of its life allotted to its instruction and improvement,—and that this era must shortly approach, we are convinced,—the regular and systematic course of intellectual study will commence after children have quitted the Infants' School. In the mean time, Infants' Schools have an important office to fulfil as preparatory training establishments.

A generation cannot pass away from the earth without leaving traces of the spirit by which it was animated. The most abiding features of the age now passing, will be those connected with educational and moral reforms. No opinion is more prevalent at this time than that society is improved in every grade; and that it is susceptible of still higher improvement, is evident to the most superficial thinker. It is also acknowledged that the infant mind may, if placed under timely direction and cultivation, help forward this moral progress; and that the years of precious time which were formerly lost to the mass of the people, or worse than lost, for they tended to engender evil habits, are the most valuable years for restraining vicious inclinations, developing the social and kindly feelings, and implanting the germ of those virtues which exalt a people.

It will be truly enough concluded from these remarks that we think Infants' Schools the most suitable preparatory seminaries for the children of all classes. Our opinion has not been hastily nor unadvisedly formed. If we consider for a moment the various circumstances connected with the domestic arrangements of the different ranks of society, we shall find that many of the most valuable elements for early moral training are not only wanting, but that they are alike inaccessible to parents of all classes. In the case of the mechanic, the labourer, the smaller shopkeeper, and the less wealthy tradesman, the mother, as well as the father, has to toil daily in procuring the means of subsistence. The elder brothers and sisters, if such there be, of these families, are employed in similar labours to their parents—in earning a maintenance. To whom can the babes of such families be committed?

In the class of professional men, merchants, and the higher order of shopkeepers, nursery-maids and gover- nesses may certainly be employed to assist the mother in the training of the infant mind. But if the mother and her assistants were, in every case, thoroughly qualified to accomplish this important task, which it is well known they are not, the work could not be carried on with the systematic efficiency which is afforded in the Infants' School, the discipline could not be sustained, the im- portant element to good training of *numbers* would be wanting, the variety of dispositions and habits which re- quire and which elicit some of the most valuable devices of the teacher would be absent, and it would be found that, even under the most favourable circumstances, the success of family instruction could bear no comparison with the modes of development practised in the well- conducted Infants' School. The experience of the writer of this article is most strongly confirmatory of the evi- dence of James Simpson, given before the Select Com- mittee on Education, in July 1835. "I do not know," says this intelligent educationist, "in the present state of education in the middle and upper classes of society, that I could point out, within my own knowledge, half a dozen mothers who I should say are qualified to educate their own children; and that is one of the results of the low state of education in the middle and upper classes."

By the position which the highest classes of society occupy, by the unnatural demands made upon their time, and by the bondage of conventional observances with which a few only are inclined to struggle sufficiently to

free themselves, the difficulties of educating their offspring are to them increased; and their wealth cannot
purchase the scope for developing and correcting the
moral and intellectual faculties of their children at home,
which is to be found in an Infants' School. Persons who
are accustomed to the government of children, do not
make those mistakes into which parents are liable to fall,
who are oftentimes placed in difficult circumstances by
the apparent caprice of temper manifested by their children. The latter are consequently led into the exercise
of undue severity, against which every child will rebel in
thought, word, or deed, or to the expression of affection
and applause which may, or may not, be merited. The
child, however, learns what value to attach upon these
parental manifestations; and, according to its natural dispositions or endowments, will be the sort of ascendancy
it will obtain over its parent. Neither must the character
of the parent be altogether left out of our consideration,
whose treatment of the child will depend, not only upon
the advantages which have been enjoyed by such parent,
but also upon the natural bias which controls and directs
each motive and action. The influence of servants is
powerful over the young; the weak, the ignorant, the
unskilful, and too often the vicious, are placed in constant
contact and communication with them. These persons are
sometimes indifferent to the happiness of families; often
they are ignorant of how large a mass of man's happiness
or misery is under their sway.* It is evidently impossible
for parents to be constantly with their children; all that
they can do is to unite to provide schools on a system
whose value is demonstrated by its effects, and to take
such a personal interest in such schools as shall ensure
the introduction of all rational auxiliaries to education.

The evidence of those who have paid the closest attention to the effects of Infants' Schools is in the highest
degree favourable. Facts might be adduced which speak
most strongly on the improvement in health, habits, man-

* This is a result consequent partly on the distance which is kept up
between masters and servants—an evil which has grown enormously of
late years, and partly from the neglect shown in the education of the
poorer classes.

ners, dispositions, and intelligence, which they have accomplished. Our inquiries as to the effect of these schools on the minds and characters of infants have been made in various districts; their result has led to the conclusion we have adopted; but we will here refer to evidence which must be considered as satisfactory, and it is accessible to all who feel interested in this inquiry. The following queries were forwarded in 1836 to the parents of the children attending six of the infants' schools in Glasgow.

1. Do you find your child's health injured or improved since it went to the infant school?

2. Do you find your child less or more obedient since attending the infant school?

3. Do you find any alteration in your children's general behaviour at home or amongst companions?

4. Do you find your child has acquired useful knowledge? and please state what kind of knowledge, and to what extent.

To these questions answers in writing were received from 221 parents; others who could not write waited personally on the teachers, and expressed most favourable opinions upon the system as it had been pursued. For examples of the parents' answers we must refer to pp. 220–227 Stow's Training System.

So satisfied are we that no other system for infantine management can be placed in comparison with this in the happy results it is capable of producing, that should schools be created throughout the country to the extent required for the infants of the middle and working classes, and should the system be amplified in all those details which only practical teachers can execute, " there would be reason to expect that, in the course of time, the class enjoying it would rise higher in character than the class rejecting it, and thereby higher in social rank. This would settle the question whether, or not, Infants' Schools are suitable for the higher classes of society."*

The objects of Infants' Schools are so important, and, generally speaking, so little comprehended, and even

* Simpson's " Necessity for Popular Education."

misunderstood, that it becomes necessary to state what they are, in order to show that *they are not* what have, in some instances, usurped their place. Some of the most important aims have been wholly neglected, or over-looked, by the promoters of such schools; or it may be that the supposed plans of instruction have been mecha-nically worked, while the *spirit* and *life* of the system have been unknown or unregarded. In some instances these objects have only been partially carried out, from a lack of teachers; this want can only be effectually sup-plied by the creation of Normal Schools, where the sys-tem shall be wrought out in all its details, and where teachers shall have those advantages without which they must too often labour in vain, or, at best, with only par-tial success.

Infants' Schools contemplate the training of children between the ages of two and six years. They receive infants from the parental roof to become to them " father, and friend, and tutor, all in one." Every aid which is necessary for the proper nurturing of a young child must be found among their provisions, or they are imperfect. Every device which the most judicious parent or well-experienced teacher can worthily employ in promoting the welfare of a child committed to their guidance, must be put in requisition in these schools, or they will ill deserve the expressive title given to them by Lord Jeffery of " well-regulated, systematic nurseries." The home and the school are to be in them united; the kindness, the love of the indulgent and faithful mother, is to be blended with the intelligent firmness of the enlightened teacher. The bodily health and strength are to be sustained by such appropriate and varied exercises as will tend to the equal development of every part of the physical system. The moral dispositions and habits are to be conformed to the standard of the Christian Scriptures by every example that can be made to bear upon their elucidation, and the precepts of the Saviour are to be made their rule of life. The mental energies are to be cultivated by correct ob-servation, the senses being duly exercised and educated; this will lead to the acquisition and application of lan-guage, in which accuracy of expression is to be strictly cultivated. Things rather than words, or, at all events, things and examples *before* words and explanations, must be the course of the Infants' School teacher if he would be successful in his labours.

Constant cheerfulness must reign in an Infants' School; occasional excitement is good, but the frequent recurrence of such a stimulant becomes a burden to all. The school must not be allowed to become a plaything, nor the frequent scene of light and frivolous amusements, nor yet an exhibition-room for the display of a few acquirements which surprise the multitude, but which neither improve the minds nor the hearts of the children. The rhymed couplets on arithmetical rules, geometrical figures and definitions,—the technical terms, and unconnected portions of scientific knowledge, acquired by rote, and above the comprehension of the pupils, are a very questionable good, we had almost said a positive evil. They were tolerated by the best friends of the system in its early days, because it was thought difficult to adapt wholesome instruction to the narrow faculties of babes: but they are a poor substitute for that knowledge which teaches how to live well,—for that instruction which is to form useful and intelligent beings; and they should be abolished as soon as rational modes of imparting information are established,—as soon as teachers can be formed to carry forward the real intents of the system, and lessons provided in harmony with its design and spirit.

Physical Training.—The first care of an intelligent parent is for the health and physical comfort of his children. A young child should be at all times light-hearted. Under the endurance of bodily pain or functional disorder, arising from a bad state of health or some temporary inconvenience in its dress, a child cannot be even-tempered. Experience among children will lead those to whom their management is committed to seek for every cause of irritation of this nature. A child who is labouring under personal inconvenience, cannot be expected to exhibit a pleasant countenance, nor to go through any course of discipline with equal pleasure and facility as those who have to bear no such annoyances. Even if it be impossible to remove any temporary obstacle to its comfort, it is desirable that the teacher should know of its existence, that due allowance may be made for fretfulness or apparent sullenness in the child, and that it may know that it is an object of sympathy.

One especial object, then, with every Infants' School, should be the physical welfare of the children. Their health is to be sustained and improved ; everything conducing to such improvement, as food, clothing, cleanliness, exercise, must be made an object of care and watchfulness. We do not say that this object is to be solely and separately pursued for any given period; but that it is to be a feature of primary importance, and consequently to occupy a portion of daily regard in every Infants' School. Physical exercises are best carried on simultaneously with the development of the reasoning faculties, in the pauses which are needful for the repose of these faculties; they afford that relief which is so essential when the mind has been actively engaged. The means in use at some of the Infants' Schools, and others that are recommended, are, 1st, a well-ventilated and lofty school-room ; 2nd, muscular motion, introduced both into their lessons and their amusements; 3rd, easy gymnastic exercises, adapted both for the open air and for the school-room; 4th, social games, or plays ; 5th, useful employments, to accustom them early to habits of industry.*

The better the idea of community can be sustained, the more successful will the teacher be in communicating sentiments of mutual dependence, good-will, and forbearance among the infants; and the higher will be their tone of moral feeling. To the provisions here mentioned for their bodily welfare, we would also suggest an open shed, for shelter and exercise in wet weather. To sustain a healthy atmosphere in a school-room where a large number of children is assembled, it should be vacated at least twice in the course of each half-day, when the windows should be opened for the free admission of air. No lesson addressed to the mental powers of infants should

* Threading beads, working wire buttons, preparing lint for hospitals, are among the employments which have been introduced ; but there is an objection to these from their sedentary nature.

ever exceed half an hour in length; and it should invariably be followed by another half-hour of bodily exercise, either in or out of the school. The design of the infant system is not to produce precocious babes,—this is one of its abuses; but it is to provide every necessary exercise for the culture of children as creatures endowed with a bodily organization which is to be sustained for healthy action, and made equal to the demands it has to fulfil,—and with intellectual capabilities to receive and retain that variety of knowledge, those portions of information, which it is found desirable to convey to them. The exercise of all the powers of man, physical and mental, tends to his well-being. In the due cultivation of all these powers, every teacher ought to be employed; and especial care should be taken not to sacrifice one to the cultivation of another. If the bodily health be not sustained, the mental action will be feeble, and hurtful, and productive of disease; and if the mental powers are overtasked, the physical system will be debilitated.

There is a very useful chapter on the diseases and accidents to which children are peculiarly liable in Wilderspin's Infant System, which we mention rather than quote, supposing this work is to be found in every Infants' School, or accessible to the teachers. We do not approve of every portion of Mr. Wilderspin's works, as will be judged from some remarks we have made, and others which will appear in the course of this article; but the spirit of the infant system is conspicuous in his writings, and we should rejoice if there were many thousands of teachers possessing his untiring zeal, and his devotedness to the cause, which he, more than all others, has advocated and promoted.

The second care of teachers of infants should be the *moral and social training* of those committed to them. It is not that we regard moral training as an object of *secondary* value that we place it here; but that the condition of *health* is indispensably necessary to the culture of the moral and social affections and the intellectual powers. The education of the animal system, the control and direction of the moral dispositions, the development of the senses, and through them of the intellect, and the communication of the great truths of religion, may be made to accompany and sustain each other; nor would it be desirable to separate one of these great objects from the rest. At the same time, a large amount of attention must necessarily be devoted to that branch of education on which the others so mainly depend.

The tender age of the inmates of Infants' Schools incapacitates them for deep or protracted mental exertion, and the too long continuance of such exercises would have a baneful effect on the brain. It is manifest to every one that while nothing can be more improving than the beautiful precepts of Christianity,. exemplified by the actions and words of Christ, and the illustrations which he has left us for our instruction, imitation, and warning; yet there is scriptural knowledge too high for infants to attain to. The nature and capabilities of their mind thus instruct us what branches of education may be carried forward without hesitation, and what subjects should be more cautiously adopted as topics for development. We ascertain that those exercises which are not only not injurious, but positively beneficial, are those in which infants most delight, and which their powers and faculties are best fitted to sustain. Nothing, then, should be allowed to impede the acquisition and regulation of physical power; and, next to this, no exercises can be more important than those which belong to the education of the heart.

The elements which conduce to the development and habitual practice of good principles, are to be found in every society of children,—the same in their nature, though not equal in extent with those which exist among those who are older and wiser than children. The passions and prejudices of the human mind early take root and thrive, unless care be taken to eradicate pernicious tendencies, and to modify ardent temperaments which are so liable to fall into error. Precept must be illustrated by example; and the pleasures resulting from the habitual exercise of things " lovely and of good report," must be made manifest and dilated upon. Every encouragement must be given to the practice of kindness, generosity, docility, submission, truth, mercy, honesty; these must be constantly shown to be the ways of pleasantness and the paths of peace. Every example that occurs to illustrate these social virtues should be treasured up in the memory or the note-book of the teacher. Circumstances will arise for calling forth these treasures, so as to make a favourable impression on the minds of the children; and their effect *must* be to regulate and influence their life, to sustain and direct their conduct. They will thus be furnished with a panoply which will be proof against the allurements and encroachments of vicious conduct and principles; they will be strengthened in virtuous feelings and commendable habits by every high and worthy motive which can be placed before them. While it is powerfully inculcated that *happiness* awaits those who are guided in their thoughts, words, and actions by *obedience;* the *misery* of *disobedience* to the law of love must also be unceasingly dwelt upon. That pains, unhappiness, and punishments follow carelessness, idleness, violence, cruelty, injustice, dishonesty, vanity, pride, insolence, obstinacy, greediness, covetousness, can be readily shown. That these vices are contrary to the word of God, hateful to him and to good men; that each brings its own punishment, and thus produces misery,—can be made evident to the narrow limits of a child's understanding. Thus the inevitable consequences of transgression—the connection between the fault committed and the punishment by which it is attended—whether pain of body or anguish of mind, will constantly occur to them; and even a regard for their own happiness, an anxiety to avoid these serious consequences, will make them thoughtful, and cause them to refrain from many faults and follies. While *wilful* disobedience is thus visited with inevitable punishment, and while we feel less sorry for the personal inconvenience felt than for its cause, it must not be forgotten that infants are peculiarly liable to transgress *ignorantly.* These are transgressions which claim our sympathy. Want of knowledge, want of experience, occasion much suffering in the world, and in infants should not be harshly visited. The first time that a child gets possession of a sharp instrument, it is not aware that such instrument may inflict pain, if not cautiously handled. Should such a result follow, the child is not to be punished with blame,—blamed for its *ignorance*, when probably

no pains have been taken to give it *knowledge ;* yet such
occurrences are very common both among infants and
men.   The state, condition, and general qualities of things
are among the first lessons which an infant begins to learn ;
and this self-instruction commences at the earliest possible
period,—immediately after its birth.   It is in this process
of self-instruction that it requires assistance and guidance ;
and the most skilful infant teacher will be the man who
can " humble himself as a little child,"—be content to
follow at first, that he may afterwards lead, not only in
things physical, but in things moral and spiritual,—

> " Allure to brighter worlds, and show the way."

The mental constitution of the teacher will exercise a
most direct moral influence upon the pupils.   He must
be " slow to anger, and of great mercy ;" he must be ever
ready to forgive transgressions, but he must by no means
clear the guilty.   He must be well qualified to discern
what are faults in his pupils, and what are merely errors ;
and, while he suffers no enormities to be passed over as
trifles, he must allow largely for inexperience and the
troubles consequent on it.   An absolute authority must
be established—established in love—parental love, which
the pupils must never be permitted to violate.   This
authority can only be sustained by moderation and
firmness.   As every direction given by the teacher
is to be obeyed, care should be taken that no command
is given that cannot be enforced.   Modesty, courtesy,
gentleness, kindness, neatness, a love of mercy, a strict
regard for truth, an absence of every selfish consideration in the teacher will tend more to establish
these qualities in the pupils, than all the moral lessons
that can be delivered verbally.   The life and conduct
of the teacher thus becomes the model for the pupils ;
it will be the standard to which they will most constantly
refer, and the pattern on which their habits will be formed.   We have very frequently seen the truth of these
remarks confirmed in schools, and in families ; and we
have even more frequently seen the confirmation of
Salzman's creed, that the educator should always seek for
the faults of his pupils in himself.   Salzman says, " If

trouble arise in my school, I *examine myself*, and generally find that I am the cause of it,—that either my body
is out of order, or some unpleasant event has affected my
spirits, or I am wearied out with excessive labour. The
more attentive I am to myself, the more seldom do offences arise." He speaks of teachers who misunderstand
and misrepresent children's remarks and motives; not
considering that their minds are undisciplined, they seek
fruit in the time of blossoms, by demanding such a course
of conduct as can only result from a cultivated understanding. He illustrates his meaning somewhat in the
following manner. It is complained that children run, and
halloo, and jump about, and do nothing that is right and
proper. To which he answers, that children should not
move like puppets,—they feel their strength, and they
exert it. But it is remarked that such conduct in no way
forms habits of reflection; to which he replies, that children whose reason is not matured cannot be expected to
have powers of reflection to the same extent as their
teachers. It is said that they do nothing but childish
tricks; and he answers, that this is because they are children. It is complained that they go to study slowly, and
to play with gladness. Without offering a severe remark
upon this complaint, which it would be easy to make, he
observes in reply, that a love of labour and study must be
gradually instilled into a child's mind, by making such
studies and labours improving and interesting. Salzman
goes on to remark that " teachers often exaggerate the
number of faults among their pupils, and class them
all together, without any distinction. Suppose, now, in an
institution for education, all the boots of the pupils should
be made from one last. Is it not obvious that only a few
of them would be found to suit, while all the rest would
be too large or too small? And what is to be done in
such a case? Are the feet which the boots will not suit
to be considered as faulty? Must something be pared
off from the feet of one pupil, and something added to
those of another? You smile. Do you wish to know what
this has to do with the subject? I will tell you. As the
feet of every boy have their peculiar form, so have their
characters and talents. Would you now work for these

boys, with their various characters and talents, with one foot for a standard, or, in other words, with one last? If this is done, only a few will be suited. Would you, then, consider this as a fault of the boys, and strive to force them to your standard? If you do this, you will act with as little discretion as those who should strive to form the foot after the boot."

These quotations from one of the most successful educators of children cannot but be of use. If important in ordinary schools, among grown boys, they have a tenfold importance for Infants' School teachers; for the first moral habits a child forms, influence his mind and conduct, and affect his principles more strongly than any that are formed at a later period; and it is in this view that Infants' Schools are to be considered as Institutions of first-rate importance.

It is in their *intellectual system* that we consider Infants' Schools, as at present conducted, to be the most defective; and we shall therefore enter more minutely into this division of the subject than we have into the physical and moral departments of training. We are fully satisfied that valuable knowledge may be imparted during infancy, without endangering the health of the pupil, provided sufficient time for recreation be also given. But this knowledge must be of a nature within the capacity of a child to understand; and it must be presented at such times, and in such a manner, as to be acceptable, and even received with eagerness. It may be well to specify distinctly and separately some of the great deficiencies which we, in common with many others, have remarked in Infants' Schools. We know some teachers who most heartily wish they were supplied, and who would be glad if there were a central establishment where they could make known their wants, with the hope that attempts, at least, would be made to supply them.*

* Since this article was written, the British and Colonial Infant School Society has been brought into active operation. It has a model school and a training school, and it has supplied some very useful practical lessons. It is to be hoped that this Society will be enabled to publish a variety of reading lessons, drawing lessons on a large scale, collections of objects, and other mechanical aids, for teachers.

1. *There is a generally acknowledged want of lessons on suitable subjects, in language simple, in matter appropriate, and in pictorial illustration accurate.*

Only those persons who have been placed in a difficulty of this nature can know how it presses upon the mind of a conscientious teacher. He is unwilling to make his teaching unproductive—to have recourse to school-books which his pupils are not prepared for—to teach them by rote matters too high for their comprehension—to proceed with them by those empirical methods upon which alone nearly all school-books are prepared, and thus prepared because the generality of teachers will not give themselves the trouble to *teach*, nor exert their intellect in ascertaining those rational processes which have been found successful in communicating knowledge. Very few teachers can teach extemporarily, and it is highly desirable that there should be much previous arrangement of all subjects they propose to bring before their pupils. Other teachers cannot satisfy themselves in the choice of subjects for teaching upon. The provision, therefore, of appropriate lessons, both in matter and arrangement, becomes a very important consideration, as it would tend, perhaps more than any other arrangement, to improve the character of Infants' Schools; it would remove a heavy burthen from the teachers; it would furnish them, not only with a plan, but with models also on which to frame new series of lessons to diversify their course of instruction; and it would relieve their minds, at the hours of teaching, on the subjects of instruction, the language, and the means of illustration. But while we advocate the preparation of every aid of this nature, we would not confine the master literally to the language of such lessons; he cannot reach every child's mind by the same track; and, in diversifying his lessons by such familiar allusions and processes as his pupils may require, he will be diverted from the one path chalked out, and the circumstances of his pupils, as visible in their future progress, will justify such departures, and such adaptations to ·their various faculties and endowments. No good teacher will ever be enslaved to the *letter* of any educa-

tional work that is ever likely to be produced, for no
work can provide everything that is necessary for the
different gradations and combinations of the human intellect.

2. *The lessons which have been written for Infants'
Schools have generally been, both in language and subjects,
above the comprehension of infants.*

There are four or five volumes, by different authors and
compilers, on the infant system. If we take up any of
these, and duly consider their contents, we shall find that
sound has, in most of the lessons, usurped the place of
sense; that the capabilities of the infant mind have been
miscalculated; and we must conclude that they have
been produced by persons who are more skilful in rhymes
and tunes than in simplifying knowledge. Instead of
considering the kind of instruction to be imparted, and
the beautiful and simple methods of those who have left
rich legacies behind them, — the fruits of experience
crowned with success,—the authors of those works which
are professedly practical, have often violated the laws
which should direct elementary instruction, for they have
neither regarded simplicity of language, nor gradations of
ideas; and they have betrayed a lamentable ignorance of
the science of mind. It is our desire to be very guarded
in what we advance on this head, but we know facts may
be adduced in support of all these assertions. According to the ordinary operations of the system, the subjects
of instruction are only superficially or partially taught.
It is professed to teach Grammar, Geography, the doctrinal and historical portions of Scripture, and many
other subjects of equal importance ; and in many Infants'
Schools rhymed sentences are the only or the principal
means employed for this purpose. The fetters of rhyme,
however pleasing to the infant ear, can never compensate
for those explanations and illustrations which inform the
intellect and educate the judgment. Grammar cannot
be taught by rules, whether in prose or verse ; graduated
examples, in which new words and new constructions
are founded on what has been previously taught, can be
made satisfactory. Perhaps the grammatical picture of

Smith and Dolier might be occasionally employed with good effect. Geography must have maps, models, and diagrams, to make the subject sensible to the very young. Religion must not be commenced with the assertion of abstract truths above an infant's comprehension, nor by the communication of historical facts, which take back the mind to a period of which an infant's arithmetical powers will not allow it to conceive.* On these and on other portions of instruction the errors we deplore are to be mainly attributed to the apathy with which all exertions in favour of education have been regarded, but while we deplore them, it is a most pleasurable duty to acknowledge how much is due to those good men who have devoted themselves to the advancement and cultivation of the present race of infants. Considering the position they have occupied, and the difficulties to be surmounted,—considering the state of education in all its branches, and in every class of society,—making allowance for the apathy of one party, the uninquiring satisfaction of another, and the silly fears of over-educating of a third,—it may even be wondered at that anything good has been preserved; and it is to the powerful efforts of the few who, under all kinds of obstacles, have neither despaired of nor forsaken their self-imposed duties, that we ascribe the credit of all the more satisfactory features in the present operations for inform-

* There are other methods of conveying religious instruction as inefficient, not to say injurious, as either of the above ; these we may illustrate by the following quotation from the lectures of Dr. Biber, on Christian Education, page 175 :

"In one infant school I have known the children to be made to laugh or cry, or to look happy or unhappy, or kind or angry, at the master's command; in another school, in which the picture of a farm-yard was hung up on the wall, the master assured me that he was expressly enjoined by his committee to ask the children for Scripture references to every object represented in that picture. Thus, when he pointed to a cow, the children were to quote him chapter and verse of those passages in Scripture in which a cow was mentioned; the same with the sheaves, the clouds, and whatever else the picture contained; this was considered by the committee as an excellent method of *connecting* religious instruction with all other subjects. To enumerate all the nonsense that has been practised, and is still practised, in this manner, would be an endless task."

ing the popular mind, not only in Infants' Schools, but in
all the establishments where simultaneous and mutual
instruction are used as auxiliaries. We look with somewhat of hope and expectancy to a state of education
when all the principles which have been in operation
shall be examined by persons duly qualified to ascertain
their value, and with the power to give prominency to
those which merit encouragement.

3. *The teachers who have been engaged in carrying out the
details of the infant system have too generally been deficient in that kind of training which would have tended to
fit them for their office.*

Most willingly do we acknowledge the moral worth of
those who have " borne the burthen and heat of the day "
in this hitherto unsatisfactory labour. The system, in an
imperfect state, was too prematurely adopted, and the
spread of Infants' Schools created a demand for teachers
before it was possible to prepare them duly for their
work. The small stipends that could be afforded by
schools with only a local, and, in very many cases, a *partial* local patronage, prevented the employment of persons
with all those qualifications necessary for carrying out
the generous views which led to the formation of such
schools. An infant teacher, and every other teacher who
has to influence the heart and to instruct the understanding, should be a person of a devotional frame of mind,
with a strong moral sense, abounding in practical piety,
devoted to his labour, firm, fond of children, and of extensive information on all common subjects. He should
possess a facility in imparting knowledge, and an un-
wearying zeal in his office; not " a man severe and stern
to view," but one who can unbend, and take pleasure in
those little things which are great to little men, who can
feel sympathy in those trifles which are the serious occupation of young minds, and who will find and make opportunities to draw from common scenes and circumstances
such lessons as shall make enduring impressions on the
minds and the hearts forming and growing beneath his
culture. Such a person, thoroughly imbued with correct
principles of education, might, when not employed in

school-duties, provide lessons, and other illustrations, for effectually working out his principles. But few, very few, persons with these endowments have been practically employed as teachers of Infants' Schools; the instruction of infants has not, therefore, had a fair trial. In lieu of such persons, but compelled by circumstances which could not be controlled, recourse has been had to a class of persons who have oftentimes been deficient either in the natural or acquired requisites for such an occupation; and they have had to toil on without guidance, perhaps with no general principles, perhaps with minds not fitted for the comprehension of such principles,—unable to supply that which should have given life and intelligence to their labour: consequently the occupation has become, in most cases, one of mere mechanical drudgery, both to the teachers and the taught.

In addition to these primary causes of failure, there are others which will disappear when these have been provided against. The unnatural desire to have pupils engaged on subjects which shall produce an effect beyond the walls of the school-room, rather than to train them in the knowledge of common things, is one of these. The cultivation of the *verbal memory* is one of the forms in which this ridiculous proceeding manifests itself, leaving the intellect unfed and unexercised. Words may excite wonder abroad, and amongst those who are not accustomed to bestow time and thought on the true objects of all instruction; but they are a poor substitute for rules, practices, and sentiments, which should direct and control the passions, and humanize the child. This habit has prevailed too much in all our schools, it has been a prominent feature in Infants' Schools, and it has been one of those fertile sources which have led to a corrupt and vitiated taste in parents, of which numberless instances obtrude upon the notice. We cannot but condemn a course so adverse to a child's interests and improvement, and so unsatisfactory to a child in every stage, if we except that very exceptionable satisfaction which nearly all children feel at being wondered at in the family circle.

We hope not to be misunderstood : it is the teaching of words alone, without their corresponding ideas, to which we object. We find no fault with the teaching of *long* words, which are commonly called *hard* words merely because they are long, and which can be readily explained. Many long words express ideas which can be at once made sensible, as *perpendicular, horizontal, oblique, opaque, inanimate ;* and others are merely the names of objects, as *caterpillar, rhinoceros, calyx, ichneumon,* all of which can be represented, and are therefore free from objection. Even scientific terms may be sometimes introduced with good effect, provided their meaning is made evident; but to task a child's memory with words of which no explanation which they could understand would convey a correct idea,—to load their minds with matter of sufficient difficulty for the ripened intellect,—is undoubtedly to transgress the laws of nature and experience. To babes " the milk of the word" must be offered; to be successful instructors of children, we must " speak as a child, understand as a child, think as a child."

Very little knowledge of the powers and capacity for progress of infant minds has been manifested in the choice of the books and lessons ordinarily used. It must be confessed that there is some difficulty in the selection and arrangement of subjects sufficiently appropriate, and rendered into easy language; but much less in the choice of subjects than in the methodical construction and arrangement of lessons. Works written professedly for children never abounded so much as at the present time ; none of these possess all the excellencies which should characterize works of this nature. In some instances they illustrate the art of education, but never the science ; for they are founded on no settled observations of the phenomena of the infant mind. Perhaps, in the present state of our knowledge of these phenomena, it would be impossible to produce a system of infant education on scientific principles, comprehending all the matter, arrangements, and methods of carrying it out, in the form of graduated lessons on all subjects which are acknowledged to be within the compass of a child's faculties; but this should not prevent attempts to approximate towards an end so desirable, and Infants' Schools should not be suffered to languish for want of this kind of aid. There is a multitude of sources, isolated it is true, but which might be made available for such purposes. There are lessons on various subjects calculated for such schools, which have never yet been brought together and arranged in a systematic form. We are satisfied that nothing is wanting but encouragement and support to lead to the publication of many such aids to infant development. This encouragement may be obtained when a board of public instruction shall exist; and our schools may then derive similar benefits to those which have been conferred on the schools of France by the cheap dissemination of methods, lessons, and illustrations for elementary instruction.

For the more efficient support of the existing Infants' Schools, two objects require immediate attention,—books of a first-rate quality, and accomplished teachers. Books or lessons are even more indispensably requisite, considering the present position of such schools, than teachers. Even if there were an abundant supply of well-qualified teachers, it would be an unwise act to supersede all those at present engaged in the task; but it will take some years before a new race of teachers can be prepared for carrying out the best plans that can be devised for Infants' Schools, and in the mean time something can be done towards making the teachers at present engaged more efficient. By a well-arranged and well-executed series of lessons, advancing from such as are suitable to the young and wholly ignorant, to such as are calculated for the instruction of children of greater age and attainments, and by a well-organized plan for visiting the schools at present established, and bringing such lessons into use, many of the present class of teachers would be improved, and their schools incalculably benefited. Through the mere detail,—the construction, the language, the arrangement—of such lessons, correct principles would, in many cases, be inferred by the teacher, which would be brought into practice, and made to bear on new subjects and various branches of education. By such a measure, the best of the present teachers would be assisted

to as great an extent as is feasible, considering their
disadvantageous position; the worse would be improved:
at all events, the mere mechanism thus brought to bear
upon the schools would help forward the progress of the
pupils, if the spirit were not evoked in the teachers.
The carrying out of this measure would be attended with
but a trifling expense, though accompanied, as it must
needs be, with such aids to instruction as pictures, diagrams, models, and other auxiliaries addressed to the
senses of the pupils. In another part of this paper we
shall suggest several of the branches of knowledge which
should have immediate attention, with such hints in detail as will show their practicability.

Method is an element which all schools cannot claim;
without it, teachers are often at a loss, pupils are disorderly, and every attempt to advance them in knowledge
is abortive. Method includes order and arrangement,—
it is not confined to modes of illustrating this and teaching
that; it should be seen in every act of the masters and
the pupils, whether as individuals or collectively: it
should not only be visible in all the operations, combined
and single, of the teacher and the taught; but it should
also determine and regulate the division and the disposal
of time to be employed on such operations. The absence
of those means by the application of which alone schools
can flourish, has to some extent precluded the employment of method in Infants' Schools to such a degree as is
needful for success. We do not wish to see a slavish
uniformity prevail in all Infants' Schools; the modifications of situation, resources, local influence, and the mental constitution of the teacher, will always be causes
productive of dissimilarity in certain details. A general
plan should be adhered to in all; the differences will have
their origin in circumstances which no foresight can control, and they will not be without their value. No school
can pursue a prosperous course where a due division of
time, with relationship to the objects of attainment, is
disregarded. This is one of the details which will be
more or less modified by circumstances. The well-
managed public and private schools throughout the coun-

try pay a particular attention to this important feature in the economics of teaching. It need scarcely be said how much it facilitates the business of a school. From all we have seen and heard, we may venture to say that no school, either of a public or private character, can be well conducted where the teachers and pupils are unacquainted with the subjects which are to occupy their attention during every day, and the hours at which their changes of occupation are to take place. With these views, and to give a general outline of the subjects which we consider appropriate for infant instruction, as well as to show the hours at which the changes of business should take place, and the space of time to be allotted to each subject, the accompanying plan has been framed. In Infant Schools, simultaneous instruction, with all its advantages, can be more extensively carried out than in schools of any other class. The pupils are seldom divided into forms or classes. One subject occupies the attention of all at the same time; and their voices, or their observing or their reflecting powers, are all called into action together. This character of Infant School discipline simplifies the form of the division of time here proposed, inasmuch as a provision for the employment of several classes at the same time on different subjects is unnecessary. To those who may be unacquainted with the nature and uses of these tabular divisions of time, it may be remarked that, in schools where the pupils are of mixed ages and attainments, it is found necessary to modify these tables every three or four months, according to the progress of the pupils, the changes of classes, or the subjects to be taught. Some change of this nature will also be occasionally, though not frequently, desirable in Infants' Schools; they will also be modified by circumstances of a similar nature to those which affect higher schools. The subjects proposed for attention in the plan are such as may form a portion of daily business in every Infants' School that has been established six months. As we shall treat of the occupation of each portion of the day under a separate head, we shall indicate the kind of help of which teachers should avail themselves in sustaining the interest of each subject, so as to impart pleasure to their pupils, while they supply them with such knowledge as they can understand and appreciate.

We admit a well-founded objection which has been often and powerfully raised against Infants' Schools, as they have sometimes been empirically conducted; namely, that their tendency has been to overtask and excite certain of the intellectual faculties. In the arrangement of subjects for instruction, and modes of imparting it, we wish to bear in mind the capabilities, as well as the gratification and improvement of the infant. The different changes of business are such as may succeed each other with propriety, and without keeping the attention too long occupied with any single subject; while the pauses for physical exercise are sufficiently long and frequent in recurrence to give vigour to the animal system, and to enable the pupils to return to lessons recreated both in body and in spirit. It would be desirable that recreation should partake of toil, diversion, and gymnastic exercises, wherever favourable circumstances will admit of these three kinds of recreation being introduced: they will be modified by the seasons of the year, and open air exercise may sometimes be wholly prevented at the specified hours by severity of the weather. Whenever this is the case, as during rain or intense cold, the exercise should be taken within doors, with the windows opened, so as to admit a free circulation of air into the room.

School-hours and Division of Business.

Morning.

	$9—9\frac{1}{2}$	$9\frac{1}{2}—9\frac{5}{6}$	$9\frac{5}{6}—10\frac{1}{6}$	$10\frac{1}{6}—10\frac{1}{2}$	$10\frac{1}{2}—11$	$11—11\frac{1}{2}$	$11\frac{1}{2}—12$
Monday.	Singing hymns, text and explanation of Scripture, prayer, and questions on explanation, every morning.	Reading.	Exercise, Play, &c.	Number.	Lessons on Objects.	Exercise, Play, &c.	Singing.
Tuesday.		Reading.		Geography.	Lessons on Objects.		Singing.
Wednesday.		Reading.		Number.	Lessons on Objects.		Singing.
Thursday.		Reading.		Geography.	Lessons on Objects.		Singing.
Friday.		Reading		Number.	Lessons on Objects.		Singing.

Afternoon.

	$2—2\frac{1}{2}$	$2\frac{1}{2}—3$	$3—3\frac{1}{2}$	$3\frac{1}{2}—4$	$4—4\frac{1}{3}$	$4\frac{1}{3}—4\frac{2}{3}$	$4\frac{2}{3}—5$
Monday	Elder Children, Writing. Younger ditto, Being read to.	Exercise, Play, &c.	Morality & Religion.	Exercise, Play, &c.	Objects.	Exercise, Play, &c.	Text of Scripture, questions on Scripture, prayer, hymn, every evening.
Tuesday	Elder Children, Writing. Younger ditto, Read to.		Natural History.		Form.		
Wednes.	Elder Children, Writing. Younger ditto, Read to.		Morality & Religion.		Objects.		
Thursday	Elder Children, Writing. Younger ditto, Read to.		Natural History.		Colour.		
Friday .	Elder Chi'dren, Writing. Younger ditto, Read to.		Morality & Religion.		Objects.		

9—9½. (30 minutes.)

We can conceive of no better commencement for the business of each day than singing. There is in the simple vocal melody of children, themselves being the melodists, an incitement to cheerfulness, which, on moral grounds, renders it a valuable auxiliary in a school, especially as it disposes them to pleasurable feelings when first congregated in the morning; it has also other advantages at this particular time, such as inducing all to be present to join in an exercise pleasing to all, and giving stragglers a few minutes longer for assembling previous to the scriptural explanations and prayer which immediately follow the singing. The hymns for commencing and concluding each day's business should be of a very simple devotional character, in language and in sentiment within the comprehension of infants, or such as admit of explanation. There is at present no perfectly unexceptionable collection of hymns with these requisites; very few of those in the Infant School manuals are suitable, and, as we do not think it would be a labour of great difficulty to select a sufficient number for such a purpose, it is matter of surprise that some selection has not been made. The five first hymns in "Treasures for the Memory," a small collection of sacred poetry, published by William Crofts, Chancery Lane, are very suitable, and are not to be found in any of the manuals of infant instruction. We copy one of them :—

I.

Must little children love the Lord?
Must little infants often pray?
And will God mind the very words
    That little children say?

Oh! yes, if truth be in the prayer,
And children wish the words they say,
Then God will surely bless them there,
    And love them every day.

As on their little beds they lie,
They think of heaven and sweetly say,
"My Saviour! hear me when I cry,
    And make me good to-day.

" E'en in my play be near me still ;
My heavenly Father, think on me !
Teach me to do thy holy will,
    And draw my thoughts to thee."

Thus little children love the Lord,
Thus little infants sometimes pray ;
And then God minds the very words
    That little children say.

After singing a hymn of a character similar to the
above, the devotional sentiment is awakened; and the
reading of a few verses of Scripture, with or without explanation, according to the choice made, may be appropriately proceeded with.   Explanations should always be
of a practical nature, such as will influence the life and
conduct of the pupils ; allusions being sometimes made,
but with the greatest delicacy,—for children are creatures
of feeling,—to circumstances connected with the conduct
of the pupils : at such seasons the expression of a teacher's countenance will often have more weight than the
most pointed rebuke or encouragement.   After the reading and explanation above recommended, a simple prayer
should be read, the sentiments expressed being ascertained to be not higher than their power of comprehension ; the nature, the end, and the efficacy of prayer
being occasionally made familiar to them.   To enable a
teacher to enter fully into these preliminary, but most
important duties, it seems desirable that a manual should
be prepared, containing a selection of hymns, a summary
of Scriptural texts, and a sufficient number of prayers to
admit of occasional change, their diversity being intended
to show the scope and nature of the three elements of
prayer,—adoration, petition, and thanksgiving.

$9\frac{1}{2}$—$9\frac{5}{6}$. (20 minutes.)

In proposing that *reading* shall occupy a portion of an
infant's time at school, we are aware that we differ from
some who have been engaged in infant instruction.   The
objections which are made to reading are of such a nature as may be easily combated; its advantages, if capable of being accomplished, no one will dispute.   The

great objections belong more to the old system of teaching to read, than to the method we shall suggest. Mr.
Stow, in his training system, remarks that, if reading is
introduced to any extent, it will injure the health of the
children by confining them too much to their seats. He
also fears that the teaching of children to read at an early
age would tend to abridge the period of education rather
than to extend it, the greater proportion of parents considering that "mere verbal reading and being educated
are synonymous terms." In reference to the first objection, the present article was commenced with the conviction that the cause of infant education would be re-
tarded rather than advanced by the advocacy of any
course of study that would tend to injure the infant constitution by debilitating the body, or by inducing preco-
city of intellect. These are dangers which more than
any others it is our wish to avoid. For the remedy to the
second objection, we must look to the increasing intelligence of parents, and *they* must be furnished with sources
for obtaining correct views.

Under no circumstances could we think it proper to
exclude the elder children of an Infants' School from
learning to read, nor even from learning to write. Indeed, we are persuaded that such an inducement to regular and continued attendance must be offered after a year
or two's training. It is not our wish that children should
any longer conquer this "most difficult of human attainments" through the medium of A, B, C; a, b, ab; b, a,
ba; &c. neither would we encounter with them any system of syllabic classifications, on which several meritorious elementary reading-books have been recently published; and the naming of the letters, as in spelling, we
would altogether discard. Neither the individual nor the
mutual-instruction systems are necessary in teaching the
mother-tongue, or any other living language. Simultaneous instruction to acquire the art of reading, and conversation for the acquisition of popular grammar, are all
that is needed. A modification of the system of Jacotot,
with a series of interesting lessons printed so large that
all the children could see them, would be found to be
the only needful auxiliaries to be employed. The lessons

must be graduated, and every sentence contained in them must possess a meaning level to the comprehension of the children. Monosyllabic lessons, though almost universally employed in early teaching, are not of that value which is generally attached to them; indeed, such lessons are so filled with particles,—words which only possess a meaning in connection with others,— and so deficient of the language of ordinary life, that they have less interest for children than exercises apparently more difficult, but which are less cramped and more natural. The best plan in the construction of reading-lessons is to follow nature, —to use those words of which children may early obtain an accurate acquaintance. Many long words are called "hard words," but it will be found that some of the hardest words in the language are the shortest. No word is "hard" to a child if he can pronounce it, and attaches to it a correct idea. We do not begin to talk to our children in monosyllables, and it will be found that most children understand polysyllabic words before they can utter them. The first lessons for reading should convey simple facts to them, without reference to the length of the words; the advance from simple to more difficult lessons must not be an advance in the measure of the words, but a progression in the subject-matter of the lesson. A few sentences read by the teacher, who is to point to them, and simultaneously repeated by the children, will be enough for the first lesson: after frequent repetitions, it will be seen that the children will name any words pointed to in those sentences. The difference in the length of the words is an advantage which is not to be found in lessons confined to two, three, four, five, &c. letters. Children soon perceive that words are arbitrary pictures; they express different things, qualities, motions, &c. and children naturally expect them to have a different appearance, as much so as they expect to see a lion of a different figure to a horse, after hearing facts which show their different habits and modes of life : the very dissimilarity of the words assists in their acquisition. The children have to remember the entire combinations,— not the letters, nor the syllables, but the words,—so that they may at once recognise them whenever they see them. Their eyes are engaged on the forms of the words, their ears on the sounds, their voices on the utterance. To assist in the framing of lessons of this nature we have given a few models which those accustomed to infant teaching will be able to complete, should the plan here suggested be attempted.*

The subjects of lessons first taught to infants, and such as it would be proper to adopt in Infants' Schools, should refer to objects with which the children have some acquaintance; as, the parts of their body, their food, clothing, animals, pictures in the school-room, flowers in the garden, productions in the fields and woods, the furniture of the house and the school-room, habits, instincts, and formation of animals, employments of mankind, &c. These should precede a more advanced series on similar subjects; the first series to include prominent characteristics, the second to be more especially the vehicle of correct information: thus the acquisition of knowledge would go hand in hand with the acquisition of the mechanism of the art of reading.

The subject of the human frame is amply developed in one of Pestalozzi's little works, a translation of which we have not seen; there are, however, some lessons smiliarly constructed in Biber's Christian Monitor.

1. *Body.*

this is the body,
this is the head,
this is the face,
these are the eyes,
this is the nose,
this is the mouth,
these are the jaws,
these are the ears,
this is the neck,
this is the trunk,
these are the arms,

these are the legs,
these are the hands,
these are the feet,
these are the fingers,
these are the toes.

2. *Head.*

this is the skull,
this is the crown,
this is the forehead,
this is the hair, &c.

* An article in No. XV. of the Quarterly Journal of Education, which is republished in "The Schoolmaster," gives the views of the writer *on teaching reading* at greater length than can be afforded here. As a testimony to the efficacy of the principle, he may add that a lady taught a very young child to read ordinary books upon it in a few months.

3. *Face.*

these are the temples,
these are the eye-brows,
these are the cheeks,
this is the chin, &c.

4. *Eyes.*

these are the eye-sockets,
these are the eye-lids,
these are the eye-lashes,
these are the eye-balls.

The above lessons may be carried out so as to form a most useful series, well adapted from the repetition of certain words, and the presence of the needful illustrations, to be successful as first reading lessons.

Colour.

the sky is blue,
milk is white,
coal is black,
gold is yellow,
grass is green,
flowers are red, purple, &c.

Form.

this table is oblong,
the walls are perpendicular,
a pencil is cylindrical,
an egg is oval,
a shilling is round,
a pen is pointed.

Size.

the ceiling is high,
this bench is low,
that pointer is long,
this pen is short,
that pen is long,
this book is thick,
that book is thin.

Animals.

a lark is a bird,
a butterfly is an insect,
a shark is a fish,
a lion is a beast,

a toad is a reptile,
a fly is an insect,
a pigeon is a bird,
an elephant is a beast, &c.

A Primrose.

here is a primrose,
this is the blossom,
this is the stem,
this is a leaf,
these are the leaves,
this is the calyx,
this is the root,
these are the fibres, &c.
the blossom is yellow,
the stem is stiff,
the leaves are green,
the roots are brown, &c.

Actions.

the dog barks,
birds fly,
a horse neighs,
an ass brays,
frogs croak,
a pigeon coos, &c.
the milk-maid milks cows,
the wood-cutter fells trees,
the shepherd minds sheep,
the ploughman ploughs land,
the rabbit eats leaves,
the horse eats hay, grass, and corn,
the dog watches the house, &c.

With care and attention, these lessons might be so arranged as to introduce all the common grammatical rules of the language in the best of all ways, by illustra-

tion;* and such lessons would afterwards serve as models
for composition; or, if this be too high a term for Infants'
Schools,† for the exercise of their observation, and the
invention of new sentences on any subject within the
knowledge of the children, according to a prescribed form.
Reading should be preceded by conversational exercises,
in order to invite questions from the children, to elicit
what knowledge they already possess on the subject of
the lesson,. and to give the teachers an opportunity of
explaining and illustrating any new words or phrases
which are to occur in the course of the lesson. The lesson itself is expositive, the conversational exercise is to
amplify to its fullest capability the subject of the lesson,
so that it may be entered upon with that degree of intelligence without which it would be not only uninteresting,
but unimproving. Catechetical exercises should always follow reading, to ascertain if the lessons have been understood; and we are satisfied that a hundred pupils may be
occupied and interested for the time proposed by one
teacher, without weariness. We have reason to think that
with lessons of this description the youngest children might
be sufficiently engaged to acquire the art of reading; but,
if it were found otherwise in practice, they might be differently employed during this fraction of the day. We have
placed reading thus early in the morning, because, as it
requires close observation on the part of the children,
and as this acquisition is generally considered to be the
most tedious of all a child's occupations, it is well that
they should proceed with it while their mental and physical energies are in all their strength.

In corroboration of the views we have advocated for
teaching reading, we beg to refer to the following extract
from a lecture by President Lindsley, of the Nashville
University, which appeared in Vol. VI. No. 3. (March
1836,) of the American Annals of Education.

---

* We have the testimony of Locke, Lord Kames, and others, that a
language is better taught by such illustrations than by rules. The rules
may be generally inferred from the illustrations when the intellectual
powers become matured.

† Oral composition is successfully cultivated in the junior school at
Bruce Castle. See second publication of this Society, page 246.

"In order to learn to read, it is by no means indispensable that the long tedious method of the schools for children should be adopted: the process may be rendered extremely simple and easy. It is not necessary to commence even with the alphabet, or to go through a course of spelling in Dilworth or Webster. Adults have very recently been taught to read in penitentiaries, and elsewhere, in a very short period,—even within one or two weeks, in some cases,—who previously did not know a letter. The chaplain, or teacher, opens his Bible,—directs the eye of his pupil to the first verse of the first chapter,—reads it distinctly,—points out each *word* to the learner, and makes him repeat it,—and so on to the end of the verse: in a few minutes the pupil can read the verse backwards or forwards. He now knows the *words* by their *phases* or *appearances* in the book."

Under the peculiarly uninviting title of " The Teacher's Treasure, or Dunce's Delight," there is a little book, the merit of which consists chiefly, though not entirely, in the mechanical construction of its lessons. To this feature it is desirable to call attention. United with the practice we have here recommended, a somewhat satisfactory system of reading might be framed for infants, and other schools where the art has to be acquired. We have not the book to refer to, but the following example will show its object, and we do not recommend the adoption of its plan without having more than once tested its efficiency.

the
the horse,
the horse eats,
the horse eats hay,
the horse eats hay, grass,
the horse eats hay, grass, and
the horse eats hay, grass, and corn.

$9\frac{5}{6}$—$10\frac{1}{6}$. (20 minutes.)

Among other auxiliaries much needed for Infants' Schools, is a manual of gymnastics, plays, and games. Grown-up persons are too apt to forget the amusements of their youth, and too inconsiderately condemn them as useless, or as a waste of time. Teachers of infants must possess flexibility of body and mind; they must be content to be infants, to form infants into men and women. It must be borne in mind that on entering an Infants' School, the child, or rather the parents on his behalf, sacrifice those plays and feats which add to the strength and tend to the development of the animal system; a substitute must therefore be provided, and the exercises of the body and the mind must be so contrived as to relieve each other. It does not derogate from the teacher's authority to be the foremost in games and plays during the hours of recreation, but it contributes to sustain it. In boarding-schools it is observable that those teachers who devote each hour of recess to themselves and their books, are the least popular among the pupils; those who join in the sports of the pupils have deservedly the most esteem and the most influence. Gymnastic exercises for infants must be suitable for their strength, and not too prolonged; and a portion of each pause for exercise must be left entirely to the children, unrestrained. On this subject we cannot do better than refer to " Exercises for the Body," forming Part III. of " Exercises for the Senses." (C. Knight.) Though we should desire to see a manual produced with illustrations of all the positions, and got up in an inexpensive form. Mere outline figures would be sufficient, somewhat similar to those which illustrate the very admirable series of papers on gymnastics in the Anthropological Magazine. The exercises on positions of the body, and on single members, (see Exercises for the Senses,)—should always terminate with brisk walking, commencing with the *ordinary* step, proceeding after a while by the *double* step, and followed by moderate running. The teacher will be occupied not only with the direction of the exercises, but in cases of falls and accidents—to which children are more prone than those who are stronger — to keeping up the spirit of good-humour among the whole party.

10⅙—10½. (20 minutes.)

The occupation of this portion of the morning is made to change on alternate days for two reasons; first, that as many subjects of school instruction as can be made interesting and improving may be introduced; and, again, that too much time may not be devoted to the more scientific branches of instruction, branches which must be resumed on their admission into more advanced schools.

The first notions of number are early formed, to a limited extent; but correct notions cannot be imparted by a repetition of their mere abstract names; a fact which is lost sight of too much by all instructors of the young. Sensible objects must be employed; as beads, beans, cubes, or a handful of grain. The use of the abacus, arithmometer, or bead-table, is pretty generally known; by its help the principles of Addition, Subtraction, Multiplication, Division, Reduction, and Proportion, can be explained. After the simple elements of numbers, including some of their combinations, have been conveyed to the children, the signs for the numerals may be taught them; these will be exhibited by means of chalk and a black tablet, or on one of the painted walls in front of the children. At this state of progress, or even sooner, recourse may be had to the "Arithmetic for Young Children," published by C. Knight; a little work which will be found of great service to those teachers who have not been accustomed to simplify number for the young. Other manuals on this subject are "Lessons on Number," Taylor and Walton; and "Lessons on the Arithmometer," Seeleys. All these works develope the Pestalozzian principles of teaching arithmetic, and these principles have received the sanction of all who have devoted their attention to this branch of instruction. The "Arithmetic for Young Children" is the most familiar, the "Lessons on Number" the most scientific; by scientific we do not mean difficult, for every step is made sure, plain, and easy, the consequence of a strict adherence to the principles on which the lessons are constructed.

The occupation of this portion of time is proposed to be given to geography on alternate days. This subject is to be surely, cautiously, and rationally commenced, or the infants will derive no benefit from it. The children are already aware that objects can be represented on paper; the first lesson to be used should be a representation of the spot whereon they stand—the school-room; in this, let the benches, the gallery, the openings in the walls for doors and windows, be carefully marked; they will, in looking upon it, perceive its relative proportions, and identify it at once. For the next representation, the scale may be decreased; the school, the play-ground, garden, and other appurtenances, should be marked in it, with a portion of the neighbouring country: this will be as readily recognised as the former plan. Still decreasing the scale, and extending the sphere of observation, the next representation may be the plan of the town or village where the school is situated. In this, the street, or other locality, where several of the children reside, may be shown to them; and a comparison made by those who live nearest to the school, those who live farthest, and those at intermediate distances, of the length of time they are occupied in reaching the school, and in returning home. During this procedure, they will be actively engaged in making comparisons, forming analogies, and will at length get a pretty correct idea, aided by the promptings of the teacher, of the size of the town or village they inhabit.

These plans must be prepared by or for the teacher,—they are all of importance; the first to show how perfectly large objects may be drawn on a small scale on paper, for it must be remembered that these children may never have seen a plan or a map before; the others, to take in objects of much greater magnitude on a still smaller scale, and to lead to the inference which, if not seen by the children, must be deduced by the teacher, that much larger portions of country may be thus portrayed.

The next step in geography is one in which we hope to see Infants' Schools assisted, for it is one available to all; a series of county maps should be executed in a bold style, and so as to be furnished at a small expense. Each school will, in most cases, only require the map of the county in which it is situated. On this map will be pointed out the neighbouring towns and villages; such as are known to one or other of the children, and such as they have heard of, being particularly noticed. From this, the transition to the map of England, to that of Europe, and to the globe, becomes perfectly easy. The chief advantages in introducing geography to children thus early, are to be found in the exercise of certain faculties which are not so well developed by any other subject of study, and in the positive knowledge of the extent, productions, (natural and manufactured,) employments, means of communication, &c. of their own and other countries.

$10\frac{1}{2}$—11. (30 minutes.)

A very large collection of objects, both natural and artificial, should have a place in every Infants' School. They are the materials of instruction which can be dispensed with less than any others. Nothing is more easy than to form such a collection; every walk, every shop, retail or manufacturing, every plant, tree, flower, animal, mineral, may be made to contribute to this store. The waste materials and productions of the spinner, weaver, carpenter, worker in metals, are all fraught with instruction, all possessed of properties external and evident to the senses, or hidden and capable of being brought forth; are all works of nature or of art; have all their uses, and are brought or produced in certain localities, or under certain circumstances, which are to be explained when the teacher has drawn forth the ideas and the knowledge which the children may have previously acquired of them, correcting them if they are in error, confirming them when they are right.

At first, a greater variety of objects will be produced for each lesson than will be needed as the children advance in their knowledge of words and properties. The teacher will have to be content with the naming of a few prominent qualities possessed by each object, with some very general information as to its uses, &c.; afterwards, a single object will afford them sufficient scope for a long lesson. It has been found a good plan, at first, to lead the pupils to classify every substance that may be presented to their notice under the terms animal, mineral, vegetable; after that, into natural and artificial objects. Another exercise would be the naming of prominent qualities; *coal,* for instance,—*mineral, natural,—black, hard, opaque,* &c.; then how obtained, as, *dug out of the earth;* next its uses,—*to make fires;* and, lastly, where procured,—as, in *Staffordshire, Shropshire, Northumberland,* &c. This last portion of information would, in a great many instances, have to be conveyed to them by the teacher, and cannot be introduced till they have obtained general ideas in geography, when the situation of some of the coal-basins might be pointed out on the map. The same kind of exercise, modified in detail, but in its general features similar to the above, would be found generally eligible in instruction on objects. A teacher who has never been engaged in teaching from objects, can have no idea of the excitement and attention such lessons invariably produce. Observations on colour, form, size, weight, resistance, number, parts, are continually brought forth, and even the barren soil cannot resist the culture thus invited. The adventurers from Spain who first saw the distant swelling of the Pacific Ocean, were not more elated with their discovery, than are the band of little ones who discover properties in bodies which till then, from lack of observation, or from the want of opportunity to derive sensuous impressions from real objects differing in form, texture, weight, &c. were involved in obscurity. Miss Mayo's " Lessons 'on Objects," and " Exercises for the Senses," before referred to, will assist the teacher; but a more useful compilation than either of these might be made, having especial reference to the wants of Infants' Schools. " Infancy," says Bichat, " is the age of sensation. As everything is new to the infant, everything attracts its eyes, ears, nostrils, &c. That which to us is an object of indifference, is to it a source of pleasure." This is an admirable testimony in favour of lessons from real objects.

11—11½. (30 minutes.)

Walking or marching round the play-ground, or garden, if there be one, may be the recreation for the present half-hour. As the first recess was devoted to somewhat severe exercise, this may be confined to milder kinds of relaxation. The children might be formed into

companies of two, three, four, or even more, abreast;
and go through a series of simple evolutions which would,
for the time, bring new thoughts and feelings into operation, and dispel those connected with their previous
lessons. The more objects of interest could be crowded
without the school-room, and accessible to them, the
better would their hours of exercise be rendered times of
interest and improvement: trees, shrubs, flowers, vegetables, large toy-bricks for building, are objects of this
description. Social games should also be introduced; and,
at least once during the day, all the children should be
engaged together in some game in which they can all take
a part. Such plays help to form the character; they
become practical lessons, and may be made to inculcate
justice, sympathy, self-denial, humility, kindliness, charity.

$11\frac{1}{2}$—12. (30 minutes.)

It is proposed that the business of the morning shall
close with singing. The space of time allotted for this
exercise will be fully occupied with the recitation which
should precede the song, and the song itself. It is desirable that the children should be able to enunciate the
words of their song very distinctly, and this distinctness
will be gradually acquired. The " Singing Master " is a
cheap and fertile source of children's melodies, which
might immediately occupy a place in Infants' Schools.
(*See p.* 305, *First Publication of the Central Society.*)
Mrs. Barbauld's Hymns set to music, and chanted, would
be a delightful change. Many of them are eminently
suitable for such a service; and, provided the music were
simple, and appropriate to the measured sentences and
the subject of the hymn, the effect of such chants would
be pleasing in a high degree.

2—$2\frac{1}{2}$. (30 minutes.)

Our arrangements for the management of Infants'
Schools involve the employment of two persons. During
the present half-hour their labours would be divided: one
of them would superintend those children employed in
writing, or those learning to sew, according to the occupation of the day; the other would be engaged in reading

to the junior ones, and in finding out what impressions were conveyed to their minds by this exercise.

With regard to *writing*, we have known little children write words very well upon slates at four years of age, so that there can be no doubt of their capacity to learn at that age; and sooner we would not begin. The first lessons should be on the elementary forms; the following comprise all these forms, and each should be written till it is conquered.

These being acquired, their progress in the formation and the joining of letters will be rapid. If a copy be not placed before each child, there should, at least, be one between two children. In some schools, we have seen a single large word on a black tablet placed before a long desk full of writers; thus the children opposite to the board see the letters as they should be written, but those receding from such situation, towards the ends of the desk, see such copy more or less in perspective: the distortions thus produced are liable to be imitated. After the elementary forms are acquired, the first and second sheets of the writing copies published by the Commissioners of the National Schools for Ireland may be used: they contain the best examples published of single forms and combined letters. We cannot recommend the three succeeding sheets of these copies; we find fault with such words and phrases as the following :—*Commonwealth, Knight-errant, Mathematical, Give due application to literature, Temperance should guide passion,* &c.; which are unintelligible to most children, not to infants alone. As soon as words can be written, the names and properties of objects, facts in natural history, astronomy, geography, &c. might be chosen, and thus instruction would be going on while the mechanism of writing was acquired. Copies need not be printed from copper-plates, but in a bold script; this type is now so perfect that it offers every advantage that could be needed at a fraction of the expense of copper-plates, thus affording a great diversity in the subjects of the copies. A good drawing of the right hand, with a pen in it, placed constantly before the children when they are writing, facilitates instruction on this point; indeed, too much stress cannot be laid on the importance of mechanical auxiliaries of this description. Ruled slates are very superior to every other material for commencing writing. The lines should not be too wide, as it is impossible for the unaccustomed hands of children to give the pressure and size necessary to show the proportionate strength of large-hand writing. A smallish text-hand is, perhaps, preferable to all others for the first year or two of practice, large enough to admit of the perfect shape of every letter, but not so large as to distress the fingers.

With regard to *sewing*, the kind of work which has the greatest charm for beginners is the acquisition of the different kinds of stitching in coloured cotton, and on a white ground. The work is, to a certain degree, ornamental, and the contrast of colours shows its regularity or irregularity.

$2\frac{1}{2}$—3. (30 minutes.)

This half-hour's exercise should be similar to that of the first half-hour in the morning, with such variations as time and practice will enable a teacher to introduce; such as beating time with the feet or the hands; the actions of trades, as sawing, planing, filing, making shoes; the motions of animals, as flying, swimming, climbing, &c. It is well said by Pestalozzi, in his letters to Greaves, that " physical education ought by no means to be confined to those exercises which now receive the denomination of gymnastics. By means of them strength and dexterity will be acquired in the use of the limbs in general; but particular exercises ought to be devised for the practice of all the senses. How many are there of us whose eye would, without any assistance, judge correctly of a distance, or of the proportion of the size of different objects? How many are there who distinguish and recognise the nice shades of colours, without comparing the one with the other? or whose ear will be alive to the slightest variation of sound? Those who are able to do this with some degree of perfection will be found to derive this faculty either from a certain innate talent, or from constant and laborious practice. Now it is evident that there is a certain superiority in these attainments which natural talent gives without any exertion, and which instruction could never impart, though attended with the most diligent application. But if practice cannot do everything, at least it can do much; and the earlier it is begun, the easier and the more perfect must be the success." In reference to the kind of toys which it is proper to put in the way of children,—and toys of a useful and very permanent description ought to be provided for the out-of-door exercises of all children,—after speaking of the natural manifestations of children to imitate, Pestalozzi says, in another of the letters to Greaves, "Children, who evince some curiosity in the objects brought before their eyes, very soon begin to employ their ingenuity and skill in copying what they have seen. Most children will manage to construct something, in imitation of a building, of any materials they can lay hold of. This desire, which is natural to them, should not be neglected; it is, like all the faculties, capable of regular development. It is, therefore, well done to furnish children with playthings which will facilitate these their first essays."

3—3½. (30 minutes.)

The employment which we have set down for the present half-hour is to exercise a direct moral tendency on the life and conduct of the pupils. Children are generally good listeners when they are talked to on subjects of interest, and within the compass of their understanding. A fund of stories exemplifying good and bad conduct must be at the command of every one who would succeed in making permanent impressions on the minds of children. It is scarcely necessary to point out the sources whence such materials can be obtained, they are so abundant. It is the kind of literature of which, perhaps, the greatest quantity is produced, both in prose and verse; yet great care should be exercised in the selection. It would be very proper that appropriate selections should be made by persons of judgment and experience, in order to economise, as much as possible, the time of teachers. During the reading of them the teacher will occasionally pause, in order to ascertain if the children are receiving the impression which is intended to be conveyed; for these readings are to be the vehicle of direct moral instruction. We repeat that the subject chosen must be well read: the teacher is the model on which the children's style of reading will be formed. It is a practice in some Infants' Schools to set up one of the pupils, whose memory is good, without regard to other qualifications,—as, a correct pronunciation, and freedom from provincialisms,—to lead the others in recitations. This may occasionally be done as a relief to the teacher; but, when this is the case, care should be taken that the *leader* has no vicious habits of speech, lest such should be perpetuated in the school.

As a change of subject for this half-hour, natural history is suggested. Pictures, showing the relative size of beasts, birds, fishes, and reptiles, should be prepared. Insects might be represented of their natural size.* Lessons to accompany these pictures would be desirable, but are not of such great importance as the pictures. A few common minerals would illustrate this portion of natural history, which would occupy a place in the cabinet of objects. Plants would be collected and dried, and thus the pursuit of natural history would be placed under a favourable aspect. The fabulous histories of Mrs. Trimmer might occasionally be read to the children during this lesson; they will enter into their spirit, and apply the moral.

$3\frac{1}{2}$—4. (30 minutes.)

We again refer to what has been said on the subject of physical exercise under the forenoon recesses, and to the use of the " Exercises for the Body," there mentioned.

* There is a cheap series of pictures of this description published by Cotes, Cheapside.

4—4⅓. (20 minutes.)

The exercises on objects are here occasionally varied by lessons on form and lessons on colour. There is, perhaps, no objection to commencing with the elementary forms by drawing them on paper; the name would be given, and illustrations from real objects. Soon after, the common solids, the *sphere, prism, pyramid, cylinder,* &c. and the regular solids, would be introduced to them, and their sides and boundaries would furnish ample illustrations. For a school of a hundred children a cube of not less than three inches should be used, and other solids of similar proportions. The " Lessons on Form," published by Taylor and Walton, will be an excellent text-book for the teacher. Colour is a less important subject than form; but to young children it is always amusing, and fruitful of examples. Nothing that draws forth their observations can be unimportant; we have therefore assigned colour a place, for it should receive decided attention at least once a week. On every colour to which the attention of the children is directed, they will be ready with. their observations. *Blue, red,* and *yellow* will be the first to be taken; and afterwards the shades of these, and the compound colours into which they are capable of being formed. Wafers, bits of coloured paper, printed cotton, cloth, silk, &c. will all find a place in the cabinet of objects, to be called forth on occasion of these lessons.

After the conclusion of this lesson, another recess will take place for twenty minutes, and the children will then return to the school-room sufficiently invigorated to go through the devotional exercises of the evening; these will be conducted in a mode similar to those of the morning, except that the singing takes the last place instead of the first.

We have not mentioned recitation, natural philosophy, or drawing, amongst the exercises to be brought within the range of studies. It is intended, however, that these shall be included under one or other of the heads we have adopted. Recitation is one mode of exercising the verbal memory, and it is included in the art of reading with propriety and elegance. Children are generally close imitators of manner, and success will more probably attend the efforts of the teacher, if, when he tells his pupils *what* to learn, he also shows them *how* it is to be learned. Natural philosophy is always attractive; and there is a multitude of experiments common enough for every one to perform, which may be performed under the most ordinary circumstances of convenience, and which are always interesting. For a guide-book, " The Little Philosopher," by Jacob Abbott, may be mentioned. Drawing comes under the head *Form*. Occasionally the elder pupils may be employed in the mechanical practice of drawing, while the younger ones are engaged in their verbal lessons A little work, entitled " Drawing for Young Children," lately published by C. Knight, is a very commendable attempt to introduce this art to the young, by setting before them the forms of well-known objects.

The higher departments of instruction will not at present be followed up in the generality of Infants' Schools. There is, however, a class of schools now coming into existence, such as the junior school at Bruce Castle, the preparatory schools attached to the Colleges at Hull, and the junior school belonging to the Mechanics' Institution at Liverpool, where facilities will exist for proving and perpetuating all that is good in the infant system.

We have thus exhibited a plan for conducting Infants' Schools, and shown how it may be filled up and brought into operation. There is a considerable diversity of opinion as to the number of hours children should be occupied during the afternoon. Some persons think two hours after dinner long enough to confine infants. This is a consideration of no great importance. During four months of the year, dismissal must take place at four o'clock; with the provision here made for bodily exercise and recreation, we cannot consider six hours a day too long a time for the school to be opened. These hours of recreation we would on no account abridge.

We believe the employment of *masters* in Infants' Schools has originated under some mistaken idea. It is clearly the province of women to take charge of the little

ones. Nature has ordained it in the especial constitution
of women. They are the first friends, the guides, the
helpers, the comforters, of little children; their softer
feelings, their larger endowment of the affective faculties,
their early education, so to term it, in the modes of managing infants, their knowledge of the nursing, clothing,
and amusements which are required, point to them as
the most proper persons to be employed in rearing, instructing, and educating infants. Such a class of teachers
has to be formed. Respectable young persons in the
middle ranks of society abound who have received sufficient instruction to become pupils in a normal and training school, and who would then be qualified to direct and
sustain the schools over which they might be placed.
At the same time, the inducement so to devote themselves
must be sufficient to enable them to live in comfort, and
to provide for future years. We cannot conceive of an
Infants' School being thoroughly well managed but by
two teachers: one of these should be the mistress, and
the other an assistant; the latter might have undergone
the course of instruction imparted at the normal school,
and have been removed thence for actual experience in
training, and in the mechanical parts of teaching. In
almost all schools a division of the infants into *elder* and
younger must occasionally take place; at such times, none
must be left unengaged; two persons are therefore necessary: besides this, among little children there are
various causes of discomfort and uneasiness which occasionally require the aid and oversight of one person
while the other is occupied in teaching.

The circumstances at present most unfavourable to a
more perfect management of, and system for, Infants'
Schools, are the want of teachers, and the want of good
lessons and manuals on the different subjects of instruction. The former can only be supplied by liberal aid
from government in the establishment and support of
normal and training schools.

The objects in selecting or compiling appropriate books
or lessons are, *good matter, and a suitable manner of conveying it.* The instruction to be conveyed must be such
as shall tend to the improvement of the infant mind, and

such as can be comprehended; the arrangement must be suitable to the subject with reference to infant teaching, and each lesson so graduated as to be founded on that which has preceded it both in sentiment and language.

The mistakes most commonly fallen into by those who provide instruction for the young can only be corrected by repeated trials, reiterated failures, and, at length, slow but certain success. *No books of instruction ought ever to be published till they have been repeatedly tested in manuscript.*

There is one consideration connected with this subject which has never been brought with sufficient force and distinctness before the public. Infants' Schools are available to the richer classes of society; and, under the auspices of wealth and intelligence combined, they might realize advantages which the schools for the poor can never accomplish. (See Second Publication of this Society, page 229.)

These schools might be of three classes:—first, as day schools; secondly, as weekly boarding schools; thirdly, as altogether boarding schools. They might, in either case, be established by a proprietary body consisting of the parents of the children there to be educated. Each plan has its advantages, but, for various reasons, we should consider the weekly boarding school as the most eligible; it would unite school with home education, and give the teacher an influence which could never be attained by the daily school system; the course of education would also be less liable to interruption than in the daily school. It would, besides, give freedom to the teachers from the Friday evening to the ensuing Monday morning,—the time when the pupils would be at their various homes. As daily schools, supposing each to contain sixty children, they would be sustained at an expense of four pounds a year for each pupil; as weekly boarding schools, at an expense of about sixteen pounds a year for each; and as boarding schools of the ordinary kind, for about twenty pounds a year for each child. If the premises belonged to the proprietary, the expense in each case would be proportionally diminished. The amounts here mentioned would in any case include every expense;

remunerating salaries to a sufficient number of teachers
and other attendants, an ample supply of books and apparatus for the school,—in fact, everything that could be
devised to render the children intelligent and happy, a
credit to their teachers, and a blessing to their parents
and society.

Infants' Schools have been sustained for the poor as
creditably, under all circumstances, as could be expected ;
their wants have been made known, the obstacles to complete success may be removed. Let Infants' Schools be
formed for the rich ; let attempts be made to supply
those aids which have been indicated as wanting, under
the direction of those who can command talent and experience. The press will multiply successful auxiliaries
to instruction, so as to afford these benefits to the schools
for the poor at a cheap rate ; and the blessing of instruction may then be diffused throughout the country. If
this be not done, to the legislature alone can we look for
that support, that encouragement, those pecuniary means,
and such other arrangements as shall enable the infant
system to be perpetuated and improved as its importance
deserves.

C. BAKER.

COUNTY COLLEGES OF AGRICULTURE.

IF the various ways in which a farmer has to deal with nature be considered, it can hardly be denied that he must either be possessed of an intimate acquaintance with it, or be continually committing errors, which, if they are not entirely fatal to his success, must, at all events, materially lessen it. The objects of living, paying rent, and putting by a something annually, are, no doubt, attained by many hard-working and frugal persons who are possessed of a very small proportion of accurate knowledge respecting any of the many objects upon which they are daily engaged. But with how much waste of labour are their gains acquired? and how much less profit do they realize than they might? and it should always be remembered, that advantages neglected are money lost; power misapplied is money lost; and resources unknown are money lost. Nor let it be thought that mere experience will cure this; if the alternative were either success or total failure, the wits of the farmers would be quickened to discover the right from the wrong, and experience would be attended with profit; but such is not the case. In the business of a farmer the degrees of being wrong are infinite; his gross results may be right so far as securing himself from positive ruin, and even obtaining a competence, but they may be wrong as being greatly inferior to what they might be; and if inferior to what they might be, inferior to what they ought to be.

In manufactures the relative advantages of different processes are soon known from the circumstance of manufacturers living in large towns—and those in the same line for the most part in the same town, as at Manchester and Birmingham. There the intercourse which results from proximity enables the parties to compare the results of different modes of proceeding with regard to the same thing. That which falls short of the maximum of result is soon thrown aside and abandoned by all. People thus become alive

to the manner in which modes can vary, and know how to
appreciate the advantage which one has over another:
the minds of people are thus quickened to the possibility
of improvement. Again: that which is best for one
manufacturer is best for all in the same line; so that
when a manufacturer has ascertained the modes by
which another has been enabled to increase his produce,
he knows the mode by which he can do the same.
The probability is, that if a person were to attempt
to engage in any one of the leading manufactures in this
country, and were to live away from one of the great
towns at which it is carried on, he would soon fall
so far behind as to be unable to bring his produce into
market at a profit. Farmers have none of these advantages; in the first place, they cannot so associate together as to know the results of all the successful experiments which concern them; and in the second, as
not only the soil and other physical characteristics of
large tracts of country differ from each other, but that of
every farm also, the practice of each individual farmer
must consequently be a modification of the general practice to suit his own local circumstances. The results,
moreover, of any new experiment in agriculture are
more tardily worked out. A season, at least, necessarily
elapses before the success of a single new vegetable introduction can be satisfactorily tested; several years are
requisite for ascertaining the superiority of one rotation
of crops over another. Thus the farmer has not one
unvarying subject matter to deal with which will permit
him to adopt wholly the practice of any other person
with a certainty of success; and even if he could, his
insulated position would not enable him to acquire
accurate information with regard to the means of producing the greatest results, while his own individual
and unaided experience must, as we have shown, be
insufficient. Can anything be done to better his position, and what? We shall endeavour to answer this
question. A farmer may be accurately instructed, among
other things, in the nature and qualities of the things
by which he is surrounded; he may be made acquainted
with the form of animals which best adapts them

for different purposes; the characteristic qualities of different soils; the modes of qualifying and improving each; the power of different descriptions of manure and other improving substances; the circumstances from which each derives its power, so far as they are known; the effects of different soils upon different crops; the rotation of crops most approved, with the reason thereof; the different machines which have been invented for shortening labour; the different modes of feeding animals in different places, with the economical advantages of each. He can further be habituated to test, by a series of varied previous experiments on a small scale, changes which it is proposed to execute on a large one. He can be taught how to apply mechanical power to the greatest advantage, and thus save labour; he can also be instructed in keeping accurate accounts, in order to enable him to judge with precision not only respecting his gross profits, but of the profit and loss in each detail of the system pursued. He can, in fact, have that enlarged and accurate knowledge of principle imparted to him, and those habits of careful practice formed, which will enable him to proceed in a manner not only intelligent, but safe; and that to a degree which no person who could not also take advantage of the variety of circumstances, and avoid the many mistakes which he, if he could, would be enabled to do. " Lavoisier, the celebrated chemist, is a remarkable example of the advantages which may be derived from the application of science to agriculture, even without a minute knowledge of the art of farming. By following an enlightened system, he is said to have doubled in nine years the produce in grain of his lands, whilst he quintupled the number of his flocks."*

In order that the force of the above observations may be brought more distinctly before the reader, it may be as well to adduce a few instances which have been drawn from Sir H. Davy's Agricultural Chemistry, and the works upon British and Flemish husbandry, published by the Society for the Diffusion of Useful Knowledge, which elucidate some of the points with regard to which

* Notice sur Lavoisier in Bibliotheque du Chimiste, tom. vii. p. 121.

it would be advantageous to communicate accurate knowledge to farmers. These must be considered as only a few out of a multitude, which our space does not permit us to enumerate.

" It is scarcely possible to enter upon any investigation in agriculture without finding it connected, more or less, with doctrines or elucidations derived from chemistry.

" If land be unproductive, and a system of ameliorating it is to be attempted, the sure method of obtaining the object is by determining the cause of its sterility, which must necessarily depend upon some defect in the constitution of the soil, which may be easily discovered by chemical analysis.

" Some lands of good apparent texture are yet sterile in a high degree ; and common observation and common practice afford no means of ascertaining the cause, or of removing the effect. The application of chemical tests in such cases is obvious; for the soil must contain some noxious principle, which may be easily discovered, and probably easily destroyed.

" Are any of the salts of iron present ? They may be decomposed by lime.—Is there an excess of silicious sand ? The system of improvement must depend on the application of clay and calcareous matter.—Is there a defect of calcareous matter ? The remedy is obvious.—Is an excess of vegetable matter indicated ? It may be removed by liming, paring, and burning.—Is there a deficiency of vegetable matter ? It is to be supplied by manure.

" A question concerning the different kinds of limestone to be employed in cultivation often occurs. To determine this fully in the common way of experience, would demand a considerable time, perhaps some years, and trials which might be injurious to crops ; but by the simple chemical tests the nature of a limestone is discovered in a few minutes; and the fitness of its application, whether as a manure for different soils, or as a cement, determined.

" Peat earth of a certain consistence and composition is an excellent manure ; but there are some varieties of peats which contain so large a quantity of ferruginous matter as to be absolutely poisonous to plants. Nothing can be more simple than the chemical operation for determining the nature and the probable uses of a substance of this kind.

" There has been no question on which more difference of opinion has existed than that of the state in which manure ought to be ploughed into the land; whether recent, or when it has gone through the process of fermentation ; and this question is still a subject of discussion : but whoever will refer to the simplest principles of chemistry, cannot entertain a doubt upon the subject. As soon as dung begins to decompose it throws off its volatile parts, which are the most valuable and most efficient. Dung which has fermented, so as to become a mere soft cohesive mass, has generally lost from one-third to one-half of its most useful constituent elements; and that it may exert its full action upon the plant, and lose none of its nutritive powers, it should evidently be applied much sooner, and long before decomposition has arrived at its ultimate results.*

" The total ignorance or disregard of the power of urine on vegetation cannot be better shown than by the fact that a large cowkeeper, near London, having built a reservoir for the urine of several hundred cows, thinking to make some profit by the sale of it, found so little demand for it at a very low price, or even for nothing, that he destroyed the tank, and let the urine into the common sewers, to add to the variety of rich impurities which daily flow into the Thames. A gentleman from Flanders to whom this was mentioned asserted, that in his country there would have been many applications to contract for the urine at the rate of 2l. per cow per annum."†

" There is probably no species of manure so generally neglected, and yet so deserving of attention ; for, although the largest portion of what is produced in most farm-yards is there necessarily absorbed by the litter, and consequently profitably applied, yet large quantities are constantly allowed to run to waste."‡

In a paper addressed to the Board of Agriculture by

* Davy's Agricultural Chemistry. † Flemish Husbandry, p. 94.
‡ British Husb. vol. i. p. 274.

Baron Schulenburgh, one of its honorary members, he states, that in Sweden the urine is collected from the farm offices, and pumped over the dung and other substances in a state of compost: it is then diluted with water, and laid chiefly upon meadow land; but it is also applied to green crops; and the effects upon the soil, though gradually diminishing, are generally considered to last for years.

" In Switzerland also the mistwasser or manure water is sprinkled over the surface of the meadows by means of large water casks and perforated water troughs, immediately after the cutting of the scythe, which makes the grass to spring up again with great vigour in a very short time."*

Mr. Harley, proprietor of the celebrated dairy near Glasgow, says, " That the advantage of irrigating grass lands with cows' urine almost exceeds belief: last season some small fields were cut six times, averaging fifteen inches in length at each cutting."†

" At an arable farm near Courtray, consisting of 120 acres, thirty cows are constantly kept, and six horses, besides young heifers and colts."‡

" It would startle a farmer of 400 acres of arable land if he were told that he should constantly feed 100 head of cattle, and yet this would not be too great a proportion if the Flemish system were strictly followed." §

" The liquid manure is the great secret of the Flemings, by which they have converted poor sands into rich mould, and produced in the lightest soil crops of wheat as fine and as heavy as we do in our best clay looms."||

An eminent agricultural author, Mr. Malcolm, complains " that he has not in any one instance been able to find anything like system in the mechanical arrangement of the components of farm-yard mixens, which he generally found put together as they arise, according to circumstances, and without any regard to rule. Hence it follows that their real value as manure can never be distinctly known to the farmer; nor can he apply that

* British Husb. vol. i. p. 275.   † British Husb. vol. i. p. 277.
‡ Flemish Husb. p. 82.   § Flemish Husb. p. 94.
|| Flemish Husbandry, p. 94.

proportion which a more accurate knowledge of the contents would enable him to apportion to different kinds of
grain, or to the particular times and seasons in which
they can be most advantageously applied." After quot-
ing an opinion opposing Mr. Malcolm with regard to the importance of separating different kinds of manure, the author
of the work on British Husbandry remarks, that warm and
cold soils require manures of a contrary nature; an advanced stage of their fermentation is in some cases less
favourable to vegetation than in others; and in the instance of potatoes it is well known that stable dung is employed with more effect alone than when mixed. It may,
therefore, be advisable that horse-litter in particular should
be separately kept in the yards, not merely for the purpose
just mentioned, but that, as being of a hotter nature than
any common dung, it may be mixed with that of other
cattle in such proportions as may be thought best adapted
to the purposes for which the compost is required.*

From ignorance respecting the mode in which lime
operates in fertilizing land, it is often used so injudiciously,
that " many thousand acres in every part of the kingdom
have been run to a state of almost total infertility."† A
farmer who knows not the reason why one dose of it
is effective, would expect similar results from repeated
applications. Mr. Falkner, a gentleman who has for many
years been conversant with agriculture, thus writes upon
the subject of lime :—" The application of this manure is
most suitable when soils contain a great quantity of rough
vegetable matter, which quick lime breaks down or de-
composes, and thus renders a portion of it soluble in
water. Though this operation is understood by some,
they are not aware that in this case a portion is taken up
by the lime, from which it cannot afterwards escape, and
is therefore lost to the uses of vegetation as soluble matter or manure. This is, however, an unavoidable condition of the benefit afforded by lime under such circumstances. But the ignorance of this operation leads often
to a great misapplication. The author has often seen
farmers mix quick lime with dung or half decomposed

* British Husbandry, vol. i. p. 236.   † British Husbandry.

manure, and even put it upon land recently folded with
sheep, which is obviously improper, for the reason above
stated, as the lime in this case unites with a portion of
the soluble manure, and destroys it."

Some very efficient manures are not generally known :
burnt clay, for instance ; of its power some extraordinary
effects are recorded : and again, all fish and oily substances
should be reduced into a compost before being used for
most crops, although, in a crude state, they may be favourable to some ; for barley, for instance, they are good; but
for oats the land " is poisoned."* In some counties fish
is often put upon the ground in its crude state.

A knowledge of mechanics is necessary for the simplest
purposes. In order that power of any sort may be turned
to the best account, we must be acquainted with the principle upon which its application depends. If a farmer had in
his stable two horses, one small and muscular, and another
heavy and weak, how is he respectively to harness each of
them to draw different carriages, so that the strength of
the one and the weight of the other shall be duly taken
advantage of? That the observations which all the world
make are not sufficient, is evident from the fact of the
powers of horses being often paralyzed by a misapplication of their respective qualities.† And Mr. Falkner informs us that he has seen very good machinery thrown
aside as useless, merely because the farmer had experienced some inconvenience from the machine being out of
order, when the least mechanical skill would have recti-
fied the fault.

Proverbial sayings, without a knowledge of physiology,
are not sufficient to preserve from error. Plant shallow
is such a saying; but after observing this rule as far as
regards planting the root no great depth in the ground,

---

* British Husbandry.

† The general practice of harnessing horses in a team one before
another, by which so large an amount of power is lost in most farms, is
often referable to a similar ignorance of mechanics. There are, however, localities and employments in which the practice is retained for
substantial reasons. For instance, when in ploughing it is desirable
that the horses, in consequence of the stiffness of the soil, should walk
in the furrow.

we have seen the turf and stones piled up to some height against the stem of the tree, by which practice the evils of deep planting are to a considerable extent incurred. Such information as the following would prevent the possibility of either such an error, or the contrary one of leaving any portion of the root exposed. "The green colour of parenchyma depends on the exposure of its epidermis to the light and air, for when a portion of the stem of a tree is excluded from light, as is sometimes done in planting, when the tree is placed deeper in the soil than it stood before transplanting, the green colour is destroyed in that part of it which is covered with the soil, and which in course of time assumes the colour of the root, and if much moisture exists in the soil, and the tree be not young, the bark so covered decays, and the tree dies. Should the soil be dry, however, and the plant young, the bark in question is gradually converted into root-bark; during this conversion of the stem-bark into that of the root, the plant advances but little, if any, in growth, but exhibits an unhealthy appearance by the paleness of its leaves and the weak growth of its shoots. The same effects are in a great degree observable from the opposite error of planting too shallow, which is when a portion of the root nearest to the stem is left above ground."* "Thousands of acres of woods and planta-tions in most of our counties," says Mr. Falkner, "are utterly ruined from a want of the knowledge of the pro-cess of vegetation, and that the free admission of air and light are indispensable conditions to the healthy growth of trees, and the progressive increase of timber. The author speaks from actual observation, extended over large districts, when he asserts that gross and wretched neglect of this subject is the rule, and tolerable attention to it the exception. If the national loss from the neglect of planting, and the mismanagement of existing forests and plantations, were duly estimated, it would appear in-credible to those who have not devoted their attention to the subject, and more particularly when the improvement of climate, and consequent fertility which planting effects, is taken into the account. Immense advantage, therefore,

* Planting. Publication of the Useful Knowledge Society.

would be derived to this department of rural management from a knowledge of principles."

With regard to animals, not only should the points be well known, but the principles upon which their value depend. The depth of hock, the slant or straightness of the shoulder or pasterns in horses, should have their reasons, as without them the judgment of the eye with regard to the fact has but half its value. Although the advantages of drawing are by no means confined to this point, still for the purpose of assisting the eye to scrutinize the form of an animal with accuracy, it is of great importance. If a young man is not only familiar with the anatomy of horses and cattle, but has himself delineated the most approved forms with his pencil, he will find that it will give him great facility in appreciating the differences in animals which would escape the eye which is less disciplined to form; he will judge accurately of the width of chest, the hooping and depth of barrel, the width of loin, shortness of legs, and smallness of bones, in cattle.

It is admitted generally that farmers for the most part keep but indifferent accounts, and many of them none at all; they look to the money they have at the end of the year after paying the outgoings, as indicating the success or failure of their practice. This rough mode of proceeding is quite incompatible with any systematic improvement in agriculture, because it is not only the largeness of the crops which is a test of the goodness of the system, but also the cost at which they are raised; and although the sum in hand at the end of the year may indicate this with regard to the entire crops of the farm, it does not enable an analysis to be made which will show the losses and gains upon each crop, so that an accurate judgment may be formed as to what should be abandoned and what continued. Again, if the account at the end of the year is in favour of the farmer, he may rest contented if he likes, without inquiring as to the means of improving his system; but if the contrary be the case, he has nothing to look to, which will indicate with precision the false calculations which he has made, and thus enable him to correct his practice. The late Mr. John Billingsby, a very distinguished agriculturist, attributed the success and superiority which he attained in his profession " to a strict adherence to the plan of not only settling annually the profit and loss of the farm in the gross, but also the profit and loss of every crop."* How much some of the most intelligent agriculturists are aware of their deficiencies, the following passage is an evidence.

Mr. Love, the chairman of the Sevenoaks Union, thus writes :—" What, sir, as a body, do we know of the chemical properties of the various soils we cultivate, or even of the different manures most generally used and approved by us to assist production? Positively nothing. We have learned by the experience handed down to us for several generations, that on some soils a fallow is the best season for wheat; on others a clover lay. But the why and because, who can tell us? Now, sir, this is precisely the information I could wish that we, as a body, could give each other, and this I am sanguine enough to believe we might do if we were to apply our minds to the study of chemistry. The more I learn of my business, the more sensibly am I impressed with the very trifling amount of my knowledge; and I am compelled to admit that, as a science, agriculture is even now but in its infancy."

An intelligent gentleman who farms a large tract of land, and is deservedly considered one of the best agriculturists in the county of Kent, informed us, as a proof of the defective character of the education which he had received, that although he knew pretty well the number of cart-loads contained in one of his own dung-heaps, he knew no means of calculating the contents of one which did not belong to him.

From the best information which we have been able to obtain, the character of the schools attended by the children of farmers is as follows: firstly, those for the wealthy, in which the instruction given does not differ materially from that imparted to the children of the higher classes generally. It comprises for the most part reading, writing, ciphering, and the rudiments of a

* British Husbandry.

classical education; that is to say, by the time a boy
quits school he has learned to construe a little Latin poetry, and perhaps one or two of the easiest prose authors,
to write a few Latin verses, to conjugate a few Greek
verbs, and possibly to translate a little of some Greek
author. He may also have learned some French, but
not enough to enable him either to speak the language,
or even to read it with ease.

In geography, if he is a clever boy, he will probably
know where to find in an atlas of the ancient world most
of the towns and rivers of ancient Greece, Italy, Asia
Minor, and Gaul, while the localities of the most important places in civilized Europe, and even in his own country, will probably not be known to him; and if the localities are, the important statistical information connected
with them certainly will not be. In fact, when, at the age
of fifteen or sixteen years, he returns home from school,
his father will probably have reason to complain, that although he has been at school for seven or eight years,
he cannot keep farm accounts, survey a field, calculate
the weight of hay in a stack, measure a piece of timber;
that he is ignorant of the points and diseases of animals,
the natural history of the plants which he will have to
cultivate, the application of the mechanical powers in the
simplest manner, or of any other matters which will enable him to enter upon his business with a groundwork
qualifying him to receive advice, and use his own experience with profit. Not only will he be found deficient in
all this, but in all probability unable to write with propriety a letter of business for his father; added to which,
there will be some danger of his despising the business
for which he is destined, and the acquirements requisite
for the intelligent prosecution of it. In this state it is
believed that many wealthy farmers receive their sons
back from school. Can it be wondered that they do not set
any great value upon an education such as this? For any
practical end, what can the boys do? The entire stock
of knowledge which is to stand them in stead in future life,
even from the first principles, has yet to be acquired at
home.

At the schools attended by the children of the poorer

class of farmers, little more than reading, writing, and arithmetic is taught, and these arts in an indifferent manner, while the children, for the most part, remain but a short period of time, too short to be of any permanent service to them, even if the discipline they were submitted to was good. To all such as these the principles of their business are for ever sealed: they can have no opportunity of knowing more than the practice of the immediately surrounding district informs them of.

If the description of schools here mentioned is in reality that which is attended by the children of farmers, it is evident that farther than as the children are taught to read, write, and cipher, they learn nothing which can be turned to account in their future profession, and that they are by no means calculated either to advance the application of science to husbandry, or to give any advantages to their children which will enable them to do so.

The truth of the statement which has been made with regard to the character of existing schools, and the importance of giving the advantages which have been mentioned, will perhaps be admitted. But how is the thing to be done? Granted that it is desirable, is it practicable? Very extensive and peculiarly-constructed premises would be requisite,—houses, schools, dormitories, farm-buildings, workshops, and these too surrounded by a farm of such extent and of such variety of soil as to be made available for the purposes of practical instruction in the principal divisions of the subject. Several thousand pounds of capital must be expended in making these preliminary arrangements; added to which, masters of high ability, of various descriptions, and in considerable numbers, must be engaged from the first at high yearly salaries. Skilled persons too must also be employed to give instruction in the several mechanical arts, and in fact all the train of expense necessary for the successful execution of the plan, must be incurred from the moment that the doors of the school are opened to receive pupils. Besides this, the farmers generally could not afford to pay more than a very limited annual sum for the education of their children; so that, as the surplus, after furnishing board and lodging, would be small, large

numbers would be absolutely requisite. Could an individual, and an individual of the rank (supposing him to
be otherwise qualified) generally engaged in conducting
schools for this class of society, calculate with any certainty upon such a number of pupils from the first as
would make the thing a reasonable speculation? and
could such an individual command a capital sufficient for
such a purpose? or if he could, would he so apply it?
We think not; we think that he would not be able either
to command sufficient confidence to enable him at once,
if at all, to obtain the large number requisite for the success of the scheme, or the capital for carrying it on efficiently, if even he could obtain the requisite number of
scholars—while there would be even still greater difficulty
in finding a person having the funds who would be willing
so to apply them. The profits arising from success would
not be large, and people who have money ever consider
(and with propriety too) how they can put it out to the
greatest advantage to themselves and families. An undertaking then, such as this, is not for an individual. It
is true that we have one great example of an individual
not only founding but perfecting such an establishment
as we desire to see, in De Fellenberg. But De Fellenberg is a man of an age; we must not wait until his like
arises in this country. He has shown us what to do;
and if we would do it, and do it upon such a scale,
and so generally throughout the country, as to be of
material service, we must do it by such means as will
not call for more than moderate sacrifices from any person, while the agents employed in carrying it out must
not only not be called upon to make a sacrifice, but see in
what they are employed to do the certain means of an
honest and honourable livelihood; and even those who
are called upon to make a small immediate sacrifice
should have a prospect of such great eventual advantages,
either in the education of their children or in the improvement of their estates, as would operate forcibly upon
the minds of all intelligent and reflecting persons.

We should then suggest, that a sum of 10,000*l.* be
raised by shares of 25*l.* each, as a loan, upon which
interest, at the rate of four per cent. should be paid,

and that this should be applied to the purposes of purchasing a piece of land of eight or ten acres in extent, and erecting and fitting up upon it buildings suitable for such an establishment as is proposed. This land should adjoin the property of some nobleman or gentleman, who would engage to let to the establishment any number of acres, from 100 to 400, upon a long lease of twenty-one years, at a fair rental.* In any of our large agricultural counties it would not, it is conceived, be difficult to find 300 children whose parents now pay 25 guineas per annum and upwards for their education, who would be happy to obtain for them the advantages which such an institution would afford, provided they could do so without any larger pecuniary sacrifice than they now make for what is so totally inefficient. Supposing, then, that 300 children entered the school at first, the parents of each of whom paid 25 guineas per annum, this would give an annual income of 7,875*l.* It has been ascertained that boys can be boarded upon good substantial food, with plenty of it, even when the food is purchased, for the sum of 15*l.* per annum each. Supposing, then, that this sum be allowed, 4,500*l.* will be applied to maintaining the children. A staff of ten masters would, we should conceive, be requisite for the government of such a school; and we should propose that their salaries should be as follows:—

A head master 350*l.* per annum, and 1*l.* 1*s.* per annum for each pupil	£665
Second master	250
Third master or head bailiff . .	150
Fourth master	100
Six assistants, at 50*l.* per annum each . .	300
Making a Total, per annum, of . .	£1,465

Supposing the borrowed capital to be 15,000*l.*, 600*l.* would have to be paid annually for interest; leaving 1,310*l.* per annum to the payment of miscellaneous ex-

---

* If either there could be raised, or the government would give, a sum sufficient for the purchase of an estate, it would be very desirable. An institution of the public character of that proposed ought not to depend for its efficiency upon the manner in which the neighbouring proprietors of land were disposed with regard to it.

penses, and making such additions and changes as circumstances might suggest. This calculation leaves entirely out of consideration all profit to be derived from the cultivation of the farm, which, as it would be cultivated by the pupils, and upon the most approved principles, ought to be considerable. This profit, whatever it might be, should be applied, together with all other surplus, to the admission of the children at as low a rate as possible. When the school shall have been made efficient, this should be the great object to attain ; as the greater the number who can be made to participate in the advantages of such an establishment, the more certainly would its effect upon agriculture be generally felt. The sum of 25 guineas, which must necessarily be required in the first instance, would, without doubt, serve to confine the school too much to the higher class of yeomen ; but the process of saving, such as has been marked out, together with the gradual increase of numbers and the profits of the farm, would, after a time, reduce the sum required from the parents to 20*l*. or 15*l*. ; as, when it is considered that the food will be directly supplied from the land cultivated by the boys, the sum indicated as being required for their maintenance will be deemed too large.

It would not, then, be hard to find the funds for the establishment of such a school as has been proposed, provided that the parents of the children could be made to feel a confidence that the advantages proposed would really be afforded. This confidence, it is conceived, might without difficulty be obtained; and for this purpose it is suggested,—I. that the shares by which the capital is to be raised should be small, say of 10*l*. each, so that a large proportion of the yeomanry and farmers might be possessed of them. This arrangement would not prevent those noblemen and gentlemen who were anxious to further the object in view from taking ten or twenty shares, or any number they might please. 2. That the directing committee or council should be chosen out of the shareholders, and that the holder of each share should be entitled to vote at their election.

This constitution would bring the proposed establishment within that denomination of schools called proprietary. These schools have in many instances not been successful, owing, as we have reason to believe, to an indiscreet interference on the part of directors and proprietors in their immediate management. This, as may easily be conceived, is an evil of considerable magnitude, and such a one as no master fitted for the high office of superintending an establishment of the character proposed, either would or ought to submit to. As this, however, is a known evil, it might be provided against at the first establishment of the association for obtaining the object in view. The utmost discretion should be used in the selection of the head master; but, having selected him, the whole government of the establishment should be vested in him; and for the purpose of effectually giving it to him, he should, it is conceived, have the power of appointing and dismissing the under masters and assistants. Having thus the sole control, the head master would have the entire responsibility, and should annually give an account of his stewardship to the body of shareholders; and, as the committee would be continually inspecting, they could, in the event of any gross mismanagement, call a special meeting, and oblige him to give an explanation of his conduct at any time. But it is suggested that it would be highly inconvenient to permit any parent or shareholder who chose, to have the power of intermeddling with and obstructing the course which it might seem to the master fit to pursue. The absolute power of the master and the superintendence of a society might thus, it is conceived, be advantageously combined.

It may, however, be desirable that we should state more at length our reasons for placing the appointments of under masters and assistants in the hands of the head master. All societies which have the disposal of good places have a tendency to job. This will be most effectually checked by giving the appointments to a person who is responsible for, and whose character is involved in their efficiency. If the subordinate appointments were to be made by the body of shareholders, numerous inconveniences would arise. Firstly, it would be impossible to fix the responsibility anywhere. Members of the society would then be privately canvassed;

and, as it would not be the peculiar business of any one of them to scrutinize the qualifications of the candidates, they would vote in favour of those in whose success they had been interested from other causes than that of fitness. Bad appointments would thus take place; nor would there be any method of securing that when one bad one had been cancelled, the appointment which succeeded it should be any better.   Secondly, supposing the greatest anxiety on the part of all the shareholders to make good appointments, no person could be so good a judge of the qualifications which ought to be required as he who, from the circumstance of directing, must be thoroughly acquainted with all the deficiencies of the school; added to which, the head master would have the institution more completely under his control in all its bearings, if the under masters depended upon him solely.

These reasons for not intrusting the appointments to the body of shareholders apply also, although not with equal force, to the committee of management.   A divided authority with them would, we think, place the head master in a false position.   It is true that the committee would probably attend to the suggestions of the master, but they might not.   The utmost direct authority that should be given to the committee in this particular should be that of exercising a veto.

The success of the school will then entirely depend upon the choice of the head master.   But who is to choose him?   A most important question.   Certainly not the body of shareholders, for they might job this all-important situation.   The appointment should be made by a number so few that they might be pointed at as responsible for it.   The committee of management should, we conceive, perform this duty; but under restrictions as to the class of persons from whom the master should be selected.   The body of shareholders, although for the reasons before stated, not those with whom the appointment of the individual should rest, are precisely the persons who can best determine the class from whom he ought to be selected.   And it may be as well to observe, that in order that the institution should, from the period of its foundation, command that respect to which, for the sake of the great object it would be directed to, it is to be desired that it should obtain, the head master ought, it is conceived, to be looked up to as a person not only distinguished for those high moral qualifications which are indispensable for the schoolmaster, but also for his scientific acquirements. He should also, it is conceived, be conversant with the application of some department of science to practical purposes.

Although we would thus vest absolute power in the head master for the purpose of enabling him to direct efficiently the studies and employments of the school, we would relieve him entirely from any trouble or responsibility with regard to the pecuniary affairs of the society. These we would place entirely in the hands of the committee and the officer whom they might appoint for the purpose of assisting them.

Respecting the character of the instruction which it would be desirable to impart, a general idea has already been given. The greater proportion of it should be selected as bearing directly or indirectly upon the future business of the pupil; and the point to which many studies should be carried should be determined by the point to which they can be rendered practically useful. It would not, we conceive, be desirable to allow any of the pupils, for instance, to devote themselves so exclusively to any one science as to prevent their giving attention to all the other departments of knowledge with which it is necessary that they should be made acquainted for the successful prosecution of their profession. There will at all times be pupils of high talent disposed to do so: but the proposed institution will not be the place for them; there are other places of learning already in existence, to which, if they would thus study, they can go. But this institution is for the education of farmers, where science will be pursued indeed, but pursued only so far as it bears upon the subject in hand. A chaplain should be appointed, part of whose duties would consist in giving religious instruction, according to the doctrines of the Church of England; but in order that the school should be open to the reception of the children of Dissenters; arrangements ought to be made to prevent their religious peculiarities from being interfered with.

Besides knowledge, skill in various mechanical arts ought also to be acquired. The farmer, when wealthy, although it may not be necessary for him ever to make use of his own hands as a carpenter or smith, must, for the purpose of forming a just estimate of the character of the work done for him, himself have some skill in these matters. A person having such a skill will not submit to slovenly carpentering, and his horses will never be lamed by a clumsy and ignorant smith; while the poorer farmer may save many a pound from the circumstance of being able himself to work at the bench of the carpenter and the anvil of the smith. Many a long winter's evening which he now spends in sleeping by the fire-side, would then be profitably occupied; and fences and buildings, which a few nails would preserve, would not be so often seen falling in ruins. The isolated situation in which many farmers live, makes it necessary that they should themselves have skill in many things. Carpenters, smiths, glaziers, and gardeners cannot, in distant parts of the country, be called in at a moment's notice, as in the neighbourhood of large towns. Besides, there is a positive pleasure in seeing the neatness and efficiency of a place supported by or contributed to by one's own handywork. Added to this, the fact of farmers being well acquainted with the manner in which work of the above description ought to be done, would operate directly upon the persons engaged in these employments.

The circumstance of having the work at all times submitted to accurate criticism, would of itself cause them to improve, while many might be induced to frequent the workshops of the institution for the purpose of acquiring an amount of knowledge and skill sufficient to enable them to make their work of the requisite character. Arrangements for this purpose might be made ; indeed, as the improvement of agriculture would be the aim of the institution, all the advantages which could be offered to any class connected directly or indirectly with agriculture, and which do not interfere with the main design of the institution, should be so. For it ought to be borne in mind that no individual can be below the work required of him in his peculiar department, without the whole business, of which it is a part, suffering; the tooth of a wheel in a machine is a little thing, but if it be displaced, the whole machine will suffer. The principle of the old story of the nail in the horse's shoe, and the loss of the life of the rider, is every day exemplified in real life : *no necessary part of a whole is contemptible.* And it is the deep conviction of this,—a conviction operating upon practice, that constitutes the secret of success. But besides possessing knowledge and mechanical skill, the young farmer should learn himself to perform with his own hand all the operations of husbandry; he should be a handy, active, skilful person. For this reason we would have the institution surrounded by a model farm, which the pupils should cultivate with their own hands. It is a good thing for all persons to be able to put forth their physical powers continuously, skilfully, and powerfully,—and for farmers necessary. He should be able to take the shafts of the plough from his ploughman, and say, "this is the way to do it;" and similarly with every operation of husbandry. If he himself can perform and has performed a good day's work, he will know what a day's work means, and not allow himself to be plundered by idlers.

Nor let it be thought that bodily exertion, such as we propose, would at all interfere with intellectual progress; from the success of M. De Fellenberg we are confident that the reverse is the case; there is no time when the mind is more willing and able to exert itself than when the body is kept in a state of vigorous health by strong exertion. If the hours were to be equally divided between study and labour of various kinds, including mechanical arts under the latter head, the attainments of the pupils would, we are assured, benefit by the arrangement. Nor must it be forgotten that much practical knowledge—an acquaintance with the application of the knowledge of the study to the realities of life, may be best acquired under a master in the field. The sappers and miners at Chatham are thus instructed; at Hofwyl this mode is adopted; and if the proposed institution is to be successful, it must be adopted in it also.

Of the humanizing effect upon the disposition and pursuits of an extended and accurate education, it is unnecessary here to speak at length. For we argue not only that it is desirable for these latter reasons, but that for the purpose of agriculture it is indispensable. Something, however, must be conceded to humanity ; and if, in addition to the necessary information and skill which we would impart, and habits of accuracy and industry which we would form, we throw in something that will add to the cheerfulness of the Christmas fireside and the happiness of the domestic circle, we shall perhaps not be blamed. For this purpose, we would give the young farmer an acquaintance with the sterling literature of his native country, and desire that he should cultivate a taste for music, both vocal and instrumental.

The ages at which pupils should enter and quit the schools are subjects of considerable importance, particularly the latter. It is most highly desirable that some mode should be devised for detaining the pupils at the establishment until their intellects shall have attained such a maturity, and they shall have profited by their studies to such an extent, as to enable them to enter upon their profession with advantage. Besides, the credit of the institution would be materially affected, if young men were to be permitted to go forth into the world as having been trained in it, who had not benefited by the full course of the instruction there imparted.

Our attention has been drawn to this subject by the following excellent observations of Mr. Love:—" If they (the pupils) are expected to leave the proposed school about the same time (say fourteen or fifteen) they leave schools in general, I am afraid it will prove too soon. Their bodily strength will not have permitted them to acquire much practical knowledge of the more laborious parts of our business ; and the period of profiting from reflection—the desire for ascertaining and treasuring up the why and because, will not have arrived. Besides, if they return home at that age, it can hardly be expected their parents will give up the management of their concerns into their hands, whatever progress or advances they may have made in their different studies. I certainly have a very strong opinion, that if such a school is established, the pupils should not be permitted to leave until (like others engaged in the study of their different professions) they have attained to such proficiency in the knowledge of the different branches of their business as will enable them either to afford useful assistance to their parents at home, or to start in business for themselves with a reasonable chance of success."

The object then is to secure that the pupils shall come early enough and leave late enough, to take full advantage of the benefits which the institution can hold forth. The age at which the pupils are to be received may without difficulty be fixed, but there would be considerable inconvenience in stipulating with the parents that their children should remain a certain number of years. All, as it seems to us, that can be done, is to encourage them to remain by dispensing certificates of attainment and competency, which none should be entitled to compete for who had not attained a specified age, and remained at the establishment for a certain number of years. The names of parties who periodically became entitled to these certificates might be published in the county newspapers, and there can be but little doubt that the obtaining them would be a distinction which most pupils would be eager for, and most parents desirous that their children should obtain. It would be, in fact, a degree, and no pupil could be considered as a fair sample of the establishment who was not in the possession of one. What the respective ages should be at which the pupils should enter and leave, it is difficult at once to say; perhaps they should enter at nine or ten, and leave at seventeen or eighteen years of age.

Athough (as has been said), for the purpose of deriving full advantage from institutions such as those proposed, it would be necessary for the pupils to enter early, and to remain until they have gone through all the most important classes; still, as there probably would always be (more particularly at first) young men desirous of becoming agriculturists, who would be anxious to avail themselves of the advantages which the arrangements of such Colleges would afford, it would, it is conceived, be desirable to open their doors to them. Such an addition would make the discipline more complicated, particularly as we agree in opinion with those who hold it to be absolutely necessary, for the morals of a place of education, that the younger pupils should be separated from those of a more advanced age. The arrangements requisite for such a purpose would be attended with expense; but the following extract from the letter of a Kentish yeoman will show that the sum to be demanded for the education of boys, viz. 25*l*., might, in the instance of young men, be more than doubled without difficulty, which, if a number varying from twenty-five to fifty were admitted, would add so materially to the funds of such an institution as to make the expense of the requisite arrangements a matter of little importance :—

" It has often occurred to me how desirable an establishment for the reception of adults would be, if every branch of agricultural instruction, theoretical and practical, could be imparted in it. Much difficulty is, I believe, experienced in procuring situations of any sort in which youths can learn the art and mystery of farming; and there is still more difficulty in getting them placed in really eligible situations and with respectable families. Now in an Agricultural College, established as the present plan proposes, the agricultural instruction afforded would far, very far, surpass what could be obtained from any single instructor, however experienced or talented he might be. In this respect, therefore, success might confidently be calculated upon. The premiums usually paid in placing out youths for agricultural instruction vary from 80*l*. to 120*l*. per annum, though I have known as much as 200*l*. given."

The advantages of the proposed institutions would not be confined to the farmer at home. Persons intending to send out their children as settlers to any of our colonies would, it is conceived, readily acknowledge how well the combination of skill with instruction would be adapted for training them to surmount the difficulties with which a primitive state of society must necessarily surround them. Lads who had acquired a considerable portion of skill in the use of the tools of the carpenter

and the smith, and who, in addition to a practical knowledge of husbandry, were also alive to many of the resources of mechanical and chemical science, would not
find themselves on the shores of a lately colonized country the helpless creatures which but too many of our
settlers have done to their great cost and suffering.

Such then is the plan of the proposed institutions ; but
when they became once established, with buildings, farms,
workshops, and masters, they would be capable of further
development : other departments might be added which
would naturally grow out of the original scheme, and form
an almost indispensable part of it.

Such an enlarged education of the farmers as is here
proposed, would immediately have the following effect,—
the farmers would be the first to perceive, that for a man
to be a good workman he must be an intelligent and skilful one, while their own superior acquirements would remove all idea that it is possible for the labourers to be, in
point of knowledge, their masters ; which we believe to be
an idea now generally entertained, and is one of the principal causes of the opposition which is so generally offered
by them to the efficient education of their labourers. The
farmers, instead of being the opponents, would, on the
contrary, be the most zealous promoters of the education of the labourers. As soon as this began to be
felt, a peasant school might be attached to, and made
dependent upon, the institution. In this an education
upon the plan detailed in Vol. I. of the Central Society
of Education, might be given, and the pupils in the
institution made to direct their labours. Indeed, this
ought to be one of the lessons which should be learned
by the young farmer. When he comes to be in business,
he must not only know how to manage machinery and
cattle, but also to direct men—not only to give effect to
brute force, but to turn human intelligence, skill, and industry to the best account; and he will here learn that the more
intelligent the husbandman is, the more will all the duties
which are confided to him be performed with accuracy.
The stupid and brutalized hind is not to be depended on
from one moment to another; as soon as the eye of the
master is off him, he relaxes in his exertions; he only dif-

fers from the slave in that the slave starts into activity upon the application of the whip, while the labourer does so at the impending loss of wages: both relax their exertions the moment the fear of the master is removed. And as in a large farm the eye of the master cannot be everywhere at the same time, the unknown loss of all farmers from this cause must be very great. A man must be actuated by some other principle than the fear of immediate punishment, or he can never be depended upon. Added to which, it is continually found impracticable to introduce many known improvements, from the fact of labourers being too stupid and obstinate to assist in adopting them. The farmer is most deeply interested in the education of the labourer; and if it were for this reason alone, we should suggest the addition of a school for labourers to the institution.

An institution of the character of those now proposed, from the fact of the children of the chief farmers from all parts of a county attending it, would be generally known throughout every district in it. Parents would often take their children to school, they would observe the superior system of husbandry pursued, and their own minds would soon become interested in what was going on. The masters, too, from the circumstance of being superior in the very line which the parents were pursuing, would be looked up to by them. These circumstances would tend to point out the locality of the school as the place in which arrangements might be most effectually made and superintended for the encouragement of improvements in agriculture by other means. It might be the repository of a county agricultural library, and improved agricultural instruments. Periodical agricultural meetings might be held there, at which prizes might be awarded. A normal school for the masters of village schools throughout the county might also be attached to it. All this should, however, be attained by a series of judicious steps; if one county were to set the example, others would soon follow; and institutions thus calculated to give stability to the agricultural interest, and shed a dignity upon the occupation, while it increased the profits of the agriculturist, would become general throughout England. The larger counties would each have institutions of their own, while the smaller would unite for the purpose of having one amongst them.*

But these institutions would be independent; each would rely solely upon itself for its own efficiency. Now it is to be feared that, after a time, these unconnected institutions would vary greatly in their value; the directors of some would become supine, jobbing would enter into the elections of others, and the masters would in some instances become inferior. There would be little to stimulate the directors of such institutions to exertion; they would possess a monopoly of the education of the sons of the farmers, and it would be difficult to dispossess them of it. These are evils in the prospect — they have their appropriate remedy. At the Universities, it is not an individual college which confers a degree or honours upon its pupils, but the Universities themselves. The examiners are appointed by the Universities, and each college, as well as each pupil, is thus placed upon trial; a spirit of emulation is generated between the different establishments, which cannot fail of being attended with benefit to each. An arrangement grounded upon this suggestion might be made for the purpose of securing the progressive improvement of the institutions which are here proposed. Scattered as they would be throughout the country, they might still be considered as forming one Agricultural University; and examiners might be annually appointed for the purpose of visiting all the institutions in rotation, examining the pupils, granting certificates of proficiency, and reporting upon the comparative and positive efficiency of each.

Institutions such as those here proposed are by no means novel. We are in expectation of receiving de-

* The soil of an institution, such as has been described, should, it is conceived, be not the best and richest of the county, but, on the contrary, of a character to require the application of science and ingenuity to obviate physical difficulties. It should be one pervading a large district of the county ; and, if it could be practicable to found it upon a spot in which two or three soils of different character exist, it would be a great advantage. Such a spot may sometimes be found. In Kent, upon and below the Dover range, for instance, there may, within a moderate distance, be found the heavy plastic clay, the chalk, the galt, and the green sand.

tailed accounts of some established in Sweden, Germany, France, and Switzerland; and it is with much pleasure that we are now enabled to lay before our readers the following interesting extracts from the Report of the Agricultural Seminary at Templemoyle, in Ireland, where for the small sum of 10*l.* children receive the advantages of a superior education, with boarding, lodging, and washing. Before doing so, however, it may be as well here to state that the Irish Education Board are occupied in founding even still more economical schools of this class in the different counties of Ireland, having already established one in Tyrone (Loughache), and another in Donegal (Clogham).

" Eleven years have now elapsed since the Agricultural School at Templemoyle commenced its operations; and, in preparing their Report for this year, the Committee of management hope they will not be deemed too sanguine when they offer to its supporters their warmest congratulations on the degree of success which their combined efforts have attained, and on the proof afforded that such an establishment can be maintained in Ireland, even with very limited funds, and that it has been and will be of the most decided advantage.

" The house at Templemoyle is situated on a gentle eminence, at the foot of which runs a mountain stream; the valley above it, narrow and with steep banks, opens here into the demesne of Foyle Park, immediately in front of the school, and expands rapidly till it is lost in the plain extending to Lough Foyle.

" The house is distant from Muff one mile, from Londonderry six, from Newtown-Limavady about eight, and about a mile and a half from the mail-coach road, which leads from Derry to Belfast, through Newtown-Limavady.

" The seminary derives its origin from the North-West of Ireland Society, many of whose members had individually experienced the great difficulty and expense that attended all their attempts to improve their property, and the frequent failures that arose from their tenants not being capable, from their education, to appreciate or imitate them. To remedy these evils and obtain the desired advantages, the Agricultural School at Templemoyle was founded in the year 1827, in connexion with, and strongly supported by, the North-West of Ireland Society : the plan of M. Fellenberg, at Hofwyl, in Switzerland, was taken in some degree as a model ; and a large sum was subscribed by the noblemen, gentlemen, and public bodies anxious to try the experiment.

" The original plan embraced two schools : one comprising every branch of education, and requiring a considerable payment from the pupils ; the other embracing every useful attainment, and adapted to the more limited means of the majority. It was hoped that the industrial school might have its means of support increased by the profit from the principal establishment, and that the general lectures of the professors of the head school would have afforded a valuable and gratuitous source of improvement to the agricultural pupils : but a short and very expensive trial convinced the subscribers that neither their funds nor existing circumstances would enable them to prosecute the whole scheme ; and they then abandoned the more expensive school, and devoted their whole attention to the other. A large and commodious house and offices were built at an expense exceeding 2,400*l.* ; 1,200*l.* of which the Grocers' Company, their liberal landlords, contributed. The house contains a school-room, 40 feet long, 21½ wide, 15 feet high ; four dormitories,—No. 1, 40 feet long, 21½ wide, 13 feet high ; No. 2, 40 feet long, 21½ wide, 13 feet high ; No. 3, 35 feet long, 16 wide, and 13 feet high ; No. 4, 23 feet long, 21½ wide, and 15 feet high. The dormitories contain 76 beds, each pupil having a separate one ; the dining-room is 45 feet long, 15½ wide, and 15 feet high : besides these, there are rooms for the different masters, matrons, servants, and committee ; kitchen, storeroom, and other requisite offices. The out-door buildings consist of two large rooms for pupils' boxes, washing-room, dairy, stables, harness-room, tool-house, cow-houses, feeding-houses, piggeries, barn ; which, together with the farming utensils, are kept with the greatest attention to neatness.

" To qualify a pupil for admission it originally required a nomination from one of the 25*l.* subscribers ; but the right of nomination has been extended by the Committee to annual subscribers, who pay 2*l*. for the first pupil, and 1*l*. for each additional.

" The in-door establishment consists of a head and second master, who instruct the pupils in spelling, reading, grammar, writing, arithmetic, geography, book-keeping as applicable not only to agricultural but commercial accounts, Euclid's Elements, algebra, trigonometry, with its application to heights and distances, and land surveying, together with the use of the water-level, theodolite, and chain; and the proficiency displayed by the pupils at the different yearly examinations, many of them in every one of the different branches of education enumerated, has been such as to surprise the talented persons who, on these occasions, have kindly acted as examiners, and to afford the best proof of the judicious selection that has been made of the master.

" Of the pupils, one half are at their studies in the house while the others are pursuing their agricultural studies out of doors: this is the arrangement for the morning. In the afternoon they change, so that the in-door and out-of-door education proceed *pari passu*. The arrangement of these hours, &c. will be seen in the Appendix.

" The domestic management of the house is confided to a highly-respectable matron, who superintends the cooking, dairy, the house and scholars' linen, and controls the female servants.

" The agricultural branch of the seminary is entrusted to a skilful and talented young man, a native of Scotland, and whose ability would be better ascertained during a walk round the farm than described by the pen: he has under him a gardener and a ploughman.

" The farm consists of 135 Cunningham, or 169 statute acres, with a north-eastern aspect, rising gradually from the house, which is 180 feet above the level of the sea, till it attains the height of 313 feet; the soil is mostly a thin retentive clay, on a micacious sub-soil, which, together with the height and aspect, will account for the small produce when compared with the skill and labour expended on it. These circumstances occasion the patrons of this establishment a much greater expense than if the soil had been more grateful in its returns; but the disadvantage is lessened, when it is considered that it presents a much greater field for the instruction of the pupils, who are taught increased vigilance in watching the seasons for ploughing, sowing, and reaping, rendered particularly precarious by the above circumstances. The school might have been situated where draining could only have been taught in its theory: here every field is, and, we may say, always will be, a practical lesson, as pecuniary means are the only limits to draining such retentive sub-soils.

" Every description of draining is here practised during the period of the year at which it is practicable; and furrow draining, which is carried to as considerable an extent as our means and time have permitted, already shows its beneficial influences on the crops that have succeeded it.

" The whole farm is laboured by the scholars in the alternate hours of their school education; and many of the senior lads, during their hours of recreation, have surveyed and mapped not only the Templemoyle Farm, but some of the neighbouring ones, in a manner that would do credit to a professional surveyor.

" Within the last year a nursery of forest trees has been made; the spring was particularly unfavourable for planting, but, with the care and attention that was employed, few of the trees failed. It will prove an additional source of instruction to the pupils, and we trust will not be without its profit.

" The garden, of which the nursery is an enlargement, has, within the same period, been rendered more ornamental; and by means of it, and the system and neatness required about the other portions of the establishment, it is hoped that what is now taught as a lesson may hereafter be adopted from principle, and from the persuasion that in that, as in every thing else, neatness is economy.

" An experienced veterinary surgeon, who had been lecturing in the adjacent towns of Derry, Newtown-Limavady, and Coleraine, and had given great satisfaction, was engaged to give a course of lectures comprehending the treatment of the horse, both as to his food and medicine, under the different uses to which he is applied, and the most approved method of shoeing.

" The system of cropping adopted on the farm is the
four and five shift rotation; 36 Cunningham, or 45 statute
acres, being under the four shift, and 94 Cunningham, or
nearly 118 statute acres, under the five shift course.
The situation and division of the fields cause the dis-
parity in the number of acres in each rotation; not that
a prejudice existed towards the one rather than the other,
but it was thought necessary that the pupils should see
each in operation. The five shift consists of, 1st year,
oats after ley; 2d, turnips, potatoes, vetches, beans, or
flax, with manure; 3d, wheat, barley, or oats, sown with
clover and grasses; 4th, clover for soiling, or hay; 5th,
pasture. The four crop rotation is the same, without the
5th or pasture year.

" Amongst the particular circumstances of the school
we would earnestly call the attention of all those who at
present, and those who may hereafter be inclined to support it, to one point, a compliance with which would
lighten the labours and ease the minds of the visiting
Committee, and would add to the character of the school,
by increasing the efficiency of the pupils when leaving it
—we would impress on the minds of the nominator of
pupils, that it is not by simply sending a youth to Templemoyle, hoping that he may be induced to comply with
the regulations there enforced, or that he may be inclined to follow those studies for which the institution
was solely founded; but it is a most imperious duty, not
only to the institution, but to the scholars, and the only
means of attaining satisfactorily the end desired, that the
intended pupil should be made most thoroughly acquainted with the rules, manner of living, &c. to be observed
at the seminary; that he should be informed that the
strictest discipline is required; and it ought to be a well-
grounded principle in his mind, before admission, that no
person can be qualified, or entitled hereafter to demand
the obedience of others, who has not been accustomed to
yield it in his own person promptly to his superiors.

" The character of our young countrymen is greatly in
opposition to this most valuable qualification; and many
of the young men at Templemoyle, having attained the
age of twenty without even the slightest restraint from
childhood, find it extremely difficult to submit to those

wholesome regulations which the very existence of such
an institution requires.

" Many have left the seminary after a short sojourn, unwilling to brook the slightest restraint; and, though their
places were immediately supplied, yet, probably, some of
the new comers would act from a similar impulse. We
would request all persons disposed to send pupils, to
ascertain, by a personal examination of them, whether
they are likely to be benefited by their fitness at the time
of entrance. The pupil should be at least fourteen, able
to read and write, and disposed to pay that obedience
which the rules require, and which his own discretion
might know was necessary. In order also to do justice
to the seminary and themselves, they should remain there
at least two years; and, should they not have had any
previous acquaintance with agricultural pursuits, a longer
time would be absolutely necessary : for want of attention to this point, many lads have left after six, twelve,
or eighteen months; and if they state, as they may naturally be supposed to do, that they have been at Templemoyle, their acquirements would be any thing but favourable to the character of the seminary. We are happy to
say, however, that there are at present many stewards
of noblemen and gentlemen, as well as men conducting
their own farms, not only in the north, but in other
parts of Ireland, who, having passed a sufficient period at
the seminary to have obtained all the advantages it affords, can testify, both by their talents and conduct, the
incalculable advantage it presents to that class of the
population to which they belong, and who will, by its
means, become what Ireland so much wants, that valuable and influential body, an enlightened and well-conducted yeomanry.

" Twenty-one counties having sent scholars, as may be
seen in the Appendix, may justify its being termed a National Establishment, and afford another proof of the disinterestedness of its founders and supporters. The improvement of their own properties, or even the surrounding country, was not the limits they assigned to this institution. They hail, with pleasure, the satisfactory intelligence that its beneficial effects are already felt in some

of the remotest parts of their country; and they trust that ere long they may see similar establishments rising in every province of Ireland. Should their best and most sanguine wishes, in that way, be realised, they will then have obtained the highest and only reward to which they have ever aspired,—that the agricultural seminary at Templemoyle has been the parent of establishments productive of prosperity and happiness to their native country."

"APPENDIX.

"*Templemoyle Work and School Table from* 20*th March to* 23*rd September.*

" Boys divided into two classes, A. and B.

" Hours.		At work.	At school.
5½—	All rise.		
6——8	. . . .	A.	. . . B.
8——9	Breakfast.		
9——1	. . . .	A.	. . . B.
1——2	Dinner and play.		
2——6	. . . .	B.	. . . A.
6——7	Play.		
7——9	Prepare lesson for next day.		
9—	To bed.		

" On Tuesday B. commences work in the morning, and A. at school, and so on alternate days.

" Each class is again subdivided into two divisions, over each of which is placed a monitor selected from the steadiest and best-informed boys; he receives the head farmer's directions as to the work to be done, and superintends his party while performing it.

" In winter the time of labour is shortened according to the length of the day, and the hours at school increased.

" In wet days, when the boys cannot work out, all are required to attend school.

"*Rules for the Templemoyle School.*

" 1. The pupils are required to say their prayers in the morning before leaving the dormitory, and at night before retiring to rest, each separately, and after the manner to which he has been habituated.

" 2. The pupils are required to wash their hands and faces before the commencement of business in the morning, on returning from agricultural labour, and after dinner.

" 3. The pupils are required to pay the strictest attention to their instructors, both during the hours of agricultural and literary occupation.

" 4. Strife, disobedience, inattention, or any description of riotous or disorderly conduct, is punishable by extra labour or confinement, as directed by the Committee, according to circumstances.

" 5. Diligent and respectful behaviour, continued for a considerable portion of time, will be rewarded by occasional permission for the pupil so distinguished to visit his home.

" 6. No pupil, on obtaining leave of absence, shall presume to continue it for a longer period than that prescribed to him on leaving the seminary.

" 7. During their rural labour the pupils are to consider themselves amenable to the authority of their agricultural instructor alone, and during their attendance in the school-room to that of their literary instructor alone.

" 8. Non-attendance during any part of the time allotted, either for literary or agricultural employment, will be punished as a serious offence.

" 9. During the hours of recreation the pupils are to be under the superintendence of their instructors, and not suffered to pass beyond the limits of the farm, except under their guidance, or with a written permission from one of them.

" 10. The pupils are required to make up their beds, and keep those clothes not in immediate use neatly folded up in their trunks; and to be particular in never suffering any garment, book, implement, or other article belonging to or used by them, to lie about in a slovenly or disorderly manner.

" 11. Respect to superiors, and gentleness of demeanour both among the pupils themselves and towards the servants and labourers of the establishment, are particularly insisted upon, and will be considered a prominent ground of approbation and reward.

" 12. On Sundays the pupils are required to attend their respective places of worship, accompanied by their instructors or monitors : and it is earnestly recommended to them to employ a part of the remainder of the day in sincerely reading the word of God, and in such other devotional exercises as their respective ministers may point out.

" *Regulations for the Farming Department of Seminary.*

" The following directions were given by the Committee to the head farmer at Templemoyle for the government of his conduct:

" 1. The great object being to make the boys practical farmers, the one half of the scholars to be constantly employed in manual labour on the farm, when they will receive instructions from the head farmer, under the charge of whom or of a monitor they are to be kept closely to their work. Every pupil is to be made a ploughman, and taught not only how to use, but also how to settle the plough irons for every soil and work ; and he is to be instructed and made acquainted with the use and practical management of every implement generally used.

" 2. Their attention is also to be drawn to stock of all kinds ; and the particular points that denote a good, bad, indifferent, hardy, delicate, good feeder, good milker, &c. are to be pointed out to each.

" 3. At the proper season of the year, the attention of the boys is also to be directed to the making and repairing of fences, that they may know not only how to make a new one, but, what is of infinite advantage, how to repair and make permanent fences of many years' standing.

" 4. The head farmer will deliver evening lectures to the pupils on the theory and practice of agriculture, explaining his reasons for adopting any particular crop or rotation of crops, the most suitable soil, and most approved mode of cultivation for each. The proper treatment and management of working, feeding, and dairy stock, the most improved breeds, and their adaptation to different situations and soils. He will point out the best method of reclaiming, draining, and improving land, and will direct their attention to the most recent inventions in

argicultural implements, detailing the respective merits
of each.

" 5. One of the more advanced pupils will be selected
weekly to act as superintendent ; the dietary account,
the labourers' book, and the account of the employment
of the pupils are to be kept by him in the manner fixed
on by the Committee, and these books are to be regularly
laid before them at their meetings.

" Unobtrusive on the public, and perhaps culpably so,
as the Committee may appear to have been in their statements, they would appeal to the annexed return of the
pupils admitted since May 1827, and the names of the
counties whence they came :

*" Table of Pupils admitted to Seminary since opening, and
the Counties whence they came.*

Derry.	Tyrone.	Donegal.	Fermanagh.	Monaghan.	Antrim.	Down.	Louth.	Dublin.	Kildare.	Queen's Co.	Carlow.	Waterford.	Wexford.	Limerick.	Cork.	Kerry.	Galway.	Leitrim.	Roscommon.	Sligo.	Scotland.	Total.
155	52	25	11	7	3	3	1	7	5	1	1	10	1	2	12	6	3	1	2	3	2	313

*" Pupils in Seminary on 1st September 1838, and the
Counties whence they came.*

Derry.	Tyrone.	Donegal.	Fermanagh.	Monaghan.	Down.	Dublin.	Kildare.	Carlow.	Waterford.	Limerick.	Cork.	Kerry.	Galway.	Total.
25	10	2	2	2	1	3	2	1	6	1	5	3	1	64

" Although the seminary was originally intended for
the education of young men destined for agricultural pursuits, yet the Committee have to state that several individuals have availed themselves of the advantage derived
from the course of education there pursued, to qualify

themselves for other avocations; and of those who have already left the seminary,

    29 are employed as Land Stewards,
    2 ————— as Assistant Agents,
    5 ————— as Schoolmasters,
    1 ————— as Principal of an Agricultural Day School,
    8 ————— as Writing Clerks,
    6 ————— as Shopkeepers,
    1 ————— as Civil Engineer,
    2 ————— as Assistants to County Surveyors,
    124 ————— at home in Agricultural Pursuits,
    32 have emigrated to America, West Indies, and Australia,
    39 left seminary since September 1835, not having remained 12 months, and 64 remain in seminary on 1st September 1838.

" The Committee have the gratification of stating that in every instance, when young men have been sent from the seminary with the necessary certificates of qualification, they have been found to give entire satisfaction to those by whom they have been employed; and in those cases when they are engaged in farming at home, it is satisfactory to know they are imparting the knowledge which they had obtained at Templemoyle to their friends and neighbourhood."

                                    B. F. DUPPA.

STATE OF THE PEASANTRY IN THE COUNTY OF KENT.*

IN the discussions in parliament respecting the late extraordinary occurrences in Kent, reflecting persons must have been struck with the importance attached to the fact of the liberation of the lunatic who was the chief actor in those scenes, in preference to what all must feel should be the proper subject for consideration, viz. the condition of the population amongst whom such events could take place. Is it to be supposed that the peace and order of society are to depend so materially upon the vigilance with which madmen are guarded? And when a considerable portion of the population of a district has been led into the commission of grave offences against the laws, are we to receive as an explanation for their conduct, that a lunatic has been imprudently liberated? These questions answer themselves. The proper subject of inquiry, for whatever reasons evaded, was evidently that which has just been stated,—the actual condition of the population of the district in question.

To ascertain this point before the interest awakened by the late events should subside, appeared to the Central Society of Education an object of primary importance. There was reason to hope that the existence of such an interest would insure to the minute, but important, details upon which the information sought for must be grounded, that attention which, under ordinary circumstances, it is so difficult to obtain for them. At the request of the Committee, the writer of the following pages (a member of the Society) undertook to visit the district in question, for the purpose of conducting the proposed investigation. The alarm and excitement produced by

* A few errors have been pointed out in the statements contained in this paper. In order that the public may judge of the degree of their importance, the original text is preserved, and corrections are made in foot notes.—EDITOR.

the disturbances had not ceased at the period of his arrival in the neighbourhood; and the appearance of a stranger going from cottage to cottage, and making minute inquiries, created at first some mistrust. Several persons concerned in the disturbances were in prison awaiting their trials, and their families were naturally suspicious that the information so collected might be used to their prejudice. These alarms, however, were generally dissipated by an open statement of the motives and objects of the inquirer. No sooner were these understood by many, than they seemed anxious to render every assistance in their power. That some, especially those who were conscious of unatoned delinquencies, should preserve their mistrust of all inquiry, was natural; but there is no cause to doubt that even these gave, in the main, correct answers to the questions put to them concerning the actual condition of their families and themselves. Indeed, in most cases their answers were confirmed by the personal observation of the writer; and, where that was not possible, by comparison of the accounts of others in similar situations, and by the testimony of neighbours.

With very few exceptions, the whole of the persons implicated in the late events belonged to the parishes of Herne-hill and Boughton, and the ville of Dunkirk, an extra-parochial district bordering upon both the above-named parishes. Of these, by far the greater number were from Herne-hill; Dunkirk furnished the next largest proportion; while that from Boughton, which is much more populous than either of the preceding, was very inconsiderable. Of the persons killed, five were from Herne-hill, two from Dunkirk, and only one from Boughton; and of the fourteen now in confinement awaiting their trial, ten are from Herne-hill, none from Dunkirk, two from Boughton, and the remaining two from the neighbouring parishes of Selinge and Whitstable. These facts determined the writer to confine his inquiries to the three first-mentioned places, Herne-hill, Dunkirk, and Boughton.

The scenery of this district is peculiarly English. Gently rising hills, and picturesque vales, covered with a rich herbage, or bearing the show of a minute and skilful husbandry, succeed to each other. Fields of waving corn are interspersed with gardens, hop-grounds, and orchards.—What pity that the moral condition of the inhabitants of so fair a spot should stand, as will be seen, in such mournful contrast with its order and beauty!

The circumstances of this lamentable outbreak have been so often and so minutely detailed, and are still so fresh in the recollection of the reader, that it would be a waste of time to repeat them here. It is sufficient to say upon this point, that the results of the investigation agree with the statements of fact put forth by the journals. But as the existence of the gross ignorance and delusion to which they have been attributed, has been much questioned by many, I shall, previously to submitting the results of the statistical inquiries, first show that, improbable as the credulity and ignorance of those who could be deluded by the monstrous imposture and absurd pretensions of Thoms may be, they did most undeniably exist.

For the purpose of ascertaining the truth with regard to this important point, the writer of these pages questioned almost every person with whom he came in contact in cottages, in beer-shops, and the fields; and their testimony was all concurrent to the effect, that the greater part of Thoms' followers believed him to be Jesus Christ, and considered that they were not only justified in obeying him as their lord, but that disobedience would entail upon them eternal damnation.

Once being in a beer-shop in Dunkirk, where four or five persons were present, the writer expressed, in the course of conversation, some hesitation to give credence to the existence of this belief. Several of them affirmed that there was no doubt at all about the matter, and that they had often conversed with believers in Thoms' divinity, who had begged them, as they minded their salvation, to join them. Incredulity upon the point was still affected, when a dark-looking person, a charcoal-burner, who had thitherto been silent, said with some earnestness, " Well, sir, I suppose seeing is believing. A man as I knows well, heard Sir William preach, and then he giv' 'em all the sacrament, and after that he anoints himself

and all of 'em with oil, and tells 'em that then no bullet
nor nothing could harm 'em;—and Sir William, he sat
upon the ground with his back against a tree like, and
there was all the women a crying and praying to him, —
and they says to him, ' Now do tell us if you be our blessed Saviour, the Lord Jesus Christ !' and says he, ' I am he ;'
—and then he shows 'em the mark of the nails in his hands
which was made when he was put on the cross. — Now
that's no lie, and I knows him well as see it." The charcoal-burner probably spoke of himself, though he did not
choose to say so, for fear of consequences. I (for it will be
more convenient to speak in the first person) still persisted
that a few only of the most ignorant could have believed in
such things; but my companions, and especially the charcoal-burner, stoutly maintained the contrary. " Why,"
said the latter, who warmed in proportion to my opposition, " there was Edward Wraight, a man who held his own
land, and William Wills, who has had the best of education, quite a learned man, *beleft* him; and, besides them,
there was Foad, and Griggs, and others, who had all had
a Bible education, and was in no sort of want at all, *beleft*
him; and William Wills told a man as he wanted to persuade to go along with 'em, that, for all Sir William was
a mile off, he knew every word they was a saying."
     I afterwards went to the house of Edward Wraight,
son of the old farmer who was shot. The man was in
Maidstone jail; but I found his poor wife surrounded
with five or six young children in the cottage. It was a
melancholy sight; the poor creature was hurrying about
her little household work, half suffocated with her sobs;
at one moment petulantly scolding her children for being
in the way, and the next caressing them as if about to
be snatched from them. She was at first startled at my
appearance, but a few expressions of sympathy and hope
reassured her. There is no difficulty in leading to the
subject of their afflictions with the poor. We began to
talk immediately of the late disasters, and I soon found
an opportunity of asking her if she really had believed
that Thoms. was our Saviour ? I wrote down her answer, as nearly as possible in her own words. " Oh yes,
sir, certain sure I did believe him; and good warrant I

thought I had. , William Wills, you see, sir, came one day to our cottage, and we had some ale; and, says he, 'Have you heard the great news, and what 's going to happen?' — 'No,' says we, 'William Wills; what be it?' And he said, the great Day of Judgment was close at hand, and that our Saviour had come back again; and that we must all follow him. And he showed us in the Bible, in the Revelations, that he should come upon a white horse, and go forth to conquer; and sure enough, sir, the day after, as we were coming in our cart from market, we met the groom leading Sir William's white horse; and he told us that all the country would be up, for the great jubilee was to come, and we must be with 'em. And so, sir, you see, next day poor Edward certainly did go to join 'em, little thinking what was to happen. And the day after, as they were all passing by the house, I looked out, and Muster Foad was just at the tail of them. And I said, 'Do you, Muster Foad, believe he is our blessed Saviour?'—'Oh, yes,' he says, 'Mrs. Wraight, for certain sure he is, and I 'll follow him to the world's end.' "—" Well," I replied, " but his death con-vinced you he was an impostor?"—" Not at once, sir; for we was told he would surely rise again; and, for certain, after poor Edward was taken prisoner, me and a neighbour sat up the whole of that blessed night reading the Bible, and believing the world was to be destroyed on the morrow."—" And did all your neighbours believe that Thoms was the Saviour?"—" I can't say for all, sir, but many of them did. There was Mrs. —— opposite, who asked him to a tea-party; and she said afterwards to me, 'You may be sure he isn't one of us; he isn't like to us. To hear him talk, and see him, it 's not at all like talking to a man. He sings the beautifullest hymns, and talks the finest words that ever you heard.' " This poor woman corroborated the story of Thoms' adminis-tering the sacrament, and anointing his men to render them invulnerable. She said she was present at the time, and heard him declare that nothing could hurt them, and that he was not afraid of ten thousand sol-diers. In imitation of Christ, he took up the children and blessed them; and the women who were present

wept over, and kissed, and worshipped him. She added,
that she saw Alexander Foad worship him, and heard
him ask him if he might go home, and be present in the
spirit, though absent in the body; but Thoms would not
hear of his departure, and threatened, if he left him, to
rain down upon him fire and brimstone. This poor
woman and her husband were in tolerably comfortable
circumstances. He was the son of the farmer of the
same name, who was shot; a man of a reserved gloomy
temper, who was reckoned a shrewd character by his
neighbours, and who yet at the age of sixty became a
victim to this strange infatuation.

A Mrs. ——— had been mentioned to me as a rather
superior person, and who had been one of Thoms' chief
agents in establishing his influence. She was the wife of
the bailiff of a landed proprietor, and had formerly been
the mistress of a day-school in the village. Everybody
spoke of her as having " had the best of education," and
as being able to dispute with any parson on the Bible.
I found her residing in a neat comfortable house; and, on
presenting myself at the door, received an invitation to
walk in. A large Bible, which she had been reading, was
lying open on the table. This circumstance enabled me
to lead at once to the subject; and, after a little conversation, I asked her if she had really believed in the
divinity of the unfortunate man who had paid for his
imposture with his life. She said, she could scarcely
answer the question; her thoughts had been so disturbed
by what had happened, that she could hardly say now
what she believed. He had informed her that Christ
had selected his body for his second appearance; that
Christ dwelt in his heart; and that his body was the
temple of the Holy Ghost. I told her, that to a certain
degree that was said by the Scriptures of all true believers; but that Thoms had pretended to much more, for
he had asserted himself to be identically the Saviour,
and for the truth of his assertion appealed to the marks
of the nails in his hands and feet. She was confused at
this, and repeated that her mind was too much disturbed to be able to speak with certainty as to her
former convictions. She persisted, however, in affirm-

ing, that, even if Sir William (for, notwithstanding his celestial dignities, she always gave him his earthly one,) had been deceived in some respects, he was nevertheless a holy man inspired by God, and that if he had even gone astray himself, he had led her (to use her own expression) into heavenly paths. A very little conversation showed that her boasted knowledge of the Scriptures was of the most superficial kind, and that she was in truth scarcely more enlightened than her ignorant neighbours.

Among these simple people the capacity to read, and to converse with any degree of fluency upon the subjects treated of, is an infallible proof of superior talents; and, as Mrs. ———— possessed these attainments, she became the oracle of the community. Her egregious vanity, and the influence she possessed amongst her neighbours, rendered her a very desirable tool for Thoms; who, whatever might be his aberration of intellect, seems to have had considerable art in selecting the best means for accomplishing his views. From her account of the conversations he held with her, it was evident he had spared no pains to enlist her vanity in his service. She was made the depository of his inspiration; and, flattered with this distinction, she greedily listened to the tale of his coming elevation to power, in which she hoped to share. He had assured her (as she told me) that the millennium was at hand, and that the reign of the saints was approaching, in which, no doubt, she expected to bear an important part. Under this influence, she exerted all her efforts to induce her relatives and neighbours to join the standard of the new prophet. Among the other victims to her persuasions are her brother William Wills, and her son. The first is now a prisoner, under a charge of wilful murder; and the other, a fine youth of only sixteen, is lying in a dangerous state, having had his thigh broken in the affray by a musketball. So great was her infatuation, that she positively refused at first to credit the account of the death of Thoms; and it was only after she had received repeated assurances of the lamentable fate of her son, as well as of Thoms, that she could be induced to believe the fact:

even then, so reluctant was she to part with the bright visions and delusive hopes upon which she had so long gloated, that, remembering an assurance given her by Thoms, she bade those who brought the news wait a little, and they would see him rise again on the third day. Of course, at the time of my visit, these delusions were at an end; but so great was the impression made by Thoms' eloquence upon her fancy, and so reluctant was her vanity to acknowledge she had been the dupe of an impostor, that she persisted in affirming her belief that, however he might have deceived himself and others in supposing that he could render himself and his followers invulnerable, he was nevertheless a holy man, and had been inspired by God.

To ascertain still further how far these occurrences were connected with a religious delusion, I made minute inquiries into the characters and circumstances of those who were killed, as well as those who are now in prison, or are at large upon recognizances or otherwise. The result was, to establish the fact indisputably, in the majority of the cases, that a belief in the divine mission of the impostor absolutely existed. How far, or in what sense, they believed the assertion of his divinity, cannot be known; probably it was not so to themselves. But that they regarded him as a being superior to ordinary mortals,—that as such they implicitly obeyed his commands, and relied on his power to render them invulnerable, and protect them against human force,—is unquestionable. At the risk of repeating what many of our readers have already seen, I shall add a concise account of the circumstances of those who have lost their lives in this melancholy business. Those who have fortunately escaped the observation of justice, it would not be proper to name; and of them, as well as of those who will have to answer for their conduct, a general description must suffice.

The men killed are :

1. Edward Wraight.
2. William Foster.
3. William Rye.
4. George Branchett.
5. Stephen Baker.
6. William Burford.
7. George Griggs.
8. Phineas Harvey.

EDWARD WRAIGHT was a substantial yeoman, farming about sixty acres of his own land. He had received the usual education of persons of his class, and could read and write. He is represented by those who knew him, as a man of a sullen, uncommunicative character, extremely tenacious of his rights. He never 'went to church or chapel; and, when pressed upon the subject, said he would not go to hear a man who robbed him every day of his life by taking tithe. He was not in the habit of reading much, and had only a few books, chiefly of a religious character. He was more than sixty years of age ; and his children are all capable of providing for themselves.

WILLIAM FOSTER was a labourer, in the service of Mr. Smoulton of Canterbury, and received two shillings and sixpence per diem. He was a good workman, always employed, a quiet well-behaved man, and in the constant habit of attending church. Foster could read ; and in his cottage were a Testament and a few religious books. He has left a widow and five children.

WILLIAM RYE, an industrious labourer, in constant employment, receiving two shillings and sixpence per diem; an attendant at church. He has left a widow and four children. Rye had never learnt to read, and had no books in his cottage.

GEORGE BRANCHETT had been a private in the East Kent Militia. He was a labourer, an industrious man; but during the last winter had fallen into great distress, and was taken, with his family, into the Union workhouse at Faversham. While there, his wife and two of his children died; and shortly after leaving it, two more children died. He has left three other children, two of whom have since his death been received back into the workhouse. This poor man had received no education ; and his misfortunes and distresses left him peculiarly open to the alluring promises of Thoms.

STEPHEN BAKER was an inoffensive young man ; in constant employment at the rate of two shillings and threepence per diem. He could read a little, and was in the habit of attending church. He has left a widow, but no child.

WILLIAM BURFORD was a labourer, and the only one killed who was known as a decidedly bad character. He was a reputed sheep-stealer, and suspected to be concerned in several depredations that had been committed. I could not ascertain whether he had received any education. In his cottage were a Testament and one or two other books of a religious nature. He has left a widow and child.

GEORGE GRIGGS was a regular farm-servant with good board and wages. He had been in his youth a constant attendant at the Sunday School, and is mentioned as having made great progress in religious knowledge, and as being capable of returning very suitable answers to questions on such subjects. He was unmarried.

PHINEAS HARVEY, another single man, was a sober industrious labourer. He was in constant employ, and receiving two shillings and threepence per diem. I could not ascertain what degree of education he had received; but he was represented as a quiet, well-conducted man, and usually attended church.

Of the sixteen persons now in gaol at Maidstone, and eleven others discharged on their own recognizances, nearly the whole were men of steady, reputable characters. Four only of them were in distressed circumstances; the remainder were either labourers in well-paid, constant employment, or possessing tenements of their own. Of these last there were no fewer than six.

The kind of education received by these persons was of the lowest and most inefficient description. The only one who had had the benefit of the common instruction given in the middling class of schools in country towns, was William Wills, who, with his sister Mrs. ——, before spoken of, were regarded as prodigies of learning by their simple neighbours. Very few could write their own names; and those who could read, rarely ventured upon any other book than the Testament or Bible. Indeed, the usual answer in the district to the question " Can you read?" is, " Yes, a little in the Testament."

The houses generally appear to be tolerably provided with Bibles and Testaments, but beyond these and a few tracts scarcely a book is to be found in

a cottage in the district. That these are not mere ran-
dom assertions, hazarded from a hasty glance at a few
cottages, will appear from the details given further on,
and which are the result of a careful and minute investigation. A little consideration of the nature of rural
life will show the danger of leaving the peasantry in
such a state of ignorance. In the solitude of the country,
the uncultivated mind is much more open to the impressions of fanaticism than in the bustle and collision of
towns. In such a stagnant state of existence the mind
acquires no activity, and is unaccustomed to make those
investigations and comparisons necessary to detect imposture. The slightest semblance of evidence is often
sufficient with them to support a deceit which elsewhere
would not have the smallest chance of escaping detection. If we look for a moment at the absurdities and
inconsistencies practised by Thoms, it appears at first
utterly inconceivable that any persons out of a lunatic
asylum could have been deceived by him. At one time
he had assumed the title of Baron Rothschild, at another
of the Earl of Devon, then of King of Jerusalem, and
afterwards of a knight of Malta;— and all these absurdities had been openly practised before the eyes of the
very persons among whom he afterwards ventured to appear as the Saviour of the world. To support this last
assumption, his chief advantages were a commanding
person and a handsome countenance, which he made in
some degree to resemble the common portraits of Christ,
by wearing his hair parted at the crown, and a long flowing beard. To these advantages were joined a considerable fluency of speech, and the power of interlarding his
discourse with Scriptural phraseology. That an imposture so gross and so slenderly supported should have
succeeded, must teach us, if anything will, the folly and
danger of leaving the agricultural population in the debasing ignorance which now exists among them. There
is not the slightest ground for ascribing these events
to the discontent occasioned by the late change in the
poor-law. Upon this point the inquiries made were numerous and minute; and those who were most likely to
be acquainted with the views and motives of the persons

engaged in these proceedings, — their friends and relatives,— all concurred in saying that a dislike to the poor-
law had nothing to do with the matter. Indeed it may be
asserted, as the statements already given will confirm, that
not more than two of the persons implicated in the transac-
tion had been affected by the change in the law ; although,
as will be seen, these three parishes sent their full proportion of paupers to the Union Workhouse during the last
winter. It is rather to be feared that, if any feeling of
dissatisfaction in regard to property existed in the minds
of these persons, it partook more of the character of a
general dislike and envy of the wealthy classes, than of
a definite objection to any particular law; a feeling, no
doubt, infinitely the more dangerous of the two, and
which is founded on a total ignorance of the advantages
resulting to society at large from the institution of the
law of property. But upon this subject I shall have
occasion to offer some remarks hereafter.

I shall proceed now to give the results of the statistical
inquiries that have been made; from which the reader
will be enabled to form some estimate of the physical
and moral condition of the population amongst whom
these extraordinary events took place. I shall begin with
the village of Herne-hill.

HERNE-HILL,

This parish contains 2619 acres ; the rental is estimated
at 3,300*l.* and the amount of poor's rates levied for the
year was 275*l.* 10*s.* 7*d.* The village contains eighty-eight
families, who compose a population of four hundred and
seventy individuals. In the quarter ending on Lady-day
last, five men, two women, and eight children were inmates of the workhouse ; and ten men, sixteen women, and
eighteen children were receiving out-door relief,—forming
a total of fifty-nine ; being very nearly one in every eight
persons.*

* Although this statement was taken from the books kept at the Union
Workhouse, it is not correct: the error was caused by the mode in
which entries are made. The average number chargeable in the different parishes alluded to in these pages is considerably below what is
here stated.

The vicar is the only gentleman resident in the parish. There is no medical man, no apothecary, nor a shop of any description. The land is divided into farms, varying in extent from sixty to one hundred and fifty acres. The holders of these farms, engrossed by their own affairs, and possessing scarcely any information upon other subjects, are not in a condition, even if they were willing, to assist much in the moral improvement of the people. The principal person among them, who appears to be the only one who takes any interest in such things, has himself received no other education than what was usually given to the labouring classes in the rural districts forty years ago. He is, however, a very meritorious individual, who, by dint of steady industry, persevering economy, and undeviating good conduct, has raised himself from the condition of a labouring man to his present respectable position. Upon his shoulders falls the whole burden of the secular concerns of the parish: he is churchwarden, guardian of the poor, and surveyor of roads; and the duties of these offices he performs, not only for his own parish, but for the ville of Dunkirk, which is the larger district of the two. It would not be easy to point out a man more truly useful in his sphere than this well-meaning but uncultivated yeoman. From this statement it will be seen that all the expense, as well as the trouble, of whatever is done for the moral improvement of the inhabitants, falls chiefly upon the vicar, whose income from the parish does not exceed 300l. per annum. It is very clear that the greater part of what can be devoted to charity out of such a sum must be absorbed by the physical wants of the poorer parishioners, and that very little, if any, will be left for the purposes of education. In looking at the condition of the parish, it is right that this fact should be borne in mind, that blame may not be thrown upon a quarter where it would be most undeserved.

The employment of the inhabitants is entirely agricultural. Of the eighty-eight families distributed through the parish, about seventy are those of labourers working for others, although some of these hold an acre or two of land, and, in one or two instances, as much as nine or ten acres. The wages at present given are, — to able-bodied men, from 2s. to 2s. 3d. a day; in some few instances 2s. 6d.; to women 1s. a day; to lads of thirteen, 6d. a day; and to other children, 3s., 2s. 6d., and 1s. 6d. a week, according to their age and strength.

Of these seventy families, the condition of fifty-one was investigated upon the system adopted for that of eight rural parishes in the neighbourhood of Maidstone, a report of which appeared in the first publication of the proceedings of this Society, p. 342. The result of this investigation will satisfactorily show that the physical condition of the villagers of Herne-hill is superior to that of many rural populations in the country, and scarcely inferior to any; so that their participation in the late lamentable occurrences can in no degree be attributed to their poverty or suffering. They are nearly all lodged in separate cottages, the generality of which exhibit both externally and internally unquestionable signs of neatness and comfort. The only exceptions are the inmates of a large house, which is portioned out among six different families. Among these, there are two families occupying only one room each. The others have two rooms, for which they pay about the same rent that is paid by their more fortunate neighbours for a neat cottage and garden. They also have gardens; but this herding together, though to an extent infinitely less than is common in large towns, is unfavourable to the feelings which induce a man to take a pleasure in the comfortable appearance of his garden and dwelling. The contrast between them and the cottagers in these respects was very remarkable. It is satisfactory to observe, however, that they felt this contrast themselves, and were eager to point out the causes of it. With this exception the villagers of Herne-hill may be considered as exceedingly well lodged; a most important point in their moral as well as physical condition. Indeed, it was impossible not to be struck with the air of neatness and comfort pervading so many of their dwellings. Many of them, in addition to a sufficiency of well-made chairs, contained well-polished tables and chests of drawers. The walls were garnished with shelves loaded with crockery and culinary utensils; and not unfrequently a corner was filled with a respectable-looking clock, which seemed to vouch for the character of the little household. A more questionable article, which was seen oftener than could be wished, was a fowling-piece, suspended, with many other things, from the ceiling.

The neighbourhood had formerly a character for poaching, but the practice is much lessened, it is said, since the farmers have become interested in the preservation of the game; and the guns are now chiefly used to frighten the birds from the cherries, of which there are great quantities. Whatever truth there may be in this, there is one inference to be drawn from the existence of these weapons, in favour of the deluded peasants who were concerned in the late events, which is worthy of observation,—that, whereas all of them might with very little difficulty have procured fire-arms, there was not one of them so armed; which seems of itself sufficient evidence that, at the time they joined Thoms, they did not contemplate the desperate actions to which his rashness or madness urged them.

Of the fifty-one families examined, two only were found living in one room for each family; eight families had each two rooms; twelve families had three rooms; eighteen families had four rooms; eight had five rooms; and five had six rooms. The rooms were generally sufficiently airy; in the principal apartment the windows all opened and shut, and this was the case, with very few exceptions, in the sleeping-rooms. There was considerable difficulty in ascertaining whether the children of both sexes slept in the same room or apart, or in the bed-room of the parents. The usual answer was, that the arrangement was not always the same, and that they were in the habit of doing all three. The gardens attached to the cottages varied generally in size from eight to sixteen perches. A few contained half an acre, and in two or three instances that quantity was exceeded. The admirable manner in which the gardens were cultivated bore testimony to the readiness and ability of the cottagers to turn land, if they could get it, to good account. In not more than three or four, was there any appearance of slovenliness or neglect. The returns represent forty-eight of the gardens as well cultivated, and three only as being otherwise. All the labourers concurred in estimating the value of a garden to them. Without it, they said, they could not get on at all. By its means they contrive to procure sufficient vegetables for their families for a great part of the year. In thirty of the gardens flowers were cultivated, and in twenty-one they were not. As this point may to some seem trifling, it is worthy of remark, that the cottages of the cultivators of flowers generally exhibited greater proofs of comfort and cleanliness than those of others.

In a hilly district like Herne-hill, there is usually a plentiful supply of water. To this advantage the cottages owe much of their cleanliness. Out of the fifty-one cases, forty-nine are returned as being plentifully supplied, and two only where a sufficiency is not immediately at hand. The general appearance of the families and dwellings, in regard to comfort and cleanliness, is expressed in the returns under the heads of "very comfortable," "middling," and "poor:"— to the first head the returns give thirty-two; to the second, thirteen; and to the last, six.

It is a great advantage to a poor man to be able to use carpenter's tools. Independent of the money to be made by repairing the chairs and tables, cupboards, doors, &c. of his neighbours, which would amount in many places to a considerable sum in the year, he may always keep his own dwelling weather-tight, and everything about him in order. If he cannot do these things for himself, he must be continually paying small sums to others, or, what is worse, allow everything to go to ruin. Much of a carpenter's work is, besides, so clean and pleasant, that it would seem almost an attraction for an idle man. Yet, with all these incentives, it is astonishing how few country-men are handy at this work. In the fifty-one families, three men only are returned as capable of using their tools in a workmanlike manner; twenty-four could use them a little; and twenty-six not at all. The twenty-four in the second class could only use them in the roughest way: they could put together a pig-stye, but they could not make, nor even repair a door, a cupboard,

or a table. One of the great advantages to be hoped
from the establishment of industrial schools, is, that the
peasantry may be taught to do many things for themselves
for which they are now compelled to pay others; this
would be a positive increase of income.

The women, generally, are more handy than the men.
In the above number of families, thirty of the wives could
sew, wash, brew, bake, and make butter; fourteen could
sew and wash only; while four, from age and infirmity,
could do nothing. It is to be observed, however, that, for
some of the qualifications of those in the first list, we have
no other proof than their own assertion; for, unfortunately,
they have no means for brewing or making butter.

Considering that the only work the women can obtain
is in the fields, the appearance of themselves, their cottages, and the dress of their husbands and children, is
very creditable to them. An obvious means of improving their condition would be by the introduction
among them of some occupation which could be pursued
within doors ; such as the making of lace or straw plait.*

* For the purpose of enabling men to turn a long winter's evening to
account, it will be admitted that in-door occupations are desirable, as
well for them as women ; and some returns with which we have been
favoured by a gentleman connected with the Poor Law Commission,
make it evident that skill in such employments is requisite for men on other
accounts.   In the workhouses in Kent, it is found that the comparative
number of the two sexes varies materially with the different periods of life.
Young lads are more numerous than young girls, — able-bodied women
than able-bodied men, while aged and infirm men are more numerous
than aged and infirm women. On the 8th of February 1837, the numbers
under the above heads in the Kent Union workhouses were as follows.

	Males.	Females.
Young persons from 9 to 16 years of age,	688	468
Able-bodied	144	440
Old and infirm	1006	659

The two last classes of persons, viz. the old and infirm men, and the
old and infirm women, are those to which it is desirable more particularly
to draw the attention of the reader at the present time. When the greater
part of a woman's strength is spent, she is still able to do many things
whereby to earn her livelihood : she can nurse, sew, cook, sweep a
room, &c. An old man, who has toiled for a series of years as an agricultural labourer, and has no longer sufficient strength for hard work, is
good for nothing. Sheer physical force was the only commodity which
he was ever able to offer as the price of his livelihood. Confined to his
room or his chair, he can do nothing which is worth any person's money.

It is well known that both in Belgium, and in some parts of Ireland, the women add considerably to the family earnings by the spinning of flax. There does not seem to be any real impediment to the introduction of these

Although he may remain in such a state for a dozen or a score of years, with the use of his hands and his eyes, he is, and must continue a burden. But had he, while in youth, been taught to use his hands and eyes in some of the variety of skilful employments which may be pursued within doors, they would in his old age stand him in good stead, in preserving his independence, and enabling him, while engaged in some quiet kind of industry suited to his years and impaired strength, to occupy his own chair by his own fire-side, instead of being banished to a workhouse. As some may doubt the practicability of discovering a sufficient variety of in-door employments, it may be as well to give the following list which accompanied a basket of goods, manufactured by the children in the various workhouses in Kent. We are indebted to Mr. Tufnell, the Assistant Poor Law Commissioner, who was the cause of such employments forming a portion of school business, both for a view of the specimens and the information we are about to give with regard to them.

" A. Slippers made of list and leather, by the boys in the Dartford workhouse ; the expense of making these slippers is 1s. per pair. The price at which they will retail is 2s. 6d. per pair.

" B. Specimen of grass plait, made by the children in the same workhouse. This is an inferior specimen, as the grass was not well collected, but the specimen marked C is worth 2½d. per yard, and an able hand will weave ¾ of a yard in an hour. A gentleman who has taken much interest in the introduction of this manufacture, writes to me respecting the expense of conducting it ; as to the cost of the raw material, I should consider the six-pennyworth of grass, and four-pennyworth of labour in harvesting it, and I should add two pennyworth of fuel for scalding it, would furnish sufficient for two guineas worth of bonnets."

" C. A pair of cloth trowsers, made by a boy in Ticehurst workhouse ; the cost of making them is 3s. ; a similar pair of trowsers cannot be purchased under 5s.

" D. A straw hat made by the boys in the same workhouse; the cost of making it is 8d. ; the selling price is about 1s. 6d.

" E. A fustian jacket made by the boys in Thanet workhouse ; the cost of this article is 3s. 4d. ; it would not be purchased in the shops under 5s. 6d.

" F. Specimen of needle-work from the girls in the Seven Oaks workhouse. It is difficult to estimate the actual value of these articles.

" G. A cap made of cloth and leather, by the boys in Eastry workhouse ; the cost of making it is 6½d. ; it is worth 1s. for sale.

" H. Gloves made by the boys in Romney Marsh workhouse ; the expense of making them is 5d. ; the selling price of such an article in the shops is 9d.

" I. Worsted stockings, made by the boys in Uckfield workhouse ; the actual cost of these two pair is 6½d, the worth of them is more than 1s.

IN THE COUNTY OF KENT.

appropriate female occupations into the rural districts. The advantages deducible from it are obvious. Instead of being taken from her household, and exhausted with labour to which her strength is inadequate, the wife would be enabled, while she plied her work, to look after

Stockings of this description will last about twice as long as the worsted stockings purchased in the shops.

" Lastly.—The basket in which the above articles are contained, is made of rushes by the pauper children in the Cuckfield Union. The value of the material is so small as almost to elude an estimate, the workhouse having been supplied with a sufficient quantity to employ the boys during the winter at the expense of 10s., of which 5s. was incurred for cutting, and 5s. for bringing the rushes home, but the pond was deep, and five miles off; otherwise the expense would have been smaller. A basket of this description sells for 1s. 3d. The net, of which this is a specimen, may be applied to make bee-hives, hassocks, matting, and a variety of useful articles."

But it is not against old age alone that the agricultural labourer has need to provide himself with such employments as have been indicated. Although he is not so much subject to a total and lasting cessation of the demand for his labour as the manufacturer, he has another disadvantage to cope with which the manufacturer has not. If the work of the manufacturer is in demand at all, it is so all the year through without regard to seasons. But a severe winter will occasionally put all agricultural labour for a time to a stand still, while at particular seasons the demand for it is always slack ; and the chances are that, unless an individual has the good fortune to be employed by the year, there will always be a part of the winter in which he will be unable to procure work. The manner in which the number of paupers in the Union workhouses varies in the course of the year in agricultural districts, may, it is conceived, under existing circumstances, be fairly considered as the measure of the degree in which out-door labour is in demand. We have now before us a table of pauperism in East Kent, comprising the last two years ; and we observe that although the pressure of pauperism was much greater in one year than in the other, the increase and diminution was in both instances gradual, and that not only were the highest and lowest points in both years in the same months, but that each month in the year had, as it were, a fixed comparative degree of pauperism allotted to it. There can be little doubt but that the labourer, even in districts not overpopulated, must calculate upon having, in addition to his long winter evenings, whole days, if not weeks, in which he must either find some profitable employment for himself within doors or be without any a all. The very nature of the operations of husbandry causes this to be of necessity the case. This is an additional reason for making employments such as we have mentioned a part of the school instruction. Circumstances like the annual recurrence of a slack demand for labour in the winter season, and the incapacity of performing work requiring strong muscular exertion in old age, are such as all persons can foresee, and against which they ought to endeavour to provide.—ED.

her family. These occupations, too, being of a nature to be laid by and resumed at pleasure, she could always leave off in time to prepare a comfortable home and meal for her husband. Even if the amount of her earnings remained the same, the addition of comfort and happiness to herself and family would be invaluable.

Of the fifty-one families, seventeen keep pigs, and twenty-four are at present without one; five keep a horse and cart, but not one is in possession of a cow. The advantage of a pig or a cow to the cottager is obvious at a glance. Independent of the money which may be thus raised, there is the benefit of a certain supply of manure for the garden. Few, indeed, of the cottagers aspire so high as to the possession of a cow, though all are well aware of the advantages to be derived from it if they could obtain a sufficient piece of pasture. So great is this conviction among them, that several said they would willingly pay a rent of 4l. or even 5l. an acre for proper land. The farmers, however, are opposed to this system, and affirm that the labourer is more likely to be injured than benefited by the possession of such things. The true reason, however, of this objection among many of the farmers is, a lurking apprehension that the labourer would become more independent and less manageable.

The usual rent paid for a cottage and garden is two shillings a week; in some instances it is half a crown, but these cases are so rare, that the former sum may be considered to be the general rate. To those who have constant employment, with good wages, this is not an immoderate sum; but it presses very severely upon those who are not so well off. In respect of rent, however, the agricultural labourers have a great advantage over the inhabitants of towns, as they get a comfortable cottage, with a good garden, at a less rent than the latter often pay for a miserable, ill-ventilated room.

The amount of wages paid to able-bodied labourers, women and children, has been before stated; but it is of importance, in order to judge accurately of the real condition of the labourer, to ascertain the exact amount of the money received by an entire family in the course of the year. This, however, is a difficult thing to get at. The labourer will always under-state it, either from design, forgetfulness, or the inability to calculate. On the other hand, the farmer is inclined to over-estimate the amount. It cannot be made out by merely knowing the rate of wages ; because, though the man may be in constant employment, his wife and children are not necessarily so likewise. The man, too, gets more when he works by the piece, as, for instance, at ditching and draining; and both in harvest and hopping season, the gains of the whole family are considerably larger than at other periods of the year. The truth can be ascertained only when a whole family is employed throughout the year by the same farmer, and one, too, who keeps accurate accounts of his expenditure; neither of which circumstances are of frequent occurrence ; for individuals of the same family are often employed at different periods of the year by different farmers, while farmers' accounts are too often of a rough character. I however succeeded in getting from the praise-worthy individual before mentioned as the *fac-totum* of the parish, the following statement of the yearly earnings of five of his labourers and their families.

Name of labourer.	Amount of wages paid for day-work.			Amount paid in harvest-time to the family.			Amount paid in hopping-time to the family.			Total.		
	£	s.	d.	£	s.	d.	£	s.	d.	£	s.	d.
Wm. Curling, a capital labourer .	37	4	5½	3	15	4	10	4	11½	51	4	9
James Adlow, his wife, two boys, and one girl ...	57	9	3	7	0	10	0	15	0	65	5	2
George Cooke and his son	55	18	0	2	17	8	1	7	2	60	2	10
James Hawkins, his wife, and one boy	35	12	7	4	11	3	0	18	10	41	2	8
Marshal Brunger, his wife, and one boy	35	8	6	3	6	10	9	15	0	48	10	4

The condition of these individuals is somewhat better

than that of the majority of the labourers, as they were always employed. Nevertheless, it affords some grounds for estimating the daily earnings of a family; the average of which, for one containing three individuals, appears to be three shillings.

The particulars above given afford a pretty correct view of the physical state of these labourers, which, upon the whole, may be pronounced prosperous. Let us now look to their moral condition, which has been investigated with equal care, so far as the nature of the facts would permit.

Of the fifty-one families examined, seven parents only ever opened a book after the labours of the day were closed. To the inquiry how they passed their time in the long winter evenings, the answer in most cases was, "About home, doing sometimes one thing sometimes another; but, most times, going early to bed for want of something to do." In two cases only was the ale-house confessed to be the usual resource, though there is little doubt but that these candid persons were not so wholly without the countenance of their neighbours as the answers would imply. Indeed, if they were, the landlords of the two public-houses and two beer-houses (for that is the number in the village) might long ago have taken down their signs.

The number of books in the possession of the cottagers corresponded with their indifference and inaptitude to mental recreation of any sort. Out of the fifty-one families, four only are mentioned as possessing any books besides the Bible, Testament, prayer and hymn books. In thirty-four cottages, one or other of the last-mentioned books was found, and, in some instances, a few religious tracts. These constituted the whole of the mental aliment of the district. Not a Penny Magazine, nor any of the other cheap publications of the day, which convey so much useful instruction and amusement to the working classes in the towns, was to be seen.

The desire of adorning the walls with prints is always an indication of some touch of cultivation in the cottager. In Herne-hill, the prints are rather more scarce than even the books. Of the fifty-one families, thirty had two or three prints, and twenty-one were without any. In twenty-six cases the subjects were Scriptural, and in four only they were not so. The prints were of the poorest kind, and were usually such as might have been seen in cottages half a century back. The productions of modern graphic art, have not as yet found their way into these rural districts.

My observations have hitherto been confined to the adult portion of the community, the moral condition of which, in an age when the blessings of knowledge and civilization are supposed to be so generally diffused, is as mortifying as it is afflicting. But, forbearing any reflections for the present, I proceed to the condition of the children. The returns give to the fifty-one families forty-five children above the age of fourteen years, and one hundred and seventeen under that age. Of the first class, eleven only can read and write, twenty-one can read a little, and the remainder cannot. In the second class, forty-two attend school, but several of these go only occasionally. The rest do not go at all. One reason why there are so many absentees, independent of those who are too young to attend, which in a given number of children will be usually found to be one in three, is, that when a child, especially a boy, has passed its tenth year, the parents say they cannot afford to maintain him unless he contributes something by his own labour. The child is therefore removed whenever a job of work can be found for him. At sixpence a day, four days of his labour would pay the weekly rent, which the labourer always grudges to spare out of his earnings. This is generally found to be an irresistible temptation. Another reason, and certainly a very forcible one, often alleged, is, that the child makes little or no progress, and might just as well be employed in the fields. This is generally too true. Children who have been two years at school, are frequently found unable to read. Again, girls are often detained at home to look after those who are too young to go to school, while the mother is employed in the fields. There are two simple methods, however, of obviating these objections of parents to send-

ing their children to school, which may very easily be put
into practice.   The first is, to send them for two hours
only, instead, as is usually done, for the greater part of the
day.   This plan is adopted in the establishment of M.
de Fellenberg, at Hofwyl in Switzerland, at those seasons
of the year, as, for instance, during the harvest, when
the labour of the children is of considerable value.   It is
found that this small portion of time, if properly employed,
is sufficient for the instruction of the children.   If this
be the case at Hofwyl, where the instruction given is of
so varied and comprehensive a character, including such
subjects as history, geography, and botany, how much
more must that time be sufficient for the degree of instruction given in a village school in England, where
nothing beyond reading and writing is ever thought of?
Indeed, this limitation of time would be rather advantageous, than otherwise, to the progress of the children.
Of the six hours usually spent in school, four may be
considered as wasted ; and would be more profitably employed in labour, or in teaching a child some useful occupation.   After two hours his attention is sure to flag, and
no advantage is gained by forcing him to con the same
lesson over and over again in the close atmosphere
and noisy bustle of a school-room.   Another advantage
resulting from this limitation of time, would be, that, by
dividing the children into separate classes, coming at
different hours, the same instructor and the same means
of instruction would suffice for a much larger number
of scholars ; and thus the expense of education might be
considerably diminished.   At the same time, the comfort
and usefulness of the instructor would be very much
consulted by giving to him the superintendence of a
smaller number of children at once.   The other method
alluded to is, the establishment of infant schools, which
are too generally known to render necessary any description of them here.
    It appears by the returns, that out of forty-two chil-
dren attending school, six only can read and write ; of
twenty-two who can read, only thirteen read fluently,
and nine very little ; and the remainder cannot read at
all.   In twelve families, the boys are instructed in gar-

dening, husbandry, or in something distinct from reading
and writing. This, however, must be taken with some
qualification; for, in most cases where the inquiry was
pursued, it proved that the boys were merely employed
in assisting their father in his labours, in doing which
they seldom received any instruction. In fifteen families,
the girls were said to learn brewing, baking, and other
household matters, independent of sewing; while in thirty-
four families they practised nothing but washing and
needle-work.

The parish possesses a Sunday school, and three
others, in one only of which is writing taught. This
school is kept by a master, who, being from physical infirmity incapable of labour, was obliged to adopt this
mode of life. He has only eighteen scholars, and half of
this number come from neighbouring parishes. The
mode of instruction is the old system, and the instruction
itself of the simplest kind. The only books used are the
Universal Spelling Book, Vyse's Spelling Book, Duncan's
English Expositor, Entick's Dictionary, the Bible and
Testament, and one of the old manuals of arithmetic.
Not more than one half of the scholars can write, and of
these a few only are instructed in the rudiments of arithmetic. History, geography, and grammar do not form
a part of even the nominal scheme of instruction. It is,
however, the high school of the place, and those parents
who sent their children there took credit for the sacrifice
they made. The terms are,—for reading only, sixpence
a-week; and for reading, writing, and arithmetic, 13s. 5d.
a quarter. The village, however, is unable to support
even such a school as this; for, as before stated, one
half of the scholars come from other places.

The two other schools are merely dame-schools, in
which nothing but sewing and reading are taught. Many
of the children attend so irregularly, and are often absent for such long periods, that they forget all they have
learned. Owing to this, some children are unable to read;
after being members of the school two or three years.
The books in use are the Bible, the Testament, Catechism,
and some religious tracts. From being confined constantly to these books, the children imagine they cannot

read others. When asked if they could read, a common answer was, " Yes, a little in the Testament." Children, who could read this book fluently enough, instantly began to spell and hesitate when desired to read out of another. The reason is, they have read, and heard read, the same thing so often, that the sound of one word suggests the following one. They even remember some words from their length or form, and the position they occupy in the page, which they would not know in another book. This accounts in some measure for instances, not very uncommon, of boys of thirteen or fourteen, who have left school two or three years, answering, when asked if they could read, that " they could once, but have forgot now, since they left school." It is probable that this occurs much more frequently than is supposed in cases where children are only taught to read ; but it would be difficult, perhaps, to adduce a single instance of this forgetfulness in a child who has learned also to write. Whenever a poor man is in the habit of reading, you may be sure he can write.

The largest of the two dame-schools is chiefly supported by the vicar of the parish. For this purpose, he allows the school-mistress to occupy, rent free, the vicarage-house, a small building well adapted for a school, with the garden and some land belonging to it. In return, the vicar retains the right of sending to the school such children as he chooses without payment, though for some he pays voluntarily fourpence a-week. The parents of the other children pay threepence a-week for each child. The number attending the school varies very much, being sometimes as low as thirty, and at others as high as fifty. It is remarkable that the last mistress who kept this school, the husband of the present one, and the husband of the mistress of the other school, were the three staunchest adherents of Thoms, and put more faith in his absurd pretensions than any others of his followers.

The Sunday school is also supported chiefly at the expense of the vicar, and the superintendence of it is undertaken by his lady. The school is held in their residence, and they have been at great pains to increase the number of those intended to be benefited by their laudable endeavours. The instruction given, as in most Sunday schools, is entirely of a religious nature. The object (as described) has been to make the children practically acquainted with moral and religious truths. With this view, after repeating the answers in the Catechism, the children are required to give the substance of the answers in their own language. By these means many of them became (to use the words of my informer) as well instructed in the principles of religion, and were as capable of giving pertinent answers to questions concerning them, as the generality of the children of the opulent. There were, however, complaints that, notwithstanding this apparent progress, the children could never be brought to connect what they learned in school with their practice in life, and remained as idle, mischievous, and vicious as before. A young lad, named Griggs, who was killed in the affray, had been one of the most promising pupils while in the school, and she said it was impossible to attribute his conduct in joining Thoms to any want of religious instruction. Might not the ground for this complaint, which is so general, be greatly lessened, if the instruction given at Sunday schools were rendered less doctrinal, and more confined to plain Christian morals, and to subjects calling for the exercise of observation and reflection, which might be illustrated by examples drawn from the Scriptures, and by cases taken from every-day life put by the teacher?

The schools above described are the only means of instruction open to the children of the parish; and how utterly incapable they are of affording even the lowest degree of education required in the present day, need not be said. In justice, however, to the present incumbent of the parish, it should be recollected, in addition to what has before been stated, that no school of any kind existed before his appointment to it; and that, for upwards of forty years previous, there had not been a resident clergyman.

THE VILLE OF DUNKIRK.

This is an extra-parochial district, comprising an extensive tract of wood-lands of not less than five thousand acres. The whole of this property, with the exception of about twelve hundred acres belonging to a lay individual, forms part of the possessions of the Dean and Chapter of Canterbury.* Until within these few years, the district was very thinly inhabited; but, since part of the land has been cleared, it has become much more populous. At present, the number of inhabitants is about seven hundred. Their only ostensible occupation formerly was wood-cutting, which, not affording constant employment, led them to seek other means of subsistence. In those days the occupation of a smuggler was a very gainful one. The navy was so fully employed that sufficient vessels could not be spared for watching the numerous creeks and inlets on the coast, and the coast-guard had not then been thought of; or, if thought of, the number of men required rendered it impracticable during a war, when it was found scarcely possible to man the vessels afloat. The *free-trade* was consequently in those days a much more prosperous adventure than it has been for many years past. Cargoes were frequently landed, and the profits were immense. Few persons participated more largely in these illicit adventures than did the inhabitants of the Kentish coast. Many of the small farmers, who prospered so surprisingly on lands out of which their fathers could barely eke sufficient to pay their rent and support their families, had found out the secret, that ploughing the sea was a much more gainful trade than ploughing the land. The unsettled inhabitants of Dunkirk, unprovided with constant occupation, were not long in making the same discovery. The excitement of such a mode of life too was congenial to their habits. They were, besides, well situated for the purpose.

* There are some errors in this estimate and distribution of the property. It appears that the district contains, according to an admeasurement made about four years back, 5,224 acres. This property is stated by Dr. Spry, Vice-Dean of Canterbury, to be divided between *twenty-two* proprietors, of whom *five* are ecclesiastical collegiate or charitable corporations. The property of the Dean and Chapter of Canterbury, in the Ville, consists of 1,008 acres 3 roods 30 furlongs. By the last census taken in 1831, the amount of the population was stated to be 613, showing an increase of 70 since 1821; but it is uncertain whether it has since increased in this ratio.

The district is only eight or nine miles from the sea; and the neighbouring woods, which cover the hills gradually declining to the coast, offered great facilities for conceal-ment.   It was not likely, situated as they were, that they should resist so many temptations.   There was, in fact, nothing in the neighbourhood at all calculated to arrest these evil tendencies, or to inspire any regard for order and law.   Though the tenants* of the Church, and living within view of the spires of Canterbury, there was not a church where they could attend the ordinances of religion, nor clergyman to guide and in-struct them, nor even a dissenting minister to supply his place.   Even the Wesleyan methodists, who at that time were imparting religious instruction to the inhabit-ants of the Cornish mines, appear to have overlooked this neglected spot.   The place did not even possess a day-school in which the lowest degree of instruction oould be imparted.   Not to speak of a gentry, there was not a medical man, a farmer, or even a shopkeeper of any description in the place.   So situated, it is not to be wondered that the people fell into pernicious courses, and acquired the character, which they have not yet lost, of a desperate and lawless community.

Of late years, however, there has been a considerable improvement in the district.   Large portions of the land have been cleared, and several small farms established, which offer more constant employment.   The vigilance of the coast-guard, established since the war, has nearly put an end to the traffic of the smuggler; and the people have been compelled to apply themselves to occupations of a more lawful description.   But the district is still without church or chapel, and would be utterly destitute of religious superintendence and instruction of any kind, but for the gratuitous services of the present vicar of Herne-hill.   This gentleman, besides endeavouring to persuade the people to attend his church, has established,

* We are informed that the Dean and Chapter of Canterbury have only one tenant in the district.   There is some difficulty in saying what is the precise nature of the relationship existing between the cottagers and the proprietors in the district, many of the former having acquired, or at least laying a claim to, the freehold, as special occupants.

at his own expense, in Dunkirk, a day-school,* kept by a mistress, for the instruction of the children. The inquiries occasioned by the late events have, however, induced the dignitaries of Canterbury to turn their attention to the spiritual wants of their hitherto neglected tenants. They are now, it is said, taking steps for the erection of a church within the ville,† and the site of it has already been determined upon. If to the church be added a minister who will zealously devote himself to the improvement of these poor people, not confining himself to his duties as a preacher, but conscientiously fulfilling the equally important ones of a judicious friend and adviser, aiding them with his knowledge and experience in the improvement of their means, much real good will have proceeded out of evil.

The ville contains between ninety and one hundred families, forming a population, as before stated, of about seven hundred individuals; but, the place being extra-parochial, it is difficult to get at the precise amount. The number of persons belonging to the ville in the Union workhouse at Faversham was, for the quarter ending on Lady-day last, sixty-two. Of these, fourteen were men, eleven women, and thirty-seven were children. The number of those receiving out-door relief was one hundred and fifty-six; viz. thirty-four men, forty women, and eighty-two children. Thus the whole number of persons receiving relief from the parish was not less than two hundred and eighteen, being considerably more than one-fourth of the whole population.‡

The condition of fifty families, taken indifferently through the district, was investigated in the same way as those of Herne-hill. They have nearly all the advantage

* The Dean and Chapter of Canterbury contribute in common with the other proprietors to the support of this dame school.

† We are informed that the design of erecting and endowing a church in the district, originated with the Archbishop of Canterbury, previously to the occurrence of the disturbances.

‡ The same remark applies to these persons, as was before made in a note respecting those receiving relief in Herne-hill, viz.—that the return relates to a portion of the year when it is more difficult to find employment than at other seasons. The number of persons now receiving relief is considerably less.

of living in separate cottages; and, though the condition and contents of their dwellings were not quite so good as those of their neighbours in the last-mentioned village, they were, nevertheless, much better than, from the habits and character of their owners, might have been expected. Seven of the cottages had two rooms for the accommodation of the family, twenty-four had three rooms, ten had four rooms, six had five rooms, two had six rooms, and one had seven rooms. Of the fifty cottages, forty-seven had gardens; twenty-six of which contained upwards of ten perches, and twenty-one less than that extent. By the report, forty are returned as being well-cultivated, and only seven as not so. In eight gardens, flowers were cultivated; and in thirty-nine they were not. In thirty-two cases, the supply of water was plentiful; in nine tolerable, and in six deficient. The appearance of comfort and cleanliness in the cottages and families is represented as being in twenty-one instances very good, in sixteen middling, and in thirteen dirty and uncomfortable. Of the fifty cottagers, nineteen keep pigs, two keep a cow, and six keep a cart and horse, or donkeys. In respect to their capability of improving their comfort by being able to make use of carpenter's tools, so as to make or repair cupboards, tables, doors, pig-sties, &c. it seems that four men only can handle them in a workmanlike manner; twelve can use them roughly, so as to mend or put up a pig-sty; while thirty-one cannot use them at all. The capability of the wives to add to the comfort of their husbands and families is expressed in the following statement. The number of those who can wash, sew, brew, bake, and make butter, is eighteen; twenty-two can sew and wash only; and eight can do none of these things. It is remarkable that knitting is a branch of female industry very uncommon in Kent. In Herne-hill and Dunkirk not six women could be found who practised this useful occupation. Several of the cottagers live in freehold cottages of their own; but the greater part of them are mortgaged nearly to their full value. The usual rent paid for a cottage and garden varies from 2s. to 2s. 6d. a-week. The wages paid to the men, women, and children, are very much the same as those before stated for

Herne-hill; but owing to the smallness of the farms, and the great quantity of wood-land, the employment given is not so constant as in the latter place. Besides labouring in the fields, the men work as wood-cutters and charcoal-burners. It is very difficult to obtain an exact estimate of the amount of the earnings of each family in the year, as their own accounts are not to be relied upon, and there are no farmers who constantly employ the same hands, and keep strict accounts of the sums paid to them.

Of the low intellectual and moral condition of these cottagers, some idea may be formed from the following items in the returns. In twenty-six cottages books were found, and in twenty-four there were none. The books were usually the Bible, Testament, Prayer Book, and Hymn Books; in a few instances all of these were seen, but generally only two of them. In four cottages only were there any books of general information. But the supply of books, deficient as it seems, was more than ample for the use made of them. The returns state that in two cottages only did the parents employ their evenings in reading; in thirty-eight cases the time after labour was described as being spent " about home," but not in reading; and in seven instances the husband went out to seek for company at the beer-house, or in the cottages of his neighbours. No doubt this number was much below the truth, but everybody seemed anxious to disclaim acquaintance with the beer-shop, though, considering the people were totally without recreation of any kind, it was natural they should go there for society and amusement. In twenty of the cottages the walls were decorated with prints, and in thirty they were not. The prints were usually of a religious kind, such as those found in Herne-hill. In four cases only the subjects were other than Scriptural. These were all of a loyal character, being portraits of King William IV. and Queen Adelaide.

The number of children, in the fifty families, above fourteen years of age, amounted to forty-three. Of these, twelve could read and write, eight could read only, and the remaining twenty-three could do neither. Several of the girls had gone into service, and the boys found occasional employment in the fields and woods. The children under the age of fourteen were one hundred and thirteen in number, forty-three of whom attended school. Four only of the number attended a school where writing and reading were taught, and for this purpose they were obliged to go into the neighbouring parish of Boughton. The remainder went to the day-school, which is kept by a mistress, and supported chiefly, as before stated, by the vicar of Herne-hill. In this school reading and 'sewing are alone taught, and this is all the instruction the district affords. Those who are sent gratis by the vicar to the day-school are obliged to attend his Sunday-school in Herne-hill, that being the condition on which the favour is granted. In the cases where the parents pay to the day-school, the attendance at the Sunday-school is, of course, optional. Of the hundred and thirteen children, eight only can read and write, ten read fluently, thirteen read a little, and the remainder cannot read at all. An allowance must of course be made out of these last for those who are of too tender an age. In ten families out of the fifty, the parents paid for the schooling of their children; four paid sixpence a-week for each, for attending the school where writing was taught, and six paid threepence a-week to the day-school. Besides this, the parents of those who were instructed gratuitously paid one shilling a-year towards defraying the expense of a fire in the school-room. In four families the boys were said to be instructed at home in wood-cutting and husbandry; and in thirteen the girls were taught sewing and other household work.

In all respects the condition of the inhabitants of the ville of Dunkirk is inferior to that of those of Herne-hill and the neighbouring parishes. This is, of course, to be attributed to its being an extra-parochial place, and to the absence (before noticed) of any class superior to that of the smallest farmers.

THE VILLAGE OF BOUGHTON UNDER THE BLEAN.

This village contains one hundred and seventy families, composing a population of thirteen hundred. The number of acres is something less than four thousand, and the net rental is under 5000*l.* The number of adults belonging to the parish at present in the Union workhouse is thirty; viz. twenty men and ten women, and the number of children thirty-six. Of persons receiving out-door relief, there are ninety-seven adults; viz. forty-nine men and forty-eight women, and eighty-six children: the whole number of those receiving parochial aid being two hundred and forty-nine,—nearly twenty per cent. of the whole population.

The duty of the parish church is performed by the rector; he does not keep a curate. There is also a Wesleyan methodist chapel, which is served by different preachers. The village contains a few retail shops, filled with such wares as are chiefly required by country people. There are six regular public-houses, and three beer-houses. The former are chiefly supported by strangers, the village lying in the high road to Canterbury. The latter are described by the respectable inhabitants as complete nuisances. A small portion of the inhabitants are employed as servants in the shops and private houses in the village; but the great bulk of the working population consists of agricultural labourers.

Though the parish lies close to the scene of the late catastrophe, and was frequently visited by Thoms, very few of its inhabitants were among his followers at the time of the conflict. This is the more remarkable, as the number of persons in the parish at that time out of employment was very much greater than in Herne-hill, where, as has been shown, there was scarcely any distress. This difference is perhaps to be attributed to the circumstance of the inhabitants being more in the way of mixing with the world than their neighbours of Herne-hill, and, consequently, less likely to become the dupes of such a delusion.

Fifty families of the labouring population were examined in the same manner as at Herne-hill. The dwellings in general wear a comfortable and neat appearance; but many of them being in the street, have but very small gardens, and some are altogether without them. Three of the families have but one room each; seven of the cottages have only two rooms, twenty cottages have three rooms, nineteen have four rooms, and one has five. It will be seen, by a reference to the returns of Herne-hill and Dunkirk, that the average number of rooms in the cottages in those places is greater than in Boughton. Forty-one dwellings have gardens, and nine are without; three only of these gardens contain more than twenty perches, the remainder are small patches not sufficient to raise half the quantity of vegetables required by a family. Nearly all of them are well cultivated, four only being returned as indifferently so. In twenty-one of the gardens, flowers are cultivated, and in twenty they are not. The supply of water is abundant; in one case only was it represented as being deficient. The general appearance of the cottages and families is described in the reports as follows: twenty-eight are returned as comfortable, twelve as tolerable, and ten as poorly. Of the fifty families, four only keep a pig, and not one is in possession of a cow. In these respects they are still more unprovided than the people of Herne-hill and Dunkirk. The men are by no means expert in the use of carpenter's tools; three only out of fifty families can use them in a workmanlike manner, six can use them roughly, while thirty-seven cannot use them at all. The women, however, are very tolerably versed in such occupations as tend to the comfort of their households. In the same number of families there are fifteen wives who can sew, wash, brew, bake, and manage a dairy; twenty-three can wash and sew, and four are returned as being unable to do any of these things. The total incapacity in the last case arose from age and infirmity.

The rent paid for cottages, and the price of labour, in Boughton, are nearly the same as in Herne-hill and Dunkirk. Employment, however, is not so constant as in Herne-hill. By the labourers this is attributed to the ill-judged economy of the farmers, who (they say) do not employ a sufficient number of hands on their land. The latter, on the other hand, affirm that the land will not repay a large outlay of labour, and it is besides a question whether they have the capital to lay out. In the mean time, the want of agricultural employment, and

the utter incapability of the labourers to turn their idle
time to account, (and all agricultural labourers, even those
in full employment, must have some idle time in winter,
especially in the long evenings,) often occasions great
distress, and, during the last winter, compelled many to
seek relief from the parish. In these cases, the want of
good-sized gardens, and of a piece of land sufficient to
feed a cow, was severely felt. Many of the men, whose
character for sobriety and steadiness was undoubted,
asserted that, if they had possessed these resources, they
would not have thought of troubling the parish, and
would have been ready with their rent to a day.

The intellectual and moral condition of the villagers of
Boughton does not appear to be superior to that of their
neighbours in Herne-hill and Dunkirk. In the fifty families, four only of the parents had recourse to books to
beguile the long tedium of a winter's evening when the
labours of the day were closed ; and the reading of these
persons was confined entirely to the Bible and two or
three religious books. The others, when asked how they
passed their evenings, replied, " At home, in the house,
doing sometimes one thing, sometimes another ; most
times, going early to bed." In twenty-six dwellings,
Bibles, Testaments, prayer books, hymn books, and a few
tracts were found. In four only were there any books
not of a religious nature, and in the remainder there
were none of any description. Prints were found on the
walls in twenty-six houses ; in seventeen instances the
subjects were Scriptural, and in nine they were mixed ;
in twenty-four houses there were none of any kind. The
whole were of the most inferior description, many of
them apparently cut off the heads of ballads purchased
from some travelling hawker.

The above families contain thirty-five children above
fourteen years of age. Of these, seven can read and
write, nine can read only, and the remainder cannot
read at all. Of one hundred and nineteen children
under fourteen years of age, thirty-two attend school,
seven only go to a school where writing is taught, the
remainder go to the Sunday-school or day-school. Of the
latter, three can read easily, nineteen can read a little,

and the rest cannot read at all. The parents of eleven
of these families pay for the schooling of their children;
three pay at the rate of 6*d.* a week for each child, four
pay 4*d.* and four pay 3*d.* In two families the boys are
instructed in gardening and agricultural occupations;
and in nine families the girls are taught sewing and
other housewifely employments.

Boughton contains two boarding and day schools, four
day-schools, and one Wesleyan Sunday-school. The two
boarding-schools are chiefly supported by pupils who
come from other places; and the day scholars who attend them belong to the families of the tradesmen and
farmers in the neighbourhood, who are not included in
the investigation of which the results have just been
given. All the day-schools are kept by mistresses. In
one only of these is writing taught. In the others the
instruction is confined to reading and sewing. The average number of scholars in each is fourteen. The Wesleyan Sunday-school is attended by eighty boys and
sixty girls, who are instructed in reading and religious
knowledge. This large number renders it difficult to
account for the number of children among the labouring
classes who are unable to read, otherwise than by admit-
ting the great inefficiency of the instruction given. Indeed, all inquiry goes to prove that until a national system of education be established, in which the minimum
of instruction shall, at all events, be prescribed, and until
masters capable of carrying it out be procured, the instruction afforded to the peasantry, whether provided by
the charitable assistance of others, or by schools supported at their own expense, must always remain of
the most worthless and inefficient description.

If due consideration be given to the statements above
made respecting the actual condition of the population of
this district, our surprise at the nature of the events
which have occurred amongst them will be very much
diminished. It is scarcely possible to imagine a state of
things more favourable to the designs of a fanatical impostor than that in which they live. Everything around
them seems calculated to keep the mental faculties in a
state of torpor;—their isolated dwellings, never or seldom

visited by strangers or persons having different occupations from their own,—the solitude of the fields in which they live and labour,—and the perpetual routine of the same tasks, all combine to prevent the reasoning powers from attaining that acuteness and perception which they would readily acquire under other circumstances. But though the judgment is thus rendered inactive, the imagination in such cases is often morbidly alive to impressions from every unusual object. Hence people so circumstanced are more open to superstition than others ;— hence the superstition of the Highlanders and the highly-wrought religious enthusiasm of the settlers in the forests of America. The best preservative against fanaticism and superstition is the constant collision of mind which occurs in more thickly-populated communities. Among them every idea is examined and put in a thousand points of view. It is almost impossible that a gross fallacy should escape detection ; and, the moment it appears, argument and ridicule are unsparingly employed for its destruction. But the advantage so gained consists not so much in the means of exposing error when it appears *en flagrant delit,* as in creating that general activity of mind by which individuals acquire the habit of examining and pronouncing upon facts and appearances the moment they present themselves.

Another and scarcely less efficacious preservative against these disorders of the mind is to be found in amusements, and other sources of innocent and healthful excitement. But, during my stay in the district, I did not once observe the peasantry engaged in any games or sports, notwithstanding the weather was unusually favourable for such exercises. On one occasion only I observed some persons playing at cricket, but they appeared to be above the class of the peasantry. For them there appeared to be no recreation of either an active or quiet character, unless they resorted to the beer-shop, the only place open to them for enjoyment of any kind. Here, perhaps, they could have a game of bowls ; but then they must play for beer, it being a general rule in such places that no *dry games,* as they are termed, shall be played. But, with the exception of these houses, there is no place where they can assemble for dancing, singing, reading, or society; so that they know nothing of enjoyments which are not associated with expense or debauchery. It is this absence of all lively and innocent amusements which has stamped upon our peasantry the heavy clownish air which all foreigners remark. It would be well if this were the only consequence of a want of amusement; but, besides rendering men dull and heavy, it tends to make them brutal and savage, and incapable of deriving any pleasurable excitement except from debauchery or fanaticism. In these matters, not unimportant points in civilization, we have positively receded since the days of Elizabeth. That princess, who was imbued with a better philosophy than that of our ascetics, encouraged the enactment of laws not merely to promote, but to provide for, the amusements of the people. She was aware that the drunken, the idle, and the vicious are not usually found amongst the cheerful and active; but amongst those whose morose and gloomy habits render them incapable of joining in simple recreations, and who draw their pleasures from darker and more dangerous sources. Among the plans for improving and elevating the character of the peasantry, that of supplying them with the means of amusement and social pleasures, unconnected with sensual indulgence, must not be forgotten. It has, indeed, received of late some attention from distinguished writers; but it is still much too little considered by the government, and the great body of those who profess an anxiety to improve the condition of the working classes.

But to return to the difference in the nature of the circumstances operating upon the inhabitants of towns, and upon those of thinly populated districts,—it may be observed that those habits of investigating and deciding, which in towns are acquired from the advantage of perpetually mixing with the world, must in the country be mainly supplied from other sources. Hence it is that education, in the widest and best sense of the term, is even more needed by the inhabitants of the country than by those of the towns. Not only should the knowledge imparted to the former be as extended and varied as circumstances will permit, but it should be communicated

in a manner calculated to awaken as much as possible
the reasoning powers, and to fix the habit of calling them
upon all occasions into play. The advantages that would
result both to the individuals in question, and to the
community, from such a system, are incalculable. We
should not then be in danger of a rural commotion because
a madman imprudently liberated from his confinement
was traversing the country, and endeavouring to persuade
a wretched peasantry that he was the Saviour of the world
returned for the purpose of establishing the reign of the
saints upon earth; nor should we be much alarmed at
the propositions of Destructives for an agrarian law and
a community of property. The advantages and necessity
of the institution of property for the benefit of all, properly
estimated by the great body of the people, would be the
surest preservative, not only against servile insurrections,
but against that envy and ill-feeling which at present
raise so dangerous a barrier between the higher and
lower classes. But, not to confine our views to merely
negative advantages, who can estimate the positive increase to the wealth and power of this country from the
substitution of a well-educated agricultural population,
scientifically acquainted with the nature of their occupations, and accustomed to reason upon their condition and
their interests, in place of a peasantry immersed in ignorance and pauperism? Such a change, however, can be
produced only by means of an effective system of education. No doubt, the provisions of the Poor-law Amendment Act, if wisely carried out, will do much to lessen
the amount of pauperism which has so long demo-
ralized the people; but, to ensure all the advantages
derivable from it, it is essential that it should be se-
conded by a sound system of national education. Those
to whom the administration of this law is intrusted should
neglect no means of securing such co-operation; for, in
exact proportion to the extent that they do so, will be
the ultimate success of their efforts. Indeed, if the reform of the law be not followed by persevering exertion
on the part of the legislature and the wealthier classes of
society to introduce the benefits of education among the
mass of the people,—teaching them not merely to read and

write, but to cultivate the prudential virtues, and learn to provide better for themselves than any charitable assistance can do for them,—the enforcement of the law will be little better than a gratuitous cruelty. Those who have conversed familiarly with the inmates of the workhouses will at once assent to this. Out of sixteen paupers examined at the workhouse of the Union, (Faversham,) to which the parishes we have been speaking of belong, only two had ever saved up so much as 10l. notwithstanding that several of them had been in the receipt, for some time, of from 20s. to 40s. a week! and not one had ever kept any account of receipt and expenditure! The being merely able to read makes little difference in this respect, for, in the number examined, there were several who could do so. Indeed, the most prudent of the two who had saved, had received no education. He had been a workman in the Powder Mills at Faversham, and out of his wages of 30s. a week, had amassed a sum of 200l. which he afterwards lost by the failure of a bank in Faversham. He bitterly regretted his want of education, which he said had prevented his embracing many opportunities that offered of bettering his condition, and compelled him to finish a life of industry in the workhouse, instead of occupying a respectable situation in society. Several others complained that they had never been taught to look forward to the consequences of their own acts. One man, a shoemaker, about twenty-eight years of age, who was in the house with his wife and five children, attributed his poverty and pitiable condition entirely to this cause. When asked if he did not calculate, before marrying so early, his means to support a wife and family, his answer was, " No, sir,—never gave it a thought—never thought of anything—you see, sir, we an't used to look forward." When asked if he would have attended at the time to any advice given him, he replied, " Why, perhaps not, sir, if it came from the like of one of us, sir; but if it had been a gentleman like you, I think I should." These, and a thousand similar instances, all tend to show that the mass of misery which creates our pauperism, and which many people appear to regard as one of the inevitable ills appointed to humanity, is chiefly the result of our own culpable neglect, and may be diminished, if not entirely removed, in proportion as we apply ourselves to the task with intelligence and earnestness.

It is beginning now to be admitted by all that it is to education we must look for the accomplishment of this great end. But the question remains, What is the kind and character of the education required? The occurrence of the deplorable events we have been considering, and the statements made relative to the nature of the instruction afforded to the peasantry of the villages in question, tend to show that the meagre instruction usually given is totally inadequate to the object. The facts prove that merely religious instruction of the kind obtained by these villagers is not of itself sufficient to fit men for discharging their duties to society. It is shown by the foregoing statements that the majority of the persons so foolishly led into the commission of such grave offences had in their youth gone to Sunday-schools, were in the habit of attending church, and that those who could read, read and possessed only religious books; so that not only the instruction they received, but the only kind they had any opportunity of gaining, was entirely of a religious character. It is particularly to be remarked that not in a single cottage was there found any one book (not of a religious nature) capable of giving any useful knowledge of men and things,—not a Penny or Saturday Magazine, nor any one of the various cheap publications of the day, which convey so much useful instruction and amusement to the populations of the towns. It seems incredible, but it is nevertheless true, that none of the cottagers examined had even heard of such things. Those who, from their position in the country, are chiefly called upon to charge themselves with the education of the peasantry, seem almost universally to entertain the idea that the Bible, the Catechism, and a few tracts, should form the whole mental aliment of a working man. Accordingly, whether in schools or cottages, this is the only provision made. Now it may be doubted if a course of exclusive religious reading, has not a tendency to narrow the mind, and instil fallacious ideas. Without the aid of information greatly superior to their own, it is impossible that unlearned persons, while reading the Scriptures, should draw those distinctions and make those qualifications rendered necessary by the lapse of ages and a totally different order of circumstances ; and yet, without such distinctions, the narratives and lessons contained in the sacred writings may be turned, as they often have been, not merely into sources of error, but into authorities for wrong. Thus the Scottish Covenanters justified their murders by the severities practised by the Israelites at the express command of Moses ; and the Anabaptists of Germany made use of the disinterestedness of the early Christians in sharing their property in a time of emergency among each other, to justify their spoliation of their peaceable fellow-subjects. This exclusive kind of reading too is apt to beget fond imaginations in the readers,—such as that they are more than others under the especial protection of Heaven, and likely to be favoured with especial communications and directions from above. Thus, Wesley,* when in any doubt or dilemma, used to open his Bible at hazard, and take the first text which could by any ingenuity be applied to his case, and regard it as an especial direction ;—a conduct not a whit less silly and presumptuous than the appeals made to Heaven, in the feudal ages, by the wager of battle and ordeals of fire and water. Probably many of his followers copied this pernicious example ; and, if we could get at the truth, we should find they often paid dearly for this rash and ignorant presumption. From the familiar manner with which Mrs. ———, before mentioned, spoke of and quoted the Scriptures, which were always lying open on the table, it was evident she was fully under the influence of the feeling here spoken of. The result of such reading in her case is a most instructive lesson.

But, while objecting to this exclusive reading of religious books, I must not be represented as wishing to banish the Scriptures from the cottage. I know the consoling, the purifying, and ennobling effect of their sacred lessons upon the poor ; but I affirm that this effect is

---

* Vide Southey's Life of Wesley, vol. i. p. 239.

more likely to follow where the mind, accustomed to exercise its powers in other contemplations, is more capable of appreciating the purity of their doctrines, and the exalted nature of the virtues they inculcate. What is wanted, is the introduction of a useful every-day kind of literature, calculated to arrest the attention and exercise the faculties of the labouring classes. If, when the out-door work was over, the cottage family, sitting by a cheerful fire, and engaged in some light and profitable handicraft, could be entertained by a member of it reading some interesting particulars respecting the labours in which they are ordinarily engaged, or the natural objects with which they are conversant, their curiosity could not fail of being excited. In the same manner, tales of the lives of persons in their own sphere, showing the results of the prudential virtues and their opposites, could not but have the happiest effects. Such recitals would call forth opinions and give rise to constant discussions,— the hearers would compare characters and actions, and the habit of doing so would do much to diminish that mental inactivity which is the great evil of rural life. Concise accounts of different towns and cities of the kingdom, giving the number of the inhabitants, and showing by what means they are chiefly supported,— short histories of distinguished men, especially of such as have risen by their own merits from obscurity,—and plain accounts of particular trades and manufactures, would never fail of interesting. There is nothing in this at all calculated to displace the Scriptures from their rightful supremacy. On the contrary, it may be repeated, that the taste for reading, and the habits of investigating and comparing, created by such exercises, would prove a great assistance towards a thoughtful and beneficial perusal of the sacred records.

The degree of education generally supposed suited to the condition of the labouring classes in this country is fixed at so low a standard, that were it not for the example afforded by Prussia and other countries, where the noble experiment of enabling the mass of the people to participate in the civilization of the age, by the medium of a national system of instruction, has been successfully tried, one might hesitate to mention the course of instruction the best calculated to preserve the population of a country from religious fanaticism. With these examples, however, before us, it may be remarked, that the course alluded to would comprise some instruction in natural philosophy, with familiar explanations of the most striking phenomena,—a concise exposition of those parts of chemistry which most affect the uninitiated, —and a popular view of astronomy, with some explanations (if such indeed can be given to the unlearned) of the principles upon which scientific calculations are made,— that the mind may learn to regard such things without disbelief or an unmeaning admiration. To these might be added an outline of modern history in short chapters, with a commentary at the end of each, containing some explanatory remarks on the nature of the events, and the characters and motives of the principal persons.

It is very obvious, however, that such subjects will never be comprised in any plan of education for the lower classes which is not founded upon a national basis. At the present moment, they are not even considered necessary in many of the schools intended for the children of the opulent and middling classes. Yet, until the principle of such an education be adopted, there never can be any security against occasional outbreaks produced by the tampering of fanatical adventurers and impostors upon the ignorance of the working classes, especially in the agricultural districts.

One of the most useful presents that could be made to the people of these districts, would be a small book, explaining, in a familiar manner, the legal rights and duties of persons as members of society. Such a book should contain a statement of the relations subsisting between master and servant, landlord and tenant, husband and wife, and parents and children. It should show the claims and obligations mutually subsisting between the parties, and the modes by which they may be respectively enforced. Other subjects, as particularly affecting the rural classes, are arson, bastardy, poaching, smuggling, petty thefts of wood, stealing corn, turning cattle into other persons' lands, and other varieties of trespass. A point of great importance is the nature of crimes, the distinction between principals and accomplices, and especially between accessories *before* and *after* the fact. The *rationale* of the poor-laws should be distinctly explained: the grounds upon which the indigent are entitled to relief,—the nature and extent of that relief,—the purpose for which it is granted,—the duty of all to abstain from pressing upon the fund, except in cases of absolute necessity, should be forcibly pointed out. The nature of contracts and bargains, and the mode of compelling the performance of them, should be laid down. When the common relations which subsist between individuals have been examined, those between individuals and the state should follow. In treating this class, it might be advisable to reverse the usual order observed by writers, and commence with the authorities immediately in contact with the people. Thus, the office and duties of churchwardens and guardians of the poor might come first; and then those of constables and magistrates. The mode of laying informations against and apprehending offenders and suspected persons should be given; and the nature of bail explained, and the cases in which it cannot be taken pointed out. From this point the writer might proceed to the composition of courts of justice, and the forms of procedure observed by them, from the arraignment to the final judgment. This description would be appropriately followed by an exposition of the duties of witnesses and jurors. It is of importance that the nature of the trial by jury should be clearly explained; and the advantages of that mode of trial, especially the security afforded by it in political prosecutions to the liberties of the subject, carefully set forth. The objects and uses of government, and the advantages of our own form of government, might be added.

From the numerous conversations I have held with country people respecting their desire for information on the above subjects, I am fully convinced such a work would be most useful and acceptable. It must, however, be written in the most simple manner, avoiding as much as possible all technical, and even compound, words. If written in long periods containing several clauses, and in the language usually employed by literary men, the book would be of no use whatever. Even the style of the Penny Magazine is too complex and artificial for the comprehension of illiterate persons. Those who propose writing for these classes cannot be too strongly impressed with the fact,—that the usual language of writers is positively unintelligible to them.*

Although the late disturbance was undoubtedly of a religious character, it must not be supposed that it was altogether unconnected with views of another nature. Thoms, taking advantage of the occasional distress of some of his auditors, did not fail to represent it as owing to the enormous masses of wealth accumulated by the few to the disadvantage of the many. In his addresses, he often hinted at a more equable distribution of property; and declared that, when he was put into possession of the power God intended to give him, no man should have less than fifty acres of land. Aware of this, I frequently, when conversing with the peasantry, led to the subject of the inequalities of fortune, and found, in many cases, very erroneous notions prevailing respecting the rights of property.

This was more especially the case in the ville of Dunkirk, where the inhabitants are left entirely to themselves, having (as before stated) neither gentry, clergyman, surgeon, nor anybody above their own condition to connect them with the civilization of the higher classes. Is it to be wondered at, that, so situated, they should regard the wealthy as unjust usurpers of the larger part of that bounteous provision which was originally made by the Creator for all; and that, measuring the necessities of others by their own simple wants, they should exclaim against this encroachment, not only as an injustice, but as a gratuitous cruelty, which crushes and starves the many to increase the superfluous wealth and splendour of the few? Hence it is that their feelings towards the rich are not merely envious but vindictive;

* The Useful Knowledge Society, it has given me pleasure to hear, are about to publish a work of this description.

hence the charities of the latter are regarded but as the return of a miserable fraction of the wealth they have extorted from their own labours, and are received by them with ingratitude and sullenness: and hence it is, that, withheld by no feeling but that of fear from an invasion of the property of the wealthy, they are ever ready to join in such invasion whenever there is a prospect of doing so with impunity.

To show how great is the ignorance existing regarding the rights of property, and of the advantages accruing to all from a sacred observance of those rights,—and, at the same time, by how simple a process that ignorance, as well as the ill feeling towards the wealthy classes resulting from it, may be in great part removed,—I subjoin the following anecdote. Talking one day with some men in the ville of Dunkirk, I observed, it was a pity there were no gentry in the neighbourhood. "Well," said one fellow, "for my part, I see no good they are to us; all they do is to make hard laws to grind us down. There was my poor brother clapt into prison, and his wife and family left to starve, all because he had killed a few hares."—"Well," said I, "what right had he to kill other persons' hares?'—"Other persons', indeed! why weren't they as much his as another's?"—"Because he had no property in the land which fed them."—"Ay, that's just it, but he ought to have had though."—"How! do you mean to say everybody ought to have land?"—"Yes, to be sure I do; look here now, didn't God give the land to all?"—"Well, what of that?"—"Why, then a few can't have no right to the whole of it."—"But I say they may."—"Then how do you make out that?"—"Suppose every man had had his share, I suppose you'll allow he had a right to do what he liked with it?"—"Why, yes; I can't say no to that."—"Well, then, suppose one man wishes to sell his share, and another wishes to buy it, they would have a right to do so."—"Why, yes; no doubt of that."—"Well, suppose, after that, the buyer saves up more money, and sets up a shop, and clears a good deal, and other men see what he is doing and want to do the same, but they have no money, and they offer their land to him and he buys it; has he not a right to do so?"—" Yes, to be sure, if he gives them the money for it."—" Well, then, you see here is a man who has got a good deal of land, and others have lost theirs, and you own it's all right?"—" Ay, ay, that's all well enough; but our squires didn't all get their land in that way." " Perhaps not, but then those they got it from did."— " But if a man makes money and buys land, hasn't he a right to leave it to his children, or to anybody else he chooses?"—" Why, I can't but say but what he has."— " So, my friend, you see one man may have half a county, and another not half an acre, and yet the last has no fair right to complain."—" Why, sir, to be sure you do make it out somehow, there's no denying that; but then it's a hard case one man's good should be another man's harm." —" But it is not: suppose a rich man were to come and build a cotton-mill in your neighbourhood, and your children could earn 10s. a week each in it, you wouldn't think there was much harm in that?"—" Harm! no, indeed; it would be the best thing ever happened to us; for you see, sir, we are often puzzled to get work here." —" Well, but how much would it take to build such a mill, and fit it up with machinery?"—" Why, I can't tell; but I suppose a good deal."—" Then I can tell you a very moderate-sized one would cost 20,000l."—"Indeed? that's a main sum!"—" Do you think the poor people in any place could ever club such a sum together?"—" Never, sir,—not if they lived to the age of Adam, and tasted nothing stronger than water."—" So, then, if the rich man didn't come and build the mill, the poor people never could do it."—" No, that's certain."—" Then you see the wealth of the rich man in this case is a real advantage to the poor?"—" To be sure it is, sir; and I was quite a fool like not to see it before."—" But did you never read of such things?"—" No, never, sir."—" Did you ever see the Penny Magazine?"—" No, can't say as I ever did."—" But you read the newspaper?"—" No, I can't say as I can undertake for that; but I read a little in the Testament."—" But you talk of these things with your neighbours?"—" No, sir, not much of that; you see, sir, though some of us are 'cute enough in some things, we aren't quite up to what you have been talking of, and there an't no one here as can talk of these things to us."

That it may not be said I am here drawing conclusions respecting the general condition of the Kentish peasantry from an examination, which, however minute, extended over a small district only, I deem it right to add that my information is by no means confined to the district in question. About two years ago, an inquiry, similar in character to that of which the results are here given, was instituted by the Central Society of Education into the condition of the inhabitants of eight parishes, composing a district in Kent, the extreme point of which is not more than seven or eight miles distant from Boughton. If the report of the investigation then made, which is to be found in the first publication* of the Society, be examined, it will be found not to differ upon any material point with the information here collected; and as I am well assured, by those who can speak from personal observation, that the condition of the intervening district is very similar in character, it follows that the tract of country, to which my observations may be considered as applying generally, is not less than twenty-five miles in length from one extremity to the other. It is probable that in most parts of this district Thoms would have found the same encouragement as he received in Herne-hill, Dunkirk, and Boughton. This is not an opinion inconsiderately hazarded; for, independently of the fact of the inhabitants of the district being very similarly circumstanced with those of the last-mentioned places, it is well known to those acquainted with that part of the country that the former were actually the dupes of an impostor whose pretensions were almost as monstrous as those of Thoms. About five years ago, a person calling himself Doctor Crouchman traversed that part of the country, pretending to cure all kinds of diseases by virtue of his touch. Wherever he stopped, the people crowded round him, putting implicit credit in his pretensions; and many persons afflicted with diseases came from considerable distances to obtain the benefit of

---

* See vol. i. of the Proceedings of the Central Society of Education, p. 342.

his miraculous powers. The villages he visited were thrown into confusion, the houses at which he put up were besieged with applicants, and, on one occasion, the people removed a portion of the roof of a house for the purpose of letting down a patient before him.

In further proof of the credulous ignorance prevailing in this last-mentioned district, I may instance the belief in witchcraft, which still exists to a considerable extent. A gentleman connected with this part of the country, related to me two instances which lately occurred within his knowledge. One was the case of a man who acted as a waggoner's mate in the service of this gentleman's brother. The man, who had been observed to be in a desponding mood for some time, gave up his place without assigning any reason for doing so. As he had been a good servant, and had no other employment, he was asked why he had quitted a place where he was so well off. At first he hesitated to give any answer; but, on being pressed, acknowledged it was owing to the warning given him by " a cunning woman" in the neighbourhood who had predicted that, if he remained any longer in his present service, he would certainly be killed by a kick from a vicious mare. The other instance was that of a farmer occupying three or four hundred acres of land in the neighbourhood, who, having lost a cow, had recourse to the same sibyl to learn who was the thief.

It would be easy, if it were required, to adduce reasons for believing that the gross ignorance shown to exist in these districts is not confined to them, and that their condition may be regarded as a tolerably fair sample of that of the same class in other parts of the county. If such then be the state of a county bordering on the metropolis, and possessing so many obvious advantages, we can hardly hope, after making ample allowance for every possible combination of circumstances by which these advantages may be counteracted, that the agricultural classes in other parts of the kingdom can be in such a state as to leave us without any apprehension of evil to be dreaded from their unenlightened and neglected condition.* And

* Vide an account of some parishes in Herefordshire in the second volume of the publications of this Society.

yet some people are alarmed at what they term the over-education of the people! They may be perfectly easy on that score! If ever the right of property shall be violated, and the progress of civilization checked, by a servile war in this country, the disaster will come, not from the education of the lower classes, but their want of it,—not from their knowledge, but their ignorance,— an ignorance mainly chargeable, and therefore righteously visited, upon those who, called upon by the station they hold in the country to forward the cause of education amongst the people, have selfishly in some instances, ignorantly in others, and in all unwisely, shrunk from the performance of their noblest duties.

The following corrected return of the Number of Inmates in the Workhouse of the Union belonging to Boughton, Herne-hill, and Dunkirk, has been obtained since the publication of the report, by which it will be seen that the number is much less than that at first given. The error was owing to the confused manner in which the returns were originally made.

TABLE showing the Number of Workhouse Inmates belonging to each of the Parishes of Dunkirk, Boughton,
and Herne-hill, during each of the weeks of the quarter ended Lady Day, 1838.

For the Week ended Friday.	Dunkirk.	Boughton.	Herne-hill.
29th December, 1837	15	33	10
5th January, 1838	15	33	11
12th . . .	15	34	11
19th . . .	46	53	13
26th . . .	29	54	10
2nd February . .	21	51	10
9th . . .	23	48	10
16th . . .	25	51	10
23rd . . .	26	40	10
2nd March . .	12	25	10
9th . . .	18	25	10
16th . . .	15	20	10
23rd . . .	11	20	10
Average .	21	37	10
Number in the present week, ending 4th Aug.	3	22	11

F. LIARDET.

EDUCATION IN IRELAND.

Questions connected with education in Ireland have been made so much the subject of angry religious controversy, and of vehement party strife, that we should have shrunk from their discussion in the publications of a Society which seeks not the triumph of party or of sect, if we were not deeply convinced of the paramount importance of education to that country. We trust, too, that in our pages these questions may be treated with candour and moderation.

Whatever may be the success of the many other expedients which have been suggested or adopted for relieving Ireland from the complicated disorders by which its social system has been deranged, it cannot be denied that an effectual guarantee for the permanency of national improvement is only to be found in that culture of the minds, the morals, and the habits of the people, which is designated by the term National Education, when used in its largest sense. To the casual observer indeed, who has witnessed the present deplorable state of a large portion of the Irish people, destitute alike of those moral blessings and of those physical comforts which elevate the nature and augment the happiness of man, it might almost seem that no improvement of laws or institutions could retrieve a condition so hopeless. But the friend of popular education cannot thus despair. Let him visit a family overwhelmed with the greatest accumulation of miseries, or even of vices; and whilst in the condition or conduct of the parents he will find nothing but what will shock or disgust, he turns to the infant that plays upon the hearth, and sees before him a being as innocent, as capable of every thing that is good and great, as if it were the acknowledged heir of wealth, virtue, or distinction. To this child the State should stand in the relation of parent. And as the father, who may find himself unable to endow a numerous family with adequate fortunes, feels consoled by thinking that, in giving to his children a good education, he has made for them the best provision: so, in the case of the commonwealth, to ensure at all times prosperity to the industrious classes may surpass the powers of the statesman; but to provide that no child shall arrive at man's estate without having been trained in the exercise of those arts, and encouraged to the performance of those duties, which can render him an useful and virtuous member of society, is a task within his competency; and, if this highest of obligations have been neglected, the guardians of the nation stand condemned for having failed in discharging the noblest of their functions. Let us now examine how far these duties have been neglected or performed in Ireland.

In presenting a general view of the educational institutions of Ireland, accompanied by observations upon their efficiency, and by suggestions for their extension and improvement, we shall follow closely in the traces of the Report of the Select Committee on Education in Ireland, which was presented at the close of last session. That masterly report, the production of Mr. Wyse, the distinguished member for Waterford, leaves little to be said by any one who treats of Irish education; at the same time that it establishes principles applicable to the subject, in reference to whatever country it may be discussed. We shall classify the various institutions under the divisions recognised in the prospectus of the Central Society of Education, as severally embracing Elementary, Academical, University, Professional, and Supplementary Education.

ELEMENTARY EDUCATION.

Among the earliest legislative efforts to promote education in Ireland, which have left traces not yet wholly obliterated, was the enactment of a law, during the reign of Henry the Eighth, which enjoined upon every parochial clergyman the maintenance of a school within the limits of his benefice. The principal object of this law was to encourage the introduction of the English language among the natives of Ireland. Whether from the indisposition of the Irish to avail themselves of the opportunities offered by this act, or from its not having been adequately enforced, it seems to have conduced but little to the instruction of the people. The number of parochial schools established in strict conformity to its provisions appears to have been at no time considerable; and although an oath is still enjoined to be taken by every beneficed clergyman, obliging him to maintain such a school, this obligation is interpreted as cancelled upon his paying a sum of forty shillings yearly towards the support of a school in his parish. In many instances both the oath and the payment have fallen into desuetude. It is only right, however, to state that in very many instances the Protestant clergy are extremely active in supporting, assisting, and superintending within their parishes schools, the operations of which are in accordance with their own views of religious duty.

The intervention of the State in support of education was, during nearly a century, applied with singular ardour and perseverance to the support of what have been called the Protestant Charter Schools. The society under whose auspices these schools were established was incorporated in the year 1733, and enjoyed the liberality of the Irish and of the Imperial Parliaments with unabated favour until the year 1825, when, an inquiry having been made by the Commissioners of Education into the management of these schools, so many abuses were discovered, and the general principles by which they were governed appeared so little deserving of public encouragement, that the grants were gradually withdrawn, and the society is now dependent exclusively upon its own resources. Enormous sums were lavished by Parliament upon the Charter Schools; not less than 723,304*l.* was granted to them between 1800 and 1829. Whatever might have been the intention of the original founders of this society, it was subsequently converted into an avowed instrument for making proselytes to the Protestant faith. From 1775 to 1803 a bye-law existed, limiting the advantages of the institution exclusively to the children of Catholic parents; so that the State, through this society, said to the Roman Catholics of Ireland, "Give us your children; they shall be fed, clothed, lodged, educated, and apprenticed: all that we ask in return is that they shall become Protestants." It is not surprising that education offered to the people on such terms should not have been accepted with avidity or gratitude. The whole number of children apprenticed during ninety years, ending in 1825, amounted only to 12,745. The society now maintains five boarding-schools, in which 287 children are lodged, dieted, clothed, and educated; and five day-schools, in which 249 children are educated. Its annual income is 7361*l.* which is derived exclusively from endowment. This revenue is charged with the superannuations of the masters of those schools which were suppressed upon the withdrawal of the parliamentary grant. This is the reason assigned for the limited utility at present produced by so ample an endowment.

The Society for Discountenancing Vice also shared to a considerable extent the liberality of Parliament, having received 101,991*l.* between the year 1800 and the year 1827, when the grant was withdrawn. In 1826, there were in connexion with this association 226 schools, giving education to 12,769 scholars. The society is at present upheld chiefly by the exertions of the Protestant clergy. Its funds are now derived wholly from subscriptions, which amounted, in the year 1838, to 1008*l.* 13*s.* 3*d.* We have not been able to obtain a return of the present number of schools and scholars in connexion with this society.

An attempt was made during several years to diffuse education through the medium of an association which is commonly known by the name of the Kildare-place Society. This association was established in 1814; and, its fundamental principle being that no peculiar or catechetical religious instruction should be given under its sanction, it at first received the support of persons of all denominations. Differences, however, soon arose with respect to the perusal of the Scriptures, in consequence of its being also made an indispensable condition of aid to any school in connexion with the society that the whole Bible should be read, without note or comment. This principle is at variance with the views of the Roman Catholic Church, which does not permit the use of the Scriptures at large as a school-book, unless accompanied with explanations by the clergy. Suspicions also were entertained to a considerable extent by the Roman Catholics, that in many of the schools receiving aid from the society, and under the patronage of zealous Protestants, attempts were made to undermine the religion of the Catholic children. Upon these, and perhaps upon other grounds, the Catholic clergy withdrew from all connexion with the society, and in many instances exerted their utmost influence to prevent the children of Catholic parents from being sent to these schools. The aid given by Parliament to this association was very considerable, amounting for several years to 25,000*l.* per annum. These grants ceased in 1832, when the society was superseded, as a means of affording encouragement to education on the part of the State, by the present Board of National Education. According to tables published by the society, it appears that there were, in 1831, 1621 schools in connexion with it, affording instruction to 137,639 scholars ; that 1908 male teachers, and 482 female teachers, had been trained; 1,464,817 cheap books issued, and 1131 lending libraries had been formed by the society. It is now wholly dependent upon its own private funds, and upon voluntary subscriptions. There are in connexion with it about 1091 schools, which are estimated to contain about 81,750 scholars. Its receipts amount annually to between 4000*l.* and 5000*l.* of which a large proportion is derived from the sale of books and school requisites. Although a society offering education to a nation upon terms to which it is inconsistent with their religious convictions to accede, may not be the most suitable medium for affording assistance on the part of the State, it ought not, in justice to this society, to be concealed, that it introduced a very superior system of instruction to that which had previously existed; that it undertook the training of masters in an excellent model school; that it printed a large collection of interesting and useful publications, which were distributed through its schools, or were rendered accessible by purchase to the public upon easy terms; and that it encouraged the formation of lending libraries; which have been the means of affording to the community much amusement and instruction.

We now come to the period when the funds applied by Parliament to education in Ireland are no longer administered by voluntary associations, but employed under the agency of a Board nominated by the Government, and directly responsible to Parliament. Towards the close of the year 1831, Lord Stanley, then Secretary for Ireland, addressed to the Duke of Leinster a public official letter, informing him that the Government had decided upon the formation of a Board of National Education, and setting forth the principles upon which its operations were to be conducted. The members of this Board* have been, the Duke of Leinster, the Protestant Archbishop of Dublin, Dr. Sadleir (three Protestants); the Roman Catholic Archbishop of Dublin, the Right Hon. A. R. Blake, Chief Remembrancer (both Catholics); Mr. Holmes, an Arian; and the Rev. Mr. Carlisle, a Presbyterian minister, and the only member of the Board who has received a salary. The fundamental principle upon which the Board has hitherto governed its conduct has been, that united education shall alone be encouraged; that the literary instruction of the children of all persuasions shall be given in common, but that their catechetical religious instruction shall be received separately. With a view to unite the children as much as possible, even in religious instruction, a small volume of extracts from the Scripture has been compiled, in a new version, under the sanction of the Archbishops of the two churches; and these extracts are very generally read in the schools, although their perusal is not compulsory. At least one day in each week is allotted to the religious instruction of the children by their own pastors and religious teach-

* There has been a recent change in the composition of the Board. Mr. Carlisle has ceased to be a member, and Sir Patrick Bellew (a Catholic), Mr. Henry, and Sergeant Greene (Protestants), have been associated with the former members of the Board.

ers; and, by a recent regulation, the Scriptures at large, or other works of a religious character, may be read on other days at stated hours, but the children are permitted to absent themselves, if their parents so desire. The following are the principal conditions upon which assistance has been granted to schools; viz. that when aid is sought for building, at least one-third of the expense shall be locally contributed, and that the site of the school-house shall be vested in trustees approved by the Board; that provision shall be made, by local subscription, towards a permanent salary for the teacher, for the repair of the school-house, and for the purchase of school requisites; and lastly, that the school shall be conducted in conformity to the regulations of the Board, and be, in all respects subject to its control. They do not, however, insist upon appointing the teachers, but reserve to themselves the power of suspending or removing them. The Board have prepared, for the use of schools, a series of excellent books and treatises, from many of which even adults would derive much useful information. These books are supplied at half-price to the national schools; and to the public they are also sold at a price which is much too high, and which ought to be reduced to the lowest possible amount, with a view to encourage their gratuitous distribution by benevolent individuals. At the Central Institution in Dublin, there is a model school; attached to which there is also an infant school, and a training establishment for teachers. There are twenty-five inspectors, exclusive of the superintendent of the Central School. The amount granted by the Board, from its establishment in 1831 to 15th December 1837, in aid of schools, not including the general expenses of the Board, or the cost of the Central School, was apportioned as follows :—

	£.	s.	d.
For building	26,298	8	$3\frac{1}{2}$
Fitting up	9,211	8	$7\frac{1}{2}$
Salaries	54,075	18	$11\frac{1}{4}$
Books and school requisites	13,666	6	1
Total	£.103,252	1	$11\frac{1}{4}$

Upon the 25th of March 1838, there were 1,384 schools in operation under the Board, with 1,510 teachers, male and female. The average number of scholars on the rolls of these schools at the same period amounted, in the aggregate, to 169,548. There are no accurate returns of the relative number of Catholic and Protestant children at these schools; but the following summary, prepared for the Parliamentary Committee of 1837 by the officers of the Board, is supposed to indicate very fairly the relative proportion upon the whole number of scholars, though the returns do not comprise all the schools:—

	Protestants.	Roman Catholics.
Ulster	14,628 .	22,455
Munster . . .	150 .	19,009
Leinster	578 .	34,945
Connaught . . .	277 .	14,186
	15,633	90,595

It is proposed hereafter greatly to extend the operations of the Board, in every department of its functions, if Parliament should provide the necessary funds. In the second report of the Board a general view is exhibited of the plan of education contemplated; and a calculation is given, by which it appears that an income of at least 210,000l. per annum would be necessary adequately to meet the wants of the country in regard of education. The last annual grant amounted to no more than 50,000l.

Ever since the period of its first formation, the Board has been assailed from various quarters with the utmost pertinacity and virulence. That the public at large are not dissatisfied with its system is best evinced by the increasing number of schools which have sought connexion with it. That by a large proportion of the Catholic clergy it is approved, is established by the fact, that in the year 1835 not less than 1,397 Roman Catholic clergymen had given their signatures to applications for aid from the Board: but it must be admitted with regret, that a great majority of the Protestant clergy have offered their unremitting opposition to the system;

and that of late a considerable section of the Roman Catholic clergy, with Dr. M'Hale, the Catholic Archbishop of Tuam, at their head, have become discontented with the proceedings of the Board.

The grounds upon which the objections of the Protestant clergy are founded are as follows. They conceive that the study of the Holy Scriptures, in all their integrity, ought to be an essential part of popular education: they object to the use of the Scripture Extracts, first, as a substitution of a part for the whole; and next, because they are of opinion that the version adopted by the Board, and the notes by which it is accompanied, lean to that interpretation of the Bible which favours the doctrine of the Roman Catholic rather than of the Protestant church. Some of them object to connect themselves with schools of which, by the regulations of the Board, the Catholic clergy are appointed visitors equally with themselves. They observe further, that a very large number of national schools are built upon ground immediately attached to the Catholic chapels, and that a considerable number are under the immediate superintendence and tuition of monks and nuns; and they fear that, under these circumstances, the Protestant children could not attend such schools without incurring the risk of being seduced from the faith to which they belong. Other objections of detail are raised against the operations of the Board; such as, that some of the schoolmasters are persons of indifferent character; others, vehement political partisans; that the inspection is insufficient; that the rules of the Board are habitually violated in some of the schools, with other charges of a like nature: but as it is admitted, even by the Board itself, that there have hitherto been many unavoidable imperfections in the practical working of the system, owing to the want of sufficient funds to provide adequate remuneration for a superior class of schoolmasters, and for a sufficient number of inspectors, these objections, even if valid, are not of a fundamental character, and, it may be supposed, will be only of temporary duration.

The Roman Catholic clergy, on the other hand, have complained that the Catholics of Ireland are not adequately represented upon the Board; for that, whilst upon the whole population of Ireland the Catholics outnumber the Protestants of all persuasions in the proportion of $4\frac{1}{2}$ to 1, there have been only two Catholics on the Board, whilst there were five Protestants; that, in like manner, the proportion of inspectors and of schoolmasters of the Roman Catholic persuasion is not as great as in justice it ought to be; they allege further, that the superintendence of education is peculiarly the duty of the clergy, and that to them, and not to a secular board, should be committed the appointment of teachers and the general control over the funds devoted to education. They object to the Scripture Extracts as compromising many points at issue between the Catholic and Reformed churches; and are of opinion, that to allow the Scriptures to be read at large in the schools, even though the attendance of the Catholic children be not enforced during its perusal, is to expose them to the dangers which their church believes to arise from an improper use of the holy volume.

Looking at all the facts which have been above stated, and balancing these contending views against each other, we are inclined to deduce from them the conclusion, that the present system of the National Board is not unsatisfactory to the great body of the people; but that there is a very considerable number of estimable and conscientious persons who would resist any plan of joint education, and who would only be satisfied with such a system of instruction as should enable them to carry on education upon exclusive principles, conformable to their peculiar views of religious truth. What, under such circumstances, is the course most advisable to pursue with a view to reconcile conflicting opinions, and to secure to the whole community the benefits of education? Our answer is, — Adopt such a system as shall exclude no portion of the people. In a country in which opinion is much divided upon religious questions, the only footing upon which education can be conducted, under the auspices of the State, in a manner satisfactory to persons of all persuasions, is that the Government shall abstain from attempting to propagate any peculiar religious tenets in

connexion with secular education; but that instruction
in the particular doctrines of each persuasion shall be
left to the clergy of the several denominations of Christians.   Consistently with this principle, it is the duty of
a National Board to provide for the people at large sound
moral and literary education, combined with so much
instruction in the fundamental doctrines of Christianity
as shall find a common acceptance on the part of all persuasions.   That system ought, therefore, to be viewed
with peculiar favour which shall unite on terms of affec-
tionate intercourse children belonging to various religious
sects in the same school.   But, if the deep-rooted and
conscientious convictions of a portion of the community
will not allow them to communicate to their children
general knowledge apart from that religious teaching
which appears to them of essential importance to their
eternal welfare, we are not prepared to say that they
should be altogether debarred from the advantages derivable, through the means of a National Board, from
funds to which they have equally with their fellow-citi-
zens contributed.   According to this view, the nunnery
school, if it be conducted conformably to the regulations
of the Board in regard of secular knowledge, ought to
receive aid from the public grant, even though the
Catholic Catechism be habitually taught in it, and though
it be on that account attended by none but Roman
Catholic children.   In like manner, the school which has
been established under the immediate superintendence
of the Protestant clergyman should also be held eligible
to receive assistance, even though the religious instruction given in it be of an exclusively Protestant character.
With a view to obviate one of the principal objections
which have been urged against the present system of the
Board, it might be desirable that the Scripture Extracts
should be presented to the Protestant child in the Protestant version, and to the Catholic child in the Romish
version.   This principle was adopted by the Kildare-
place Society with regard to the whole Bible; and it is
considered by many of the clergy of both persuasions
much less objectionable than any thing like an attempt
to evade and confound the points at issue between the

churches by a new version. The claim of the Roman Catholics to a more just representation on the Central Board appears to be irresistible, inasmuch as about five-sixths of the children in the national schools may, under any circumstances, be expected to belong to the Roman Catholic faith. As a general rule also, it would be desirable that the religion of the master should be the same as that of the majority of his scholars. The assistant might, in large schools, be of the same persuasion as the minority.

We have hitherto noticed only those features of the system of the Board of National Education which have occasioned virulent party contention; but there are others, to which public attention has not been equally directed, at least as much deserving of serious consideration. The point to which we shall now especially advert is the condition upon which the funds granted by Parliament are distributed throughout the country. We have seen that the Board professes to give aid in no case, unless a considerable portion of the expense of maintaining the school is provided by local subscription. Whatever may be the abstract merits of such a principle, its practical effect has been, and must always be, to direct the national bounty to those districts in which education is most prized, and in which the people by their circumstances are best able to provide funds for its extension. In many parts of Ireland there are no resident gentry; in others the few who are resident are opposed to national education. Under such circumstances, if the bulk of the population be very poor, a subscription for the purpose of establishing a school can rarely be obtained, and without such subscription no aid can be obtained from the Board; so that those parts of the country which are least civilised, and where education is most required, derive no advantage from the public grant. This is a result which might have been foreseen, and which does not rest upon mere assumption, but is fully established by the returns laid before Parliament. In the Report of the Commissioners appointed, in 1834, to inquire into the state of public instruction in Ireland, the per-centage of the population receiving education from every source is given in detail for each diocese ; so that we have an opportunity of comparing the relative state of one part of the country with another. If we refer to this Report, and to the returns from the National Board, we shall find that the public aid has been chiefly directed to those districts in which the percentage of the population at school is the highest. We shall elucidate our argument by only one example. In 1835 the comparison as regarded two dioceses stood thus :—

	Population.	National Schools.	Per-centage of population at school.
Diocese of Connor	361,618	86	$9\frac{11}{100}$
Diocese of Ardfert and Aghadoe	304,687	5	$4\frac{63}{100}$

It is not necessary to multiply examples. The same inequality will be found throughout the different dioceses. We will, however, refer to a more recent return, in order to show how little the distribution of these funds has been governed by a regard to relative population. It appears that, on the 15th December 1837, the number of national schools, of scholars, and the total amount of aid granted to the following counties, stood thus :—

	Population.	National Schools.	Scholars.	Total amount of money granted in aid of education.
County of Monaghan	195,532	45	5611	£3133
County of Roscommon	239,903	11	1698	1067

The county of Monaghan is in the diocese of Clogher, in which the per-centage of the population receiving education in 1835 was computed to be $9\frac{7}{100}$. The greater part of the county of Roscommon is in the diocese of Elphin, in which, at the same period, the computed per-centage at school was $7\frac{37}{100}$.

We now proceed to notice the exertions made in support of education by several societies not yet mentioned, which do not derive aid from Parliament.

The London Hibernian Society is supported wholly by voluntary subscriptions. Its income for the year 1837 amounted to 9991*l*. 10*s*. 9*d*. There were in connexion with it 1143 day-schools educating 85,673 scholars, and 1279 Sunday and adult schools educating 53,418 scholars.

The teachers of 813 day-schools were paid according to the number and progress of the children, as ascertained by the inspectors of the society. The attendance of scholars at the several inspections was 58,201. The fundamental principle of the society is, that the Bible at large shall be taught in the schools ; and also that through the agency of Scripture readers it shall be read and disseminated throughout the country. The attendance of Roman Catholic children on the day-schools is stated to have amounted in 1837 to 31,285 ; but the Catholic clergy give every opposition in their power to the proceedings of the society, as tending to proselytism, and as inconsistent with the views of their church.

The Sunday School Society is also supported by voluntary contributions. Its receipts during the year 1837 amounted to 3057*l*. 1*s*. 6*d*. ; of which about 600*l*. were derived from the sale of Bibles and school-books, which it distributes largely throughout the country. The number of schools in connexion with the society on the 1st of January 1838, is stated to have been 2975, in which instruction was given to 214,164 scholars by 20,885 gratuitous teachers. As the instruction given is of a Protestant character, the Catholic clergy do not encourage or sanction these schools.

The Irish Society for promoting the education of the native Irish through the medium of their own language, is another association which depends exclusively upon voluntary subscriptions. Its income for the year ending the 17th March 1838, was 5157*l*. 15*s*. 2*d*. There were 770 schools in connexion with it, giving education in the Irish tongue to 18,843 scholars, of whom 14,776 were adults. Scriptural education is the paramount object for which the society was founded, and it is to this object that its labours are chiefly directed.

In connexion with the Irish branch of the Baptist Society, there were, in 1838, forty-one schools, containing about 3000 scholars.

There exists in Ireland a fraternity connected with the Catholic Church, who are entirely devoted to education. They are called Brothers of the Christian Doctrine. In the Catholic Directory for 1838, the number of children taught by persons in immediate connexion with the Roman Catholic Church in Ireland is stated to be 14,870. Of these schools a considerable proportion are in receipt of aid from the National Board. By a return made to the Parliamentary Committee of 1837, it appears that at that time twenty-six national schools were taught by nuns, and eighteen by monks.

We may here notice, in connexion with Elementary Education, a very ample endowment which exists in Ireland, arising out of a bequest by Erasmus Smith. The estates placed under the administration of the governors of this charity are stated to comprise 7593 acres, giving an annual rental of 7584*l*. These funds are applied to the encouragement of education of every description. A considerable number of elementary schools for the poorer classes are maintained; several academical seminaries have been partially endowed; and in Trinity College, at Dublin, three professorships, viz. mathematics, modern history, and Oriental languages, have been founded by the aid of this charity.

The education afforded by the societies and institutions comprised in the foregoing enumeration is for the most part given gratuitously. Where a school fee is required, in the case of schools not deriving aid from any society, it ranges from one shilling and sixpence per quarter to half-a-crown. For instruction in the higher branches of elementary knowledge it seldom exceeds seven shillings per quarter. The education given in the ordinary elementary schools of Ireland is limited to reading, writing, and arithmetic; but in those of a somewhat higher description, a slight knowledge of geography, history, mensuration, geometry, and algebra, is not unfrequently communicated. The monitorial system of teaching has been adopted by the National Board, and by the various educational societies, and has in other schools been brought into very general operation. The books used in schools which are under the patronage of the societies are of a very excellent description, and though works of an objectionable kind are sometimes to be found in the hedge schools, yet a great improvement has taken place in this respect since the time when the earlier parliamentary commissioners made inquiries into the state of education in Ireland. The general character of the teachers has also been much improved, but it is still very far from having reached that standard which ought to be attained by those who are charged with the care of youth. In the case of those masters who are dependent upon the different societies, or upon benevolent individuals, the fear of losing their situations, in case of misconduct, must operate as a restraint; but where such influences do not exist, the check of public opinion, and the fear of being deserted by their scholars, do not appear to act as motives sufficiently strong to prevent occasional irregularities of conduct. The emoluments of those who devote themselves to the education of the poorer classes in Ireland are so inconsiderable—seldom reaching twenty pounds per annum,—that there is not sufficient inducement to tempt persons of character and attainments to apply themselves to a pursuit which does not hold out the recompense which it deserves, either in regard of public esteem or of pecuniary remuneration. With reference to industrial training as a part of education, we regret that scarcely any attempt has yet been made to unite with literary instruction any knowledge of the industrial arts, or the practice of any manual occupations. In all well-regulated female schools, however, needlework, knitting, straw-plait, &c. form a part of the occupation of the children. Of the general character of the moral training which prevails in the schools of Ireland, it is difficult to convey a correct impression. It necessarily varies in every school, and it has not hitherto been made the subject of any formal inquiry. The last education commission—that of public instruction—does not appear to have considered this branch of the subject as falling within the scope of their investigation. In forming a judgment how far this duty has been performed or neglected in Ireland, we must remember that it is, above all things, necessary that the teacher should in his own conduct afford an unexceptionable example of self-government. In such proportion, then, as the teachers of Ireland are found defective in point of character and conduct, may we infer that the moral training of the

children has been perverted or neglected.   In so far as
moral excellence can be inculcated by precept, we may
observe that the main object of the religious societies in
promoting education has been to diffuse, as widely as
possible, a knowledge of the Bible, and they trust to the
efficacy of the Scripture morality as the best guide to the
practical conduct of life.   The school-books in circulation in all well-regulated schools have also been framed
with a view to lead the pupil to cherish the better feelings of our nature, and to subdue the passions which are
destructive of our own happiness and that of others.
Upon the whole, however, we are inclined to doubt whether, even in the best-conducted schools in Ireland, the
attention of the teachers has been as much directed to
the moral culture of the children as it has been to the
developement and improvement of their intellectual faculties.

We shall now exhibit the general summary of the
state of education in 1835, as ascertained by the Commissioners of Public Instruction, to whose labours we
have already adverted.   We must premise, however, that
if the more recent returns from the Board, and from
some of the societies, indicate an augmentation of the
number of their scholars, it would not be right to infer
that the aggregate amount of education had been thereby
considerably increased; because many of the schools
which appear in such recent returns as connected with
the Board, or other associations, formerly subsisted as independent schools, often under the same master, so that
the number of children taught in such schools may not
have been increased, but simply the character and denomination of the school have been changed.

	Province of				Total in Ireland.
	Armagh.	Dublin.	Cashel.	Tuam.	
Number of daily schools	4,482	1,612	2,322	1,241	9,657
Number of daily schools supported wholly by payments from the children	2,396	830	1,577	850	5,653
Number of daily schools supported wholly, or in part, by endowment or subscription	2,086	782	745	391	4,004
Number of schools in connexion with, or receiving support from, { The National Board	461	204	137	90	892
Association for discountenancing Vice.	112	48	37	6	203
Erasmus Smith's Fund	61	25	22	7	115
Kildare Place Society	195	17	15	8	235
London Hibernian Society	460	26	37	95	618
Number of daily schools of which the books containing lists of the children were produced	4,235	1,403	2,126	1,122	8,886
Number of children on the books of these schools { Males	169,118	52,346	85,133	47,212	353,809
Females	105,234	40,481	52,586	25,599	223,900
Sex not specified	2,089	1,644	1,361	610	5,700
Total	276,441	94,471	139,080	73,421	583,413
Number of schools of which no lists were produced	247	209	196	119	771
Computed number of children under daily instruction in such schools	16,055	14,003	12,740	7,735	50,886
Computed total number of children under daily instruction	292,496	108,474	151,820	81,156	633,946
Total population in 1834	3,128,016	1,247,290	2,345,471	1,233,323	7,954,100
Proportion of daily schools to total population	as 1 to 698	as 1 to 774	as 1 to 1008	as 1 to 994	as 1 to 824
Proportion per centum of children under daily instruction to total population { Total on books	8 84/100	7 57/100	5 93/100	6 8/100	7 93/100
Computed total	9 35/100	8 70/100	6 47/100	6 58/100	7 97/100

From the foregoing table it appears that not more than about eight per cent. of the population of Ireland are in attendance upon school; whereas, if education were sufficiently prized, from twenty to twenty-five per cent. of the population would be in course of instruction. It is also to be remembered that the above return does not exhibit the average number in actual daily attendance at school, but only the number on the books. Nor does it take into account the wretched quality of the instruction given in many of these schools, which is not unfrequently of such a nature as to render such education a very doubtful benefit. Let us take the lowest computation that can be made of the proportion of the population that ought to be at school, and we shall then more clearly perceive how lamentably deficient is the present supply of education in Ireland. The number of children between the ages of five and twelve years is rather more than eighteen per cent. We may fairly say, that no child can be considered as educated who does not receive constant instruction during this period of life in at least such intermitted attendance upon school as is indicated by the expression " on the books of a school." We shall then arrive at the conclusion that not one half of the children of the people of Ireland now receive education. The present population of Ireland probably amounts to 8,500,000. Upon this number eighteen per cent. would give 1,500,000 children to be educated; of whom 1,200,000, or, at the very lowest computation, 1,000,000, belong to those classes for the education of whose children it is the especial duty of the State to afford peculiar facilities. In this view of the subject we have not taken into account the children between three years old and five years, although in our opinion infant schools ought to be provided for this portion of the national offspring. In this paper we have not attempted any separate notice of the infant schools at present existing in Ireland, because they are not sufficiently numerous to obtain a place in our general classification. To provide a suitable education for one million of children would probably cost above 300,000*l.* per annum; and herein lies one of the main difficulties, which terrifies our

statesmen. The same minister who cheerfully asks from
Parliament above a million and half sterling every year
to provide a military and police force for the purpose of
coercing the people of Ireland to the observance of order,
would shrink from the duty of proposing an annual grant
of 200,000*l.* to instruct the rising generation in their
duties as subjects and citizens. Those, however, who
demand education for the people as a right, or solicit it
as the greatest of moral blessings, do not come before
Parliament as mendicants. They only ask of the Legislature to declare that schools open to children of all persuasions shall henceforth be considered at least as essential an adjunct to our social organization as a road, a
bridge, or a gaol; and that an adequate machinery shall
be by law provided for their erection, support, and administration. It is strange, indeed, that many of those
who, in reference to religious instruction, abhor the voluntary system, yet in regard of national education rely
entirely upon the casual success of individual exertion.
We have seen how inadequate these exertions have
hitherto been in Ireland; we have seen that, even when
assisted by Parliament, they have failed to direct the
public aid to those quarters in which it is most needed.
For our own part, therefore, we are prepared to adopt
the remaining alternative, and to accede to the recommendation of the Parliamentary Committee of last session, that each locality shall be enabled to raise by a local
rate a portion of the funds required to establish and
maintain its schools. It would lead us into too much pro-
lixity if we were to attempt to elucidate all the details
appertaining to a system founded upon such a basis.
They would be framed with a view to do no violence to
the conscience of any one; to provide for the proper selection and training of the teachers; to secure a constant
and vigilant inspection and superintendence; to ensure a
supply of books of the best quality, as well as of other
useful accessories to education; to teach the rudiments of
the industrial arts; in fine, to send forth into the world a
succession of young persons trained in the knowledge
and exercise of their moral and religious duties, and competent by mental and physical qualification to apply their

industry to the best advantage both for themselves and
for their country.

ACADEMICAL EDUCATION.

We trust that we shall not be considered as under-
rating the value of the education of the poor, when we
express it as our opinion, that the proper instruction of
the superior classes is an object of national concern even
more important than that of the less wealthy grades of
society. To them the poor most naturally look for example and guidance: in their hands lies the productive
capital of the country; and according to the skill, knowledge, and prudence which they possess, will be the more
or less profitable and provident application of those resources upon which the prosperity of the community
depends. To them also our free constitution has delegated almost all the functions which are connected with
the maintenance of the social system. It is obvious,
therefore, that the well-being of the whole state must
depend upon the manner in which these duties are performed. If these classes act under the guidance of an
enlightened judgment, sustained by private virtue and
public spirit, we may justly hope to enjoy all the blessings of order and of well-regulated freedom: if, on the
contrary, they be deficient in high moral principle, or be
blinded by a wayward ignorance, we may expect corruption in every department of our institutions, or a mis-
guided pursuit of objects conducive neither to the happiness nor to the moral dignity of man. It is sometimes
argued with respect to these classes, that, inasmuch as
they possess the means of defraying the expenses of the
education of their children, there is no necessity that the
State should intervene to aid or to guide it. If the instruction of the people at large depended upon considerations of expense, there might be some weight in
arguments of this nature; but we regard the pecuniary
part of the question as an object of the most trivial kind,
when compared with the great moral results to which we
have adverted. We have then only to ask ourselves
whether the unaided operation of the voluntary principle, in regard of educational institutions, has hitherto

generated these results, or whether it be sufficient hereafter to produce them; and if we are compelled to reply
in the negative to both these questions, a case is made
out for the intervention of the Legislature as an assisting power, which shall give to the seminaries of the
superior classes the character of national institutions.
Let us now examine how far the academical instruction
at present existing in Ireland is calculated to answer
these requirements.

A certain degree of attainment in classical learning,
as well as in the elementary branches of mathematics, is
by no means rare, even amongst the humblest classes in
Ireland. The writer of this article has found, in schools
supported exclusively by payments from the pupils not
exceeding from 7s. to 10s. per quarter each, boys whose
knowledge of Homer, Livy, and other classics, would not
be considered discreditable to a student at Oxford or Cambridge in the first year of his college course; and upon one
occasion he discovered a considerable number of peasant
children learning their lessons under a hedge, who were
very considerably advanced in geometry and algebra.
The children of the farmers and shopkeepers in Ireland
receive, in general, a good elementary education, using
the term in its ordinary application to reading, writing,
and arithmetic; and a certain proportion of them, probably with an occasional hope of entering upon the
learned professions, obtain the superior kind of tuition
which we have just described. But, as regards those
sciences which bear upon the arts and occupations of
general industry, we fear that the attainments of the
whole body of the middle classes throughout the greater
part of Ireland are altogether inconsiderable. Indeed
the opportunities of acquiring knowledge of this kind
are so rare, that we cannot be surprised at such a result.
If a person in respectable circumstances were desirous
that his son should receive instruction in any of the
experimental, natural or practical sciences, such as chemistry, natural philosophy, &c.—botany, mineralogy, &c.
—civil engineering, architecture, &c.—we believe we
are correct in stating that there is scarcely a seminary or
institution in Ireland, except at Dublin and Belfast, in

which he would have an opportunity of procuring such instruction.

Diocesan Schools.—Of the academical institutions now subsisting in Ireland, the earliest in point of origin are the diocesan schools. These seminaries were founded under an act of the reign of Elizabeth, which directed the establishment of free schools, or, as they are called in an act of the reign of William III, " Classical Schools," in every diocese, to be maintained principally at the expense of the bishops and clergy. This act appears to have been carried into but very partial operation; and, with a view to its more effectual enforcement, the Legislature passed subsequent statutes at various periods. By one of these acts, 29 Geo. II. c. 7, grand juries in Ireland were directed to present money for building diocesan school-houses, to be levied in the same manner as other grand jury presentments,—by county rate; thus establishing the principle, that local taxation for the support of academical institutions is a legitimate mode of providing education for the class for whose benefit these schools were intended. In some few instances this statute has been acted upon; but, upon the whole, the diocesan schools cannot be said to have answered the purpose for which they were originally designed. It could scarcely, indeed, be supposed that the Roman Catholics of Ireland would avail themselves to a great extent of these schools, because in every instance the master is a clergyman of the Church of England: and although they are professedly open to persons of all persuasions, yet, as they are supported mainly by the contributions of the Protestant clergy, they are naturally considered as Protestant endowments. In 1835 the whole number of diocesan schools in Ireland was twelve. The aggregate number of scholars was as follows:—

Boarders	148
Day scholars	229
Free scholars	65
Total	442

The expenses of tuition in these schools appear to

average from 30*l.* to 40*l.* for boarders, and about six guineas a year for day scholars. The endowment is, in most cases but slender, consisting chiefly of a payment to the master from the bishops and clergy of the respective dioceses, which gives a fixed salary ranging from 64*l.* to 200*l.* per annum. The masters are appointed by the Lord Lieutenant: some of them have held preferments in the church. The course of education consists of instruction in the less difficult of the classic writers; in logic, in arithmetic, and the elementary parts of mathematics, with a course of general history, geography, grammar, &c. which varies in each school.

With a view to ensure a greater efficiency, and to correct abuses which had sprung up in the diocesan and other endowed schools, an act was passed in the year 1813, by which the superintendence and control of these establishments was committed to a permanent board of unpaid commissioners, most of whom are high official functionaries in the Protestant church or in the law. Their management has not, upon the whole, been successful; which may arise partly from the want of sufficient power to enforce their regulations, partly from the want of adequate pecuniary means to provide proper inspection, and partly from the circumstance that, as none of the board are paid for the performance of their duties, they are not subjected to the responsibility which attaches to public services when remunerated by the State.

Royal Schools.—The next class of academical schools which has been placed under the control of these commissioners, are the schools of royal foundation, which were endowed by Charles I. with extensive estates. They are situated at Armagh, Banagher, Carysfort, Dungannon, Enniskillen, and Raphoe. All of them, with the exception of Carysfort, are of an academical character. The revenues belonging to these schools are very considerable, and, under an improved administration, might be made instrumental in giving the best description of academical education to a much larger number of students than at present derive benefit from them. The estates belonging to Armagh school, for instance, pro-

duce 1,415*l.* per annum, of which 650*l.* are paid to the
masters, exclusive of a residence and of their receipts
from the students; and yet only thirty-six young men
were at this school in 1835, of whom ten were boarders
at thirty-five guineas per annum, and twenty day scholars at eight guineas per annum.   The income of Enniskillen school, in like manner, amounts to 2,119*l.* per
annum, of which, exclusive of their residences, 850*l.* are
paid to the masters; and yet not more than sixty scholars
were receiving instruction in this school in the year 1835,
of whom fourteen were boarders at thirty-four guineas
per annum, and thirty-six day scholars at six guineas
a year each.   The aggregate annual income of the six
academical schools above named (excluding Carysfort,
which is a free elementary school,) amounts to 6,317*l.**
which is derived from territorial possessions, comprising
16,529 acres.   The total number of boys receiving instruction in 1835 was as follows:—

Boarders	118
Day scholars	108
Free scholars	25
Total	251

The payments required from boarders range from thirty
guineas to forty-five guineas per annum, and from day
scholars the average appears to be about eight guineas
per annum.   When it is considered that, without the aid
of any endowment, this scale of payment for tuition enables private teachers in Ireland to maintain good academical schools, it must be felt that the advantage
secured to the public from this munificent endowment
is by no means commensurate with the resources which
it commands.   The fixed salaries of the head masters,
who, with one exception, are appointed by the Lord Lieutenant, range from 200*l.* to 500*l.*   Some of the masters
enjoy preferments in the church,—an union of functions
which we conceive to be incompatible with the due per-

* Six hundred and fifty pounds per annum has been recently allocated to the foundation of exhibitions in Trinity College for students
from the schools of Dungannon, Enniskillen, and Armagh.

formance of either duty. The course of education in
these schools is very similar to that given in the diocesan
schools : in both, the natural and experimental sciences
are equally neglected.

Schools of Private Foundation.—In addition to the diocesan and royal schools, eleven endowed schools of private foundation have been placed under the control of
the Commissioners of Education; of these, nine are of
a character decidedly academical. The endowments are
not by any means so considerable as those of the royal
schools, and only afford to the masters fixed salaries
ranging from 30*l.* to 140*l.* independent of the payments
required from the pupils. The masters are variously appointed. The payments for tuition range from thirty
guineas to fifty guineas for boarders, and for day scholars from two guineas to ten guineas, averaging about
eight guineas per annum. The course of education is
precisely the same, in point of general character, as that
given in the royal and diocesan schools. The aggregate
number of scholars in these nine schools stood as follows
in the year 1835 :—

Boarders	162
Day scholars	214
Free scholars	30
	406

We are not able with confidence to state what may be
the number of academical establishments in Ireland not
comprised within the foregoing enumeration, but we apprehend that their number is not very considerable.
There are a few private seminaries for the education
of the children of Roman Catholic parents. " The Bel
fast Academy" is, perhaps, deserving of an especial notice, as having been originally founded by subscription.
It gives education of a superior kind to about 150 pupils.
As, however, we have not before us sufficient materials
for presenting an accurate view of any academical establishments, except those which have been made a subject of especial parliamentary investigation, we abstain
from submitting statements founded upon imperfect information.

The Committee on Irish Education, to whose report we have already alluded, have recommended that the royal schools should be placed under such an improved administration as shall greatly extend their utility; and that, wherever the existing provision for academical instruction is found to be inadequate, the grand juries, or other fiscal bodies to whom is entrusted the duty of levying money for local purposes, shall be permitted to raise the necessary funds for permanently maintaining one or more academies in each county; and that the first expense of establishing such academies, by erecting the necessary buildings, &c. should be defrayed by parliamentary grant. They propose that the buildings so erected, and all the fixed property of the establishment, should vest in a board, to be appointed by act of parliament; that to this board should be entrusted the superintendence of education of every description; and that, specially with reference to these academies, it should be the duty of the board to take care that properly qualified persons are appointed as masters, and to maintain a watchful inspection over their administration. They suggest that a committee should be appointed, for the purpose of local superintendence, by the grand juries, or other bodies representing the interests of those who contribute to the rate by which the institution is supported; that the masters should be eligible without respect to their peculiar religious opinions, and that the academies shall be open indiscriminately to the children of persons of all religious persuasions; that the school fees shall be moderate and uniform; that, if any free scholarships be established, they shall be awarded to such candidates as shall distinguish themselves by their proficiency in an open and impartial examination; and, lastly, that the range of instruction shall be extended so as to embrace the natural, experimental, and practical sciences.

We shall reserve our observations upon these recommendations until we have spoken of the collegiate establishments of Ireland, to which branch of the subject we now proceed.

COLLEGIATE EDUCATION.

The Belfast Academical Institution. — We have not classed the " Belfast Academical Institution" among the academies of Ireland, because it possesses rather the character of an university than of an academy. It was founded in the year 1810. In the previous year, a large subscription, amounting in the whole to above 25,000*l.*, was raised in the north of Ireland for the purpose of establishing an institution which should afford a superior education in every department of science to the children of the middle classes, and thus render unnecessary the practice which prevailed of sending the youth of this part of the kingdom to the universities of Scotland. The Belfast Institution obtained an act of incorporation in the year 1810, by which subscribers to the amount of 22*l.* 15*s.* were constituted proprietors, with power to elect a board of management, and to make by-laws. It was also enacted that every subscriber of 100 guineas should be entitled to nominate one boy, to be educated free of expense. Visitors were also appointed. The board of managers select and remove the professors, superintend the financial arrangements of the institution, and, concurrently with the visitors, exercise full control over all its affairs. This institution has been encouraged and assisted by parliamentary aid, which has varied in annual amount. In the session of 1838 the grant amounted to 1800*l.* This sum is chiefly applied in salaries to the professors. The professorships are as follows: Logic and Belles Lettres; Greek and Latin; Hebrew and the Oriental languages; Moral Philosophy; Natural Philosophy; Anatomy and Physiology. To each of the foregoing a fixed salary of 150*l.* per annum is allotted out of the parliamentary grant. To the following professors only 50*l.* is allowed: Chemistry; Midwifery; Materia Medica; Botany; Theory and Practice of Physic. There are also professors of Irish, of Elocution, and two professors of Biblical Criticism, who do not appear to receive any portion of the parliamentary grant, but are dependent upon the class fees which they receive from the students attending their lectures. There are also two professors of Divinity, who receive each 100*l.* per annum. They are appointed by the Synod of Ulster and the Secession Synod respectively, these being the two principal denominations into which the Presbyterian Church in Ireland is divided. The first class of professors, together with the Divinity professors, form a board of faculty to regulate the literary arrangements of the institution. With the exception of the Divinity professors, none of the professors are compelled to subscribe any religious test. The religious instruction of the boys is left to their parents, and to the clergy of the denominations to which they belong. The number of students amounted in the academical session of 1834-35 to 226. A very large proportion of the students are candidates for the ministry in the Presbyterian Church. The fees payable for attendance on the different courses of lectures are very moderate, the highest (Natural Philosophy class) being only two guineas and a half for the session, which lasts from November till May. Attendance on the lectures alone, without submitting to examination, exercises, &c. is allowed upon payment of half the usual fees. Examinations are held at the close of each session; and, upon the completion of the entire course of study, the student receives a general certificate, which may be considered as equivalent to a degree. In immediate connexion with the Belfast academical institution there is a flourishing elementary school, in which instruction is given in English; in writing; in mathematics; in mercantile knowledge; in the classics; in French; in drawing.

The influence of the Belfast institution has been extremely useful in improving the intellectual character of the district in which it is placed; and it has probably contributed to increase that reputation for superior civilization which is claimed, not without reason, for the northern counties immediately adjoining Belfast. Indeed, the residence alone of a body of men of high intellectual attainments, such as the professors of the institution, in a large central town, cannot fail to give a tone to the tastes, dispositions, and occupations of the surrounding community; and at once to create a thirst for knowledge, and to aid its developement when created.

The University of Dublin. — Trinity College, or the
University of Dublin, was permanently founded and endowed by Queen Elizabeth. She granted to it a charter,
which was confirmed and enlarged by her successors,
James I. and Charles I. The corporate body consists of
a provost, seven senior fellows, eighteen junior fellows,
and seventy scholars. There are also thirty sizars. The
estates belonging to Trinity College are very considerable. Its revenue arising from landed property is stated
to amount to 13,846*l.* per annum, exclusive of the fines
receivable upon the renewal of the leases, the lands being let upon the same tenure as bishops' lands. This
revenue is also exclusive of a rental of 2400*l.* per annum,
arising from a separate estate attached to the provost-
ship. The senior fellows are supposed to enjoy incomes
amounting to 2000*l.* per annum; but we are informed
that they do not exceed 1500*l.* per annum. The incomes
of the junior fellows are divided into three classes, and
amount respectively to about 800*l.* 600*l.* and 400*l.* per
annum. The fellowships are awarded, when vacant, to
such candidates, being of the degree of B.A. as shall
have distinguished themselves by their superior proficiency, as ascertained by a very severe examination,
in an extensive course of mathematics, classics, ethics,
logic, general history, and physics. With only three exceptions, the fellows are compelled to go into holy orders
within three years after they have taken their degree
of master of arts. They vacate their fellowships upon
marrying or accepting a living in the church. There are
thirty-one ecclesiastical benefices in the patronage of the
college. The scholarships are worth about 60*l.* per annum.
each. They are held for five years; so that the average
number which become vacant each year is fourteen.
They are awarded to those students who distinguish
themselves by superior proficiency in classical attainments. There are professorships and lectureships in the
following sciences:—Divinity; Hebrew; Greek; the Modern Languages; Modern History; Oratory; Political
Economy; Law; Natural History; Mathematics; Natural and Experimental Philosophy; Astronomy; Physic;
Surgery; Chemistry; Botany. The course of education

is very similar to that which prevails in the English universities, a decided preference being given to classical and
mathematical learning over the practical sciences. The
pensioner's undergraduate course is completed by attendance on eight examinations during four years. Residence is not imperatively required. There is an examination at the commencement of every term, at which
honours are awarded. The college fees required from
the students, exclusive of rent of rooms, commons, &c.
are, for a pensioner, 15*l.* on entrance, and 15*l.* per annum, with a fee of 7*l.* 17*s.* 6*d.* on graduating as bachelor
of arts, and 9*l.* 19*s.* 6*d.* on taking the degree of M.A.
The fees of fellow-commoners are double those required
from pensioners. An admirable library, a tolerable museum, a repository of anatomical specimens, and a botanic
garden belong to the college; but the access of the students to these sources of instruction and enjoyment has
not hitherto been encouraged. There is no collection of
pictures or of statuary, nor are there any of the other
accessories calculated to inspire and cultivate a taste for
the fine arts. Two hundred and eighty-three students
entered college during the academical year 1837-38. The
number of students who took the degree of B.A. during a
period of five years, ending with the year 1831, was 1336,
giving an average of 266 per annum. The average number of students preparing for holy orders during the same
period was 120. The divinity lectures must be attended
during four terms by all students who belong to the Established Church. No religious tests are exacted, either
on entrance or on taking a degree; but no Catholic
or Dissenter is eligible to the scholarships or fellowships. And here we cannot avoid attracting notice to
the fact, that, in a country in which above four-fifths of
the population are Roman Catholics, the Catholics are
excluded from all share in the administration and emoluments of the only university which Ireland at present
possesses. Such exclusion naturally alienates their feelings, and deters the wealthier classes of the Catholics
from sending their sons to the University of Dublin.
For our own part, we should regard it as a decided
improvement in the constitution of all our universities

that the necessity of entrance into holy orders as a qualification for a fellowship should no longer be exacted,
except in the case of the professorships in divinity. A
college tutor can but seldom efficiently perform the duties of a clergyman; and, though we should not consider
it desirable to prohibit the fellows of a college from taking orders, we are of opinion that the introduction of lay-
men of all religious persuasions into the university of
a country much divided in regard of religious opinions,
would tend greatly to extend its utility, and to establish
it in the full confidence of the whole community. We
regard it as a matter of infinite importance to the harmony of society in Ireland, that the Roman Catholic
youth should be educated in association with Protestants
of their own station. By mingling together in their
pleasures and their studies, they learn to respect each
other's feelings; and they form early friendships, which
the collisions of adverse creeds cannot separate. To
those who are about to enter into either the Protestant
or the Roman Catholic Church this union in youth is
more peculiarly advantageous; because the wide difference of their studies and pursuits in after-life has but too
natural a tendency to create angry and embittered feelings, such as now unhappily exist between the clergy of
the different churches in Ireland to an extent unknown in
any other country in the world. The period of peculiar
preparation for the church ought to follow the completion of a course of general study. Till that course is
fully completed, the Catholic and the Protestant ought
to be united in their education. A period of three years
after taking the degree of B.A. might be allotted in both
churches to a course of theological study, combined with
a probation in all the other essential requisites of the clerical character.

We cannot conclude these remarks upon the University of Dublin without expressing our regret that celibacy
is there, as in the English universities, made a condition
essential to the enjoyment of a fellowship. It seems to
us that the arguments which are held conclusive by Protestants against imposing celibacy upon the clergy, apply
with equal, if not greater force, in the case of those who

are appointed to superintend the education of youth ; and in reference to the habits of the students, the opportunity of associating with the families of the tutors and professors, would probably operate as a moral restraint upon young men who are too often led into vicious company by the absence of the salutary influences of domestic society. Should it be urged that, if marriage were permitted, there would cease to be any motive to relinquish a fellowship, and that, consequently, the efficiency of the collegiate instructors would be impaired by the natural advance of old age and infirmities, we reply that, in all well-regulated public institutions, provision should be made for granting superannuation allowances to those who have devoted their years of health and vigour to a particular service. The endowments of Trinity College are so ample, that either the number of the fellowships might be increased, or superannuation allowances might be provided, without diminishing to an injurious extent the average income of the fellows. Such an extension of their number, by multiplying the rewards allotted to learning, would also tend to increase competitors for university distinction, and would attach to the college a greater number of men of tried ability and erudition. Another objectional feature of the collegiate system of Dublin,—which, however, it shares in common with the English universities,—is the artificial distinction created amongst the students by their classification as pensioners and fellow-commoners, by which a position is given to wealth which ought only to be awarded to superior diligence and good conduct. We offer these few observations in no unfriendly spirit towards the University of Dublin, to the many excellences of which noble institution we pay a willing homage. There are many other minor details,—some inviting praise, others animadversion,—upon which we are compelled to refrain from observation.

There are several small Roman Catholic colleges in Ireland, some of which are chiefly destined for the preparation of young men for the Catholic Church. They partake, however, more of the character of an academy than of a university, and therefore do not require a separate description.

The Committee of last session have recommended that, in addition to the county academies of which they suggest the establishment, there should be erected a college possessing the character of a university in each of the provinces of Ireland. The existence of the University of Dublin would, in their opinion, supersede the necessity of establishing one in Leinster; and they regard the Belfast Institution as a suitable provincial college for Ulster. Already the important city of Cork, supported by a large body of the nobility and gentry of the surrounding counties, has given its sanction to this project, by applying for the establishment at Cork of a provincial college for Munster. A similar application has also been made on the part of Limerick and the adjacent counties. The Committee recommend that the expenses of building and of outfit should, in this case also, be defrayed by the State; but that the permanent maintenance of the institution should be provided for by a local rate, levied upon the adjoining counties which derive the most immediate benefit from the institution. It is proposed that the Board of education to be constituted by act of parliament, as before described, should exercise a general superintendence over these colleges; and that, subject to such control, their administration should rest with a *senatus academicus* of the professors, acting conjointly with a committee delegated by the fiscal bodies which represent the counties contributing to the support of the provincial college.

After what we have already said respecting the advantages to be derived from the education of the middle classes of society, it is not necessary for us to dwell upon the benefits which would result from placing in different parts of Ireland institutions which should give to the children of such parents as cannot afford to pay more than from 5*l.* to 20*l.* per annum for the tuition of their sons, the opportunity of receiving as complete a course of instruction in every branch of knowledge as can be obtained in any of the existing universities. The principle of maintaining such establishments by funds raised by local taxation also appears to us the most convenient, the most secure, and the most satisfactory mode of en-

suring their permanent support. This principle, having
been already recognised in the case of the diocesan
schools, cannot be considered as a legislative innovation.
We are, therefore, prepared to assent to the general
recommendations of the report, both as regards the
establishment of county academies and provincial colleges; but we think that they ought to be subject to
modifications when applied to each locality. For instance, in those parts of Ireland in which there is a
large central town, which serves as a focus to the intercourse of several counties, it may be more desirable
to erect one large collegiate institution, by the combined exertion of such counties, than to multiply minor
establishments by the erection of an academy in each
county. This remark would be applicable to towns circumstanced as are Cork, Limerick, Kilkenny, Londonderry. On the other hand, there are some counties so
much isolated as not to be immediately connected with
any large central town, and yet not sufficiently wealthy
or populous to support a college. In such cases the establishment of a county academy would probably meet the
existing wants of the district. When it is remembered
that the population of Ireland exceeds eight millions;
that Scotland, with a population not amounting to two
millions and a half, supports four universities, which have
greatly contributed to raise the intellectual character of
her people; that in almost every country in Europe institutions of this nature are to be found in equal abundance; there seems no reason to doubt that Ireland
would require and support at least five or six collegiate
establishments, besides an adequate number of public
academies. An anxious wish having been already manifested, on the part of two of the most important districts
in Ireland, to obtain the advantages of such institutions,
upon the principles set forth by the Parliamentary Committee, there is every reason to hope that men of enlightened minds, belonging to all parties in England, will
be glad to second these local efforts by giving effect to
such part of the arrangements as are dependent upon the
sanction of the Legislature.

SPECIAL OR PROFESSIONAL EDUCATION.

Under this head we are called upon to notice those institutions in which persons destined for particular professions, receive a special education. We have already seen that, in regard to preparation for the clerical profession, the University of Dublin is the seminary from which issue the ministers of the Protestant Episcopal Church; and that, in like manner, the Belfast Academical Institution supplies the Presbyterian Church with candidates for its ministry. It, therefore, only remains for us to speak of the seminary in which the Catholic clergy are educated. The College of Maynooth was founded in the year 1795. It was thought inexpedient, upon grounds of state policy, to allow the clergy of the Irish people to be educated, as was formerly the case, in foreign countries, lest they should imbibe sentiments hostile to the British dominion: it has since that time been supported by annual parliamentary grants. The vote of 1838 amounted to 8,928*l.* which is applied partly in payments to the professors, who receive out of it 112*l.* each; partly to the subsistence and maintenance of 250 students at 23*l.* each, and of 20 scholars at 55*l.* each; and partly to the other expenses of the college. The Bishops of the respective dioceses nominate each a certain number of students to be placed on the establishment. A certain portion of the students defray their own expenses of tuition and maintenance. There are professorships in the following departments of science:—Dogmatic and Moral Theology; Sacred Scripture and Hebrew; Mathematics; Natural Philosophy; Logic; Metaphysics and Ethics; Rhetoric and Belles Lettres; Humanity; English Elocution; the Irish Language. The Commissioners of Education made a report upon the College of Maynooth, from which it appears that the number of students in 1827 amounted to 391; of whom 250 were on the establishment; 110 were pensioners, 20 were bursars or scholars, and 11 were scholars on the Dunboyne endowment. It is there stated, that the course continues for seven years, and that the young men usually enter at the age of seventeen. At that time Maynooth supplied the Catholic Church annually with fifty young clergymen. From eighty to one hundred clergymen were then required to keep up the numbers of the Catholic clergy in Ireland; the remainder were supplied from Carlow and the other minor colleges in Ireland, and from foreign colleges. We believe that no material change has taken place since the time at which this inquiry was made by the Commissioners of Education. The present number of students at Maynooth is about 460.

Law.—An introduction to the profession of barrister is obtained in Ireland, as well as in England, by eating dinners, and by paying a certain amount of fees. Before a person can be called to the bar in Ireland, he must have kept law terms for two years, by attending at dinner at the King's Inns* in Dublin, and a similar number of terms at one of the Inns of Court in London. It is needless to observe, that this cannot be called legal education : the only effect of such an arrangement is to diminish the number of candidates for the profession, by rendering the process of qualification tedious and expensive. The law student at present educates himself as best he may, with such aids as his purse will enable him to procure. If he pass one year with a conveyancer, and another with a special pleader, to each of whom he must give 100 guineas, and if he apply himself with unremitting diligence to the study of the law for several years, he may be considered as educated for the bar. No opportunity, however, being afforded him of making known the success of his studies, it not unfrequently happens, that after all this preparation, and all these sacrifices, he languishes in unheeded obscurity until he is at length driven to abandon the profession in disgust. Such is the fate of many young men of the fairest talents and of the most untiring industry. The necessity of some change in a system so cruel in its operation can scarcely be denied. It seems to us that in most cases the disappointment, which now so frequently occurs, might be averted by the simple ex-

---

* Graduates of Trinity College, Dublin, are not now required to keep terms for more than one year at the King's Inns.

pedient of ascertaining the qualifications of young men destined for the bar, by a public examination held before competent and impartial examiners. We are not prepared to say, that any serious difficulties should be interposed to prevent persons of limited legal acquirements from being called to the bar, because the public cannot be injured by their incompetence; but we are of opinion that a most valuable boon would be conferred upon the assiduous student of the law, if he were to be afforded an opportunity of exhibiting, in an impartial public examination, the extent of his legal attainments. Distinction so obtained would serve as his best recommendation to those in whose hands lies the disposal of professional business. Provided one such examination, or more, take place during the period allotted for preparation for the bar, we hold it to be of little importance where the student acquires his education. It would, however, be highly desirable, that, connected with such a society as the King's Inns, there should be regular courses of lectures and examinations in the different departments of law; so that the student might be enabled to acquire a competent knowledge of his profession, on terms less expensive than those by which it is at present obtained.

The same suggestion, subject in each case to the necessary modification, applies equally in principle to the various other branches of professional training, whether in reference to the occupation of solicitor, civil engineer, architect, &c. or to any other of the higher descriptions of intellectual labour.

Medical Profession.—The character of Dublin stands very high in regard to medical education. Exclusive of the University, there are in Dublin three separate chartered bodies connected with the medical profession, viz. the College of Physicians, the College of Surgeons, the Apothecaries' Hall. To each of these incorporations is attached a corps of professors and lecturers, who give regular lectures in the different branches of medical science. These colleges are invested with peculiar privileges: thus, for instance, none but members of the Royal College of Surgeons can be appointed as surgeons to the hospitals which are supported by county rate:

---

again, a Scotch degree in pharmacy will not enable a practitioner to exercise the calling of apothecary in Ireland. As a large portion of the medical men in Ireland have been educated in Scotland or England, and have brought home Scotch and English diplomas, these privileges, conferring a partial monopoly upon the Irish medical colleges, have given rise to much exasperated contention. For obvious reasons, it is the duty of the State to take care that ignorant men shall not be allowed to practise in the medical calling with unrestrained freedom, and therefore the attainments of every candidate for the profession should be tested by some competent body; but, on the other hand, there appears to be no sufficient reason for enacting, that a person who is held qualified to practise in England or in Scotland shall not be permitted to practise in Ireland, and *vice versá.* The mode in which it seems to us that the most perfect freedom consistent with adequate qualification could be attained, would be the establishment, in each of the three kingdoms, of a public board of impartial and competent examiners unconnected with any privileged body, such bodies being naturally interested in diminishing the number of their professional competitors. Any person who, after having undergone a public examination, shall have obtained a certificate of qualification from such board, ought to be permitted to practise in any part of the United Kingdom, either in medicine alone, in surgery alone, in pharmacy alone, or in all three departments, according as the terms of such certificate shall declare that the candidate has been found properly qualified in one or in all of these branches of the science. Under such an arrangement it ought not to be made an essential condition that the medical studies of the candidate should have been prosecuted in Ireland, in England, or in any other particular country. All that is required is competent attainment; and if the student finds or fancies that it is more conducive to his advancement to learn his profession in Paris, or in Germany, than in his own country, he ought not, on account of a zeal for the science thus leading him to distant lands, to be incapacitated, on his return home, from practising the profession which he has mastered. In order to diminish the chance of abuse on the part of such a public board of examiners, it might perhaps be advisable that the professional corporations at present existing should still be permitted to grant degrees concurrently with such public board. If this course, however, were adopted, it would be necessary to make much more effectual provision by law for raising the standard of medical education, than has yet been made by many of these chartered bodies.

We are not aware of the existence of any other public institutions in Ireland for professional education, unless we can regard as belonging to this class the Hibernian Academy of Painting, Sculpture, and Architecture in Dublin, to which an annual parliamentary grant of 300*l.* is allotted ; a small School of Medicine and Surgery at Cork; and an Agricultural School at Templemoyle in the county of Londonderry. This school is of so interesting a character that it deserves a brief notice. It was established in 1827 by public subscription. It was instituted for the purpose of giving to the sons of farmers and others, the best description of instruction in practical agriculture. Attached to it is a farm of 169 acres of land, with extensive and suitable buildings. The boys themselves execute the work of the farm ; and their instruction in other general knowledge is not neglected. They enter at the age of fourteen and upwards. Each pupil pays 10*l.* per annum for board, lodging, and instruction. The number of pupils amounted not long since to sixty-four. The effect of this establishment has been to qualify as land stewards, and to prepare for the profitable tenancy of farms, a number of young men who, but for the advantages afforded by this school, would probably have continued in the same state of primitive ignorance as their forefathers. The Parliamentary Committee recommend that at least one such school should be esta‹ blished in each province. We think that there ought to be at least one in each county. The land in Ireland, which is, generally speaking, extremely fertile, is capable of producing, under improved cultivation, an increased quantity of food, the extent of which none but a practical agriculturist who has witnessed the present neglected state of agriculture thróughout the greater part of the kingdom, can rightly estimate. As Ireland is now the granary upon which England depends for a large portion of its supplies, the consuming classes in England have a deep interest in every effort which is made to increase the agricultural produce of Ireland. The cost of these agricultural schools would, after the first outfit, be very inconsiderable; since, if properly managed, they would very nearly support themselves. A large school of this kind might be established, at a very trifling expense, in the south of Ireland, upon an estate which belongs to the Crown. It is situated at Pobble O'Keefe, in the county of Cork; consists of several thousand acres; and, having been already laid out and partially reclaimed with the view of serving as a model estate, there would be but little trouble in making arrangements for the reception of young men from all parts of the kingdom who are desirous of becoming instructed in the most improved processes of agriculture.

SUPPLEMENTARY EDUCATION.

It now only remains that we should speak of that class of institutions which have been designated as subsidiary to the general purposes of education. In this class may be placed scientific and literary associations, mechanics' institutions, public libraries, museums, botanic gardens, galleries of paintings, schools of arts, &c. An enumeration of the institutions of this nature existing in Ireland, will furnish but a meagre catalogue. They are chiefly confined to the metropolis; and may be stated, in general terms, as consisting of several associations connected with the study and pursuit of the professions of law and medicine; a geological and a zoological society; a society of civil engineers; several musical societies; and a society for promoting the fine arts in Dublin; a similar society in Cork; horticultural and agricultural societies in Dublin and in the provinces; a few scientific and literary associations and mechanics' institutions in some of the principal towns. Upon the whole, Ireland is sadly deficient in these aids to education. Neither in number nor efficiency can the very few institutions of this nature which exist, be said to indicate a just appreciation of the enjoyments and advantages of literature, science, and the arts. The only establishments which appear to us to require a special notice are those which are aided by parliamentary grant. These are the Irish Academy, and the Dublin Society. The former receives a small annual grant of 300*l.* It publishes transactions which are chiefly devoted to subjects connected with polite literature, with abstract science, and with antiquities. Among its members are to be found most of the leading men of science in Ireland, and in general its reputation stands deservedly high.

The Dublin Society was founded above a century since; and was much encouraged, and most liberally supported, by the parliament of Ireland. An enumeration of the objects which it embraces, will show how comprehensive is the range of useful action which it assumes to itself. It possesses a museum, a library, and a botanic garden, which are open to the public. It maintains four professors, who give gratuitous lectures, which are numerously attended by the public, in chemistry, natural philosophy, botany, mineralogy, and geology. The botanic garden, which is one of the finest in Europe, is a practical school for young men seeking instruction in gardening. There are also four schools of art, in which several most distinguished artists have received the rudiments of their education. They are as follow :—A figure school, a school for landscape and ornamental drawing, a school of architecture, and a school for modelling in clay. Exhibitions of Irish manufactures and agricultural implements are also held once every year under the auspices of the society. Evening meetings frequently take place, for conversation and mutual instruction in regard to objects connected with literature, science, and the arts. About nine hundred members have been admitted since the Union, upon payment of a sum which has varied from twenty guineas to fifty guineas each. The society having given upon some occasions indications of party spirit, it has not hitherto fully possessed the confidence of the Roman Catholic portion of the community; but there is every reason to hope that such circumstances will never again occur.   The annual parliamentary grant is 5300*l.*; but considering the multiplicity of objects which the society embraces, and that it stands in the same position with regard to Ireland that the British Museum does to England, it will not excite surprise that this grant is found inadequate to enable the society to perform, in a satisfactory manner, everything that such an institution, if properly supported, is calculated to effect. The Parliamentary Committee, which was appointed in 1836 to inquire into its management, recommended that it should be enabled, in some degree to supply the void which exists in Ireland with regard to instruction in the experimental sciences, by sending down to the small towns either its own professors, or other qualified persons, to give lectures in this department of science.   It was proposed that a small subscription should be raised by the locality applying for such a course of lectures, partly with a view of defraying a portion of the expense, and partly in order to show that the call was made by persons who were really desirous of deriving benefit from such instruction.   The Dublin Society has recently been enabled, by the government, to act upon this suggestion, and lectures upon chemistry, natural philosophy, and mechanics, have been given by the professors of the Society in the towns of Galway, Partarlington, and Wicklow. We cannot conclude this part of the subject without expressing it as our opinion, that the municipal bodies in the different towns in the kingdom, should by law be enabled to apply a portion of their borough rate to the maintenance in each town of a public library, a museum, a botanic garden, and of other means of promoting the innocent recreation and instruction of the inhabitants.

We have now completed this review of the educational institutions of Ireland; and we deduce from the facts before us the conclusion, that the provision heretofore made for the instruction of the people, either by the voluntary efforts of individuals, or by the fostering aid of the State, is wholly inadequate; that the endowments founded by private or by royal munificence have, through a defective administration, failed to produce benefits commensurate with the means of usefulness which they possess; that the instruction at present afforded to the different classes of society is seldom the most suitable that could be given in reference to the circumstances of the individuals receiving it; and that its quality requires to be improved, and its range to be enlarged. If these results cannot be fairly deduced from the facts which are before us, we are at liberty to stand still; but if neither the facts can be denied, nor the conclusion be controverted, then we are entitled to call upon the Legislature, upon the Government, and upon the people to begird themselves strenuously to the noblest task that can occupy the human energies—that of enlightening the minds, refining the tastes, and improving the habits of a nation; and, above all, of teaching them the practical exercise of that religion which was announced by its divine herald as the harbinger of peace on earth and goodwill to man.

WILLIAM S. O'BRIEN.

WHAT ARE THE ADVANTAGES OF A STUDY OF ANTIQUITY AT THE PRESENT TIME?

THIS question, which has often been discussed, it is proposed to examine again; not with the expectation of completely satisfying either the advocates or the opponents of what is commonly termed a Classical Education, but with the view of stating the matter in dispute with somewhat more of precision than has generally characterized this discussion. When we undertake to explain the advantages of any particular branch of study, we undertake to explain *what* that study comprehends : it may also be expected that we should point out *how* such a study should be prosecuted in order to be profitable.

A Classical Education comprehends a study of the Greek and Latin languages, and also a study of the matter contained in Greek and Latin books.

One end proposed to be obtained in the study of these languages, and an end which under a proper course of instruction may be obtained, is the power of reading with facility the Greek and Roman writers. If this end be not fully or adequately obtained, one object of a classical education is not completely accomplished ; but it does not therefore follow, that the education has been of no use.

The question which we shall first consider is the study of the Greek and Latin languages, as languages. The term "language" in its widest sense, may comprehend every medium by which we express our meaning to one another, or by which such meaning is transmitted to future times. In its limited and proper sense, language is the totality of those vocal sounds, by the combination of which society converses, and by which man expresses all that he feels, conceives, and concludes. That which gives language a permanent form is writing ; a mode of representation purely arbitrary and conventional, of which the historical origin is unknown. The real matter of every language is vocal sound, of which we cannot affirm that it was in its origin arbitrary or conventional. By the use of writing, every language acquires more precision and fixedness ; and the two languages which we have here to consider are now known to us only in this form. For the purposes of instruction we necessarily assign sounds to the words of these languages, but these sounds are not or may not be the true sounds ; and it is a matter of secondary importance for the purpose which we are here considering, whether they are or not. These two languages are only known to us properly in their written form, of which it is our object to ascertain the meaning.

In order to understand generally what language is, we must study some particular language or languages : the more languages a man studies fully and exactly, the more full and exact will be his conception of what language is, the more precise will be the notions which he will attach to words in any given language, and the less liable will he be to be imposed on by sounds which have no meaning.

This assertion is proved, or attempted to be proved, thus :—Any given language consists of a great number of articulate vocal sounds, which are its matter or material. These vocal sounds are, generally speaking, sufficiently numerous to express by their combinations what the speaker would wish the hearer to understand; in other and plainer words, to convey what is commonly called his meaning. When such sounds are addressed to one who by long experience has become familiar with them, they produce, if rightly selected and arranged, the effect which the speaker intends, so far as the functions of the understanding are concerned. Whether they shall move the affections or convince the reason of the hearer, is another matter. When language has reached the understanding of him to whom it is addressed or presented, its office *as* language is performed ; if it fail to move, to please, to persuade, to convince, the fault is not in the language used, but the fault is in that which the language has been made the medium of conveying.

Any language then, which has been cultivated and improved so as to keep pace with the general improvement of society, may be considered to possess the capability of being used as a means of diffusing, as from one centre, through all the channels of society, the thoughts of an individual, and of transmitting them through the permanent form of writing to the remotest generations : but that this effect may be fully or adequately produced, it is necessary that he who speaks or writes shall select words for his purpose, that have by use obtained exact and determined meanings ; or, if such cannot be found, that he shall give to existing words such a meaning as he requires, and consistently persist in such meaning ; or employ new words that shall convey his meaning ; and further, that he shall so combine and arrange his materials, that is, his words, as to convey not merely distinct conceptions of the things of which he speaks or writes, —the objects which he has under his view, taken singly, but also of the relations to one another under which he contemplates the objects of his thought.   It will strictly follow from this that, unless a man clearly conceives the objects which he contemplates and their relations, he cannot express such objects and relations clearly ; for the expression, whether it be sound or writing, is the *form* of the thought, and it would be an obvious inconsistency to admit the possibility of a distinct material representation of any thing which is indistinctly conceived in the mind : but, on the other hand, it does not follow, because the expression is ambiguous or obscure, that the conception of the writer also is imperfect or indistinct.   It may happen in two ways that a man shall fail to express what he understands and wishes to communicate—language may be incapable of serving as a complete expression of his thought, which, however, must be considered as the rarer of the two causes of obscurity ; or the writer or speaker may be unable to avail himself of the capabilities of his language, which is a common cause of ambiguity and indistinctness in speaking and writing.

It is important to observe, that the intellectual powers are not developed and ripened before language is learned ; but are developed at the same time that language is learned. Without, then, attempting to show how this acquisition of language, and the growth of the mental capacities, mutually operate on each other, it is enough for our present purpose that this acquisition and growth are contemporaneous. Of the infinite variety of things which are the objects of our intuition, part are immediately subject to the cognizance of our senses, and in their integrity are associated with particular vocal sounds, or words, without much danger of confusion or misapprehension; such words form a large part of the language of children, and of those who, having had little mental culture, use a language almost as limited as that of children. But a very large class of words do not denote any existing things, or at least do not denote things that are subject to the cognizance of the senses; they express the relations under which the mind contemplates two or more things, or they express things which are purely objects of thought: they are, therefore, not *things* as objects of sense; though the contemplation of objects of sense is in most cases a condition necessary for the suggestion of their relations, and for the conception of those things which only exist in the mind. This class of words is almost infinite: part are the common property of every member of a society; another part are the common property of all who think with exactness, or, in other words, they belong to the common language of philosophy; while others are more particularly appropriated to the several branches of science and art, which altogether comprehend the sum total of human knowledge.

The whole existence of any given society cannot be expressed by a definite number of terms. We have a word to denote the country in which a nation lives, a figure to express the numbers of the community, a name for their form of government, and a by-word or a phrase by which we express our opinion of their national character. But these terms, let them be the exactest possible, tell us little or nothing. Those numerous living objects, that constitute the entirety called a nation, have their individual relations to the whole of the community and to each other; which relations comprehend every possible mode of pain and pleasure, of happiness and unhappiness.

These infinite relations are expressed, however imperfectly, by a finite number of words, to which, in the progress of society, notions more or less definite have become
attached. The more precisely these notions are conceived, the greater stability will there be in the use of
the words to denote them, and the fewer will be the mis-
apprehensions and mistakes as to these relations; the
more certainly also will the course of such a society be
progressive and improving. But such terms as express
any of the infinite forms or relations under which society
may be viewed, are of all terms the most vague and unsettled, and yet of all terms the most important to be
clearly and fully conceived; such are " right," " duty,"
" morality," " liberty," " equality," " government," " monarchy," " democracy," and a thousand more. In the
minds of the vast majority of every nation, the ideas
attached to such terms are unsettled, indistinct, varying,
and capricious; and it follows, that their general conduct
in life, with reference to the things comprehended in
these terms, and particularly when the affections are put
in active motion, must also be unsteady, insecure, and
dangerous to their own happiness. The fixedness of the
meaning of such terms is almost as important as the right
understanding of the things of which these terms are the
symbols or signs: the right understanding of them is all-
important; but a wrong understanding, provided it is
fixed, does not threaten society with any thing like the
amount of danger that is involved in the instability and
variableness of the notions attached to such terms.

When we learn language, which is done through the
medium of a language, the purpose is not to learn what
is the real nature of things, nor what are the relations
under which we ought to contemplate things; but the
purpose is to learn what are the things and the relations
signified by the words used, and how things and relations,
as conceived by the mind, whether rightly or wrongly,
may be expressed so as to be understood. Such learning
also does not concern the more or less definiteness of the
words or terms: if they are definite, whether they express a truth or not, they will be learned and understood
as definite; if they are ambiguous or indefinite, they will

be learned and known as such. There can, therefore, be no learning of language without a learning of things as they are understood; and the better a language is learned, the more completely will things also be learned as they are conceived and understood; not necessarily as they are, or as they ought to be understood; nor yet necessarily in contradiction to what they are, or to the way in which they ought to be understood. There is a phrase by which persons who would improve our education often express their disapprobation of the study of the classical languages of antiquity : they say that it is a teaching of words only ; that education ought to teach things, and not words ; and other remarks to the like purport or effect. Now, as to this teaching of things, it appears that the things which many of them would teach, are things only which are cognizable by the senses ; things which it is very useful and necessary to know, but which are a very small part of all the things which need to be known. Many of these persons, who would teach us things and not words, would leave us to be satisfied with the outside of things, and with things which can be seen and felt. But there are many things which cannot be seen, or felt, or tasted, and to the knowledge of which we can only arrive by the exercise of our mental faculties, of which language is the manifestation : not that language *must* express truth, but that truth cannot be expressed without language ; and, therefore, we use the expression of language as the index of the mind's operations, and so we reach the conceptions and judgments of others and compare them with our own.

It may then be asserted, that no man can either understand language when used by others, or use it with precision himself, unless he has had some discipline or training for this purpose. This will hardly be denied by those who admit the truth of what has been already said. It is true that many men of great ability and little education have been strong, perspicuous, and good writers; by which terms no more is here meant than that they have conveyed their meaning (not here considered with reference to its truth or falsehood) to others, adequately, forcibly, and in an agreeable manner. But this excellence, though it may be obtained without the advantage of early training, has never been obtained without industry and perseverance and much practice. Those who think that writing well or speaking well is a kind of gift, as they call it, which comes of Nature's bounty, confound writing or speaking well with writing or speaking much, which, for aught we know, may come of Nature's bounteous profusion, just as she scatters weeds and briers with most profusion where the hand of the industrious cultivator is wanting.

The study of language seems to belong especially to the season of youth, when the mind is daily strengthening its powers and receiving from the infinite variety of things and the words which are associated with them, the imprint which may remain to the latest days of existence.

It is not here intended to be said that just notions of language cannot be acquired by the study of the mother tongue only, or that language cannot be learned by the study of a modern language: but as to learning language by the study of the mother tongue only, there are many difficulties; and, as to learning it by the study of a modern language, there are also difficulties which do not apply to the study of the classical languages.

The Latin and Greek languages contain a sufficient number of books to enable us, with the aid of the interpretation derived from tradition, to ascertain the meaning of their writers with sufficient exactness. The matters which the best of these writers treat of are those which concern all mankind; they mainly relate to what affects the social existence of a community. The number of these writers is large enough to furnish us with sufficient materials for our study, and not so large as to bewilder us by the extent of the field to be traversed. Whatever is the meaning embodied in these writings, it is now fixed and unchangeable. The political existence of the nations has long since ceased, and their language and literature will always remain what they now are. It is not necessary for our argument to contend, that the best specimens of literary composition in the Greek or Latin language are superior to the best of modern times:

it is enough that they are of undoubted excellence, and that their value can never be affected, as that of the best specimens of any existing literature may be, by the lapse of time, and the changes which it brings with it. In studying the languages of the Greeks and Romans, we study both their meaning and their expression: their meaning, as an intellectual exercise that will always remain the same in kind for every age and every nation; their expression, for the purpose of forming and correcting our taste by something which all nations appeal to as a universally acknowledged standard and measure, if not of perfection, at least of excellence.

Our relationship to the monuments of Greek and Roman civilization, must not be measured by the advantages which we may derive from them, merely as instruments for our mental improvement. It would, indeed, require many words to exhibit in its completeness that which we can only indicate. The history of our own social existence, and that of Europe and its colonies, is only the history of the further developement of that which we read of in the extant monuments of the Greek and Roman nations. To them, as to a source, we trace the wide-flowing and ever-swelling stream, in which the civilization of modern Europe is now spreading over the globe. Other nations have their sources to which they must trace the historical origin of their social existence; that of the Hindus or the Chinese, is not ours. The light of history, which penetrates to the origin of our race and the beginning of society, fails us when we come to trace the steps by which the various nations of the earth assumed that form under which they emerge from the darkness of unrecorded ages; and the primitive relationship of all the children of men, becomes, by the lapse of years, confused and indistinct. Thus in the great mass of our actual society, the descendants of children who are sprung from common parents, in a few generations are strangers to one another. We cannot, therefore, show how all the various social systems into which mankind are distributed are related to one another, because there is no uninterrupted historic record of human society. But though we cannot show this, we can show and we know, that our social life is a link in that long chain which binds together all the nations of Europe and their colonies, and reaches backwards to the cradle of our arts and sciences,—to the earliest memorials of the nations of Greece, and the founders of the greatness of Rome: a study of their monuments is a study of our own history.

The books in the Greek and Latin languages, which form the materials for the instruction of our youth in language, are a small number selected out of many. They are chiefly books which describe political events or exhibit the public life of the Greek and Roman nations; or books, such as the different species of poetry which represent them to us in their more inward and moral character, or such as contain their philosophical speculations and systems. The matter then which they treat of, though characteristic of a particular period in the history of the world and of a particular stage in civilization, is matter of that kind which most directly concerns our most immediate social wants and interests, and can never become either unintelligible or uninstructive, since the social man of to-day is in all essentials the same as the man of two thousand years ago.

This is the matter, expressed in language, on which the student of the classical languages is employed. We shall now show *how* he is employed upon it. For this purpose it will not be necessary to describe the elementary instruction by which he acquires a certain facility in these languages, though much might be said on this part of the subject with reference to old and new methods of teaching, both in the way of commendation and censure. We suppose a certain facility acquired, such as a boy of twelve or fourteen years of age may possess. The matter expressed in language, which is laid before the youth, may be a portion of a Greek or Roman historian—a portion of Herodotus or Thucydides, of Livy or Tacitus. It will comprehend many words or terms, which, from their universality and permanency, can never become doubtful in meaning; as, man, horse, mountain, river. It will comprehend others, which, though no less universal, are subject to modifications in every country; as, house, temple, chariot, ship; and which cannot, there-

fore, be fully understood without knowing wherein the
things signified by the terms differ from the things known
by our own experience, and corresponding to and equivalent to the things denoted by such terms. It will also
comprehend many terms which though of universal use in
all countries to express certain notions, yet are distinguished in all countries by certain peculiarities, which in
effect constitute the great distinctions between the different forms under which social life exists; as, husband, wife,
parent, child, master, slave, guardian, ward. The terms
"parent" and "child," for instance, present to the mind
or suggest a relation between persons, which relation as
to some things implied by the terms possesses the character of being universally intelligible, but as to other
things has a particular force and meaning in each particular country. Akin to words of this class, but still more
technical and positive in their meanings, are all those
words which enter largely into works that treat of the
public life of a nation, and express the various modes in
which sovereign power is held, distributed, delegated, and
exercised, the various rights and duties of the citizens,
the terms by which are expressed their rights to property,
and their mode of defending it from invasion; in a word,
the terms of government, law, and administration. It
will also comprehend that large class of words by which
nations express their judgments of things as they affect
the sense of the beautiful, or what may be called æsthetic-
cal judgments; the words by which they express their
critical judgments of the faculties of the human understanding; and those by which they express their judgments of human conduct, in which is embodied the positive morality of a nation.

In order then to comprehend fully the Greek or Roman historians, the student must endeavour to ascertain
the exact meaning of all the terms used by them. He
must learn to understand the things spoken of; that is, to
conceive them as they were conceived by the writers.
He must do this partly by the help of the instructor,
partly by consulting the best books of reference, and
partly by comparing the various passages in which the
same term has been used by the same or by other clas-

sical writers. The labour of such research is often great ; the difficulty of the analysis, which it sometimes requires, may often prove more than a student can surmount ; and after all, in some cases, complete success may not be attainable by the most accomplished critic : but in the labour of the inquiry consists more of the profit than in the success of the research.

It does not appear, so far as we can see, that there is any other exercise for youth, except that of learning a language other than his own, which gives him the same occupation as this. Those who know no language but their own are seldom practised, when young, in the task of ascertaining the precise meaning of many of those general terms which they must daily use, and the precise meaning of which it is often most important to know. With increasing years, as the active business of life comes upon a man, he is often driven to the consideration of such terms, and he must then endeavour to ascertain their meaning as well as he can.   It is hardly necessary to remark on the utter inability of a large number of persons, who are by no means deficient in natural abilities, but have had no sound instruction in their youth, to give to others, or even to form for themselves, any clear notion of what is really meant by many of those general terms which are daily in their mouths,—the watchwords of political parties, the ensigns of religious sects, the signals of strife and hatred, the fruitful source of error and unhappiness.   The only other way in which a youth could be practised at an early age in this kind of analysis, would be by introducing him to those several branches of study to which such terms severally belong ; a kind of education manifestly impracticable, because the teacher generally would not be competent to it ; and as manifestly useless for the pupil, because he would be incapable of profiting by it.   Nor would it be any substitute for these studies to introduce him, as is the fashion in some places, to a course of mental philosophy,—understanding by the term, as we do here, a study of the powers of the human mind. Such a study, though proper for the teacher as a means of enabling him to direct the pupil, is not proper for the pupil till his mind has been disciplined and strengthened by previous studies.

One process on which the student is employed when he is discovering the meaning of the words and terms used by the writer who is the material for his study, is this:— he will find that the same word has various meanings in various passages,—meanings at first sight discrepant, and sometimes apparently inconsistent; a circumstance which greatly increases the difficulty of remembering them. But he will discover, and, if his studies are properly guided, he will be led to the discovery, that these varieties of meaning are often parts of, or included in, a general meaning; that there is some term or meaning so comprehensive as to embrace every variety which he has discovered. The varieties are *species*, which, viewed with respect to one another, are characterized by differences; when viewed with respect to the all-comprehensive term, they are brought under a logical unity, and, thus viewed, belong to a *genus*, or are included in a general term.

Many words or terms, at first sight synonymous or nearly so, require to be distinguished; which can only be done by a complete analysis of all that is respectively comprehended in them. The object of the pupil's study is not to discover truths, but only to ascertain the meaning of words, so as to understand what things they denote, and to understand them in the same way as the things were understood by him who used the words; the process, therefore, is purely analytical. The general notion which the word conveys, and which is conceived *generally*, though in a confused and indistinct manner, is to be separated into its parts; a process which implies, so far as it goes, a right exercise of the understanding, and the importance of which will appear from the consideration that all through life a large part of our intellectual activity consists in separating into their elemental parts the general notions which we conceive of things; it being a fact, that we conceive most things at first in their totality, and consequently in an obscure and indistinct way, and that we arrive at an exact knowledge of them only by the resolution of them into their parts. In the case of such apparent synonymes, the first process is the resolution of each respective intirety into its parts; the next is a comparison of all these parts respectively. The ascertainment of differences in all the parts has, for its result, the complete separation of the two intireties, and thenceforward the two terms are logically opposed. If in any one or more of the elements a sameness is discovered, the intireties, viewed with respect to that sameness, may be considered to have a logical identity.

When the meaning of the author's terms has thus been ascertained, or approximated to, the next operation is to choose terms from the pupil's mother tongue which shall express the same meaning. Sometimes this cannot be accomplished at all; because the thing signified by the one term is totally unknown in the other language. When it is ascertained that no equivalent term can be found, the result is the same, as to the pupil's improvement, as if he had discovered an equivalent. Sometimes he may discover a term which may be precise enough in a general sense, and yet not an absolute equivalent; if he uses the term, being fully aware wherein it is not an equivalent, the purpose of his labour is also satisfied. In many cases he may be certian that he has adopted a term in his mother tongue which shall completely and adequately express the original. Thus the learner must examine fully the terms and words, both of the language from which he translates, and of that into which he translates. But the determination of the meaning of all the several terms which contain any difficulty, is not the end of the pupil's task ; he must also *express*, in his own language, the entire meaning of the author. To be enabled to do this, he must conceive fully and correctly the import of each proposition that enters into the formation of a complete sentence, and the dependence of these several propositions or members on each other. He must perceive what is stated or assumed as a truth, what is merely hypothetical, and what is concluded or inferred from that which is assumed or premised. He must observe when assumptions are made by implication, by virtue of the comprehensiveness of the terms used, without being expressed in direct and proper words. Wherever the subject-matter of the author peculiarly belongs to the argumentative kind, he must more especially keep his attention alive to the proposition to be proved or established, and to the inter-

mixture of facts, hypotheses, and conclusions which tend
to that end.   For this purpose he must often bring the
expression of his author to the test of the syllogistic form,
in order to satisfy himself whether the conclusion which is
drawn is a necessary consequence of the premises given
or assumed ; not that it is his business to correct the
reasoning of the author, but because it is his business
clearly to see whether the reasoning is correct or not, and
so to express the author's meaning that a like process of
syllogistic reduction, when applied to his translation, shall
give the same result that is derived from this process
when applied to the original.   To do all this completely
is the work of the finished critic; to attempt to do it is
the labour and the discipline of the scholar.

It is not until the full purport and meaning of the
author are seized, that the pupil can venture on the expression of it in another form, in his own language, which
constitutes what is known by the name of Translation.
This exercise, humble as it may seem, and familiar as it
is in some kind or degree to most persons, is one that may
give full employment to the most mature mind and the
most accomplished critic.   The translator, it is true, does
not invent, combine, and arrange, as the author of the original work has done ; he does not go through the labour
of investigating, selecting, and rejecting his materials.
But he must go through the labour of attaining to a full
perception of the meaning of the original ; and must either
by previous knowledge have been prepared to seize it
easily and completely, or he must in studying his original
often go over the same field of investigation in which the
author has laboured, and must thus, and thus only, attain
to an adequate conception of the language which the
author has employed.   But this is only half his labour.
The author of the original has his mind occupied with his
subject; from the fulness of his knowledge, and from the
depth of his thought, flows the stream of language, copious
and clear.*   Apt words and forcible expressions generally
proceed with ease from him who has thought long and

* Ex rerum cognitione efflorescat et redundare oportet oratio.—*Cicero*,
de Oratore, i. 6.

patiently, and feels the full import of that which he would express. So true it is, that words then become the very body of the thought. The translator, on the other hand, with labour and difficulty, puts himself in the place of the original author, as to the conception of the subject; but he can never be so fully occupied with it as with the creations of his own mental activity: he must curb and check himself on the one hand, that he may not exceed the bounds of his original; he must rouse and stimulate himself on the other, that he may not fall short of them. He cannot give full scope to his expression in his mother tongue, because it is his business to express what his original expresses: he cannot tamely attempt to render every sentence of his translation a verbal counterpart of the original; for no language admits of such a mode of transcript, without a total loss of all the energy, force, and beauty, and consequently the meaning, of the original. Thus, while the translator must assume the air of freedom, he must never forget that he is in fetters. When he has performed his work in the best way that it can be performed, his work, as a work of art, is of the highest kind. In performing this work a man has two things to do; one is, to understand *fully* the subject-matter before him, which will employ all the faculties of the understanding; the other is, to express that which he understands, or to convey the full meaning of it to another—a process which most nearly concerns the real business of life.

This exercise which the pupil has to attempt, constitutes a most valuable part of his mental discipline. The meaning of the original, as he has conceived it, is to be expressed in his own language; his mind is stored with the rich materials of his author, to which he has only to give another form of expression. His first step to composition is lightened and made easy by the labour which his author has already undergone for him. He is not reduced to the miserable and painful necessity of lengthening out some common-place which is given him as a text; of stringing together phrases which have barely a meaning; of concluding something about which nobody ever doubted, from premises which only express the same

conclusion in other words. His business is to express, in
his own language, that which he conceives the author to
have expressed in the original. The translator thus occupies the place of an interpreter, who has to become the medium of communication between two persons who do not
understand the language of one another. He represents
him also in another respect. The interpreter's first duty
is to understand what is said, and then to express what he
has heard in a manner that will be intelligible to the person
to whom it is addressed. He may judge by the mode in
which it is received how far he has been successful. The
translator knows and feels how he has conceived the passage ; after he has expressed it in his own language, he
may subject the new expression to the judgment of his
own understanding; or he may see how far another can
derive from it the conceptions and thoughts which he has
derived from the original.

A comparison of the *manner* of expression with that of
the original, will serve to point out to him where his own
language is deficient in perspicuity, force, or beauty.
Generally, the result will appear, even to himself, far beneath the original if the original is a work of merit, and
far below what he would gladly aspire to. When he attempts to write something of his own, he may be more
successful in the expression, because he will write with
more freedom ; but this superiority of freedom, which he
finds in his own original essays, may blind him to the
worthlessness of the matter ; he may be charmed and deceived by his own words. It will not be so when he has
to render the thoughts of others ; he will see how feebly
and inadequately his language expresses even *his* conception of another's meaning. The value and the distinctness
of the original thought will contrast with the poverty and
the vagueness of the expression in which he has rendered
it. This is the effect of every essay at translation from a
valuable work, upon the mind of him who has sterling
merit enough to be capable of becoming a good writer.
His own common-places, expressed in the best language
that he can command, appear trivial by comparison with
the thoughts which he has laboured to penetrate and understand ; his expression of that which he has at last ade-

quately conceived must appear poor and lifeless when
contrasted with his original ; and thus, from feeling what
his deficiencies are, by seeing what he has attempted
without success, he may reach the first step in improvement,—a knowledge of what he has to learn, and a well-
founded admiration of that which he has proposed as his
model. Who that ever attempted a translation of any
work of genius, has not felt the feebleness of his efforts,
and the advantage that he has derived from his unavailing
attempts ?

This exercise of translation, in order to be useful as a
part of education, must be conducted under the guidance
of an able and efficient master, who can point out defects,
correct errors, and supply by his enlarged knowledge and
experience what his pupil is deficient in. It must be
proportioned in quantity and difficulty to the pupil's age
and progress. Simple narrative, of which the Greek and
Roman historians contain so many excellent examples,
forms the first stage in this exercise. The translation of
such portions as are argumentative,—for example, the
orations of Cicero, Æschines, or Demosthenes,— is a more
difficult exercise; and still more difficult is the translation
of such works as exhibit a scientific treatment of a subject,
or an attempt to treat a subject in a scientific manner,
as the dialogues of Plato, the writings of Aristotle, of
Cicero on the Orator, or the Classical Roman Jurists.

It may be collected, from what has been said, that it is
written translation to which so much importance is here
attached. It is true that a large part of the school exercises are, and must be, made orally ; but there ought to
be, in the course of every week, two or three written
translations at least. Oral translation has, doubtless,
many of the advantages which written translation has,
and some which it has not; but written translation cannot
well be dispensed with, though in some public schools it
forms a small part of the school exercises,—a fact which
may help to account for the Greek and Latin languages
being often imperfectly learnt at such schools. The
careful correction of the written exercises by the master
is of the first necessity, in order that they may be really
instructive.

It may be a useful exercise to attempt to translate some of the best specimens of the Greek and Latin poets into the corresponding, or to suitable, English measure ; an exercise that, for many reasons, we should rate higher as a means of forming the taste than the practice of writing Greek and Latin verses, though we do not join in the total condemnation of Greek and Latin versification as an exercise for young students. This exercise may certainly be so conducted as to contribute to the acquisition of a knowledge of these languages, to a nicer perception of rhythm, and to the formation of a pure taste. It may be an appropriate part of school exercises when it does not demand too much time ; but it is altogether unsuited to a course of university education, and to an age when the intellectual faculties should be actively employed on those studies which are to form the man.

The critical skill in language which may be acquired from a careful study of the best Greek and Latin writers depends, as we have already intimated, on two things : that the languages are now an unchangeable material, fixed and positive ; that they contain enough, and not too much, for the purpose : and that they possess merits as languages at least equal to those of any other. To this may be added, that the great difference between the character of these languages and our own constitutes, as it has been sometimes remarked, one advantage in the study of them which is not derived in an equal degree from the study of the modern languages of Europe.

It follows from this, that the *quantity* of the material on which the youthful pupil is to be employed should be limited by selection, if it were not limited by the actual quantity that remains. Were the quantity that remains all as valuable as the best part, we should not require so much for our purpose ; as much of it is of little or no value, there is the less difficulty about selecting from the mass ; and, if we could not trust our own judgment in this matter, the judgment of antiquity itself has already decided for us.

It is not, then, one object of a classical education to carry a pupil through all, or nearly all, the writers of antiquity ; though it certainly is one object to enable him to read any of them if he chooses. One main object is to train him to a critical study and exact use of language, by keeping him employed on a few models of undoubted excellence, whose value for all that we value them will be the same a thousand years hence that it is now. Another object is to form his taste, and lead him to a perception of all those qualities on which language depends for its perspicuity, strength, and beauty; in other words, of all that makes language of any value at all.

Those, then, who say that the writers of antiquity need no longer be studied, because all that is worth reading in them may be learned from translations, mistake the question entirely. What is worth reading in them, or what they are worth reading for, is a matter for a separate consideration. We here contend that they are worth reading, independent of the matter that is in them; though we also contend that it is by virtue of the matter with which the words are associated that they do derive much of that value for which we consider them the best introduction to the study of language, and the best material for developing the critical sagacity of youth.

It will follow, from what has been said, that we consider a solid acquisition of the Greek and Roman languages as an essential result of their study, if they are to be studied at all. This remark may appear either trifling or unmeaning; but, with explanation, it will perhaps not be open to either objection. It is possible, and not uncommon, for many years to be employed in and about the Greek and Roman languages, and yet for a pupil not to learn these languages well. When this is the result, it must be admitted that the time is ill spent; for we think that, if the master has the requisite knowledge, and a good mode of teaching, the languages will be learned adequately in a reasonable time by all pupils who have average abilities and industry. Where the pupils have such abilities and industry, and the result is a failure, the non-attainment of a competent knowledge of the languages implies want of knowledge or ignorance of proper methods in the master, and, as a consequence, no intellectual improvement in the pupils. A pupil may, however, learn the languages with a moderate degree of accuracy, and may employ much of his time on what are commonly called Greek and Roman antiquities (matters of archæology), Greek and Roman history, Greek and Roman geography; and may acquire, in these departments, much that passes under the name of learning. We shall presently discuss the value of this kind of learning, both as subsidiary to a right understanding of the languages, and as a thing independent of a critical knowledge of them. At present it is here contended that those who do make the Greek and Roman languages their study, must make the languages *as* language their first and main object; and if they study the authors in the way here insisted on, they will not fail to master the languages well. We do not here insist so much on the acquisition of the languages as a means for reading the authors with ease, but we insist on the obtaining a full perception of the author's meaning, and on the practice of expressing that meaning in another language; the former as a most valuable intellectual exercise, and the latter as being also a most useful and necessary practical discipline. In going through this discipline, the ancient languages will certainly be learned, and may then be used according to the learner's pleasure. So far as both or either of these languages is learned on sound principles, so far this discipline will be beneficial; for a good discipline is not the less beneficial in its degree, because it may be carried further. If, then, either of these languages is learned well to any degree, to that degree the exercise has been beneficial. If the mode of teaching and the intellectual discipline are bad, the pupil's time is as ill employed as if he were learning any thing else badly; but not worse, for any reason that we can see.

It now remains to consider what advantages may be derived from the study of the matter contained in Greek and Latin authors; and this is a part of our subject which requires to be treated with some precision, inasmuch as those who maintain the value of classical learning, seem to have seldom formed a clear conception of that which constitutes its value; and those who are the opponents of this branch of learning cannot be supposed to have any

clearer notion of the matter, being, so far as we have observed, entirely ignorant of the subject.

It is not pretended by any person who understands the
nature of the question, that a knowledge of antiquity,—that
is, of Greek and Latin authors, and the matter contained
in them,—has any direct bearing on many of the modern
sciences. A man who will study chemistry, botany, or
zoology, need not, for those purposes, know anything of
Latin or Greek authors ; nor is it necessary for him who
cultivates mathematics, or any of those branches of science
which require their practical application, to know any
thing of Greek or Latin authors for that purpose. It is
not here said that a man would be the less adapted for
such studies or pursuits, if he were acquainted with the
Latin and Greek authors, but it is admitted that he may
do without them ; and it is not even contended that the
advantage of knowing the meaning of the technical terms
of any of these sciences, which are derived from the ancient languages, and of forming such terms with accuracy when required, deserves any weight at all in the
consideration of this question. It is then admitted that,
for a great number of persons who could afford the time
and expense required for a classical education, such an
education is in no way necessary for any of the purposes
above-mentioned.

Those who investigate the history of a branch of
science, such, for instance, as astronomy, are seldom
satisfied unless they trace it to its origin ; and the writings
of the Greeks, on this as well as other sciences, furnish
abundant materials for such investigation. But here also
the diligence of modern scholars and men of science has
collected every thing, or nearly every thing, that can be
gleaned from the records of antiquity ; and such investigation, therefore, would, to a great extent, be either a
mere matter of curiosity, or a kind of learned amusement,
pleasing enough for those who have the leisure and the
means to follow it, but not necessary even to make a man
competently versed in the history of any science which was
cultivated by the Greeks. After these admissions, it may
be asked, for whom, then, is the study of the Greek and
Latin authors useful, and how is it useful ?

This question shall be answered thus :—Many of the Arts and Sciences are immediately concerned only about the production of wealth ; and others, which, so far as they are branches of pure speculation, furnish employment for the best powers of the understanding, are also in their practical applications mainly subservient to the same end. Man operates upon matter by separating it, combining it, and fashioning it into new forms, and thus he produces all the material objects that he desires. He also exchanges the result of his labour for the labour of others, and for this end he contrives the means of moving things from one place to another with speed and safety. So far as these operations extend, a knowledge of the literature and science of a people whose national existence has long since ceased, can be of no direct use. But man has other wants. The feeling for the beautiful and the social instincts are part of his nature ; the former is inseparable from all attempts to give form to matter; and the social union which is the result of these instincts gives birth to innumerable wants, which, acting in accordance with his nature, man seeks to satisfy, and which stimulate him to acquire a knowledge of his own inner being, in order that he may reach those springs of action, and those laws of the human mind, which must govern him in all his dealings with his fellow-men. Man has always existed in society, for a family is a society; and even in this, the most contracted conceivable sphere of social existence, are contained the elements of that more comprehensive society which we call a nation. Every nation or people that has had a long period of existence, and has left behind it the records of its social state, is an object of interest and instruction to every nation or people that comes after it. The advantages which every member of a nation derives from that union implied in the term Nation, People, or any other terms by which the masses of mankind are designated as units, need not be particularly enumerated. It is sufficient to observe that there is nothing which renders life desirable to us of the actual generation that does not ultimately owe its origin to that union of individuals called society, and that does not depend on the constitution of society for its stability. The structure of society, then, is the great problem which must occupy the first place in the human mind so long as man exists. But no society can exist unless it is based on certain fundamental notions, which must always be the same. Obedience to sovereign power, a term which also implies the will and the power on the part of the sovereign to compel obedience, is one of these notions. It is this which gives to a society its fundamental element of a unity. To know how to secure to a given society—that is, to every individual member included in the term,—the greatest amount of individual good consistent with the preservation of that unity, is the great problem which involves nearly every question that concerns man's temporal happiness. It involves not only the physical, intellectual, and moral well-being of every individual *as* such, but also the right organization of all into one coherent and consistent mass.

To express ourselves less in general terms :—Every man is interested not only in having and forming for himself the best physical, moral, and intellectual character, but it is also his interest that every other person may have the same. All are interested in the well-being of all. All being one, by virtue of the union implied in the term society, no one can fall short of a proper standard and measure without injuring others as well as suffering himself; and, in order that this universal well-being may be secured as far as the nature of so numerous an association admits, all are interested in having the best organization given to that body of which each is a living member.

A knowledge of the principles of any science which is directly concerned about the production of wealth can only be attained by those who make such principles a special study ; and the members of society will be divided into various classes, according as it is their business to be conversant about this or that science or art. All the members of a nation are interested in the successful prosecution of all such arts and sciences, because the benefit derived from them is extended to all ; though it does not directly concern all to know these sciences and arts, which can only be perfected by a great division of labour. But all the members of a nation are directly concerned in every thing by which the general well-being of the community, as a society, is secured ; though here also, owing to the great difficulty of fully comprehending the means by which this well-being is secured, it becomes necessary for the mass to rest satisfied with certain general principles, or notions, and to leave to particular classes of persons the special study of those various branches of knowledge which concern the conservation and improvement of society. The great difficulty here is to convince the mass of mankind, not that they have a direct interest in all that concerns the organization and conservation of society, for that is not needed,—they feel that they are interested deeply; but the difficulty is to convince them that the organization and conservation of society do involve fundamental principles which require as accurate a study as those of any other science, and, in tracing which principles to all their logical consequences, greater mental power is required than in any other branch of science which man has formed and cultivated. A man will readily admit that he knows nothing of chemistry, surgery, astronomy, and many other things ; but how few will admit, or believe, that they know nothing of the powers of the human understanding, of government, legislation, jurisprudence, and other matters of the kind. If pressed hard, such persons may admit that they know nothing of the artificial systems into which such branches of inquiry have been erected, and of the technical language in which they are expressed : but divest them of their technicalities, and their common sense is as good a guide for them on all such subjects as the pretended philosophy of others. Further, a man may admit that he knows little or nothing of the various ecclesiastical, judicial, and administrative systems which govern the society of which he is a member, because of their being formed into artificial systems, and wrapped up in a technical language. Such artificial systems and technical language had, he will observe, their origin in ages far less liberal and enlightened than the present, and have grown up to their actual form under the sanction and protection of those who are interested in the preservation of abuses, or of those whose views were narrow, and whose vision was dim, when contrasted with the wide range and piercing eyes of modern philosophers. Thus, many well-meaning people, whose zeal for the general well-being is undoubted, but whose powers of seeing and understanding things as they exist is far below that of those whom they denote as the dull bigoted adherents to established things, would sweep away without fear, because without knowledge, innumerable positive institutions and rules by which society is now governed. In place of these they would substitute a few plain simple rules, such as nobody could dispute about—till they came to apply them to practice. Such persons, not being sufficiently disciplined to comprehend the difficulties of determining by words the infinite relations which co-exist in society by virtue of the union which forms a society, and seeing with intuitive clearness a few principles which nobody disputes, conclude that these artificial rules and systems are a mere cumbrous machinery, which has been constructed in utter ignorance of those principles which they comprehend so clearly. It may not have occurred to such persons to consider that the notion of a triangle is fully conceived by three straight lines in a plane, surface, each of which intersects the other two. The infinite relations which subsist between the three sides and the three angles of a triangle are a necessary consequence of the notion of a triangle; though not seen or comprehended when the notion is conceived, they are created by the same mental power which conceives the triangle; but they are not *known*, though existing by virtue of the primary notion, till they are deduced from the primary notion by the operations of the pure reason. When a number of individuals form a society, the notions of sovereign and subject, of husband and wife, of parent and child, of the right to property, and of the binding force of contracts or agreements among individuals as to acts to be mutually done, when such contracts are not contradictory to positive law, are fundamental notions without which the notion of a society cannot be formed; for the notion of a society includes these other notions. Now these fundamental notions are few in number, and in every society they soon acquire a fixedness and a distinctness equal to those of the axioms of geometry. They are the sides and angles of the triangle; elements few in number, but capable of infinite combinations and relations, the determination of which, as logical consequences of the elemental notions, often baffles the utmost powers of the human understanding.

The fact that all people do form some judgment of every matter which concerns society whenever it is brought before them, proves the universal interest which all such questions excite. It proves that the things which move their affections, and on which they will pronounce a judgment, are of universal interest. But we believe that the mass can never be made to comprehend that these things are capable of being subjected to a scientific method, and of being, within certain limits, matters of demonstration. Nor is this opinion weakened by the fact, that a sound principle is often adopted by the mass of a people, and zealously maintained till it produces an effect on the governing body. Such a principle always emanates from some other source, and is often only adopted by the mass because it coincides with some passion or affection, or because it favours what they suppose to be their interest; and a wrong principle may be as generally adopted by the mass, and as zealously maintained, as a right one.

Now, as to all these notions, these merely mental existences, which form the very groundwork of every society, and govern all its operations, it seems impossible to convince those who are merely conversant with material phenomena that these other phenomena require as careful a study and discipline in order to understand them,— that is, clearly to perceive them,—as the phenomena of those which in popular language are called the sciences. Every man feels that he does know something about them, and that he is deeply interested in them; but he cannot conceive that any other person should know more of them than himself. He will admit, as already observed, that he knows nothing of the technicalities in which they are veiled by interested men; but then his plain common sense points out to him the absurdity of all such technicalities, on which, however, men with as good capacity as himself employ their time, and, as they think, not unprofitably.

Now, as it is here contended that the preservation and well-being of a nation, considered as a society, involve the consideration of an unlimited number of things, which the mind conceives as things existing by virtue and in consequence of that union of individuals called society, and that these things are in their nature capable of being clearly conceived and expressed in words, it follows that they are, like any other phenomena, capable of being the materials from which systems may be constructed, with as much certainty as any other system which is constructed upon fundamental principles. But the difficulty of constructing such systems is greater; because the phenomena which are the basis of these systems are differently conceived by different persons, and often indistinctly conceived by all persons, and in the constructing of such systems the affections often mislead the judgment. It may, perhaps, give some further distinctness to our meaning, if we add what subjects are here particularly referred to. We may mention religion, morality, legislation, jurisprudence, positive law, and, as a part of it, judicial procedure. All these are founded on principles which are merely notions, but which admit of a purely scientific treatment and developement. In their practical application they concern the very existence of society; or rather, society, as conceived by us, comprehends in the term these and many other notions equally extensive.

Out of the developement of these notions proceeds that infinite number of other notions, and of practical rules in which they are embodied, which compose the society of every particular nation; and according as they are modified, or well or ill understood, give to each society those characteristics by which it is chiefly distinguished from others.

On the right understanding of these notions depends more of the happiness of individuals and nations than on the means of their command over matter; and these notions can never be rightly understood or conceived in their full extent, except by those who have made them their study. Mankind, indeed, may be and are often

governed and directed by those whose conceptions of
these things are as confused and indistinct as those of the
mass whom they govern and direct; but no real advantage can be secured to society, except by the labours of
those who approach these difficult subjects with an honest
desire to understand them, and who labour with perseverance to conceive them in all their full import and extent.

Now, the careful study of the best classical authors
may, we think, conduce to forming the mind for these inquiries more than any other studies on which youth can
be employed. It is here admitted that classical studies
as directed do not much conduce to this end; but perhaps
no studies, if well directed, would be a better introduction
to an understanding of every thing that concerns the existence and improvement of society.

We do not, indeed, think that those who direct classical education, either in schools or colleges, have generally
any definite end in view. The Greek and Latin books
which they read are, with some exceptions, those best
deserving of being read; but the way of reading them
implies no definite end. If there were a definite end, it
might indeed be considered as indicated by the choice of
the books; for the choice of the books would imply a
choice of the matter, and a choice of the matter would
imply an end. But as the way of studying these books
seems to show that no end is clearly conceived, we must
conclude, either that choice has not determined what
books shall be used; or that, choice having once determined what books shall be read, they are now read, not
with reference to the reasons of the choice, but because
it has long been the custom to read them. The latter
conclusion seems, for many reasons, the more likely.

The studies, then, for which the best writers of antiquity
appear to us to be a good preparation, are those which are
generally denoted by the terms moral and political, and
which concern the intellectual powers mainly as applied
to the study of man as a member of society. Among the
writers of antiquity, those are most worthy of being read
who have treated on various branches of pure speculative
inquiry, on the right method of reasoning from premises,
on ethics, law, constitutional forms, and the great events
which have characterized the progress of nations—the

philosophers, the orators, the historians, and the jurists of antiquity. To these we would add those poets whose writings aid us in more fully conceiving the domestic and moral character of their age, and in whom we can trace those more finely expressed lineaments which fill up the portraiture of a nation.

The whole number of volumes which a student has thus proposed to him is not large; and out of even this limited number a few may suffice for the purposes of instruction. It is a very mistaken notion to suppose that the object, even of a good and complete classical education, is to make a man a *scholar*. To be a scholar is to adopt the study of antiquity as the business of life; and the materials are ample enough to engage the whole time of the most industrious student,—indeed, so abundant and various, that no man can merit the name of a scholar who does not make the study of antiquity his sole or his principal pursuit. Nor is it an object of classical education that a pupil should encumber himself with a number of isolated facts of history, geography, and archæology; though, if one might judge from the questions proposed to students in some of our examinations, any fact of any kind, of any value however inconceivably small, is a fact which he may be called upon, at any time, to produce : a list of barbaric kings of whom nothing is known but the names; or a conjecture of some modern critic about something which cannot be learned with certainty, and which has no connection with any thing else that is the subject of examination.

To prevent our meaning being misunderstood, a few words are necessary as to this matter of examination. When an author is selected as the material for the student's labour, every thing that may explain the meaning of that author is a thing which requires the student's attention. The thing, however small in itself, acquires an importance when it is useful or necessary to explain the author's meaning; but, independent of this use or necessity, innumerable things have no value at all. For the student to encumber his memory with them is worse than a waste of time and trouble; for an examiner to inquire about them, disconnected from that which alone gives them any value, shows a complete incompetence for the function which he affects to discharge.

The great value of the study of such a book as Herodotus, Thucydides, Livy, or Tacitus, consists in the subject-matter of the author being in a reasonablecompass. If Thucydides, for instance, be the book chosen, it being the student's business to understand his author, it is his business to examine into every matter without a knowledge of which the author's meaning cannot be fully understood. For this purpose he must often divert from the historical narrative, and seek in various authorities for information as to the places mentioned by the author, as to historical facts incidentally alluded to, and peculiar national customs. Now, as every thing which the human mind can entertain has some relation to every other thing, a student may, in following up any particular matter referred to in the text, wander into an endless field of inquiry, in which, however, he may perhaps hardly travel so far as some of his examiners. How far he should follow up such inquiries, it is impossible by any words to define; but, if his studies are well directed, he will never carry them beyond the limits which are necessary to give him the full understanding of the passage which has set him on the inquiry. He will never forget that to understand Thucydides is the business in hand; that a book which contains a connected narrative of events forming one great subject, needs comparatively little foreign illustration; and that the improvement which he will derive from the study of an author who is worth studying, will bear pretty nearly a direct ratio to the attention which he devotes to that author exclusively. Nor is it necessary for the reader of Thucydides to have a very exact and laboured knowledge of the events prior to the time when the author's narrative commences. It is only necessary to have such knowledge as will enable him to connect that which he is studying with that which precedes, and so far to connect it that there be nothing erroneous, though there may be much that is incomplete, in his knowledge. If the whole of Thucydides were carefully studied as a book, and a subject by itself, with no further reference to extraneous matter than is necessary to explain the text, such a complete study could not fail to have a most favourable effect on the understanding, and to open the mind to a consideration of many the most important political questions that affect the interests of society. The *completeness* of the study would have that effect, which nothing but a complete study of a limited quantity of subject-matter can give ; the effect of disciplining the mind to exactness, of forming it to a full comprehension of the value of thoroughly knowing a subject, and at the same time of convincing the student how difficult it is fully or adequately to comprehend even a limited amount of subject-matter,— a conviction never reached by those who ramble unrestrained over a boundless space, and so have not leisure sufficient to learn how little they actually see of the infinite which passes before their eyes. Such a book as Thucydides, if properly studied, is alone sufficient to form the mind of any well-disposed and intelligent youth ; that is, to form it so as to give it a real insight into human character and the nature of society, to fashion the mind for reflection, and to prepare it for further and more arduous intellectual labour. Such a book also, in itself, independent of all extraneous matter, would furnish a competent examiner with sufficient materials on which to try the proficiency of the pupil, without rambling into matter unconnected with it. It cannot be too often repeated that the value of these ancient books, as a discipline for youth, consists in the limited amount of the material; and that a course of study, or of examination, which shall lead the student into the endless variety of matter which a scholar might wish to investigate, is only a method of destroying the value of that for which the study of these books is mainly recommended.

Whatever be the matter on which a young student is properly employed, the powers of the understanding which are called into action, and the exercise of the reasoning faculty, are pretty nearly the same. But the study of the classical writers appears to us to offer some advantages over every other matter for a large class of students; because the matter of the best of these writers is that which has more immediate relation to our future life as members of society, and more directly conduces to form and discipline the mind for all political and moral investigations, than any other. The material on which the mind is so employed is calculated to call all its powers into action; and it has the advantage of being a kind of material similar to that on which all men must, in after-life, try the strength of their powers of understanding, and which many men must make the business of their lives,—matter historical, philosophical, moral, juristical. The sameness or similarity of these matters appears to us a most important consideration. As all correct reasoning is the same process, it has often been supposed that any matter which exercises the reason would form as good a discipline for the mind as any other matter; because such other matter can do no more than exercise the reason. But this is a mistake. People with any moderate education do not generally fail so much in their logical deductions, as in their right apprehension about the matter in hand. Some are, no doubt, much more practised logicians than others; and, supposing two men to have just the same knowledge of a thing, one will more easily detect a fallacy in any argument about that thing than another. But that which constitutes the greatest difference between men in their handling of a matter is not the correctness of their deduction, but their powers of apprehension. One will make false deductions, and the other will make true ones; and the cause of the difference will often be, not any syllogistic error in either, but it will happen that one has reasoned from complete, and the other from incomplete, premises. The power of seeing *what* any given thing is, never is strong but by long familiarity with that thing; and this is a reason for choosing for our studies those things which, while they exercise the reason, will also prepare the mind for its future labours.

In order that any exercise of the youthful mind may be healthful and invigorating, the matter must be limited. A clear and correct understanding can be formed in no other way than by working up a limited quantity of matter till the whole has been so thoroughly assimilated as to become an integral part of the pupil's knowledge. Thus we observe that many men who have laboured successfully upon any thing, be it what it may, when young, if they do not acquire knowledge that is useful in after-life, obtain at least the power of acquiring it. According to this view, we should read only a few of the writers of antiquity, and those few with much less extraneous help, and much less reference to foreign matter, than our ordinary courses of instruction now prescribe.

These remarks lead us to a few observations on that part of classical studies which may be called the historical. This branch of study has of late years assumed quite a new aspect, and, on the whole, promises to bear good fruit. True historical criticism seemed to be nearly extinct till it was lately revived in Germany. The labours of those who have, as it were, opened a new world to us, deserve our gratitude ; and it is impossible to read what they have written without deriving improvement from it. But the love of system and of establishing something new, or viewing something in a different light from what it was viewed in before, may sometimes deceive the acutest critic. The detection of error, and the dispelling of a whole set of illusions, will not always save a writer from being deceived by his own supposed discoveries and combinations; he will readily find evidence for supporting a new theory, which will appear proof to him, though it may not appear so to others.

If we were to venture an opinion, we should set little value on Grecian history, beyond what is acquired by the actual reading of Herodotus, Thucydides, parts of Xenophon, and the orators. As a subject, Grecian history has no unity, except either as viewed in connection with Persian history, or viewed as the history of Athens. From the time of the first Cyrus to the death of Alexander, the history of the Greek nation presents a coherency solely when viewed in relation to its contests with the Persian empire. Athens forms the prominent object in this contest on the Grecian side; and it also forms, through its great writers, a separate historical series, in which we trace the progress of a singular political constitution, and the developement and progress of a national literature, which, though now very limited in point of extent, is abundant in variety and rich in worth.

As to that branch of historical inquiry which attempts to trace the early history of the nations mentioned by Greek and Roman authors, including the early history of the Greeks and Romans themselves, and to deduce historic truth from fable, by the aid of the various traditions and scattered memorials found in these writers, it would be unjust to withhold from such labours the praise that is due to ingenuity and industry; but at the same time it would, as it seems to us, be unwise to turn the industry of our youthful students to so unprofitable a field. This field yields little or no fruit of real knowledge, even for the understanding of the best Greek and Roman writers; and at most we cannot do more by such labour than select and combine the discordant statements of ancient writers, so as to make something which shall, on the whole, be the most probable and consistent statement of facts. More than this we cannot do. Those statements of writers which are finally relied on as the most probable, because the most consistent with everything else that we know, are often nothing more than the statements of writers who could not possibly know the truth. It may be said that the attainment of exact truth is not the only thing to be looked to : if the intellectual training incident to such investigation is profitable, the main purpose is answered. We admit this; but contend that the orators of Athens, and the writings of Aristotle, so little thoroughly studied in comparison with their real merits, would furnish much better employment for the student than any such investigation, and may be adequately and profitably studied to the total neglect of all such investigation. Of all the parts of a nation's history, the least valuable is the beginning, and, after all, it is the part which we can never know; nor is it ever an objection to studying the best period of a nation's history and literature, that we have not thoroughly studied, or cannot thoroughly know, the earliest period. Though there is always something in a nation's history that we cannot fully understand, because we can only contemplate the nation in its progress and developement, and not in its origin, this something becomes comparatively unimportant the more thoroughly we study any period for which we possess sufficient historical evidence. Thus a man might read Thucydides and the Attic orators with much profit, and at hardly any disadvantage, if he knew nothing more of

Greece and the Greeks than what he would learn from these books themselves. A distinguished writer has observed, " that of the various combinations of things which make up the existence of a state, that of the public authorities, because they are always acting and always visible, is the easiest to understand. The totality of the private relations of the citizens is much more obscure; and it is one of the most difficult problems proposed to the historian to give asatisfactory account of the import and signification of these relations, and still more so of their origin and developement. An investigation of this kind, in order to be conducted with any certainty as to its results, must assume, first of all, a definite point of time as the starting point : where this point shall be assumed, whether in an earlier or a later part of the chronological series, is generally indifferent, provided only every thing which precedes; and every thing which follows it, be critically referred to and connected with that determined point." (Savigny *Zeitschrift*, v. 230.)

Roman history has a much higher value. It comes nearer home to us, and concerns us much more directly and in more ways than is generally supposed. But even here we should set comparatively little value on the study of the earlier and obscure periods of Italian history, a great part of which is wrapped in impenetrable darkness, and if it could be cleared up, would have little or no value. The interest which every inquiring man feels in investigating the early history of Rome is not to determine the historical existence of their kings, or the reality of many of the acts attributed to them, but to ascertain what were the constituent elements of that social system which at last acquired a stability and strength sufficient to govern the known world, and which has imprinted on the whole of western Europe the indelible traces of its supremacy. We do not doubt that, however, difficult it may be rightly to apprehend the political constitution of Rome, and as a part of that inquiry to ascertain the meaning of all such notions as entered into it, the inquiry is one which will strengthen and invigorate the understanding and form an excellent preparation for political and philosophical studies. In Germany, the profound study of the Roman law, though its direct object has been Roman jurisprudence, has thrown a clear and steady light over many things formerly obscure or unintelligible, and we may hope that much which is still uncertain in the history of this great people, will be capable of elucidation when a competent study of Roman law shall be considered as a necessary preparation for and as a part of the study of Roman history. So thoroughly and completely are the notions and the terms of law interwoven with the public and private life of the Romans, that it is hardly possible to read a single Roman author with satisfaction without some knowledge of these terms of art. It is a great merit of a recent writer on Roman history (Dr. Arnold) that he has devoted a chapter of his first volume to Roman law, and that he is fully sensible that the proper handling of the matter of the history is not to be disjoined from the matter of the law. The scientific method and precision of the Roman lawyers have long been the admiration of those who have studied their writings. In Germany, many of the ablest men in that country are diligently and laboriously employed on the exposition of the Roman law; and thus, sometimes incidentally, in other cases directly, they elucidate numerous passages of the Roman writers, which have hitherto been perfectly unintelligible, but are now susceptible of a consistent and a certain interpretation.* At the head of these illustrious men the name of Savigny stands pre-eminent, and claims our profoundest veneration. In our own country the study of the civil law certainly once flourished, and exercised no small influence on our jurisprudence, and an influence far beyond what any writer on the history of our law has yet noticed. If this study were revived and prosecuted in a liberal spirit, in connection with our own law and the principles of general jurisprudence, a great step would be made towards giving to the abundance of excellent materials which our law contains, that scientific method and precision in which it is still deficient. The great step made by the revival

* As examples, see Savigny's work on Possession; and numerous articles by him and others in the *Zeitschrift für Geschichtliche Rechtswissenschaft*.

of Roman history seems likely to bring with it a revival of the study of Roman law, which cannot.fail to be followed by important consequences. The study of jurisprudence will make little real progress unless it is founded on a knowledge of more systems of law than one; and, of all foreign systems, that of the Romans is, perhaps, best worth the labour of an English lawyer.

We may anticipate that the time will soon come when the Institutional Treatise of Gaius shall form a part of the classical studies of our youth, and so lead them to a correct understanding of those terms, without which the reading of the best Roman writers cannot produce all the benefits which may be derived from them. That in this country, where we profess to cultivate ancient learning, we should so long have neglected the study of the Roman law, the best and only original part of their literature, and should have gone on in the dark, admiring and thinking that we understood the writings of Cicero, our model of Latinity, is a proof the strongest possible of the degradation into which classical studies have sunk in our higher places of education. In one University, lectures on the civil law have ceased to be given, though there is still a professor; and in the other (Cambridge), though lectures are given, and degrees taken in civil law, it is well known in how little estimation both the subject itself and the degrees are held by those who follow what may be called the regular studies of the university. Instead of the lectures on civil law being considered as auxiliary to and part of the Latin studies of the University, which they ought to be and might be, an attendance on the course of civil law and a residence in the hall where the lectures are delivered, are generally viewed rather as a convenient means of obtaining a degree. Such being the case, it would not be an easy matter for the professor to restore the study of the civil law to its proper dignity, and to make it an integral part of the University course. This neglect of a study, which even in the reigns of our early Norman kings flourished in the schools of England, forms a striking contrast with the vigorous and scientific prosecution of it in Germany, and with its condition even in Holland, France, and Italy. Whether the neglect of the study of the Roman

law has had any effect in causing the decline of Latin
studies in this country, we cannot say; but we are disposed
to think that the decline of the one is, to some extent,
connected with the neglect of the other.   However this
may be, it is certain that in one of our Universities (Cambridge) the study of the Roman language and literature
has been greatly neglected within the present century;
and that now, and for many years past, the production of tasteful Latin verses, and a well-written essay
or declamation in that language, seem to be nearly all
that is required of the most succesful student. A full and
exact knowledge of the language has not been required,
nor a full and exact knowledge of the best writers in it.
The impulse which has recently been given to the study
of Roman history, we may hope, will have the effect of
reviving the study of the language and the literature;
especially that part of it, the neglect of which has led to
these remarks.

Perhaps we should hardly be excused, if we were entirely
to pass over that part of the study of Greek and Roman
writers which is more particularly connected with the formation of the taste and the education of the faculty for
perceiving and judging of the beautiful. The poetry of the
Greeks, like the rest of their literature, though unfortunately we have lost much that is of the highest value, presents,
in its existing remains, the developement of a national mind.
We trace this developement from the epic poems of the
Iliad and the Odyssey, the earliest extant historical monuments of the nation — from the simple memorial of
events—through all its gradations, till it exhibits its complete character in the form of the drama.   The poetry of
the drama is that kind which combines in itself all other
kinds, and is therefore the last to which a nation arrives
in the progress of its mental developement.   Between
the epic poem and the drama,—between the poetry which
belongs to the rudest state of existence, which is susceptible of being the subject of art, and is also its appropriate form of expression,—and that which combines in
itself the acts of man and his inner workings and thoughts,
the transition must be slow and gradual.   The intermediate period must have been one in which man's con-

sciousness of his internal existence was awakened by reflection. Though the history of Greek poetry, as known to us in its existing monuments, has preserved but scanty memorials of this state of transition, there remains enough to show the value of that which we have lost. Even the fragments, such as many of them are, may be cherished as models of their kind.

A study of the best ancient poets, if well directed, cannot fail so far to form the taste as to be a preservative against falling into the admiration of the absurd or the extravagant; that is, against admiring what in any given society may be the actual fashion or caprice, and may exist merely by virtue of the positive opinions of that society for the time. Good taste is nothing more than the power of perceiving what is true or false, apt or inappropriate, in each thing that is submitted to its judgment. So far as the term is applied to our judgment of the objects of sense, it is a perception of the sensuously beautiful, that is, of fitness and of form; it rejects the superfluous and the unmeaning, and every accessary which detracts from the full perception of that which is the principal object. A complete study of the ancient poets cannot be separated from the study of those works of art in which the unrivalled genius of antiquity embodied its conceptions, or represented in a sensuous shape what the imagination of the poet had conceived. The poet was the father of Grecian art, and from him the painter and sculptor borrowed their inspiration. The poet in his turn borrowed from the creations of the pencil and the chisel, and embodied in some of his noblest verses the material labours of the painter and the sculptor. Thus the poetry of the Greeks both lent and borrowed from the imitative sister arts; and its study, therefore, to us of the present day is an imperfect one, unless we associate with the reading of the poet, the contemplation of those objects without which the poet's meaning cannot always be reached.

Since the land of ancient Hellas has been freely opened to our voyagers and travellers, light has been thrown on many obscure passages, both of historians and poets, by our more accurate knowledge of the localities of this country.

A description that was before obscure is now clear; an epithet that appeared idle or unmeaning is found to be pertinent and significant; and we learn to admire the taste and good sense which could select what is appropriate without encumbering that which it was intended to adorn. This more accurate knowledge of the localities inhabited by the Hellenic race has accordingly contributed to a more accurate knowledge of the meaning of those books of which we have urged the *complete understanding* as a useful discipline for youth, and as that which gives to our study of antiquity its chief value.

To Grecian art, as exhibited in the remains of sculpture, and the beautiful designs on their coins and vases, we should look as to one of the means of forming a good taste in most of those arts which contribute so largely to the pleasure of our present social existence. While we learn to understand a passage in an ancient poet, by comparing it with the delineation of that which the poet had in his mind at the time, and perhaps often before his eyes, we may learn at the same time that beauty consists with, and is inseparable from, simplicity; that form, and not material, is that which gives us the expression of the beautiful; that ornament, however sumptuous, cannot please unless it is appropriate; and that, while we can add to the pleasures of existence by surrounding ourselves with objects which gratify our senses, true taste tells us that the luxury is a cheap one, and as much within the reach of a man of moderate means as of the wealthiest individual.

It is to be regretted that so little use has yet been made in our places of instruction of all those means of illustrating ancient writers, derivable from existing works of art; and of thus conveying to the youthful student the full perception and meaning of that which he reads, together with the formation of his eye to the just appreciation of works of art. Various books have, however, appeared of late years, which will probably tend to introduce among us a study of the arts of antiquity, in connection with the written language.

Of all the poets of antiquity who claim our serious and earnest study, the dramatists undoubtedly occupy the first place. We cannot complain that they have been neglected in this country,—at least of late years; but we may complain of the way in which they have been studied. It cannot be supposed that any man who would wish to read an ancient author in his integrity, would undervalue the labours of those who have attempted to establish the text of the dramatic writers. But the text, when established, should have a meaning given to it—a position one would suppose very obvious, and one which would not be disputed, if it had not been the case that for many years in this country it seemed as if the only object in reading the Greek dramatists was to instil into the pupil certain verbal canons (many of doubtful authority, and some positively false), to exercise his critical sagacity on an emendation, sometimes when none was necessary ; and at best to teach him to pick up a few matters as to the disposition and arrangement of a Greek theatre, and the apparatus for producing thunder and lightning. In the midst of these laborious trifles the real drama was neglected ; the whole business became a mere school-boy exercise, a puerile, inane, and unimproving drudgery.

To our kinsmen in Germany we are indebted for opening our eyes to the contemplation of the beauty which was hid from us. By them we have been led to the just appreciation of the Greek drama as one of the great features in the intellectual and moral character of the nation ; and to a study of it as a work of art founded upon a social and religious system, out of which it grew, and of which it became the ever-living expression and memorial. It may be confidently asserted that if our classical studies in this country, in the last century, had not sunk to the lowest state of degradation, the English nation would not have become so insensible, as they actually did become, to their own excellent old writers, nor would such criticism on Shakspeare as appeared have been either printed or tolerated. Within the present century, and more particularly since the close of the war, a better spirit has been gradually prevailing. With a proper reverence for our own great writers, a truer notion of the advantage of a right study of antiquity has grown up; and, though much remains to be done before this study is placed on a proper footing among us, it seems that the desirable turn has taken place, and that we are now on the way to improvement. So long as a sound, liberal, and comprehensive study of the best writers of antiquity shall prevail, so long will the best writers of our own country be studied and valued ; for the same well-founded esteem which leads us to the study of the one will lead us to that of the other. We seek in the old writers, whether of our own or of any other country, something that has been stamped with the approbation of time ; not that we value a writer because he is old, but because a writer cannot become old otherwise than through the preserving care of each successive generation ; and because that which has been sedulously maintained and transmitted to us has of necessity been considered worthy of preservation by all those through whose hands it has passed. The universal judgment of mankind, whether it be of an author or of any thing else, possesses that stamp of value which a wise man will not pronounce worthless on a slight examination. He who takes his model and his guide among the actual existing writers, and has no other standard to refer to, must run the risk of taking a bad model and a deceitful guide : for, by the supposition, he has nothing by which to determine him to a judicious choice. He who has taken his model from among those writers whose merits all acknowledge, cannot be deceived, if he possesses ordinary judgment, in choosing from the mass of contemporary writers those who are best worthy of his serious study. The press now pours forth in abundance both good and bad,— a consequence of the improved mechanical means at our command, of a general diffusion of knowledge and a general habit of reading. It is useless to complain that the worthless and that which has a mere temporary value, greatly exceeds in amount that which is calculated to be of permanent utility. This is a consequence which seems inseparable from the other consequences. But in order that a man may be enabled to choose the good from the bad, some education beyond that which contemporary productions can give, seems absolutely necessary. Without this education a man cannot be safe against the pernicious influence of many works of the day, the supply of which seems scarcely adequate to meet the craving demand of the greedy and gluttonous reader ; of such works as weaken the understanding which they affect to inform, corrupt the taste, and debase the morals, while the phrases of religion and morality are used as covers and wrappings for trite common-places, or even dangerous doctrines. This may appear a harsh censure ; but perhaps it is not an unjust judgment upon that class of publications to which it is intended to apply. He alone is secure from the contagion of such a pestilence whose early years have been passed in labouring at that which can only be attained by labour, and whose mind has been formed by converse with the wise and the great of past times.

It might be almost unpardonable if we omitted to mention as partly among the results of an improved study of the ancient languages, and partly as having contributed to such improvement, the present state of philological knowledge in that department which is commonly called Etymology.

A verbal study of the Latin and Greek languages has been, till recently, almost the only thing which was considered as appertaining to the study of these languages. The matter of the languages was neglected and misunderstood, and the words alone were looked to. But this verbal study was of the most limited and trifling kind. It was deservedly neglected and despised by many students, who found in the pursuits of the exact sciences something better worth trying to understand than hairsplitting differences between the meaning of words and the measurements of syllables. No instruction was given in our schools or colleges which led the pupil to the right method of investigating the forms of words, of reducing them to their elemental parts, and thus tracing through all its varied modifications and combinations the same simple element. Consequently, nothing was done towards disciplining the student to a correct method of tracing the history and meanings of words in the same language, or the affinities of words in different languages ; and one branch of inquiry, which is strictly and properly historical, was altogether omitted by those who professed to teach the history and languages of antiquity.

So far as we can trace back to its commencement the change in this department of teaching, it seems to be in a great measure due to the introduction of the study of Sanscrit into Europe. Our own countrymen had the merit, as they had, from their peculiar advantages, the duty imposed on them, of bringing Hindu learning into Europe; but we are indebted to the Germans for the successful study of the Sanscrit, and for showing how the etymological form and structure of a language ought to be exhibited. Independent of the value of a just etymological exhibition of any given language as a means of learning that language with more ease and certainty, the comparison of the Sanscrit with the languages of Europe has opened a wide field of historical investigation,— the results of which belong strictly to the department of discovery. As the geologist, by his examination of the crust of the earth, and of the various forms of animal life embedded in it, discovers the records and the evidence of revolutions which our globe has undergone,—so the philologist, by applying to the comparison of languages, now separated by half the circuit of the globe, the true principles of investigation, discovers, in the recorded forms of language, in the symbols of mere sound, the movement of the air which we breathe, evidence as certain of the history of man which no other monuments have perpetuated. This boundless field of investigation is but newly opened, and the labourers in this country are still few. Yet it offers perhaps the only prospect of our ever attaining a complete or even a satisfactory knowledge of that of which no memorial, except the book of Genesis, has preserved even the remembrance,—the diffusion of the human race from one centre over the surface of the globe. It points to and indicates, though it is yet far from proving, that languages are not many, but one; that the human race, therefore, is one; and that language is a part of man's being,—not, as some have weakly asserted, a thing made by him as he advanced from a supposed state of barbarism to civilization.

The application of these principles to the study of the Latin and Greek languages will make both of them more easy of acquisition; will contribute to their more exact and accurate knowledge; and will form a valuable mental discipline for the young student. The material of the Greek and Latin languages will thus be subjected to a strictly scientific method, which, while it gives the learner a more full and complete view of the matter, is that part of the training for which such a study is most valuable. That acquisition of language, which we have already considered as the principal object, will thus be facilitated and secured; and a solid foundation will be laid, on which the student may erect a superstructure of linguistic knowledge and sound philology, whatever be the language, or the form of language, which is the subject-matter of his investigation. It is certainly not very encouraging to observe how slowly in this country improvements are effected in methods of teaching; how the absurdities of the old etymologists still maintain their places in our grammars and dictionaries; and how teachers, whose example carries with it authority, still cling to absurdities which they should be the first to abandon. If our universities would in this matter begin a reform, a change would soon be effected in our schools. Many of our teachers need only to be put in the right way, in order to see the advantage of handling a subject according to fixed principles, over the unsatisfactory one of having nothing which shall enable us to tell whether what we give in the way of explanation is merely a lucky guess, which may be right or wrong, or a manifest absurdity, which never could be a truth. It may not be out of place to refer to a work* that has lately appeared in one of our universities, of which we are prevented from saying more than that it will probably contribute to that reform which is so desirable.

If the study of the classical languages of antiquity can produce such fruit, perhaps an objector may ask, is it true that it does? The answer must be a short one. It does not; at least, not to the extent that it ought and might. And why does it not? The answer is, because we have not a sufficient number of teachers com-

---

* Donaldson's new Cratylus; or Contributions towards a more accurate Knowledge of the Greek Language. Parker. London. 1839.

petent for the purpose. And why have we not a sufficient number of competent teachers in a country which
abounds in wealth, which is rich in endowments particularly designed for this branch of learning, and which perhaps is not behind any other country in the number of
persons who have ability and industry sufficient to raise
them to distinction in any department of knowledge?

The reason seems a plain one. There is neither unity,
connection, nor plan in our education; and experience
shows that education is always slow in progress, unless the
state, which alone can do it, shall give to education that
unity and definite purpose which it gives to other branches
of administration. It must be admitted that if those who
educate and are educated, are not united in such a way
that each shall derive from the union advantages the same
in their kind and degree which the individuals of a nation derive from that union called society, there can be
no progressive improvement of the whole, even if there
be improvement of parts; and there must and will be
deterioration of the scattered members of a body which
has no proper coherence.

In this country, the two universities of Oxford and
Cambridge are the only bodies that have hitherto exercised an influence on the liberal studies of this country,
which may be considered as giving to them a certain
unity of purpose and plan; and, though the effect has not
been all that we might wish, the effect has been beneficial, and perhaps as extensive as could be produced by
indirect influence. Neither university, as a place of education, is affected by the interference or direction of the
state; and neither university is affected by, or subject
to, any control of the other. Each regulates its education
as it thinks best. The indirect influence of the universities, which is most effective, is upon the schools where
youths are trained for the universities, and on their teachers. This indirect influence also extends to all teachers of the higher class, inasmuch as all suppose that
what the universities prescribe must be the best. The
studies of the two universities, though they have approximated more of late years, still present certain differences,
somewhat in the subjects, and perhaps also in the manner

of treating them. We should be inclined to think that
the studies of Oxford are, on the whole, to be preferred;
but as to this there may be a difference of opinion.
Those studies which these two universities do propose to
their members are, however, the best that they could propose; and we should see little to add to or subtract from
them as to matter, however much it might be desirable
to vary the proportions, and to change the mode of handling and treating it.

Now, as to their classical studies, these two universities
seem at present hardly to perform the function of universities. They are rather schools, in the sense in which
other places of instruction among us are schools. A very
large body of students is annually admitted into both
universities, and particularly the University of Cambridge,
whose ignorance is such, that they are incapable of profiting by any but the elementary kind of instruction, such
as they ought to have had at school. Those, also, who come
from the best schools and tutors, with a very competent,
and some with a considerable, stock of Greek and Latin,
are continued pretty nearly at the same kind of exercise
as they were working upon when they left school. The
examinations in the universities and the colleges, of
course, prescribe both the matter and the manner of the
study; and accordingly we find that youths, from the age
of nineteen till they attain the full growth of manhood
and leave the universities, are encouraged and required,
if they hope for the most brilliant success in their career,
to spend much of their time in making Greek and Latin verses, and other similar pursuits, which, for a university, are trifling, and for that age absurd. It not unfrequently happens, also, that the well-prepared scholar,
who leaves his school or his tutor, is introduced into a
college lecture-room, where he finds a lecturer who can
teach him nothing, and who is infinitely inferior to the master whom he has just left. He finds also a number of
young men, some well prepared to read the author that
is the subject of the lecture-room study, many totally incompetent, and no small number neither competent to
learn, nor willing to be taught. From the college lecture-room, therefore, in many cases, he learns nothing.

The university, as such, has ceased to teach; and, if he looks anywhere for help, he must seek a private tutor; and perhaps he will, in most cases, do best by choosing one who is only a few years older than himself. Such is the education that is given at our universities as such.

The real stimulus and direction which the universities give to the studies of their youth is by their examinations; which, in their present form, may be considered as a reformed system, and, on the whole, have had a beneficial effect. But it would appear somewhat difficult to reform the education of the universities, if we may admit that there is such a thing as university education, so long as the college system continues exactly what it is. The college system, with some advantages that are obvious enough, and which the supporters of it do not neglect to make the most of, manifestly tends, as it exists at present, to lower the character of the universities as places of education, and to bring them to the level of the schools. Such, however, is not the limited sphere of university education. A university occupies, or should occupy, a place between the school and the business of life. In a university, as we may conceive it constituted, and as many universities are constituted, those studies are mainly followed which are to form the business of life. To keep to our present subject, it is obvious that, while philological studies might to some extent be followed in our universities by all who intend to embrace what are called the learned professions, they would be peculiarly the study of those who are intended for the church, and of those who are designed for teachers in our schools. If this definite end were kept in view, the studies of which we are speaking would be prosecuted in a more worthy manner; and, while a full and exact knowledge of antiquity would be proposed as an object, it would never be forgotten that there was an ulterior object to which this was subservient.

But so long as students are admitted into the colleges of our universities with that amount of knowledge with which they now are admissible, so long is all reformation of their classical studies hopeless; and it is difficult to say how this reformation can begin, it being directly opposed to the pecuniary interests of those who have the chief direction of the colleges, to exclude incompetent persons. So far as we can learn, there are several colleges in both universities, and particularly at Oxford, where increased strictness as to the admission of students has now for some years been exercised. This highly creditable example will, perhaps, be followed by those colleges in which the conditions of admission are now so lax as to be in effect no bar to the admission of any applicant.

It is, perhaps, not generally known out of the universities, that the college lecturers, who may now be considered as occupying the same place in the colleges that the professors would properly occupy in the university system, are very indifferently paid for their services. This is at least the case in some colleges which, both in point of numbers and reputation, occupy the first rank. It is not necessary here to explain how it happens that a high or a sufficient remuneration is not, in all cases, given to college lecturers. Such, however, is the fact. The sum that is generally paid to a college lecturer is not sufficient to induce a man to devote himself actively and seriously to college lecturing as a regular business or profession. The best men, therefore, cannot always be procured as college lecturers, nor can their services be secured by the college, if any moderatively lucrative and permanent employment elsewhere is offered to them. Thus there is not, even in some of our best colleges, that regular and certain succession of able lecturers, which is necessary to maintain the high character of these institutions; and as the university instruction no longer exists, there is no body of public teachers who occupy a station like that of the great teachers of Germany. Yet this is not because men cannot be found willing to devote themselves to public teaching, and competent to discharge the duties of the office. The reason is, that an active man soon finds better employment than lecturing in a college for a small sum of money; and if he does accept the place of a college lecturer, it is generally only as a temporary matter, and he seldom undertakes it with the same zeal and temper in which a man would undertake a more lucrative employment. These remarks relate to the remuneration of those who are simply employed and paid as public *teachers* in the colleges, and they have no reference to the remuneration of those who are known and designated as College Tutors, and who may also be, as they sometimes are, college lecturers and teachers; their remuneration is probably, in most cases, amply sufficient to secure the services of persons the best qualified to discharge the onerous and responsible duties of the office of college tutor.

It is not easy to conceive a well-constituted state (and we believe no writer, ancient or modern, has conceived such a thing) in which the supreme direction of education should not be part of the general administration. The principle of the direction of education by the sovereign power is admitted and acted on both in the monarchies of Europe and in the democracies of North America; and, accordingly, under both these forms of government the state directs the education of the whole people. The amount of superintendence and direction varies in these different states; in the monarchical being generally greater and more effective than in the democratical states. But the principle of education being a part of administration, is equally recognised by both. In both forms of government, statesmen do either immediately, or through their delegated agents, administer the affairs of education as they do those which belong to other departments. Thus education is not left to be directed by those who live apart from the world in monastic seclusion, but it is governed by those who participate in the general government of the community. The results on the whole are favourable; for they prove that a supreme direction and control may consist with freedom of teaching. The state may say what shall be taught, without saying how it shall be taught; but the *how* is secured by the appointment of competent teachers, who have been brought up under men originally selected with care, and who themselves are continually forming other teachers who shall perpetuate and improve the methods of their masters. The *how* is further secured by constituting a university in such a manner that it shall be the chief school in the state for every department of knowledge which it concerns the interests of the state to cherish. The schools, being a part of the general system of education, occupy their proper place as subordinate and ancillary to the universities. For the establishment of such a university, neither large funds nor length of time is necessary. In a few years the illustrious Münchhausen erected such a university in a poor and petty kingdom, which now, for a full century, has enjoyed and sustained the reputation of being one of the best schools in Europe in every department of knowledge.*

It is not here insinuated that our statesmen should direct our education. Circumstances forbid it. And till some happy event shall render interference on the part of the state desirable, and its superintendence certainly useful, we can only hope that those who have the government of our universities may seriously consider how much improvement they can effect if they will wisely use the power which is in their hands.

GEORGE LONG.

* See an account of the origin and present state of the University of Göttingen, in the Journal of Education, vol. x.

AN ACCOUNT OF THE COMMON SCHOOLS IN THE STATES OF MASSACHUSETTS, NEW YORK, AND PENNSYLVANIA.

I. MASSACHUSETTS.

IT is greatly to the honour of the original settlers at Boston, that one of their first cares was to make provision for the education of the people. One of the earliest acts of legislation of the colony of Massachusetts Bay (which received its royal charter in 1628) was a law making it obligatory on parents to educate their own children and apprentices : Harvard College* was founded in 1636 ; and in 1647 the colony provided by law for the support of schools at the public expense, for instruction in reading and writing, in every town containing fifty families, and for the support of a grammar school (the instructor of which should be competent to prepare young men for the University) in every town containing one hundred families. For this measure they assign the following reason :—

" It being one chief project of Satan to keep men from the knowledge of the Scriptures, as in former times keeping them in unknown tongues, so in these latter times by persuading from the use of tongues, that so at least the true sense and meaning of the original might be clouded and corrupted with false glosses of deceivers ; to the end *that learning may not be buried in the graves of our forefathers in church and commonwealth,* the Lord assisting our endeavours, it is therefore ordered," &c.

In the year 1691 a charter was granted by William

---

* Harvard College is situated at Cambridge, three miles from Boston : it has at present thirty instructors and two hundred and thirty-three students. The other colleges for general education in the State are, Williams, at Williamstown, which has seven instructors and one hundred and nineteen students ; and Amherst, which has twelve instructors and two hundred and fifty-nine students.

and Mary, incorporating the province of Massachusetts Bay ; and, the year after this charter was received, the laws which had been passed under the charter of the colony for the regulation and support of free schools were essentially confirmed by an act of the Governor, Council, and Representatives, convened in general court or assembly. The constitution of Massachusetts also, adopted in 1780, recognised the importance of education, and in 1789 an express law was passed to promote it.

The requisitions of the law, as it now stands, are substantially as follows: — Towns containing fifty families or householders are required to maintain a school or schools for terms of time which shall together be equivalent to six months in each year, in which children shall be instructed in orthography, reading, writing, English grammar, geography, arithmetic, and good behaviour, by teachers of competent ability and good morals.

In towns of one hundred families or householders, schools of the same kind are to be kept for terms which together shall be equivalent to twelve months.

In towns of one hundred and fifty families or householders, schools of the same kind, and not less than two, are to be kept for terms not less than nine months each, or three or more schools for terms together equivalent to eighteen months.

In towns of five hundred families, similar schools, not less than two, are to be kept for twelve months each, or three or more such schools for terms together equivalent to twenty-four months ; and, in addition to the above, they are required to maintain a school for the benefit of all the inhabitants of the town, ten months at least, exclusive of vacations, in each year, in which the history of the United States, book-keeping, surveying, geometry, and algebra shall be taught by a master of competent ability and good morals. And if the town contain four thousand inhabitants, the teacher shall, in addition to all the branches above enumerated, be competent to instruct in the Latin and Greek languages, general history, rhetoric, and logic.—See *First Annual Report of the Board of Education*, p. 74.

The schools provided for by the law are open to children of all classes, and the expense of maintaining them is paid by a tax on the people, raised chiefly on their property. Each town (or, as we should call it, each township,) is made responsible for the execution of the law within its own jurisdiction; and it is the duty of the school committee (which consists of five persons chosen annually by the town) to overlook the schools, to visit them at least once in six months, to employ and approve the instructors, and to direct in the selection of school-books.

" New England possesses some peculiar advantages for carrying into effect its system of education. It is divided into small townships, or separate corporations, of from five to seven miles square. The responsibility of these small corporations is more likely to insure a vigilant discharge of their duty than if they were larger, and the subject of their responsibility less immediately under their inspection. As the population is scattered over almost the whole territory, and the children are often young who attend the primary schools, it has been found convenient to divide each town into smaller districts for this object. Thus a school is carried to the door, or at least into the neighbourhood, of every family. Each township constitutes from four to twelve districts; and none are so far removed from all schools that an attendance on some of them is not easy. The appropriations for schooling in each town are adequate to support a school in each district from three to six months in the year, and often longer." . . . . " These appropriations are expended, a part in the summer months for the advantage of the younger children, and a part in the winter months for the accommodation of those who are more advanced in age, and whose labour cannot be spared by their poor and industrious parents. The summer schools are taught by females; and children of both sexes, of from four to ten years, attend,—females often much older. In these schools from twenty to forty, and sometimes twice that number of children, are taught reading, spelling, and English grammar by a single instructress. In the more improved of this class of schools, writing, arithmetic, and geography are added to their usual studies. In the leisure time between lessons the female part of the school is devoted to-various branches of needle-work. These primary schools, however humble the branches taught, and young the children to whom they are taught, have a strong influence in forming the characters of the young. Although the progress in studies may be inconsiderable, yet they are important for the notions of order, decency, and good manners which they inculcate, and for the habits of attention and industry which are there formed. The whole expense of a school of this kind, taught by a female, exclusive of the house (which, in the country, costs but a trifle), does not exceed from two to three dollars per week. For this very inconsiderable sum, thirty, forty, or even fifty children are not only kept from idleness and consequent depravity, but are taught much which will be useful to them in life. In the winter months an instructor is employed; and arithmetic, geography, and history are added to the studies of the summer schools. These schools bring together for instruction those children and youth, whose labour is too valuable to be dispensed with in the season which gives the agriculturist most employment. The total expense of a school of this kind amounts to from six to ten dollars per week; and it contains from thirty to eighty or a hundred scholars."—*Letters on the Free Schools of New England, by James G. Carter.* Boston, 1824. Pp. 29. 32.

The higher description of schools, which the law directs to be kept in towns with five hundred and with four thousand inhabitants, do not appear to be maintained in all the places in which they are required. The following remarks, in reference to them, occur in the " Report of the Secretary to the Board of Education," p. 51 :—" In this commonwealth there are forty-three towns, exclusive of the city of Boston, coming within the provisions above recited. (I leave this city out of the computation, because the considerations appertaining to it in connection with this subject are peculiar to itself. I need only mention that common schools in Boston, valuable as they are, bear no proportion to the whole means of education and improvement which they do in the country.) These forty-three towns contain an aggregate of about two-fifths of all the population of the State, exclusive of the metropolis. Of these forty-three towns only fourteen maintain those schools 'for the benefit of all the inhabitants of the town,' which the law requires. The other twenty-nine towns, in which this provision of the law is wholly disregarded, contain a very large fraction over one-fifth part of the whole population of the State out of Boston." . . . . "In these twenty-nine towns, which do not keep the 'town school' required by law, the sum of 47,776 dollars is expended in private schools and academies, while only 74,313 dollars are expended for the support of public schools."

The refusal of the town to maintain the free 'town school' compels the wealthier portion of the inhabitants to establish the private school or academy, at which they may place their children, with a view to complete their education; and these institutions, when established, tend to injure the common schools, as they draw off their best pupils, diminish the funds which would otherwise be appropriated to them, and tempt away the best masters by the offer of higher compensation. This is more peculiarly a subject of regret with those who are attached to republican institutions.

The general results of the system may be judged of by the following "Aggregate Statement," which is taken from the School Returns presented to the Senate of Massachusetts at the beginning of the year 1838 :—

Number of towns which have made returns (*i. e.* all except eleven)		294
Population, May 1, 1837		691,222
Valuation, 1830	dollars	206,457,662*
Number of public schools		2,918
Number of scholars of all ages in the schools, { in winter		141,837
{ in summer		122,889
Average attendance in the schools { in winter		111,520
{ in summer		94,956
Number of persons between four and sixteen years of age		177,053
Average length † of the schools, in months and days		6*m.* 25*d.*

---

* In this and some other instances the *cents* are omitted, as being of little consequence, and tending to embarrass the eye.

† That is, the portion of the year during which they are kept.

Number of teachers, including summer and { males . 2,370
winter terms . . . { females . 3,591
Average wages paid per month, including { to males 25 doll. 44 c.
board . . . { to females 11 doll. 38 c.
Amount of money raised by taxes for the support of
schools . . . . . dollars 465,228
Amount raised by taxes for teachers' wages, including
board, if paid from the public money . dollars 387,124*
Amount raised voluntarily, to prolong common schools,
including fuel and board, if contributed . dollars 48,301
Number of academies or private schools† . . 854
Aggregate of months kept 5,619
Aggregate of scholars 27,266
Aggregate paid for tuition . . . dollars 328,026
Amount of local funds . . . . dollars 189,536
Income from the same . . . . dollars 9,571

Till lately there has been no school fund in Massachusetts; but as, on the 1st of January 1835, it was found that there was a sum of 281,000 dollars in the state treasury, arising from the sale of public lands and payments by the General Government, it was determined that this money, together with one-half of all the future proceeds of the sale of public lands, should form a permanent fund for the support and encouragement of schools, and that the income arising from it (upwards of 16,000 dollars) should be distributed in a certain ratio among the towns; but that any distribution has actually taken place does not appear from the documents received.

In reference to the above table, the secretary remarks, in his Report, p. 37, that, if from the whole number of children between four and sixteen years of age, in the two hundred and ninety-four towns which have made returns, we deduct twelve thousand as the number of those who attend private schools and academies, and do not attend the public schools at all, there will remain one hundred and sixty-five thousand and fifty-three; that a portion of the children, dependent wholly on the common schools, absent themselves from the winter school, either permanently or

---

* It is presumed that this amount is included in the preceding —S.W.
† A very great proportion of the numbers under the head of private schools and academies represent small schools, kept in the interim between the winter and summer terms of the district schools.

occasionally, equal to a permanent absence of about one-third of their whole number ; and a portion absent themselves from the summer schools, either permanently or occasionally, equal to a permanent absence of considerably more than two-fifths of their whole number ; that, on account of the voluntary absences from school, the winter and summer terms, taken together, are reduced to about four months and one week in the year ; and so much as some scholars dependent upon the common school actually attend school more, just so much do others actually attend less ; and he goes on to say,—

" Were it certain that the number, one hundred and seventy-seven thousand and fifty-three, was not an over-estimate of the children between four and sixteen years of age, and did the returns embrace all the children of all ages attending in all the public schools, it would appear that forty-two thousand one hundred and sixty-four children, wholly dependent on the common schools, have not, the past year, attended school at all in the summer ; and twenty-three thousand two hundred and sixteen neither in summer nor winter. There is some reason to believe that, from omissions in the returns, and, perhaps, from other causes, the total of the children of all ages attending all the schools is rather too low. After making every possible allowance, however, the returns exhibit frightful evidence of the number of children who either do not go to school at all, or go so little as not to be reckoned among the scholars."

The short time that the children attend school would be less a subject of regret, if the instruction which they receive were of a good quality ; but it is to be feared that this is not the case. A writer in a recent number of the *American Quarterly Review** affirms that " The common school system, as it is called, as at present administered in this country, is emphatically *a failure ;* and that not one in twenty of the boys and girls who attend upon it is educated as the public good, nay as the public safety, and his own individual usefulness and hap-

* As quoted by the Rev. C. Brooks, in his " Lecture on Teachers' Seminaries," delivered before the American Institute of Instruction at Worcester, August 25, 1836, p. 13.

piness, require him to be educated." If I may be allowed
to judge of the common schools of Massachusetts by
those which I saw, in October 1836, at Worcester, a
county town of six thousand inhabitants, they cannot certainly be placed in a very high grade. In one of these
schools (as in some of those at Boston) the boys were set
to read pieces which were much too difficult for them :
one class, which was called upon to read " The Impeachment of Warren Hastings," did not know what was meant
either by *impeachment*, or *peeresses*, or *avenues ;* the master was well aware that what was put into their hands
contained many things which they did not understand,
yet he had no idea of questioning them in an efficient
manner, or of supplying the information which they did
not possess. That the qualifications of the teachers are
not of a high order, may be inferred from the small
amount of their pay. The average wages paid per month,
including board, are, as stated above, for males, twenty-
five dollars and forty-four cents, or (taking the dollar
at 4*s*. 3*d*.), £64. 16*s*. 6*d*. for the year ; and for females,
eleven dollars and thirty-eight cents, or, £29. 1*s*. for
the year ; and, if the large towns were not included, the
average would of course be much smaller. The secretary states in his Report, p. 60, " The teachers are as
good as public opinion has demanded. Their attainments have corresponded with their opportunities ; and
the supply has answered the demand, as well in quality
as in number. Yet in numerous instances school committees have alleged, in justification of their approval of
incompetent persons, the utter impossibility of obtaining
better for the compensation offered. It was stated publicly, by a member of the school committee of a town
containing thirty or more school districts, that one-half
at least of the teachers approved by them would be rejected, only that it would be in vain to expect better
teachers for present remuneration."

As pay and qualification always mutually affect each
other, one of the most certain means of raising the pay
of the teachers is to raise their qualifications ; and this
can only be done by having normal schools, in which
they will be specially trained for the duties which they

propose to undertake. Till this is done on a large scale, and on a well-matured plan, the state of the schools must necessarily be low. At present the only institution in the State expressly for teachers is that at Andover; and even there they have no model-school as a part of the establishment, — the one which is so regarded, and to which the teachers have access, being a mere private school.

Massachusetts has much to do in the reformation of her scholastic institutions. Though it is infinitely to the credit of the ancestors of the present generation that they made such early provision for the promotion of education; and though the benefit of this is now felt in the generally sober and respectable character of the inhabitants, which character, attaching to the parents, serves in no small degree to correct and supply the deficiencies of the public schools; yet, that deficiencies exist, there can be no doubt. If not even in Boston can a school be shown which will bear a rigid examination of its merits, what must be the case with the country schools? If, in short, that ancient and venerable commonwealth would maintain the high character which she has acquired as a patron of general instruction, she must look to her laurels; she must not content herself with having done so much in times past for the cause of education; she must not point to the number of instructors whom she has supplied to every State in the Union; but she must keep pace with the advancing spirit of the times; she must send forth intelligent men to England and to the Continent of Europe, personally to visit the best schools which are to be found; and, when they return to her shores, she must remodel her own institutions with a vigorous and unsparing hand, and infuse into them a degree of life and spirit, in which they are now very deficient.

That the necessity of something more being done for the promotion of popular education is now beginning to be more generally felt in Massachusetts, is evident from the appointment by her Legislature of a Board of Education. This board held its first meeting in the council-chamber at Boston, on the 29th of June 1837; and we have before us their first Annual Report, dated February 1st, 1838, as well as that of their secretary, Mr. Mann, (late President of the Senate,) and a second by the same gentleman on school-houses. It was made the duty of the Board not only to prepare an abstract of the usual school returns, but to ascertain the actual condition and efficiency of the common schools and other means of popular education ; and to diffuse as widely as possible through the commonwealth information of the most approved and successful methods of arranging the studies and conducting the education of the young ; and further, to make reports to the Legislature of their observations and suggestions. They had also power to appoint a paid secretary. With the view of accomplishing the purposes for which he was appointed, this officer travelled through the State in the autumn of 1837, and met conventions of the friends of education in every county, except one. At these meetings the best spirit prevailed ; and in most places associations were formed for the improvement of common schools. The reports, also, which have been presented and printed, contain many excellent suggestions, especially respecting the situation and construction of school-houses, the duties of committee-men, and the pay and qualifications of teachers ; and there can be little doubt that, when the Board has had time to mature its plans, something effectual will be done. The secretary's reports are characterized by good sense and by kind and patriotic feeling ; and much benefit may be anticipated from the services of a man of so enlightened a mind, and so truly philanthropic a spirit.

BOSTON.

The schools in this city demand a more special notice.

There is no city in the world in which more ample provision is made for the education of the people, than in Boston. Every inhabitant is rated to pay a certain yearly sum for the general education of the community ; and, in return for this, he is entitled to have his sons and daughters educated free of expense, except for books and writing materials, in any of the public schools of the city. So entirely is this admission without restriction, that the poorest Irish labourer who works on the wharfs may send his ten boys, if he has so many, to the Latin school; and they will there receive such instruction as will fit them for college, with no further expense to their father than the requisite books.

The origin of free schools in the city of Boston was at a very early period. The first trace of them in the records of the city is under the date of April 13, 1635, where it is stated to have been agreed upon " That brother Philemon Purmont shall be entreated to become schoolmaster, for the teaching and nurturing of children with us." This gentleman had a tract of thirty acres of land assigned to him; and in 1641 the General Court of Massachusetts, having at a previous period granted to the town of Boston several of the islands with which the bay is so beautifully interspersed, the record states that " It 's ordered that Deare Island shall be improved for the maintenance of a free school for the town, and such other occasions as the townsmen for the time being shall think meet, the sayd school being sufficiently provided for." Various other provisions were made for the support of the school, both from the public funds and by private munificence. For many years it would appear that this was the only free school in the town; and that English and writing, as well as the learned languages, were taught in it; but others were added from time to time, as the population increased. In 1789 the first school committee was appointed; in 1818 the primary schools were instituted, in order to prepare the children for entering those of a higher description with more advantage; and now there is one public Latin grammar school, one English high school, twelve grammar and writing schools, and seventy-six primary.*

These schools are all under the care and superintendence of a committee, consisting of the mayor and the president of the common council, and twenty-four other persons annually elected by the citizens at large, two in each ward of the city. Their duty is to appoint the

---

* Accounts received since the above was in type state the number of grammar schools to be thirteen, and of primary eighty-three; and the total number of children in all the free schools ten thousand three hundred and forty-eight.

teachers, to fix their salaries, to make any regulations which they may think proper relative to the discipline and instruction, to visit the schools, and to report upon their condition. At their first meeting they choose a secretary; a visiting committee for each school, consisting of at least seven for the Latin and the English high schools respectively, and of three for each of the other schools respectively; a standing committee on books, and a standing committee of conference with the primary school committee, which is appointed by the board of the general school committee.

The primary schools are taught by women (with a salary of 250 dollars a year), and they are intended for children between the ages of four and seven; the object being to teach them to read, write, and cast accounts, and thus prepare them for entering the higher schools. The board by which they are governed consists of a chairman and secretary, and as many other members as there are schools. It is divided into district committees, consisting of from six to nine persons, who have the care of a corresponding number of schools in that part of the city in which they reside. It is ordered that every school shall be visited at least once every month, by at least one member of its district committee, without any previous notice to the teacher; and reports are made by the visiters, as well as by the teacher, to the district committee, and by them to the standing committee (of as many members as there are districts), who also visit all the schools every six months, and make up a full report, which is sent to the general school committee.

This system of supervision is very well as far as it goes; it presents an almost insuperable barrier against palpable neglect on the part of the teacher, and it will be found to be efficacious in carrying into execution a good system when once introduced; but the primary schools at Boston are far from being in a satisfactory state. The old method of reading and spelling "without note or comment" is pretty rigidly adhered to; many words are suffered to pass without the children having the remotest conception of their meaning; and when I have exemplified the interrogative method, and appealed to the mistress to say whether it was not superior to that in vogue among them, she has readily acknowledged the justness of my remarks, but has replied that the school committee expected her to hear a certain number of classes, and to carry them through a certain number of pages in reading and spelling every day, and that she would not be allowed to spend so much time on each lesson as the new method would require. Thus it is that, by being conducted on the old and now exploded system, these institutions, so valuable in themselves, are robbed of one-half their utility.

Of the twelve grammar schools, three are for boys exclusively, three for girls exclusively, and six for both. They receive children from the age of seven to fourteen. They are taught in handsome buildings erected on purpose; in which there are, where the arrangement is complete, two large rooms, one of which is occupied by the grammar, and the other by the writing school. The scholars are formed into two divisions, one of which attends to grammar and the other to writing, exchanging every half-day; and, if there are both boys and girls in the same school, they are kept separate. In the writing department the pupils are taught writing, arithmetic, and book-keeping; in the grammar department, spelling, reading, English grammar, geography, and the history of the United States, together with composition and declamation; and the following studies and books may also be introduced at the discretion of the master,— Smellie's Philosophy of Natural History (Ware's edition), Blake's Conversations on Natural Philosophy, Worcester's Elements of General History, and Parker's Exercises in English Composition. The principal teacher in each of the departments is always a man, and his assistants are commonly young women; the salary of the master being 1500 dollars a year, and that of each of his assistants (if women) 200 dollars. As the monitorial system is not adopted in these schools, at least only to a very limited extent, it is necessary to have a large number of teachers, and one is generally provided for every fifty or sixty scholars. Thus, in the Hawes school I found about one hundred and thirty boys present out of two hundred under the care of the head-master, and one male assistant, who has a salary of 600 dollars; and in the writing department there were nearly two hundred girls under the charge of one master and two female assistants. In the Bowdoin school, which is for girls, and has a total of four hundred and fifteen,—average, three hundred and fifty,—there are a master and three female assistants in the grammar department, and the same in the writing school.

The last of these schools which have been organized are the Johnson and the Winthrop: in these the course of instruction and the general regulations are the same as in the others; but each of them is placed under the charge of a master, who is responsible for the state of the school in all its departments, the instructor in penmanship being merely subordinate; and it is provided that, whenever any vacancy occurs in the writing department of the other grammar schools, they shall be organized in the same manner.

The visiting or sub-committees are required to visit their respective schools at least once in every quarter, and once every month, without giving previous notice to the instructors, according to the provisions of the statute, and as much oftener as they can make it convenient; they are required to make a report in writing at each quarterly meeting to the school committee of their examination and its results: and in the month of May in each year committees are also appointed, whose business it is to visit all the schools, and critically to examine the pupils in all the branches taught in them; to make a report previously to the annual election of the instructors; to attend the annual exhibitions, and to confer medals on those pupils to whom they have previously awarded them. The masters also are required to make regular half-yearly returns of the number of pupils actually belonging to their schools.

In the autumn of 1836, I visited four or five of these schools, and think that upon the whole they are well conducted, though they certainly admit of improvement. In all of them the most perfect *discipline* is maintained; corporal punishment is occasionally resorted to, but the principal means of enforcing diligence and good behaviour

is a system of *checks* and *merits*, each lesson, as gone
through by the pupil, having its value assigned to it, and
certain deductions being made for absence or palpable ill
behaviour : an account of all this is regularly entered in
a book against the name of each pupil, and it is thus
easily ascertained what the amount of excellence has
been during the term. I have no doubt that a solid and
useful education is obtained in these schools. That to
which I paid the most attention, and which I have reason
to believe is one of the best, is the Bowdoin (for girls) :
the master, Mr. Andrews, is a very intelligent man, with
a candid and inquiring mind; and the compositions which
he showed me, both in prose and verse, are extremely creditable to the talents and information of the young persons
who enjoy the benefit of his instruction. I also examined
them, or heard them examined, in grammar, in geography,
in ancient history, and in the elements of natural philosophy, and they answered well. In none of these schools,
however, is the interrogative method carried to its legitimate extent; much less are there any lessons on objects,
such as are given in the schools on the Pestalozzian system : sufficient pains are not taken to make the pupils
thoroughly understand what they read; and in one of the
boys' schools which I visited too much attention is paid
to the delivery of difficult and impassioned pieces, while
the time would be much better devoted to what is plainer,
easier, and of more practical importance.

One of the twelve grammar schools is intended expressly and exclusively for the children of Blacks and
persons of colour of both sexes. In the higher school
there were, in 1836, one hundred and sixty-five boys and
girls ; and in the same building there were two primary
schools, containing together one hundred and thirty.
The master told me that two years and a half ago
there were only fifteen scholars in the higher school ;
that many of these children are exposed at home to the
most corrupting influences, and that most of them have
been almost literally picked up out of the streets. They
have here the means of acquiring a good education, which,
with those who have leisure and occasion for it, is carried
even to Latin and Greek.

The teaching of religion does not enter into the course of instruction in the grammar schools in Boston. The Testament is used as a class-book only in the primary, but the morning exercises of *all* the schools commence with reading the Scriptures and prayer, and as there is a Sunday school attached to almost every church, and these excellent institutions appear to call forth the exertions of an active body of teachers, it is probable that most of the children have the opportunity of acquiring religious knowledge on the Lord's day.

The English high school was established by a vote of the city in 1821. It was instituted with the design of furnishing the young men of the city, who are not intended for a collegiate course of study, and who have enjoyed the usual advantages of the other public schools, with the means of completing a good English education, so as to fit them for active life, or qualify them for eminence in private or public stations. Here is given instruction in the elements of mathematics and natural philosophy, with their application to the sciences and the arts; in linear drawing, grammar, rhetoric, and belles-lettres; in moral philosophy, in history, natural and civil, in the evidences of natural and revealed religion, and in the French language. The institution is furnished with a valuable mathematical and philosophical apparatus, for the purpose of experiment and illustration. Boys are not admitted into it under twelve years of age, and none can remain longer than three years; in December 1836 there were one hundred and twenty on the list. It is ordered that the instructors shall be a master, a sub-master, and so many assistants as shall give one instructor to every thirty-five pupils, provided that no additional assistant be obtained for any increase less than twenty-one. The school is in excellent order, and does great credit both to those who planned it, and to the head-master, Mr. Miles, by whose ability and attention the system has been carried into effect.

The Latin grammar school was instituted about the middle of the seventeenth century: the rudiments of the Latin and Greek languages are taught, and scholars are fully qualified for the University. Instruction is also given in writing, in mathematics, in geography, history, declamation, and English composition. The boys are admitted at nine years of age, and the course of instruction continues for five years; but it is proposed that they shall not be admitted till eleven, and that writing, arithmetic, and geography shall be excluded. This school has enjoyed a high reputation, and has qualified many of its pupils for entering at Harvard and at other universities; but I was informed that not many of them are carried so far as Horace or Juvenal. After the books and exercises required have been specified in the regulations, the following passage occurs:—"It being, however, understood that there must necessarily be different degrees of proficiency amongst so many pupils, especially in the highest class, the following studies, viz. geometry and trigonometry, Xenophon's Anabasis, Juvenal, Horace, Homer, Stansbury's Catechism (on the Constitution of the United States), and Paley's Natural Theology, not being required for admission to the university, are allowed to be introduced at the discretion of the master, but are not absolutely required." The school contained, when I visited it, about ninety boys, which was less than the usual number; but a new master had lately been installed, and it was hoped that, under his care, the institution would revive.

The amount of money raised by tax in Boston, in the year 1837, for the support of schools, was 107,500 dollars, of which 78,750 dollars was for paying the wages of instructors solely. The number of scholars of all ages in all the public schools was nine thousand six hundred and eighty-three; and as, out of a population of eighty thousand three hundred and twenty-five, there are, it is stated, only seventeen thousand four hundred and eighty-five between the ages of four and sixteen, and in so wealthy a community* there are many families who prefer to send their children to private schools, it is probable that the whole juvenile population enjoy the benefit of instruction; the schools also are kept

* The "Valuation" of the city, in the school returns, is stated at *eighty millions* of dollars, or *seventeen millions* sterling !

during the whole year, with short vacations, and the
average attendance is the same in both seasons.   It
must, at the same time, be stated that these institutions
have little of the appearance of *schools for the poor.*
There are, in fact, in New England, very few persons
who are in indigent circumstances ; and many who could
well afford to send their children to a private school,
prefer those which are public, partly because they are
satisfied with the instruction there imparted, and partly
also from a republican feeling that such institutions
ought to be generally supported.   I have had pointed
out to me, in a public school at Boston, a child whose
father was a merchant worth from 50,000 to 100,000
dollars.

There are in Boston a number of infant schools, supported by private subscription ; and there is also an
excellent institution called " The Boston Asylum and
Farm-school for Indigent Boys."   It is intended to rescue from indolence and vice such children as are peculiarly exposed to corrupting influences, and to give
them an education which will fit them for entering with
advantage on the active business of life.   In order to
carry their plans into execution, the governors have purchased Thomson's Island, which lies in the bay, about
four miles from the city.   It contains one hundred and
forty acres of land, of which thirty are in cultivation ;
twenty head of cattle are kept, besides other stock ; and
all the work both of the farm and of the house, as well
as the making of many articles of clothing, is done
by the boys, (one hundred and seven in number,) with
the assistance of only a farming man, a boatman, and
a tailor, besides the superintendent (Captain Chandler)
and his wife.   I went over to the island, and am sure,
from what I saw, that these little fellows are in excellent
hands.   I examined them in their learning, and they read
and answered in a very creditable manner; and the master
also examined them in botany.   The greater part of them
are kept in school for five or six hours every day ; but one
division is always engaged on the farm, and the older
boys are all accustomed to the management of a boat :

seven of them rowed us back to the main land ; and it was beautiful to see the time they kept, and the unwearied vigour with which they plied the oar, though the distance was nearly two miles, and the water not very smooth. The institution had, when I saw it, been established only a year or two, and the good which it is to effect is as yet, in some measure, a matter of speculation ; but it promises favourably : the boys are trained in good habits and are acquiring valuable knowledge, and it is hoped that in a short time their labour will pay the expenses of the establishment. They are *absolutely* given up by their parents to the directors, and will by them be apprenticed out, when they have arrived at the proper age.

There is another school, which I cannot forbear noticing, though not strictly belonging to the same class as any of the above. It is, in fact, a proprietary school, having been instituted by a committee of gentlemen. It is for girls, and is conducted by Mr. W. B. Fowle. By the aid of the monitorial system he is enabled to teach one hundred and ten scholars, for four or five hours every morning, without having a single paid assistant ; and he teaches them well. Among other things, they are accustomed to draw maps from their first entrance into the school : and the mode in which they are instructed in composition is admirable ; it is taught even to the lowest class. First they have simple sentences dictated to them, which they write down ; then a story is read or told to them, which they are required to write in their own words ; afterwards they have the heads of a composition given them, and finally only the subject.

II.—NEW YORK.

The public provision which is made in the State of New York for the purposes of general education may be ranged under three heads, viz. Colleges or Universities, Academies, and Common Schools.

1. Of *Colleges*, or *Universities*, there are five : viz. Columbia College, in the city of New York ; Union College, at Schenectady ; Hamilton College, at Clinton ; and the University of the city of New York.

			Pro- fessors.	In- structors.	Stu- dents.
1. Columbia Coll. was founded in 1754; it has			9	4	114
2. Union College . . 1795		.	8	1	279
1. Hamilton College . . 1812		.	6	2	100
4. Geneva College . 1823		.	6	1	15*
5. University of New York city 1831		.	19	—	364

Of the students at the last-named University, three hundred and sixty-four expresses the whole number during the year; but, of these, only one hundred and fifty-three pursued the regular undergraduate course.

Most of these institutions were founded by associations of private individuals, and they do not receive any money from the public funds; but they are subject to the visitation of the regents of the University, a corporate body, who sit at Albany, and whose business it is to manage the Literature Fund, and to take cognizance of every thing that is done throughout the State relative to collegiate and academical education; and to this body the colleges and academies are expected to make regular reports.

2. *Academies.*—There are in the State of New York seventy-six public academies, from all of which except two returns were made to the regents in 1837, and most ample information respecting them is contained in the last Annual Report of that body. It appears that, in the seventy-four academies which made returns, there are six thousand three hundred and ninety-one pupils. These institutions are supported in part by the Literature Fund, from which they received last year about 12,000 dollars expended chiefly in the payment of teachers, and 5145 dollars for books and apparatus; in part by the interest or income of permanent funds, amounting to about 15,000 dollars; and in part by fees. The latter amounted last year to upwards of 102,000 dollars, and the whole amount of compensation received by the teachers was 107,826 dollars, which, distributed among two hundred and eighty-four, gives an average of 379 dollars and 66 cents, or 80*l.* 13*s.* 3*d.* for each. This is a small remuneration certainly for men who are expected to be well

* There are also five professors and sixty students in the medical department.

instructed and able to teach; but when it is considered that, in most places except the large towns, board (and it is presumed that this includes lodging) may be obtained for sums varying from 1½ dollar to 3 dollars per week, (see Report of the Regents, p. 106,) the compensation is not so small as may at first view appear. The fees paid by the pupils vary according to circumstances, the average for each throughout the State being nearly 16 dollars, or 3*l*. 8*s*. a year.

The academies hold an intermediate rank between the colleges and the common schools; and many of them include all the branches of education which are taught in schools of the highest description, as will be perceived by the following table, which has been compiled from the Report.

SUBJECTS OF STUDY.

Arithmetic, Algebra, Chemistry, Composition, Declamation (in all except the female schools), English Grammar, Geography, Geometry, General History, Orthography, Natural Philosophy, Penmanship, Pronunciation, and Reading, in all the 74.

Latin in all but 2.

Greek in all but 4.

French	in 56
Spanish	7
German	3
Italian	5
Hebrew	5
History of the United States	48
Constitution of ditto	15
History of the State of New York	2
Constitution of ditto	9
Law	18
Political Economy	2
Logic	20
Intellectual Philosophy	54
Moral Philosophy	41

Rhetoric in all except 6.

Evidences of Christianity	10
Theology	1
Natural Theology	16
Book-keeping	56
Trigonometry	29
Mensuration	22
Surveying	53
Levelling	3
Navigation	11

Astronomy in all except 11.

Architecture	1
Botany	43
Natural History	19
Geology	17
Mineralogy	11
Technology	5
Physiology	9
Phrenology	2
Drawing	1
Painting	1
Embroidery	1
Dancing	1
Music	16

I had not the opportunity of examining personally into the state of any of these academies, except those at Albany, in which, as being the seat of the State government, and otherwise a place of considerable consequence, it might be expected that the means of education would be of a superior description. The Albany Academy, which contains two hundred and seventy-six boys, provides ample, and for the most part excellent, instruction in all the branches of a liberal education; and the Female Academy, where there were, in October 1836, four hundred and twenty-three pupils from the age of four or five to eighteen, is the finest institution of the kind that I know. The course of instruction is so complete, as to leave those who go through the whole of it but little to desire of the advantages of a college. I heard classes examined in trigonometry, natural history, physiology, and moral philosophy; and, as they are all taught to sing from notes, the music at morning prayers in the chapel was very good. The terms are in the lowest department 4 dollars, and in the highest 10 dollars per quarter, with an additional charge of 5 dollars per quarter if French or Spanish is learnt. There are no boarders in the establishment, but board may be had in the town at a reasonable rate; and it is stated that the whole expense incurred by a young lady for board and tuition, including all the studies taught at the academy, does not exceed 225 dollars, or 47l. 16s. 3d. a year.

The academies distributed through the rural districts must, of course, be of a much inferior order to those just specified, as is evinced by the fact that, out of six thousand three hundred and ninety-one pupils in all the seventy-four which reported, only five thousand and forty-six were allowed by the regents to have pursued classical studies, or the higher branches of English education, or both, for four months of the year; but the very existence of such institutions, though they may not be all that could be wished, must be allowed to be a great advantage to the public.

The academies are required to make meteorological reports every year, and these are generally prepared by the principal of each institution. They have not indeed been made with uniform accuracy; but the trouble and labour of the work must be taken into consideration, and also that no pecuniary compensation has yet been made for it. To obviate the deficiency, it has been proposed that returns shall be required from only a small number of suitable stations, selected in different parts of the State, and that they shall be paid for.

3. *Common Schools.*—Nothing was done to encourage common schools in the State of New York till the year 1795, when an act was passed appropriating the annual sum of 50,000 dollars for five years for the purpose of maintaining schools in the several cities and towns of the State. The several counties were required to raise a sum equal to one half of that appropriated to each by the State. At the expiration of the law in 1800, the legislature refused to renew it; but in 1805, impelled probably by a sense of the deprivation under which the State laboured in being again thrown back on voluntary or local efforts, the legislature passed an act providing a permanent fund for the support of common schools, and this has been enlarged by subsequent appropriations. In 1811 measures were taken to organize a regular system of schools, and to provide for the distribution of the interest of the fund. In 1812 the present system was established, under the direction of an officer known as the Superintendent of Common Schools. The interest of the fund was directed to be annually distributed among the several towns in a ratio to their population, provided they should raise a sum equal to their proportion by a tax upon themselves. Each town was to be divided into

school districts, and commissioners and inspectors were to be appointed. The first distribution of money under this act took place in 1816 : in 1828, in sixteen counties alone out of fifty-five, the number of school districts was two thousand five hundred and eighty-six, and of scholars attending them one hundred and forty-two thousand three hundred and seventy-two. There were then in fifty-five counties eight thousand two hundred and ninety-eight school districts, and since that time the number has gradually increased.

On the 31st of December 1836, the number of organized counties was fifty-six, and of districts ten thousand three hundred and forty-five ; of which nine thousand seven hundred and eighteen made reports, and six hundred and twenty-seven made none.

Each of these districts (of which a town contains several) has a school, which is required to be kept at least three months out of the twelve, in order to entitle it to its quota of the public fund.

The affairs of the common schools throughout the State are administered by Commissioners, Inspectors, and Trustees. "Three persons are appointed under the title of *Commissioners* at the annual meeting in each town. Their duties are to regulate the boundaries of the school districts within the towns for which they are chosen, to alter existing districts and to form new ones when it becomes necessary for the convenience of the inhabitants. They receive from the county treasurer, with whom it is deposited, the quota of the revenue of the common school fund to which the town is entitled, and from the collector of the town the equal amount raised upon its taxable property; and they apportion these sums among the school districts of the town, according to the number of children over five and under sixteen years of age residing in each district, provided a school has been kept in it three months by a qualified teacher during the preceding year, and provided also the school monies received in that year have been applied to the compensation of such teacher. They receive the annual reports of the trustees of the school districts, and from them prepare a consolidated report, setting forth certain particulars specified in the statute to be transmitted to the superintendent," i. e. to the secretary of state who is, by virtue of his office, Superintendent of Common Schools. It is the duty of this officer to make an annual report to the legislature respecting the schools; to apportion the income of the public fund; to prepare and transmit to the officers of the district suitable forms and regulations, with necessary instructions; and to act as a court of appeal in all matters of dispute that may arise under the statute.—See the *Report of the Superintendent, presented to the Legislature*, January 6, 1836, pp. 28, 32.

"Three *Inspectors* of common schools are annually chosen in each town. Their duties are to examine all persons offering themselves as candidates for teaching common schools in the town; to visit all the common schools at least once in each year; and they may give their advice and direction to the trustees and teachers of such schools as to the government thereof, and the course of studies to be pursued therein. The commissioners of each town have, by virtue of their office, the same powers; so that there are always six persons in each town authorized to act as inspectors."—*Ibid.* p. 33.

"In each school district there are annually chosen three *Trustees*, whose duty it is to call special meetings of the inhabitants whenever they deem it necessary; to make out all tax lists, when taxes are voted by the inhabitants of the district to build or repair the school-house; to provide fuel or to purchase a lot for a school-house; to make out all rate-bills [tuition-bills] from the lists kept by the teachers; to exempt indigent persons from the payment of their proportion of such rate-bills; to have the custody of the district school-house; to contract with and employ all teachers, and to provide for the payment of their wages."—P. 37. This is done in the following manner:—"The sum of 100,000 dollars is annually distributed to the school districts from the common school fund, and is appropriated to the compensation of teachers who have been inspected by the proper authority, and received a certificate of qualification. The board of supervisors in each county are required to cause to be levied, by tax on each town, a sum equal to that which such town receives from the common school fund as its quota of the annual income. The sum thus levied is also appropriated to the payment of the wages of teachers qualified according to law. The inhabitants of each town have also authority to vote, at their annual town meeting, an additional sum not exceeding the amount directed to be raised therein by the supervisors; or, in other words, not exceeding its quota of the income of the common school fund. Thus each town is annually taxed to an amount equal to the sum it receives from the common school fund; and it may, by its own voluntary act, be taxed twice that amount." . . . . . " Several towns have local funds, the income of which is also paid into the hands of the commissioners, for distribution with the other school moneys, and is also appropriated to the compensation of qualified teachers by force of a provision of law, which requires all moneys paid by the commissioners to school districts to be so applied." The balance of what the district has agreed to pay the teacher is raised by rate-bills as follows:—" At the expiration of each term in a school district, the trustees pay the teacher so much of the school moneys as is appropriated to that term by vote of the inhabitants of the district at their annual meeting; and the residue of his wages for the term is collected from all who have sent children to school, in proportion to the number of days their children have attended. Indigent persons may be exempted by the trustees from paying any part of the rate-bill; so that the compensation of the teacher for the term, excepting so much of it as is provided for by the public money, is paid by such of the patrons of the school as are of sufficient ability to pay anything. It is proper to add that parents may, if they please, pay directly to the teacher the amount due from them. In this case, the amount so paid is not included in the rate-bill; and the fees of the collector, who is allowed five per cent. on all moneys collected by him, is saved by the person or persons making such payment."—*Ibid.* pp. 24, 25.

The whole expense of purchasing a lot, building a school-house, and furnishing it with a few indispensable articles, is paid by the taxable property of each school district, according to a vote of the inhabitants; and, if a tax for fuel is not voted, it is furnished by the persons sending children to school, in proportion to the number of days of attendance.—P. 26. Except in case of indigence, the necessary school-books must be provided by those who send the child to school.

The peculiar advantages of this system are, that, while it induces the inhabitants of the richer districts to tax themselves liberally for the education of their children, and thus supplies a powerful motive to a careful supervision of the affairs of the school, it at the same time carries its assistance to the most remote and needy neighbourhoods, which might otherwise be entirely destitute of the means of instruction.

The amount of public money expended by the trustees of school districts in the year 1836 in payment of the wages of teachers, was 335,895 dollars; of which amount the sum of 100,000 dollars was received from the common school fund of the State, 216,562 dollars were levied by tax on the property of the inhabitants of the towns and cities, and 19,332 dollars were derived from the local funds of particular towns. The amount paid for teachers' wages during the year 1836, *in addition* to the above-mentioned sums of public money, was 436,346 dollars, which exceeds by the sum of 10,702 dollars the amount so paid in the year 1835. The whole amount paid for teachers' wages in 1836 (with the exception of about 46,000 dollars, expended on school-houses, furniture, &c. in the city of New York,) was 772,241 dollars, exceeding by the sum of 33,221 dollars the amount so paid in 1835.—*Report*, p. 9.

In the Superintendent's Report for 1835 (pp. 14. 16) it is stated that, including interest at six per cent. on money invested in school-houses, the annual expense of books for the scholars at 50 cents each, fuel for the school-houses at 10 dollars each, and the estimated expense of compensation to commissioners and collectors, with the fees of collectors, &c. the whole amount of the annual expenditure for the support of the common school system in the State of New York cannot fall short of 14,000,000 dollars, or nearly *three millions* sterling. Of this amount the common school fund pays one fourteenth, taxable property and local funds pay about five four-teenths, and the remaining eight fourteenths are contri-buted by those who send children to school. As in the year 1830 the population of the State amounted to 1,918,608, and may now probably be taken at 2,300,000, this will give an average payment of 5 dollars, 64 cents, or 1*l.* 4*s.* from each individual for the purposes of public education, besides what is derived from the common school fund and from local funds.

The extent to which the people avail themselves of these facilities may be judged of from the fact, that in the year 1836, in the districts from which reports were received, the number of children instructed in the com-mon schools was five hundred and twenty-four thousand one hundred and eighty-eight, while the whole number of children between five and sixteen years of age residing in the same districts was five hundred and thirty-six thousand eight hundred and eighty-two. Allowing that some of those in attendance are under the age of five and others above sixteen, and that some, in consequence of moving from one school to another, are reckoned twice, and considering, on the other hand, that many between those ages attend private schools, academies, and colleges, it would appear that nearly the whole juvenile population take advantage of the means of instruction. It must, however, be taken into the account, that the average period during which all the schools were kept was little more than seven months; that in nine hundred and ten schools the period was less than four months, and in six hundred and thirty-four only three. To remedy this defici-ency, it is proposed by the superintendent that the amount from the public fund for the support of these schools shall be increased; and that, in return, they shall be re-quired to be kept six months, instead of three, by a quali-fied teacher.

The subjects of instruction in these schools are reading, writing, arithmetic, grammar, geography, and the history of the United States: in some of the schools only is religious instruction given, the Testament being used as a class-book in only one hundred and one towns, while the English

Reader is found in four hundred and eighty-six, and the History of the United States in two hundred and twenty. Simple and elementary as these branches are, yet, if they were well and efficiently taught, these schools might be regarded as answering the purpose for which they are designed; but it is to be feared that this is not generally the case. One main cause of this is the very low wages which are paid to the teachers; the average to male teachers being stated, in the report for 1835, to be about 12 dollars, 90 cents, or 2*l.* 14*s.* 10*d.* per month, and since that date there does not appear to have been any considerable augmentation. In " *The District School,*" by J. Orville Taylor, third edition, 1835, p. 114, it is stated that " The common school teacher, who is employed for twelve successive months, does not receive more than eleven dollars per month. There are a few who have more than this sum, yet a greater number who receive less. Now the common labourer, who hires himself to the farmer by the month, gets as much as the teacher; and the wages of the mechanic are double the wages of the teacher. It is a very common practice with young men who teach during the winter, to labour on the farm during the summer; and they make this change, because the summer wages of the farm *are more* than the wages of the summer school. There is no employment among the American people (what a reproach to our intelligence and affluence!) *which receives less pay than elementary teaching.* Yes, there is no service so menial, no drudgery so degrading, which does not demand as high wages as we are now giving for that which is the life of our liberty, and the guard of our free institutions.''

It is not surprising, then, that the teaching of a common school is regarded as a mere temporary resource, especially in a country where the facilities of obtaining a comfortable livelihood are so great. Young men who are with difficulty maintaining themselves at college, others who wish to save money in order to go thither, and others again who have been unsuccessful in some other line of life, resort to the employment of keeping a common school; and, the moment they see that they can do any thing better for themselves, they abandon it. They

264 COMMON SCHOOLS.

bring no peculiar fitness to the task; and they are chosen
by the school inspectors, partly because few others present themselves for the office, and partly because, from
the indigence of their circumstances, they are willing to
accept a very moderate compensation. With a view to
correct this evil, it has been proposed to appropriate
from the annual income of the deposite fund 110,000
dollars for the payment of teachers; and if, in the case of
this grant, as of the former, it should be made a condition that an equal sum should be raised by the towns on
their taxable property, the gross remuneration of the
teachers would be increased by 220,000 dollars.

Another principal cause of the district schools not
being in a better state, is, that till lately, no provision
whatever has been made for the training of teachers.
Within the last three or four years, however, the eyes of
intelligent men have been opened to the necessity of
something being done for this purpose; and a law has
been passed, appropriating 3,200 dollars annually for the
support of teachers' departments in connection with an
academy in each of the eight senatorial districts of the
State. In these academies also certain inducements and
facilities are held forth to those, who are disposed to enter the teachers' department. The term of study is
three years, but only eight months in each year are devoted to instruction. There is a vacation of four months
in winter, to enable the students (many of whom will, it
is supposed, need such a resource) to teach a district
school, and thus earn something to support them in completing their course of preparation. At the end of the
term each student is to be examined publicly, and if
he passes a satisfactory examination in all the prescribed
subjects of study, he is to receive a diploma under the
seal of the academy. It is clear, however, from the reports, that the great majority of the students attend only
two or three quarters. These departments have now been
in operation three years, and the whole number of pupils
who have during the last year been in a course of preparation for teaching is two hundred and eighty-four, exceeding by sixty-six the number reported in the preceding year. The influence of these institutions is felt in

raising both the standard of the qualifications, and the pay of the teachers. Instructors have been eagerly sought for from these departments, and in some instances it has been found impossible to supply the number required. In the report of the Washington academy at Salem, it is stated that " of the male students in this department, fifteen are now engaged in teaching district schools. They generally receive a preference, and command more wages than ordinary teachers ; and, as an evidence of the estimation in which they are held, it may be noticed that they receive from 18 to 20 dollars per month, whereas formerly the usual compensation of teachers was only from 10 to 12 dollars." This plan has been productive of so much benefit, and has obtained so strong a hold on the public mind, that it is suggested by the superintendent in his report, that the number of academies having these departments connected with them should be increased from eight to twenty-four, and that the annual appropriation to each of them should be 500 instead of 400 dollars. That the number eight should be increased, is certainly desirable ; but it is still more to be desired that *model schools* should be established. Of these there are at present none : the young men who are placed in the teachers' departments of the academies have the means afforded them of acquiring much valuable knowledge, and they have also lectures given them on the principles and the art of teaching ; but they have no opportunity of seeing a superior school *actually in operation*, and of taking part in its management; consequently they cannot be expected to possess much skill in teaching, and little or no improvement is to be looked for in the methods adopted. If *four* model schools were to be established on a liberal scale in different parts of the State,—say, at New York, Albany, Potsdam (St. Laurence county), and Canandaigua,—and if pains were taken to introduce into them, all the latest improvements which have been applied to similar institutions in Europe, their good effect would be incalculable; old methods of teaching would be exploded, and new ones adopted ; and the moral and intellectual benefits resulting from the common schools would be infinitely increased.

It is also much to be wished that the whole general charge of the common schools should not be left to the secretary of state, who is, by virtue of his office, superintendent of these institutions. In the discharge of the general duties of his office, and in attending to the distribution of the common school fund, he has already more than enough on his hands, without troubling himself with modes of teaching and other internal arrangements, with which, indeed, from the very terms of the statute, he considers that he is not authorized to interfere. If more life and vigour are to be communicated to these schools, if the bounds of instruction are to be enlarged, and the methods of teaching to keep pace with the growing improvements of the age, the regulation of these matters must be intrusted to a distinct minister of instruction,—to some one specially fitted for the task, who will give his whole attention to the subject, and travel through the country with the view of obtaining information and carrying his plans into effect. Then only may we hope to see these schools, so admirable in their external organization, approach more nearly in their internal discipline to what they ought to be. It is, at the same time, only an act of justice to say, that the reports of the superintendent evince great care and labour, and may well serve as models to those who have occasion to prepare similar documents; and the same may be observed of the report of the regents of the University, already referred to.

[In the Connecticut Common School Journal for February 1839, there is a long account of the common school system in the State of New York, from which the following particulars are taken :—

" Columbia College has now 157 students, Union College, 300, and Geneva, 50. In 79 academies, subject to the visitation of the regents, there are about 10,000 students ; and the sum to be annually distributed to them hereafter is 40,000 dollars, being an addition of 28,000 to the preceding annual appropriation. The number of organized common school districts is 10,583, of which 9830 maintained schools during an average period of eight months in the last year. The number of children between the age of five and sixteen in the school districts is 539,747, of whom 528,913 received instruction in the common schools within the year.

By an act passed in 1835, the inhabitants of the school districts are authorized to vote a tax not exceeding twenty dollars, to purchase a library for their common use, and a further tax, not exceeding ten dollars in any one year, to make additions to the library; and, by an act of 1838, 55,000 dollars of the income of the United States Deposit Fund is appropriated for three years to the purchase of libraries in the several districts, on condition that the districts raise as much more.

All these are gratifying proofs that education in the State of New York is obtaining more of the public attention and resources.]

CITY OF NEW YORK.

The public schools in the city of New York are on a different footing from those in the other parts of the State. In the year 1805, on the petition of De Witt Clinton, and other benevolent individuals, a bill was passed by the State Legislature, constituting a body corporate for the establishment and management of public schools in the city. They elect their successors on the second Monday in May in each year, and their number has been gradually augmented till it now amounts to seventy-five. At their first meeting after the annual election, the trustees are divided into school sections, one section being attached to each public school-house, of which there are sixteen. They appoint a paid agent, who takes charge of the general depository of books, stationery, &c. and distributes the supplies to the schools, as they apply for them, once a week. At the same meeting there are also appointed an executive committee, a primary school committee, a finance committee, and others. The executive committee appoint the teachers and monitors of the several schools, with such salaries as they may think proper, not exceeding such limits as the board of trustees may have settled; and on the application of a section or otherwise, they may remove a teacher and appoint another in his place. It is their duty to visit and carefully examine all the schools annually, and to report to the board of trustees on their general state; but with respect to the primary schools, this duty may be omitted at their discretion. They have also to prepare the annual report, and to examine all books proposed to be introduced into the schools. It is the duty of each section to attend to the interest of the schools to which it is attached, to examine them from time to time, and to make a quarterly report upon their state to the board of trustees; in conjunction also with the primary school committee, and a consulting committee of ladies, they are required to inspect and regulate the primary schools in their own neighbourhood.

There are, as has been mentioned above, sixteen public school-houses. These are handsome brick buildings, containing two large rooms, one on the ground floor, and another above, appropriated to the pupils of the respective sexes. In ten out of the sixteen there is also a *primary department* for younger children, kept in the basement story; and there are, besides, thirty-two *primary schools*, distinctively so called, taught in hired rooms, frequently the basement story of churches: there are also six schools for the children of the Blacks. The rooms in which the higher departments of the public schools are taught are light, airy, and commodious; and, where the arrangement is complete, they have two smaller apartments attached to the larger for the use of separate classes. In most of them the Eastern and Western Hemispheres, six feet in diameter, are painted in strong colours on the wall; in some is added a representation of the solar system, or of the eclipses; and most, if not all, of the schools are furnished with libraries. Nor let me omit to state, that the apartments, especially those in the primary schools, are kept beautifully clean, chiefly by the use of fine white sand, which is sprinkled on the floors.

These schools are all taught on a modification of the monitorial system, there being always one or more paid teachers to assist the principal. Thus, in Public School

No. 3, in the boys' department, with three hundred and sixty-four on the list, and an average attendance of about three hundred, there is a head-master with a salary of 1000 dollars, a second master with 500, a first monitor with 200, and a second with 50 : in the primary department, in the same building, where I found two hundred and fifty children present, there were four teachers, all females, with salaries of 250, 200, 75, and 50 dollars. The teachers in all these schools are required to make quarterly and annual reports of the number of children admitted and discharged, the actual attendance, and other particulars; and no alteration can be made in the system or discipline of the school without the sanction of the board of trustees.

In order to provide a sufficient supply of efficient monitors, a school is opened in which the young female teachers and monitors receive additional instruction on the Saturday morning ; and there is one for the young men and boys, taught on five evenings in every week during winter, and on Saturday mornings during the rest of the year. Besides these, there are several evening schools for the instruction of apprentices, domestics, and others, whose employments during the day-time prevent their attendance during the usual school-hours.

In the primary schools the method adopted is a modification of the infant school system, and, as far as I had the opportunity of judging, it is efficiently applied. In the higher departments the course of instruction for boys embraces spelling, reading (including definitions and questions concerning the meaning of the author); writing, making and mending of pens ; arithmetic, geography, the use of the globes, and drawing maps; English grammar, composition, and declamation ; book-keeping; the elements of history, astronomy, algebra, geometry, and trigonometry. The course of instruction for the girls is the same, with the exception of declamation, algebra, geometry, and trigonometry, and with the addition of needle-work.

In the last annual report, p. 7, it is remarked that " the constitution of the society and public sentiment wisely forbid the introduction into these schools of any such religious instruction as shall favour the peculiar views of any sect; and the trustees endeavour so carefully to guard them in this respect as to give no just cause of complaint, leaving this subject where it rightfully belongs, to the parents and guardians of the children. They wish, however, not to be understood as regarding religious impressions in early youth as unimportant; on the contrary, they desire to do all which may with propriety be done, to give a right direction to the minds of the children entrusted to their care. Their schools are uniformly opened with the reading of the Scriptures, and the class books are such as to recognize and enforce the great and generally acknowledged principles of Christianity. A large proportion of our scholars attend the various Sunday schools of the city, by direction of their parents; and the trustees are happy to bear testimony to their great usefulness, believing them to be very valuable auxiliaries to the cause of public instruction."

In January 1837, I visited several of these schools, and think that on the whole they are in an efficient state: in geography and the elements of astronomy some classes which I examined answered very well; the style of penmanship, too, is superior to what I have seen anywhere else; but it is much to be regretted that the interrogative method, as illustrated by Mr. Wood of Edinburgh, and exemplified in all the best British schools, is not adopted to a greater extent: it *is* partially adopted in the higher classes, but not so as to produce that quickness of perception, that readiness and felicity of illustration, and that general briskness and animation of manner, which are the certain results of the method, if thoroughly and faithfully applied. "*Let well alone*" is the principle on which too many of the school trustees both in New York city and in other cities are disposed to act; and because they have effected and are still effecting much good, they are slow to acknowledge the value of improvements in the methods of teaching, which would double the amount of the benefit conferred, and produce an effect on the mind and manners of the great mass of the community, such as every well-wisher of his country would be proud to witness.

The public school trustees of the city of New York have the greater motive to exertion, as they are surrounded by an indigent, ignorant, and vicious population, continually poured into their port from foreign nations. That their efforts, praiseworthy as they are, have as yet but very imperfectly accomplished the object which they have in view, is evident from the fact that on the 1st of May 1838 there were, on the registers of the public schools of that city, only fifteen thousand two hundred and eighty-nine children, while the entire population at that period must have amounted to two hundred and eighty thousand. Now, if in Boston there are seventeen thousand four hundred and eighty-five children between the ages of four and sixteen, out of a population of eighty thousand three hundred and twenty-five, there must in New York be upwards of sixty thousand between the same ages; and allowing that five thousand more attend during some portion of the year, that twenty thousand go to private schools, and five thousand to infant and other charity schools, we shall still have the alarming number of fifteen thousand children unprovided with the means of education.

The poor appear to avail themselves of the means of education so far as they are provided for them, for I found most of the schools full; and they would have no excuse for not doing so, since the advantage is offered them entirely without cost: they pay nothing either for the instruction itself, or for the books or other school materials which are required.

These schools derive their quota from the general school fund of the State; but the main part of their support is derived from a tax of a twentieth of one per cent. on the assessed value of the real and personal estate within the city and county. The account presented in July 1837 shows 13,668 dollars to have been received by the school commissioners from the State, the same sum from the city, and 72,651 dollars from the tax just named, and of this gross sum 92,730 dollars were appropriated to the Public School Society.

III. PENNSYLVANIA.

1. *Colleges.* — With respect to these institutions in Pennsylvania, a great error has been committed in having a number of them, instead of concentrating the available resources on one or two. The consequence has been that scarcely one of them can be said to have flourished. In the year 1836, there were in the State fourteen colleges for general education; but as only nine reported in 1837, and one of these was not in operation in a collegiate capacity, it may be presumed that in the course of time six have become virtually extinct. Of the eight in operation there are only five which have so many as four professors and one hundred students, and the aggregate number of the latter is only seven hundred and ninety. The medium price of tuition for one year is about 35 dollars, or 7*l.* 8*s.* 9*d.* and the whole expense 115 dollars, or 28*l.* 8*s.* 3*d.* The whole property of these colleges is estimated at 623,150 dollars, and the value of the money and land which they have received from the State at 97,530 dollars.

2. *Academies.*—About fifty county academies have received aid from the State, varying from 2000 to 5000 dollars each, exclusive of land. Of these only twenty-one reported during the last year, the total number of their students being eleven hundred and eighty-eight. The studies generally pursued were all the branches of an English education, the Greek and Latin languages, and in some of them French. The average cost of tuition is about 18 dollars, or 3*l.* 16*s.* 6*d.*; and the whole average expense to each student, including board, &c. 165 dollars and 77 cents, or 35*l.* 4*s.* 7*d.* The value of money and land which has been bestowed upon these institutions by the State is 34,231 dollars; and, if they are to be maintained in an efficient condition, they must receive further assistance from the same source, for their buildings are estimated at only 64,061 dollars, their invested funds at 17,408 dollars, and their whole property at 51,484 dollars; but, in respect of the last item, the printed statement is not very clear.

3. *Common Schools.*—Much less has been done for the

promotion of general education in Pennsylvania than in the north-eastern States of the Union. Although, by a clause in the amended constitution of 1790, it was required that "the legislature should, as soon as conveniently may be, provide by law for the establishment of schools throughout the State, in such a manner that the poor may be taught gratis," yet, so far as relates to common schools, nothing was done in compliance with this article of the constitution till 1809, when an act was passed "for the education of the poor gratis." Partly from an idea that the poor were thus designated as a distinct class, and partly from indifference to the subject, but little progress was made for many years in the execution of the provisions of this act; and a few years ago so strong was the prejudice against the system, that the cry at the contested elections was 'Down with the free schools!'" In 1834 an act was passed, appropriating large funds for the encouragement of common schools, and entitling districts to avail themselves of their quota of these funds by levying a poll-tax to a certain amount. This law, which was objectionable in some of its provisions, was amended in 1836; and the conditions on which the districts now receive their State appropriations are, that they accept the common school system, and assess a tax at least equal to their proportion of the appropriation; but the directors may increase the tax to double that amount *without* the assent of the citizens, or to any extent *with* their assent. The number of districts which accepted and acted upon the system was at first only about half; and it is a singular circumstance that the counties in which it met with the most strenuous opposition were those which had been the longest settled. At length, however, the opposition is dying away; out of one thousand and one districts (which is the whole number in the State, exclusive of the city and county of Philadelphia and the city of Lancaster), seven hundred and sixty-five have accepted the condition of the law by assessing a tax; there are now four thousand and eighty-nine primary schools taught in the districts which have reported, and the whole number of scholars in these districts is one hundred and eighty-two thousand three hundred and fifty-five, out of a supposed aggregate of two hundred thousand between the ages of five and fifteen, whereas, so far as returns have been received, the whole number taught in schools of all kinds in the same districts before the adoption of the system was only eighty thousand. It must, however, be taken into the account that the *average attendance* is not given, and that the aggregate duration of the teaching is only six months out of the twelve. Of the whole number of children taught, three thousand six hundred and twelve were exclusively German, nine hundred and twenty-two were in endowed schools, and seven hundred and fourteen Coloured.

The following statement, taken from the "Fourth Report of the Superintendent of Common Schools," (Mr. Thomas H. Burrowes,) p. 34, will exhibit at one view the progress of the system since the date of the preceding annual report:—

	1837.	1838.	Difference.
The whole number of districts	987	1,001	14
The number of paid districts	603	765	162
The number that reported	573	664	91
Whole number of schools	3,384	4,089	705
Whole number of teachers	3,394	4,841	1,447
Whole number of scholars	139,604	182,355	42,751
Average compensation of male teachers* dollars	18·38	18·89¼	·51¼
Do. do. of female teachers	11·96	11·79½	·16½
Duration of teaching	4. m 3 d.	6 m. ⅓ d.	1 m. 27⅓ d.
Cost of each pupil per quarter dollars	1·06¼	1·27½	·21¼

" It will be perceived," observes the superintendent, " that there is an increase in nearly every one of the items in the foregoing statement since last year; all being favourable to the system, except those of the salaries of female teachers, and the cost of instruction per scholar. It is believed that this last average is not exactly correct, many of the districts having included under the head of *instruction* expenses that should have been embraced elsewhere. The superintendent would estimate the average at 1 dollar 10 cents, being little more than that of last session. The cost of teaching will, beyond a

* *i. e.* per month.

doubt, be further reduced. When all the children of each primary district get into the habit of attending school (which is by no means the case at present), the average will be proportionably diminished, as no additional expense will thereby be incurred."

The whole number of completed school-houses in the districts which have reported is two thousand and ninety-eight; the number in progress, six hundred and nine; the number yet required, eight hundred and eighty. Their average size is twenty-four feet by twenty-four; with high ceilings, large windows, and comfortable seats and desks, in such as have been recently built. The public money voted last session but one for the building of school-houses, viz. half a million of dollars, has been of great service to the system. The buildings are at least fifty per cent. better than they were twelve months ago, and have improved one hundred per cent. in the last three years.—*Report*, p. 41.

The ordinary annual appropriation of the public money for these schools is 200,000 dollars, payable to the districts in the ratio of their taxable inhabitants; and in addition to this there is the 500,000 dollars voted by the legislature two years ago for the building of schoolhouses, making 700,000 dollars to be distributed in the last year: as, however, many of the districts did not accept the terms, the sum actually distributed (including 89,536 dollars to Philadelphia, and 23,509 dollars of arrears,) was only 500,598 dollars. If to this sum be added the tax assessed on the accepting districts during the last year, being 231,552 dollars, the whole amount of money at their disposal for school purposes, including the school tax of Philadelphia, which was 59,999 dollars, was 792,151 dollars, or 168,332*l*. In the State and County treasuries there is a gross total of undrawn balances, amounting to 307,520 dollars, awaiting the action of the non-accepting districts. It is stated that the amount, viz. 231,552 dollars, raised by tax in the accepting districts, (exclusive of Philadelphia,) is about double the amount of their annual appropriation from the State.— *Report*, p. 49.

The whole government of each school district is lodged

in a board of six directors, with an appeal to the superintendent in certain cases. They are assisted by a treasurer; and there is also in each primary district a committee of three individuals, who act in subordination to them. These directors and commitee-men are chosen, it may be presumed, by the inhabitants.

The branches of study in the country primary schools are generally reading, writing, grammar, geography, and arithmetic; and, in towns, history, composition, book-keeping, and some portions of the mathematics, with various other branches, have been successfully taught. A higher description of schools than those in the country will soon be generally wanted, and it is to be hoped that *secondary* or *high schools* will be established; but it is not easy to see the utility of having both these and the county *academies*, as well as four *practical institutes*, as proposed by the superintendent, *Report*, p. 11—16. From their number and variety, these institutions, if established, would starve each other. It would be far better to have primary schools for the young, and to make the secondary schools of so high a character as to supersede the necessity of most of the academies.

During the last summer and autumn the superintendent visited the principal town in each of thirty-three counties of the State, for the purpose of ascertaining the condition of the system, and of settling on the spot such controversies as were subject to his jurisdiction. This tour was found to be of so much use, that he proposes to complete it this year. The results which have been ascertained are such as were to be desired. The superintendent considers that, in a large majority of the accepting districts, the crisis of the system is past; the contests which now arise are not *against* the law, as formerly, but *under* the law, for its benefits; more regularity is introduced into the transactions of the directors; the profession of teaching is much elevated; the compensation of instructors is increased, while the cost of the common schools to each scholar is at the same time diminished; " the odious distinction between rich and poor scholars " is every day becoming less apparent; all are learning to meet as equals on the broad platform of education; political animosities are laid aside in the desire to promote a great public object; and, above all, there is a general discussion of the merits of the new system, and of the nature and the best means of education generally.

It is evident that the whole State is awakening to an attention to this vital subject; and, if the judicious suggestions of the superintendent should be put in execution, there can be little doubt that Pennsylvania may soon dispute the palm with any State in the Union in the support of public education. The superintendent proposes that the annual State appropriation shall be made equal hereafter to one dollar for each taxable citizen, making an addition to the present grant of 108,919 dollars ; and, secondly, that there shall be a liberal grant to establish two seminaries exclusively for improving the present generation of teachers. After their immediate purpose has been answered, these are by degrees to " rise and widen into practical institutes," already mentioned, where all the branches of a liberal education are to be taught, with the exception of the languages, and where the course is to occupy two years. To these all are to be admitted who desire the kind and degree of instruction which is there offered; and it is hoped that, of the aggregate number of students at these and three other similar institutions, such a proportion will be disposed to become teachers as will supply the wants of the schools. It is justly observed that the " art of instruction " should form a special branch at the two teachers' seminaries; but the idea of a model school in connection with them appears to be very imperfect, for it is proposed that the " scholar teachers " themselves shall be formed into such a school, whereas it would be much better that they should teach the children in the neighbourhood. Unless this be done, the " art of teaching " will not be acquired.

PHILADELPHIA.

In the year 1818 the city and county of Philadelphia were erected into a district, called "The First School District of Pennsylvania." It is divided into ten sections, in each of which a school committee is chosen by the councils in the city, and by the commissioners in the surround-

ing districts, and these are elected by the inhabitants.
These committees have the whole management of the
schools, subject, however, to the revision of the controllers, a body of twelve men, chosen by the committees
from among their own number. It is the duty of the
committee-men, otherwise called directors, to visit the
schools once a week.

The public schools under the charge of the controllers
are supported, like those in the other parts of the State,
partly by the public fund, and partly by a tax levied on
the inhabitants of the city and county. From the former
source the controllers received last year (for buildings
and for teachers' wages, &c.) 89,536 dollars,—from the
latter source about 60,000 dollars; and they had at the
beginning of the year a balance in hand of 61,086 dollars.
The whole expenditure during the year was 191,616 dollars, of which 110,864 dollars were for the purchase of lots
and the erection of houses, and 80,767 dollars for instruction, school furniture, books, stationery, fuel, &c. When
I visited these schools in the spring of 1837, the principal
teacher in each of the boys' schools received 1000 dollars
a year, and his assistant 400 dollars: in the infant schools
connected with the higher the teachers are females, of
whom the principal had 400 dollars, and the assistant
200; and in the primary schools the teacher's salary was
250 dollars.

The want of sufficient means of education for the
poorer classes of the community in Philadelphia was till
lately very great; but, during the last two or three years,
the controllers have been making very laudable exertions
to remove the evil, and the report which they have issued
this spring presents gratifying evidence of their activity.
" A retrospect of the present year," they observe,
" will exhibit greater activity, larger expenditure, increased accommodations, more numerous pupils, and in
all departments more important results than have characterized any previous period;—abundant means, aided to
a munificent extent by the enlightened liberality of the
State government, have enabled the controllers to extend
their permanent improvements in new edifices, and in re-
building and enlarging their former school-houses, as well

as in carrying out several of the plans of former sessions for the establishment of primary schools, of the high school, and of adding to the number of efficient teachers in the large grammar schools. The aggregate amount of expenditure appears very large, but, when duly analyzed and applied to its distinct objects, presents a result at once striking and satisfactory. Whilst by far the greatest portion has been invested in valuable lots and well-finished and enduring buildings, the residue will be found to have sufficed for the instruction of at least SEVENTEEN THOUSAND pupils throughout the whole year, at an average cost, including books, stationery, fuel, &c. of 4 dollars and 75 cents per scholar, or 1 dollar and $18\frac{3}{4}$ cents per quarter."

Seventeen thousand pupils is an increase of five thousand upon the preceding year. It should also be mentioned that there are fourteen schools under the charge of the Friends, called Corporation Schools, under the charter granted by William Penn in the year 1687 ; these contained, in April 1837, about six hundred children, and there were three or four hundred more in other schools under the care of the same religious body.

"The entire number of primary schools contemplated by the controllers has now been established, amounting to sixty, and containing, it is believed, nearly six thousand scholars. The wise policy of this measure continues to manifest itself; and the effects produced by it, not only in gathering up those infants and very young children who would otherwise receive no instruction, but in relieving the larger schools from pupils who have hitherto only embarrassed the teachers and the more advanced learners, are striking, and have been noticed with special approbation by the committees of our legislature at their recent visit."

The controllers go on to state that the corner-stone of the new high school was laid in September last; that they expect it to be opened and organized during the present summer; and that there will be added to it an astronomical observatory, with a very superior collection of instruments. "The conduct and condition of several of the schools," they remark, "has been essentially changed by the employment of additional teachers at suitable rates of compensation; and, although the expenses of some are considerably increased thereby, there is reason to believe that the advantage gained in higher and more general instruction to the whole of the pupils is more than commensurate with the advanced charge."

" At the commencement of the monitorial system here, it will be remembered that one teacher, aided by monitors from amongst his own pupils, was considered sufficient for the care, and government and instruction, of three hundred children. The fullest experience has induced the controllers to question the efficiency of this arrangement, which they think cannot be defended on any but narrow and parsimonious views. Wherever a crowded school existed under that organization, it was found that a very large portion of the scholars rarely or never received direct instruction from the master himself, but was thrown entirely under the care of juvenile monitors, often incompetent, and always indifferent, to the improvement of their fellows. The effort now made is to furnish, even at considerable increase of pay, an adequate number of well-qualified teachers to a suitable proportion of scholars, so as to secure to each child a due share of instruction from its teacher, and also, by mingling male and female teachers in every school, to obtain the peculiar benefits to be derived from the presence and influence of females in every school, male or female. As to the result of this experiment, and the expediency of making it general, the controllers reserve a positive opinion until time and practice warrant its expression. A constant endeavour is also made to keep pace with improvements in teaching, in different branches to be introduced, and in the adoption of the best books as they appear; always keeping in view that the utmost that can be hoped for is to furnish to the pupils in these schools the foundation of a plain substantial English education, and to those only who can devote future years to it, the complete course of instruction which the board hopes to accomplish by the due organization of the high school."

The directors do well to reserve for the present the expression of " a positive opinion" as to the result of their experiment; for it is clear that an increase in the

number of adult assistants will effect but little, unless
this be accompanied by a sounder method of teaching.
That some improvement in this respect is much needed,
I can myself affirm from what came under my own observation in the spring of 1837. If the style and manner
of reading may be taken as any test of general intelligence, the public schools of Philadelphia must be placed
in a very low grade : in very few of the spelling drafts
were any questions asked as to the meaning of the words ;
and of all the children it might be remarked, that they
wanted that briskness and animation, which are infallibly
found where a system of interrogation has been fully and
thoroughly adopted. If this delightful method were
more efficiently practised, we should then hear but little
of the defects of the monitorial system ; the elder boys
would then be *qualified* to instruct the younger ones ; and
that they are not *now* qualified to do it is a decisive proof
that they have not been well taught themselves. The
monitorial system, in fact, has never had a fair trial in
America. The peculiar circumstances in which it was
introduced were such as to create a prejudice against it ;
the genius of the national institutions is decidedly unfavourable to it ; and they who have adhered to it have
not united with it those later improvements with which it
is now uniformly associated in the best British schools in
this country, and without which some of its peculiar advantages must in a great measure be lost. If, in short,
the conductors of the public schools in Philadelphia
would make them what they may and ought to be, they
must do much more than what they have as yet attempted ; they must not content themselves with sending
a deputation of their own body to New York and Boston,
and then assimilating their own schools to the " enviable
models " of those great cities : they must take a far bolder
flight ; they must depute some man of education and
intelligence to cross the Atlantic, and make himself intimately acquainted with the far superior " models " which
are to be found in England, in Scotland, in Holland, and
in Prussia. This is what the governors of the Girard
College have done in reference to that noble institution ;
and, till the same thing is done with special reference to

the public schools, they cannot be expected to make
any material advance beyond their present imperfect
state. Their external arrangements may be good, but
the method on which they are taught is essentially defective; and, till this is reformed, the real ends of instruction will be but partially attained.*

It is perhaps only an act of justice to add, that, of the
schools which I examined in Philadelphia, the best were
the infant department of what is *called* the Model School
in Chester Street, and the South-Eastern Girls' School.
There was also a very active and intelligent master in
the boys' school in Third Street, above Brown; and I was
glad to see there a good library of eight hundred volumes
and a small mineralogical cabinet, and to learn that there
is connected with the school a lyceum, which meets for
lectures and mutual improvement once a week. The
master of this school is very strict in enforcing regular
attendance; the want of this is one great evil against
which the teachers have to contend. When I spoke
to one of them of the advantage which would result
from the training of monitors, he replied that he could
do nothing with so *fluctuating* a set of boys as he had.
There is, he assured me, no dependence to be placed on
the attendance of any child for any length of time: the
mothers want the girls at home; and, after attending for a
few months in the winter, many of the boys go off to brick-
making, hat-making, or any other trade by which they
can earn a dollar and a half a week in the summer time.
This, along with the unreasonable prejudice of the pa-

---

* On the recommendation of the superintendent, there have been
printed, at the expense of the State of Pennsylvania, three thousand
copies (two thousand in English and one thousand in German) of " A
Report on Elementary Instruction in Europe, made to the Thirty-sixth
General Assembly of the State of Ohio on the 19th of Dec. 1837 ; by
C. E. Stowe." This Report contains much interesting and useful information, chiefly relating to Russia and Prussia ; but more good would
perhaps have been done by reprinting and distributing " Mr J. Wood's
Account of the Edinburgh Sessional Schools ;" or the " Lessons on
Objects, as given at a Pestalozzian school at Cheam in Surrey." The
former of these works has indeed been reprinted at Boston, but I have
reason to believe that neither of them is as much known and appreciated
in the United States as they deserve.

rents, must be allowed to be a serious obstacle to the success of the monitorial system; and another obstacle exists in the intractable spirit generated by republican institutions. From what I saw of the children in the United States, I do not believe it would be *practicable* to get a set of monitors to work over-hours, as I have seen them work in England: they would not submit to the drudgery; consequently they and their country lose the benefit to be derived from it. There can be no doubt, however, that much more might be done, than what has yet been attempted, to overcome these difficulties.

I cannot conclude this paper without suggesting that the cultivation of vocal music would be a most desirable improvement in the common schools of the United States. During the twelve months that I was in America, I spent many hours and days in inspecting public schools, not only in the three great States of whose institutions for education I have now endeavoured to give some account, but in others through which I passed; and in none did I ever hear the voice of song,—the female academy at Albany, and one infant school at New York not properly forming an exception to the remark. They who are familiar with some of our best schools for the labouring classes in London (to say nothing of the Continent), need not be informed how much the cultivation of this taste tends to promote cheerfulness and good manners, how greatly the children enjoy the exercise, and how favourable an influence it appears likely to have on the future character. From the following passage, which appears in the Sixth Report of the American Lyceum (for 1836), it appears that a society has been formed with this object in New York; and it is much to be wished that its laudable efforts may meet with the general enouragement which they deserve :—

" Actual experiment has proved in School No. 10, under the gratuitous tuition of an agent of a society established for the general cultivation of music, that one hour's instruction in a week is sufficient to make children practically acquainted with the rudiments, and to sing a number of rather difficult tunes with taste and effect. The good influence produced upon the pupils has been acknowledged by both the teachers and the trustees of those schools.   The exercise is generally highly popular among the children, and promotes order, obedience, good manners, and activity in study.   A youth who had long been indolent and ill-behaved, probably in part owing to disadvantages at home, was animated by the introduction of music, for which he was naturally well prepared, so that his manners became improved, and he was soon found advanced from a low class to the highest. In many instances, and in different schools, the same branch of instruction has been found to afford encouragement to the awkward and the backward, like a kind of balance-wheel in the machine."

S. WOOD.

August, 1838.

THE EDUCATION OF PAUPER CHILDREN IN UNION WORKHOUSES.

THERE are now upwards of forty-five thousand orphan children in England permanently chargeable, who can have no education but what they receive in the school of a workhouse. It is therefore a matter of importance to consider what is the education which they receive?— what is that which they ought to receive?

In country districts the guardians regard this subject sometimes as a matter of indifference, at others they express a dissatisfaction and jealousy at any proposition which has a tendency to improve the education of these poor children. They consider the children as so many paupers whom it is sufficient to feed and clothe, so as to keep them alive; but, as to learning, the question is, " *What business have they to do with learning?* " And when an effective system of education is proposed, they become timid, and are afraid of the paupers knowing more than themselves.

The consequence has been, that in many workhouses great difficulty has been experienced in persuading the guardians to do more than appoint some superannuated pauper to drill into the children, by the means of a cane, a little reading and writing. Upon the head of industrial training they are, however, more open to conviction; but, even with regard to this, there is a difficulty in persuading them to act with efficiency. Confined within the walls of the workhouse, where such a spirit reigns, it is difficult to conceive anything more joyless and miserable than the life of these poor creatures. Surrounded by nothing which can elicit a spark of intelligence, it would be expected that their countenances should be characterized by vacancy, or passion; and such is the case. At Marylebone, about two years ago, the writer of these pages saw a lad of fifteen years of age, who had never but once

been out of the house from the time of his birth; he was
well grown, but, as may be easily supposed, deficient in
intelligence. It is not more than two years ago since the
children were taken out of the workhouse for a walk for
the first time; and a person who saw them (and who has
been greatly instrumental in introducing an improved treatment of the children in that workhouse) stated that it was
a most affecting sight to witness the delight and surprise
with which they first beheld the green fields near Primrose Hill. They rolled upon the grass, and appeared incapable of being satiated, so great was their joy. The poor
fellow before alluded to fell into every drain and ditch;
he had never before experienced such holes in the earth,
and a jump or a long step were motions unknown to him,
for he had never walked upon anything but the flags of
the Workhouse.

Some of the assistant commissioners have not been
idle in endeavouring to cure this state of things. They
have viewed the subject in the right light; and have
thought it their duty to strive that the poor children
should be brought up, not as paupers, *but in a manner to
prevent them from remaining so.*

In the country districts one great difficulty has been
experienced from the circumstance of there not being in
any one Union children enough to enable the commissioner to press for a salary sufficiently high to secure a
superior master; so that it becomes necessary, on economical as well as on other grounds, that the children should
be taken out of the workhouses of three or four Unions,
and educated in a school apart. Endeavours have been
made to effect this; but it has been impossible to persuade the guardians anywhere to consent to this measure,
although they would be the pecuniary gainers by it.

But, notwithstanding these impediments to a general
adoption of a good system, several schools have been
founded under the auspices of the Poor Law Commissioners which are well deserving of attention, as being
the best for the labouring classes known to us in this
country. The first of these is but a few miles distant from
London,—at Norwood. It is a school at which children
are received at a stipulated annual sum by Mr. Aubin

from the different London workhouses. It is five or six years since the writer first visited this establishment; there were then a large number of children there, whose sole employment was the sorting hair for brushmakers. They were taught a little reading and writing; and there was a court into which they might run out, or get cold, as they pleased. Mr. Aubin, however, is a benevolent person and ready to adopt any improvement pointed out to him. A gentleman who accompanied the writer to the school suggested how much the condition of the children might be improved by the introduction of an infant school; and an infant school was established by Mr. Aubin shortly afterwards.

When Dr. Kay became commissioner of the London District, the school at Norwood immediately attracted his attention, and the changes in that establishment are probably the result of his intercourse with Mr. Aubin. Such masters as Dr. Kay suggested were engaged; arrangements were made for industrial training; provision was made to secure the happiness and well-being of the poor children in every point of view; and an education was prepared calculated to send them out into the world, not paupers, but active, intelligent, and good members of society. Four masters from Scotland have been obtained. A tall mast, rigged in due form, which cost 160*l.* has been planted in the play-ground, for the purpose of training children as sailors.

Near it is a gymnastic apparatus for the younger boys.

Around the yards are carpenters', blacksmiths', whitesmiths', tailors', shoemakers' shops; in all of which little hands are busily at work, tasking their skill and ingenuity.

There are to be gardens also.

The girls are taught washing and ironing.

The intellectual instruction is of a high character; and the writer knows of no school for the poor, whether out of London or in it, that is so efficient.

The children sing both hymns and songs; and this not in a loud monotonous manner, which is generally the case, but with some feeling and a variation of intonation. This singing in a poor school is a cheering thing. The faces of the poor orphans brighten up as though all was not so cheerless to them, and there was hope for them beyond its walls. There was one exercise which particularly pleased us. The master gave them a lecture upon the properties of some object; and, when he had done so, he bade them get their slates, and write down what he had told them. Some of these compositions were by no means discreditable.

Dr. Kay, whose mind appears to have been actively engaged upon the subject of appropriate education of the working classes, and giving an industrial character to all instruction, has had some maps prepared for teaching geography. These are, however, industrial maps; on which are designated the places at which important trades and manufactures are carried on. The particulars of these the boys will be made acquainted with; so that, in after-life, they may know to what points they must direct their steps for the purpose of obtaining labour of the character which suits their genius and habits. Other maps are, I understand, in preparation,—for instance, of the healthy colonies,—accurate accounts of which, and the prospect of success there, will be pointed out.

But, beyond labour and study, these poor children *play;* and Mr. Aubin has been at some expense to afford them the means of doing so, and it is found to operate beneficially.

The religious instruction and religious exercises occupy a due portion of the day; and are not likely to leave the less impression from the circumstance of the children being made happy in the first instance.

The other school which we have visited is in the country, in Kent, where Mr. Tufnell is the assistant commissioner. The system is, for the most part, the same as at Norwood, but on a much smaller scale, there not being more than seventy or eighty children, while at Norwood there are eleven hundred.

There is, however, a Scotch master, who teaches so as to excite interest; and there are workshops for the boys, but not so efficient as they might be if three or four Unions were joined together. Among the employments at this workhouse there was one peculiarly appropriate to the country. In order that some of the children may learn to be grooms, a number have to clean the horses, bridles, saddles, and carriages of the guardians. This they do very well; and we heard, but do not say how true it may be, that with a good many of the guardians the board-day is the only day in the week on which their bridles and saddles are cleaned at all. But be this as it may, however rusty a bridle may come into the workhouse stable, it is bright enough when it leaves it.

Mental arithmetic is taught in this as well as the school at Norwood. The children do not perform the feats exhibited in the Borough Road School; but the following are some of the questions which they answered :—

49 articles at 4*d*.
50 articles at $3\frac{1}{4}d$.
100 articles at $4\frac{3}{4}d$.
$\frac{9}{10}$ths of 30.
13 articles at 3*d*.
37 articles at $4\frac{1}{2}d$.

It may be asked what has been the effect of this education upon the children. The head-master of Norwood states that the children are as ready to labour in the workshops as to play ; that they like work; and that, from the circumstance of having worked, they also like to learn ; that, when he first came, thieving of money, knives, handkerchiefs, &c. was ever occurring; but that now, whatever is lost is found again ; that the children used to run away continually, but that the change of system has now taken away the desire of doing so; that the children get places soon, people being willing to take them as apprentices, whereas, at another school close by, the children hang on hand for several years longer.

The following are extracts from the reports made to the Central Board by Assistant Poor Law Commissioners in different parts of the country.—The first is taken from Dr. Kay's, which, from the able manner in which he has dealt with the subject, is deserving of particular attention :—

" The pauper children maintained in Union workhouses are dependent, not as a consequence of their errors, but of their misfortunes.

They have not necessarily contracted any of the taint of pauperism. They are orphans, or deserted children, or bastards, or children of idiots, or of cripples or felons ; or they are resident in the workhouse with their parents, who seek a brief refuge there.

" The dependence of certain of these classes of children cannot be transient. The care of their natural guardians is at an end, or is suspended for so considerable a period, that the children have claims on the Board of guardians, not for food and clothing merely, but for that moral sustenance which may enable them, at the earliest period, to attain independence.

" The physical condition of the children who are deprived of the care of natural guardians ought not to be elevated above that of the household of the self-supported labourer. Their clothes, food, and lodging should not be better than that which the labourer can provide for his child. But, whenever the community encounter the responsibility of providing for the education of children who have no natural guardians, it is impossible to adopt as a standard for the training of such children the average amount of care and skill now bestowed on the moral and religious culture of the children of the labouring classes generally, or to decide that their secular instruction shall be confined within limits confessedly so meagre and inadequate. The privation of such agencies cannot be proposed as a means of preventing undue reliance on the provision created by the law ; but, on the contrary, education is to be regarded as one of the most important means of eradicating the germs of pauperism from the rising generation, and of securing in the minds and in the morals of the people the best protection for the institutions of society.

" The dependence of the majority of the pauper children is unavoidable and absolute. The burthen of their dependence cannot cease, even temporarily, unless the children be reared in industry. The consequences of a neglect of training in the old workhouses may be ascertained by such inquiries as were conducted by Mr. Hickson in the gaols, at the request of the Poor Law Commissioners, when he found that crime had recruited its ranks, to a large extent, from the workhouses under former management. Whether the state acknowledge its interest in the education of the masses or not, the consequences, of a neglect of the pauper class evidently were, prolonged dependence, and subsequent chargeability as criminals in the prisons and penal colonies.

" The State is *in loco parentis* to the pauper children who have no natural guardians, and the interest it has in the right discharge of its responsibilities may be illustrated by supposing the government had determined to require direct, instead of indirect service, in return for education. If the army and navy were recruited by the workhouse children, it is evident that it would be the interest of the state to rear a race of hardy and intelligent men—instructed in the duties of their station—taught to fear God and honour the Queen. The state has not less interest, though it may be less apparent, in supplying the merchant service with sailors, and the farms and the manufactories of the country with workmen, and the households of the upper and middle classes with domestic servants : it has the most positive and direct interest in adopting measures to prevent the rearing of a race of prostitutes and felons.

" The workhouses of thirty-five Unions in Norfolk and Suffolk are now completed, and are in full operation. These Unions contain five hundred and thirty-seven thousand and twenty-seven inhabitants, or about one twenty-sixth part of the population of England and Wales. In the week ending 9th December 1837, the workhouses of these Unions contained—

" Youths from 9 to 16	. .	483
Girls from 9 to 16	. .	420
Boys from 2 to 9	. .	547
Girls from 2 to 9	. .	456
		1906

or one thousand nine hundred and six children, from two to sixteen, were in that week maintained and educated in thirty-five Union workhouses now in operation in Norfolk and Suffolk.

" The questions presented for the consideration of the Poor Law Commissioners are —

" 1. What number of children maintained in the Union workhouses will remain there during periods which will render them chiefly, if not solely, dependent on Boards of guardians for education.?

" 2. How far would the absence of a well-devised system of education for these classes of children tend to increase the extent of hereditary pauperism, and what would be the consequent pecuniary burthen? and—

" 3. What means can be legitimately adopted to train these children in such a way as to render their future dependence on the rate-payers improbable?

" The children of able-bodied labourers are resident for short periods only in the Union workhouses, and their temporary dependence on the care of the Boards of guardians does not entail upon those bodies so serious a responsibility as arises when a child has no natural guardians, or when its natural guardians are prevented from performing their duties by physical and legal disabilities. In such cases the child is dependent on the Board of guardians for more than maintenance : it must be trained in industry, in correct moral habits, and in religion ; and must be fitted to discharge the duties of its station in life.

" Perceiving that a very large proportion of the children maintained in workhouses, were not protected by natural guardians, or could not receive effectual protection from them, I was anxious to ascertain their exact number, and for this purpose I issued a circular to the masters of workhouses throughout Norfolk and Suffolk ; in which I inquired, 1st, What number of bastards, orphans, children deserted by their father, children deserted by their father and mother, children of men undergoing punishment for crime, children of persons dependent on parochial aid on account of mental or bodily infirmity, was resident in each workhouse. These children will evidently owe the greater part, if not the whole, of their training in industry and religion to the care of the Board of guardians, on account of the loss of their parents, or their inability to perform their natural duties. I also inquired, 2nd, What number of children of able-bodied widows, of able-bodied widowers, and what number of children belonging to large families of able-bodied labourers admitted into the workhouse as relief to their parents, were resident in the workhouses. These latter classes are likely to remain in the workhouses longer than a third class, viz. the children of able-bodied parents who seek a temporary asylum there with their families, but whose dependence is generally transient. In the two former groups of classes, the children will be mainly, if not entirely, dependent for their training on the guardians, or they will remain so long dependent as to render their education a subject of great importance, when considered only in relation to its probable effects on the amount of pauperism, which has formerly been directly reproduced from such sources, and which would probably be perpetuated without such care.

" The results of my inquiries in Norfolk and Suffolk are contained in the following table, which exhibits the number of children, from two to sixteen, resident in the Union workhouses in the week ending 9th December, in each of the classes likely to be dependent on the Boards of guardians until they are fitted by their education to earn their own livelihood. Besides the children enumerated in this table, the workhouses contained in the same week fifty-nine children of able-bodied parents, who were also resident in the workhouses, and two hundred and fifty-nine infants too young for instruction.

" Bastards	543
Orphans . . . . : . . .	382
Children deserted by the father	279
Children deserted by father and mother . . .	54
Children of men undergoing punishment for crime .	171
Children of persons dependent on parochial aid on account of mental or bodily infirmity . . .	116
Children of able-bodied widows resident in the Union workhouse	144
Children of able-bodied widowers resident in the Union workhouse	36
Children belonging to large families of able-bodied labourers, admitted into the workhouse as relief to their parents	122
Total . . .	1847

" It is difficult to perceive how the dependence of the orphan, bastard, and deserted children, and the children of idiots, helpless cripples, and of widows relieved in the Union workhouses, could cease, if no exertion were made to prepare them to earn their livelihood by skilful labour, and to fit them to discharge their social duties by training them in correct moral habits, and giving them knowledge suited to their station in life.

" It may be important to consider what is the usual training of an agricultural labourer's child under his father's roof, and in what respects it may be proper to imitate that training in educating those children who are necessarily maintained in workhouses.

" The child of a labourer reared beneath its parent's roof is trained to labour. At a very early period the lad follows his father a-field—he rides the horse home or to water—he is employed to scare the crows from the recently sown corn. By-and-by he assists his father when threshing in the barn—he drives the plough-team. At hay-time the whole family, both boys and girls, find constant work ; at harvest they are very early employed in gleaning ; at seed-time they work, at a very tender age, at wheat-dropping.

" The boys gradually become thus initiated in the duties of husbandry, until, by assisting more or less in ploughing, harrowing, threshing, milking, and the charge of horses, they take their station in some department of husbandry, commonly first as team-men ; and afterwards are gradually employed in those departments of labour requiring greater skill, and implying more confidence in their integrity and industry.

" This is the industrial training of a labourer's boy, when resident under his father's roof.

" The girls do much work a-field. I have already alluded to their services in the corn and hay harvest, and at wheat-setting. They are also employed in carrying their fathers' provisions to the field—in stone-gathering—in hoeing—in turnip-topping, and other agricultural work, which is not deemed too laborious to be performed by a female in the rural districts. In the labourer's own household (the more appropriate scene of female exertion and care) the girls learn to scour the floors, to wash the linen, to sew and knit, and to clean the few utensils which their father may possess ; to assist their mother in baking or in cooking their frugal meal, or in nursing a younger child. The girls thus acquire a knowledge of domestic duties, and become fitted (too frequently, it is to be feared, not so fully as could be wished) to perform the domestic duties, and to encounter the domestic cares of a labourer's household.

" Little can be said respecting the training which the children of labourers receive in useful learning suited to their station in life ; because few schools exist in the rural districts, and the instruction in many of those which do exist is meagre.

" Neither can it be said that the religious instruction of the labourer's family is always satisfactorily promoted by the existence of customs such as prevail in the household of the Scottish peasantry ; but the domestic and social sympathies are awakened and cherished by mingling with their father's family, and associating with their neighbours.

" But if an orphan, bastard, or deserted child, or the child of an idiot, helpless cripple, or felon, or of a widow, be maintained in the Union workhouse from the age of three to the age of fourteen, the age when he ought to go to work, one of two results must ensue —

1. Either the child must at that period have acquired such habits of industry, such skill in some useful art, and such correct moral habits, as to render his services desirable ; in which case he will go to service, and his dependence will cease :

" Or, 2ndly, by neglect, or by the adoption of a system of training not calculated to prepare them for the discharge of the practical duties of their station in life, the pauper children maintained in workhouses are not *qualified for service*, and then it becomes necessary to adopt the old expedient for the removal of the burthen created by the absence of a correct system of moral and industrial training ; viz. *to apprentice the children* to a trade or calling, by paying a premium to some artisan to instruct them in an art by which they may earn their subsistence.

" The payment of premiums for apprenticeship has been shown to be a system having many most pernicious tendencies, and which has altogether failed to promote the well-being of the children for whose benefit this expedient was adopted. That it should have proved inefficacious cannot be a legitimate subject of surprise, when, apart from all other sources of failure, it is borne in mind, that a child apprenticed from a workhouse under the former system had been brought up in listless idleness, or useless and inappropriate work, to which it was subjected as a task ; and that it was in constant association with all the vicious adult males and females congregated within the workhouse of the incorporation or parish, without any means being used to teach it how to earn its livelihood, or to rear it in the habit of performing its duties.

" It will be deemed a moderate computation if I suppose, that, out of the one thousand eight hundred and forty-seven children more permanently supported in the workhouses of Norfolk and Suffolk, one hundred and eighty would have to be annually apprenticed, if the children were not prepared for the discharge of their duties in after-life by careful training. In the Samford hundred alone, containing only eleven thousand inhabitants, thirty-three children were apprenticed annually for a series of sixteen years, at an average premium of about 10l. each. If, therefore, one hundred and eighty children were apprenticed from the present workhouses of Norfolk and Suffolk every year, four thousand three hundred and fifty-six, or, in round numbers, four thousand three hundred children would have to be apprenticed annually in England and Wales, at an expense of 43,000l. per annum, provided means cannot be adopted for training the children educated in workhouses in such a manner as to avoid any necessity for having recourse to the system of apprenticeship in future. This expense could only be regarded as the final expense attending a neglect of the industrial and moral training of the children, upon the assumption that the future dependence of these children would be *averted* by their apprenticeship ; a consequence which is contrary to all previously ascertained facts. Even if this preliminary expense were incurred, and the apprenticeship of the children were conducted with much greater care and skill than it formerly was, under the management of parishes or incorporations, a large number of the children whose training had been neglected up to the period of their apprenticeship, would be found so ignorant, idle, and vicious, that the efforts of the best master would be vainly exerted for their reformation, and they would sooner or later become a disgrace and burthen to the country, either in its gaols or in its workhouses.

" It is found in the schools of the Children's Friend Society at Hackney Wick and Chiswick, that the reformation of the vagabond children trained there is extremely difficult, if not impossible, when they are admitted after the age of twelve. The success of the apprentice's master would probably be less when he received a child from a workhouse, where no care had been taken to form habits of industry and good conduct, and where the instruction of the children in knowledge suited to their station in life, and in religion, had been neglected.

" The number of children maintained and educated in the workhouses of Norfolk and Suffolk is greatly less than in some other parts of England. Thus I am aware that the workhouse-schools in the county of

Kent contain a much greater number of children in proportion to the population, whereas probably in the north of England a smaller number of children might be found to be dependent on the rate-payers.

" If the children maintained in the workhouses of the rest of England be admitted to bear the same proportion to the population as in Norfolk and Suffolk, the workhouses of England would contain forty-six thousand one hundred and twenty-five children between the ages of two and sixteen, and forty-four thousand six hundred and ninety-seven children between the ages of two and sixteen who are longer resident in the workhouses.

" If the want of classification, and the absence of correct discipline, which prevailed in the old workhouses, continued in the new, a great number of these latter children would acquire the habits of hereditary paupers, or even of felons, and (which would by no means be improbable) if *one-tenth of them only became dependent during six months of each year*, with families of the ordinary size, they would occasion a burthen of 104,574*l.* 12*s.* per annum.

" It is certainly impossible to exhibit the consequences of such neglect by direct statistical calculations, and a moralist would probably deprecate the adoption of such a method of appreciating the effects of this mismanagement, or, if he admitted it, would urge that a mass of hereditary paupers could not fail to prove a demoralizing leaven which would corrupt society, and, by its vicious influence, vastly increase the charge which the public would sustain in relieving the indigence of an enervated, vicious, or turbulent race, and in protecting society from their assaults.

" The commissioners will not be insensible to any consideration which could influence the mind of a moralist in estimating the effects of different systems of training on the probable future destiny of forty-four thousand six hundred and ninety-seven children ; but such considerations are so inseparably connected with that single object which the commissioners can legitimately propose to accomplish, viz. the cessation of the dependance of these children on the rate-payers at the earliest period, that means must necessarily be employed which would satisfy the moralist that all he can desire will be attained when these objects are fulfilled.   I, therefore, proceed to inquire what means can legitimately be adopted to train these children in such a way as to render their future dependence on the rate-payers improbable.

" In discussing this question it will be more convenient to consider—

" 1. Whether the general arrangements for the maintenance of children in workhouses could be improved, before deciding

" 2. What methods should be adopted respecting—

    " A. The industrial training of the children.

    B. The methods of instruction and moral discipline.

    C. The extent of secular instruction.

    D. Religious instruction.

" When these subjects have been considered in relation to a proposed improvement in the general management—

" 3. The applicability of these principles to existing arrangements in Union workhouses will be determined.

" The establishment of two county or district schools of industry in each of the counties of Norfolk and Suffolk appears to be rendered desirable by various important considerations.

" 1. The number of orphans and other children of the first class maintained in each Union workhouse throughout these counties is not sufficient to afford an opportunity for correct classification, so as to conduct the general and industrial instruction of the children on such a system and by such methods, in each workhouse-school, as to procure the largest amount of benefit from a careful training of the children. The children of able-bodied labourers, for the most part, are received into the workhouses with their parents, who seek only a temporary refuge there ; and their period of residence is so short, that the children rather disturb the routine of school arrangements adopted in the workhouses, than, by their numbers, increase the efficiency of the system adopted.

" The industrial training of the children who have no natural guardians, and who are therefore altogether dependent on the Board of guardians for instruction in the practical duties of life, is thus impaired by two circumstances, which would cease to exist provided such children were sent to a district school.

" The classification of the children separately from the adults (excepting their parents) is preserved with care in the workhouses of Norfolk and Suffolk, but cannot be rendered perfect in any workhouse as at present regulated.

" A child should not be degraded in his own estimation by being a member of a despised class. A child cannot be a pauper in the sense in which that term is commonly understood,—that is, he cannot be indigent as the consequence of his own want of industry, skill, frugality, or forethought ; and he ought not therefore to be taught to despise himself.

" The dependence of these children is probably the natural consequence of the crimes or follies (but it may also be of the misfortunes) of their parents ; and in any of these cases it is the interest of society that the children should neither inherit the infamy, nor the vice, nor the misfortunes of their parents.

" This stigma, and consequent loss of self-esteem, would be entirely removed if the children were taught at a district school, with other children, not received from the workhouses, nor the offspring of pauper parents.

" When the whole arrangements for the Unions of Norfolk and Suffolk are completed, those counties will contain thirty-nine Unions or incorporations, for the workhouses of which it will be necessary to provide efficient schoolmasters and schoolmistresses. I find it impossible to secure the services of schoolmasters from Scotland at a lower sum than 35*l*. or 40*l*. per annum, with a separate apartment and maintenance in the workhouse. The salary for a good schoolmistress is 20*l*. per annum, with a separate apartment and maintenance. Several Unions have consented to give 35*l*. per annum to their schoolmaster, and 20*l*. per annum to their schoolmistress, with separate apartments and maintenance. One or two Unions have agreed to higher salaries. Where the salaries are lower, the schoolmasters and schoolmistresses have never received any regular instruction in a correct system of training children ; and, though exertions have been made to improve their methods by sending them to better schools for short periods, or by sending well-trained teachers to their schools, these teachers are still very imperfectly acquainted with their duties.

" The salaries offered in the various Unions for the services of schoolmasters and schoolmistresses are often not sufficient to secure efficient instructors, and persons trained in the model-schools in the metropolis and in Scotland have some aversion to a residence in a workhouse.

" A combination of Unions for the support of a common school for the instruction of the children who have lost their natural guardians, would enable the Boards to provide the most efficient schoolmasters and schoolmistresses, and, at the same time, to reduce their annual expenditure. The objections entertained by duly qualified teachers to a residence in the workhouse would not exist with respect to a central school separate from all the workhouses.

" In thirty-nine workhouses the cost of this arrangement may be thus estimated :—

" Lowest salaries at which the efficiency of the schools of thirty-nine workhouses could be maintained.

	£.	s.	d.
" Schoolmasters, 35*l.* per annum each .	1365	0	0
Schoolmistresses, 20*l.* per annum each .	780	0	0
Maintenance of schoolmasters, at 8*s.* per week, 20*l.* 16*s.* per annum	811	4	0
Maintenance of schoolmistresses, ditto, ditto	811	4	0
	£3767	8	0

" Besides this outlay, a pauper shoemaker and tailor, employed in assisting the schoolmaster, are generally maintained in each workhouse, at an outlay of 3*s.* or 4*s.* per week each, or 7*l.* 16*s.* per annum each, which, in thirty-nine workhouses, would amount to an outlay of 608*l.* 8*s.* or 811*l.* 4*s.*

" In each of these thirty-nine Unions at least 80*l.* must also be expended in Bibles, Testaments, Prayer-books, catechisms, lesson-books, apparatus in gardening, and carpenters' tools, shoemakers' and tailors' implements, &c. and in fitting up a separate wash-house and laundry for the girls. As the lowest sum, an outlay of 3120*l.* must thus be incurred, and 20*l.* would have to be expended in fitting up the apartments of schoolmaster and schoolmistress ; making a total outlay of 4000*l.* Many considerable advantages as respects discipline would be secured by assembling the children, now more permanently maintained in the thirty-nine workhouses, in four district schools, which should each contain four hundred or five hundred children.

" These four schools might be provided with the most efficient schoolmasters and schoolmistresses, &c. for the following annual outlay for salaries, and abundant maintenance :—

" Four schools containing four hundred or five hundred children each

		£.
" Four principal schoolmasters, } Four principal schoolmistresses, } salaries 100*l.* . . .		400
Maintenance, 10*s.* per week each		208
Four assistant schoolmasters, } Four assistant schoolmistresses, } salaries 60*l.* . . .		240
Maintenance, 10*s.* per week each		208
Four tailors' wages, 10*s.* per week, } Maintenance, 5*s.* . . ditto }		156
Four shoemakers' ditto, ditto		156
Four laundresses, 15*l.* per annum wages		60
Maintenance, 5*s.* per week		52

£1480

Four chaplains, 100*l.* per annum 400

£1880

" A clear saving of 2000*l.* per annum in the salaries and maintenance of officers would be thus accomplished in thirty-nine Unions, and the Boards of guardians would be enabled to obtain efficient schoolmasters and schoolmistresses by affording sufficient salaries and more liberal maintenance and accommodation.

" If such Unions as, upon a careful estimate, are likely to supply to a district school four hundred children of the classes who have lost the guardianship of their parents were united for the purpose of maintaining such an establishment, it ought to be so conducted as to insure the cessation of the dependence of the children trained there at the earliest period.

" Having been impressed with the importance of considering the principles on which such an establishment should be conducted, the commissioners are aware that my colleague, Mr. Tufnell, and myself visited Scotland for the purpose of inspecting the Sessional School, conducted by Mr. Wood, in Edinburgh, and the model schools of the Glasgow Normal Seminary. The commissioners are also aware that we have visited various industrial schools in quest of similar information, particularly the schools of the Children's Friend Society at Hackney Wick, and at the Victoria Asylum, Chiswick, and Lady Noel Byron's school at Ealing, &c. More recently I have had an opportunity of inspecting the principal schools of Holland and Belgium.

" The attention which my duties have required me to give to the improvement of the methods of instruction pursued in the schools of Union workhouses, and the necessity of placing clearly before myself the principles on which the schools should be regulated, induced me to prepare a slight sketch of a school, which I submit to the commissioners as the result of inquiries and observations respecting plans pursued in the schools previously alluded to, but into which I have carefully avoided the introduction of any plan which has not been thus tested by experience.

" The object which can be most legitimately proposed as a ground for the interference of the Poor Law Commissioners in the training of children maintained and educated in the workhouses is the effect which such training must have in the formation of habits of industry, and thus enabling them in after-life to support themselves by the labour of their hands.

" A. I therefore propose to consider, in the first place, what methods should be adopted for the *industrial training* of the children.

" The great object to be kept in view in regulating any school for the instruction of the children of the labouring class, is the rearing of hardy and intelligent working men, whose character and habits shall afford the largest amount of security to the property and order of the community. Not only has the training of the children of labourers hitherto been defective, both in the methods of instruction pursued, and because it has been confined within the most meagre limits, but because it has failed to inculcate the great practical lesson for those whose sole dependence for their living is on the labour of their hands by early habituating them to patient and skilful industry.

" An orphan or deserted child, educated from infancy to the age of twelve or fourteen in a workhouse, if taught reading, writing, and arithmetic only, is generally unfitted for earning his livelihood by labour. Under such a system he would never have been set to work. He would therefore have acquired no skill ; he would be effeminate, and, what is worse, the great practical lesson in patient and skilful industry, which he would have acquired had he been so fortunate as to live beneath the roof of a frugal and industrious father, would be wanting.

" In mingling various kinds of industrial instruction with the plan of training pursued in the model school, it is not proposed to prepare the children for some particular trade or art, so as to supersede the necessity for further instruction ; it is chiefly intended that the practical lesson, that they are destined to earn their livelihood by the sweat of their brow, shall be inculcated ; to teach them the use of various tools, so that they may be enabled to increase the comfort of their own households by the skill which they have acquired, or to obtain a greater reward for their labour by superior usefulness.

" The district school should be surrounded by a garden of six, eight, or ten acres, in which the system of instruction in gardening adopted in Lady Byron's school at Ealing, in conformity with the plans pursued in De Fellenburg's establishment at Hofwyl, in the school of the Children's Friend Society at Hackney Wick, and also by the Earl of Lovelace, Mr. Allen, and others, ought to be pursued. The schoolmaster should, at the appointed hours, accompany the boys into the garden, and superintend their instruction in digging, hoeing, planting, and careful gardening. They will thus be initiated in employment closely resembling rural labour, which, if it were only followed by the useful result of enabling them in after-life to cultivate their cottage allotment with greater skill, would be a desirable acquisition. The schoolmaster should be provided with some simple elementary works on gardening, from which some of the oldest boys should read extracts daily to the school ; after which the master should ask such questions, and make such comments. as he may deem desirable, to awaken and sustain the attention of the children.

" The plans pursued at Ealing Grove would require considerable modification in a school containing pauper children. It would not be possible to afford the stimulus of wages for labour on land not allotted to the children, nor could the profits of the allotments be given to children maintained at the expense of the rate-payers in the county school ; but it would be desirable that the land should be divided into allotments among those boys who had acquired a certain amount of skill in gardening, and that a separate account should be kept for such allotment of the seeds and manure furnished and their value, and of the crops produced and their value ; and the accounts thus rendered should from time to time be examined and certified by the master, and compared before the school. When an orphan or deserted child was about to leave the school to go into service, the account of his labour in the garden and elsewhere should be carefully examined before certifying his diligence ; and the produce of his allotments and work might be considered in reference to the nature of the outfit granted him on leaving the establishment.

" The products of the children's labour would have a certain value. Thus, for example, the establishment would be altogether supplied with vegetables from the garden cultivated by the boys. It is therefore desirable, before proceeding further, to remark that the object of setting the children to work is, *not to make a profit of their labour, but to accustom them to patient application to such appropriate work as will be most likely to fit them for the discharge of the duties of that station which they will probably fill in after-life.* If the hope of profit from the labour of the children be not considered subordinate to the great object of enabling them to earn their livelihood by the employment of the surrounding district, or in assisting them to contribute to the comfort of their households by the exercise of their skill during periods of leisure, the establishment would necessarily fail as a means of promoting the independence of the children unavoidably chargeable to the rate-payers from the ordinary casualties of life.

" I now proceed to consider what other employment could be usefully taught the child of an agricultural labourer.

" Several of the workhouse schools are supplied with carpenters' tools and rough boards. The boys make their wheelbarrows, erect any small outhouses which may be required, fit up their toolhouses, make the desks, forms, and fit up the closets of the school, and do any other rough carpenters' work which may be required in the establishment. They are thus prepared to do any work of a similar description which might be required in ordinary farm service. A husbandman who could weatherboard a barn would be preferred by a farmer, and would probably obtain superior wages. The premises selected by the Children's Friend Society for their industrial school at Hackney Wick were, when first occupied, in an almost ruinous condition. The dilapidations have been repaired, the breaches have been filled up, the roofs restored, and the woodwork renewed almost solely by the labour of the boys. When I visited the school, they were engaged in erecting a new building. The children have thus acquired a knowledge of the way to make mortar, to set a brick, to saw and plane a piece of wood, to drive a nail in a workmanlike manner : all which skill cannot fail to be useful to them as farm-servants ; or in repairing dilapidations in their own cottages, or enabling them to make a bench to sit on, or a box to hold their clothes, or to put up a shelf. In a large establishment, coopers', cabinet, and other descriptions of woodwork, might be introduced.

" The guardians of certain of the rural Unions consider it desirable that the children should learn to make a hurdle, an osier or a 'frail' basket, or a net; and such arts may be taught by procuring the attendance of an artisan during a certain portion of the day, twice or thrice weekly, until the schoolmaster and the children have acquired sufficient skill to pursue their employment without such assistance.

" Some other employments might be taught with a view to enable the future agricultural labourer to contribute to the comfort of his household, without an expenditure of his earnings. Thus the whole of the boys' clothes of the establishment should be patched and mended by them ; and a certain portion of their clothes, at least, might be made by the boys, even if it were considered undesirable to rear any of them to the employment of a tailor. In the same way, the whole of the shoes worn in the house should be mended by the boys ; and, if it were considered desirable to train certain of the boys to earn their livelihood as shoemakers, perhaps a large portion, if not all the shoes used, might be made in the house. Neither of these trades should, however, be further pursued than, upon a careful consideration, may be thought desirable ; first, to train a few children as tailors or shoemakers,—or, secondly, to give the rest of the children sufficient skill to contribute to the comfort of their households without an expenditure of their earnings. The hope of profit ought not to induce the guardians to allow these employments to be pursued to the exclusion of others more appropriate to the future situation of an agricultural labourer.

" In the prison for the correction of juvenile offenders, which has, within the last two years, been established on an improved system by the Dutch government at Rotterdam, many of these employments are taught the children, who appear to have acquired considerable skill ; and this part of the moral discipline of the prison is considered eminently important, in combination with the religious instruction and the rest of the training adopted.

" The boys are also employed in the workhouses in plaiting straw hats, making straw mattresses, whitewashing the walls whenever necessary, in cleaning out their rooms, lighting the fires, &c. The domestic management of the house affords opportunities of instructing the boys in cleaning knives and forks, shoes, windows, &c. ; and, at the weekly meeting of the guardians, the oldest lads are most usefully employed in receiving and taking charge of the horses, when they are taught to wipe and clean the bridles and saddles, to take them off and put them on, to clean whatever gigs or chaises are in the coach-house, and afterwards to clean the stables, make up the bedding for other horses, &c. They are, on such occasions, required to manifest to the guardians habits of prompt attention, which the master is requested to inculcate.

" The employment adopted in similar establishments in the manufacturing districts would, of course, bear a relation to the trades of the neighbourhood, similar to that which the above-mentioned occupations have to the pursuits of an agricultural labourer. In seaports, the example of the Stepney Board of guardians, who have determined to form a maritime school for the training of children belonging to the parishes of Wapping, Shadwell, Limehouse, &c. is worthy of all imitation.

" The domestic management of the establishment will afford considerble facility for the industrial instruction of the girls. The whole of the domestic arrangements should be made subservient to the training of the girls in all the arts of household service. For this purpose they should be divided into classes, which should be successively employed, during such periods as may be found convenient, in every part of the household duty. Thus, one class of girls would be engaged in scouring the floors, lighting the fires, and making the beds in the several wards ; another class would be employed in the wash-house, where all clothes of the establishment should be washed ; a third class would, in rotation, work in the laundry ; and, among the officers of the establishment, it would be desirable to have a laundress to superintend the girls employed in washing, ironing, and making up the clothes of the establishment.

" A separate establishment for children would enable the commissioners to regulate the dietary in such a way as to assist the schoolmistress in affording the children valuable instruction in such frugal cookery as it would be desirable that the wife of a labouring man should know. Books treating on this subject should be provided for the use of the school, and the reading and explanation of them should form a part of its regular routine ; while the oldest girls should be employed, in rotation, in the kitchen, under the superintendence of the schoolmistress, in learning to cook such food as the wages of a labourer could ordinarily supply, in such a way as to ensure the most economical management of his means. The whole of the other duties of the kitchen and scullery should likewise be performed by the girls.

" A portion of every day would, of course, be devoted to the ordinary instruction in knitting and sewing ; but the children should likewise be taught to cut out and make their clothes.

" No part of service is of greater importance than a proper attendance on the sick ; and cases may occur in the school where the older girls may be employed, not to supersede, but to aid the proper nurses in attendance on the sick, under the direction of the medical officer.

" From time to time the girls might be occupied in weeding and hoeing in the garden, as a means of instructing them in the out-door employments of females in rural districts. They might also learn to wait upon the schoolmasters and schoolmistresses.

" The success which has attended the efforts of the Children's Friend Society to reclaim juvenile offenders, by the adoption of a similar system of industrial training in their establishments at the Brenton Asylum Hackney Wick, and the Victoria Asylum Chiswick, and of the directors of the Refuge for the Destitute in their institutions in Hackney Road and at Hoxton, would warrant the commissioners in requiring its adoption in a district school, or throughout the ordinary Union workhouses of England and Wales ; and, without such instruction, it is evident that, whatever other system of training is adopted, the education of the pauper children can afford no effectual guarantee for their future independent subsistance by the wages of industry.

" B. In proceeding to describe the methods of instruction and moral discipline which it might be desirable to pursue in a district school, no mention will be made of any plan which has not been subjected to the test of experience, and the utility of which has not been ascertained by personal observation.

" Every district orphan school should, like the Glasgow Normal Seminary, consist of—

" 1. An infant school ;

2. A juvenile school, comprising

A. An industrial school for boys ;

B. An industrial school for girls.

" For the attainment of the largest amount of benefit, it would be desirable that the child should have the advantage of the entire system of training proposed to be pursued,—first, in the infant, and next, in the juvenile and industrial classes ; though the prior instruction in the infant school is not absolutely necessary to the attainment of much of what the juvenile and industrial schools are calculated to convey, unassisted by the previous instruction of the infant school.

" Board of Management.

" If a district school were established on the foregoing principles, it would become necessary to construct a Board to superintend the management of the house and the training of the children. For this purpose two or three of the most intelligent guardians of each Union should be selected ; and it might be desirable to require in some districts, as a qualification for the important duties confided to the Board of the district school, that each member of that Board should have served one year at least as a guardian of his Union. It would probably be sufficient that the whole Board of management should meet monthly at the school, but rota of three or four members should attend weekly to superintend the execution of the directions left by the General Board of management, and to meet any emergencies which might arise.

" Children might be admitted into the school at the end of each month from the several workhouses of the district; and it should be required, wherever such a school was established, that no child of the classes enumerated as more permanently dependent on the rate-payers for maintenance and education, should reside longer than one month in the workhouse of the Union to which he belonged. It would thus be necessary that the master of each Union workhouse should, once every month, convey such children to the district school ; he would on that day attend the Board of management, and would receive from them a report concerning the progress made by the children of the Union to which he belonged, and especially enumerating those to whom the Board could grant certificates that their moral conduct, industry, and skill, warranted the Board in recommending them as prepared for domestic service.

" If it were necessary to purchase or hire land or buildings, or to erect a suitable house, the Board of management should be entrusted with the requisite authority, as well as to enter into contracts for supplies, and to direct contributions for the current expenditure.

" The Board should also be required to render full accounts quarterly to each Union of the whole expenditure incurred for establishment charges, and for the maintenance and clothing of each child respectively.

" The establishment expenses should be distributed as a common charge to the Unions, in the proportion of their averages, and the cost of the maintenance and clothing of each child should be carried to the account of its parish.

" Improvements have been introduced into the schools of workhouses :

" 1. By procuring teachers from various establishments for education. The Central National School, Westminster, the Borough Road School, the Edinburgh Sessional School, the Glasgow Normal Seminary, &c. have been resorted to for a supply of teachers, who have been procured with great difficulty. Some of these, and of the provincial teachers, have undergone further training in the processes of industrial instruction pursued at the Brenton Asylum Hackney Wick, at the Victoria Asylum Chiswick, and at Lady Noel Byron's school Ealing; which methods are also successfully adopted by the directors of the Refuge for the Destitute in their establishments at Hoxton and Hackney. The general acquirements and the knowledge of methods of instruction attained by the teachers trained in the Edinburgh and Glasgow model schools have occasioned numerous applications to be made for assistance from these establishments.

" 2. The employments of gardening, carpenters' work, tailoring, shoe-making, straw-plaiting, basket-making, or net-making, &c. &c. have been introduced into several of the workhouses for the instruction of the boys. The girls have been trained in knitting, sewing, scouring, bed-making, washing and ironing, straw-plaiting, and sometimes in cooking. The girls need a wash-house and laundry separate from that used by the adult females, with whom, for obvious reasons, association should be avoided. In the selection of persons qualified to instruct the children in the various handicrafts, the fullest inquiry should be made into the moral character of the candidates, and it is of great importance that they should be persons of cheerful dispositions and good temper.

" 3. Care has been taken to supply the schools with the Bible, the Testament, the Book of Common Prayer, the lesson-books of the national schools, of the Society for Promoting Christian Knowledge, of the Edinburgh Sessional School, &c. Some workhouse schools contain small libraries of religious and useful works, which are read with great interest by the children.

" 4. The schoolmaster and schoolmistress have been furnished with approved works on the art of teaching, describing the methods of instruction which have been most successfully adopted. Among the books have been comprised ' Wood's Account of the Edinburgh Sessional School,' ' Stow's Moral Training,' ' Abbott's Teacher,' ' Dunn's Normal School Manual,' ' Wilson's Manual of Instruction for Infant Schools,' ' Wilderspin's Infant System,' ' Chambers's Infant Education,' ' Brigham on the Influence of Mental Cultivation upon Health," ' Forss's Account of the Brenton Asylum Hackney Wick,' &c. books on gardening, frugal cookery, &c.

" 5. Suitable apparatus has been supplied to many of the schools.

" The small schools of the rural workhouses must, however, for some time remain defective in many important characteristics of a well-regulated school.

" It is desirable to exhibit continually to the Boards of guardians the great importance and honourable nature of the functions of a teacher. In order that the schoolmaster of the workhouse may be placed in his proper station in the household, he should be supplied with a separate apartment, comfortably furnished, and should be allowed to take his meals in private, or with the superior officers of the household. The visiting committee should not permit the time of the schoolmaster or schoolmistress to be expended on duties connected with the internal economy of the workhouse, it being desirable that their whole time and attention should be devoted to the school. Though the master of the workhouse is superior in authority in the household, he should remember that the schoolmaster or mistress ought on all occasions to be consulted concerning the domestic management of the children; and that their moral training and instruction are committed to his or her care, subject to the directions of the Board of guardians alone. The emoluments of many of the workhouse schoolmasters are so meagre as to prove how low an estimate of the services of a teacher has been made, but a juster view of their importance is rapidly diffusing itself.

" In a small workhouse school one-half the floor should be covered with desks and forms, arranged according to the Dutch method, as described in a previous part of this paper, the rest of the floor being left vacant for the division of the children into separate classes whenever that is expedient. The master's or mistress's seat and desk should be placed on a stage, about six inches high, in front of the first row of desks.

" The master should be furnished with a shelved closet or cupboard for books, apparatus, &c. The books, apparatus, and tools, previously alluded to, should be furnished to such an extent as may be required by the number of the scholars. Whenever the chaplain attends the school to superintend the religious instruction of the children, the master should relinquish the task to him, and assist in the instruction to such an extent as the chaplain may require.

" The chaplain's reports will relate to the department of religious instruction and moral training.

" In the other departments of instruction the schoolmaster should, with the assistance of pupil-teachers, or of his most advanced scholars, be required to keep books in the following forms, which should be presented with the chaplain's report every week to the Board of guardians :—

" *Journal of Religious and Secular Instruction.*

Name of Child.	Monday.												Tuesday.											
	Reading Bible and Testament, and Religious Instruction.		Reading and Spelling from Lesson-books.		Writing.		Arithmetic.		Catechism.			Reading Bible and Testament, and Religious Instruction.		Reading and Spelling from Lesson-books.		Writing.		Arithmetic.		Catechism.		
	From	To	From	To	From	To	From	To	From	To	From	To	From	To	From	To	From	To	From	To	From	To	From	To

And so on for the rest of the week.

* " *Journal of Moral Conduct during the Hours of Instruction and Recreation for the Quarter ending*

Name.	Week ending							Week ending							Week endiug							Week ending						
	Sunday.	Monday.	Tuesday.	Wednesday.	Thursday.	Friday.	Saturday.	Sunday.	Monday.	Tuesday.	Wednesday.	Thursday.	Friday.	Saturday.	Sunday.	Monday.	Tuesday.	Wednesday	Thursday.	Friday.	Saturday.	Sunday.	Monday.	Tuesday:	Wednesday.	Thursday.	Friday.	Saturday.

And in like manner for the rest of the quarter.

* See previous account of plan pursued at Ealing Grove School.

" Boys' Journal of Instruction in Industry.

Name of Boy.	Monday.												Tuesday.											
	Gardening.		Tailoring.		Shoemaking.		Carpenters' or Cabinet-makers' work.						Gardening.		Tailoring.		Shoemaking.		Carpenters' or Cabinet-makers' work.					
	From	To	From	To	From	To	From	To	From	To	From	To	From	To	From	To	From	To	From	To	From	To	From	To

And in like manner for the rest of the week.

" Girls' Journal of Instruction in Industry.

Name of Girl.	Monday.										Tuesday.									
	Knitting and Sewing.		Scouring and Bed-making.		Washing and Ironing.		Cooking.		Straw Plaiting.		Knitting and Sewing.		Scouring and Bed-making.		Washing and Ironing.		Cooking.		Straw Plaiting.
	From	To	From	To	From	To	From	To	From	To	From	To	From	To	From	To	From	To	From	To

And in like manner for the rest of the week.

" The arrangement of the school routine, and the punctual observance of it, deserve the special attention of the visiting committee. This routine may be variously settled; but it may be useful, in order, to facilitate such arrangements, to give a specimen of the succession of employments, during a single day in summer, in a rural workhouse school. In this example the industrial training is pursued in the morning, both because work can be more easily performed in the garden at that part of the day, and because the employments of the girls require their absence from school in the morning; while, in a workhouse containing few children, it may be necessary to instruct the boys and girls at the same hours. But the scheme of engagements may easily be modified by transferring these occupations to the afternoon :—

" Six o'clock A.M.—Rise, wash and dress. The monitors are to preserve order.

" Twenty minutes past six.—Assemble in the school-room ; rolls read by schoolmaster and schoolmistress, each child answering to his or her name ; absentees noted. Children inspected, to insure cleanliness of dress and person.

" Half-past six.—The children proceed in an orderly manner to the dining-hall ; prayers are read ; a hymn sung, in which all the children join. Breakfast.

" Quarter-past seven to eight.—Recreation in the yards ; gymnastic exercises and healthful games.

" Eight to eleven.—In weather suitable for out-door employment, the boys shoulder their tools and proceed to the garden, where they are employed in skilful culture under the instruction of the schoolmaster. At other seasons useful in-door employment (such as making baskets, carpentering, shoemaking, tailoring, whitewashing, and repairing the premises) is pursued ; and an effort is made to mend and make all the boys' clothes and shoes in their department of the house.

" During the same period the girls ventilate the bedrooms, make the beds, scour the floors, clean the dining-hall. Certain of the older girls are employed in the wash-house and laundry, or in the kitchen, till noon, or to a later hour.

" The children should return to the school-room, carefully wash their hands, arrange themselves in a line to be inspected by the schoolmaster and mistress at eleven.

" From eleven to twelve the oldest boys and girls read a chapter in the Bible or Testament; after which, the master and mistress ascertain how much they remember of the narrative, &c. read, interrogate them respecting its purport, and instruct them in its relations to the rest of Scripture, and the practical influence it ought to have on their conduct. In such instruction the directions of the chaplain guide the teacher. The younger children meanwhile learn to repeat a hymn, which is read to them for that purpose by a pupil-teacher, or monitor.

" Twelve.—Children proceed to the hall, and dine.

" Half-past twelve to two.—Recreation, gymnastic exercises, and games in yards.

" Two to three.—Reading in lesson-books; questioned as they proceed concerning the lesson : explanations and general instruction given.

When the lesson is read, the books are closed; and they repeat what they remember of the lesson read.

" Younger children reading on tablet lessons to pupil-teachers, or learning numbers.

" Three to four.—Younger children reading to schoolmaster or school-mistress, with interrogations and explanatory remarks.

" Elder boys and girls writing names of animals, seasons, days of the week, months of the year, senses, remarkable towns, &c. ; or writing passages (concerning the morning's labour, or such as would be used in a familiar correspondence by a child) read by the monitor, or on other occasions writing from copies. On other days arithmetic on slates, or mentally.

" Four to five.—Hour at which catechism may be taught, or children be visited by their licensed minister, or general instruction imparted by the simultaneous method. (If this hour be inconvenient, another is to be selected.)

" Five to six.—The children are all instructed in singing in the dining-hall.

" Six o'clock.—Supper. After supper prayers are read, and a hymn is sung by the whole of the assembled inmates.

" The children then return to their schools, where the schoolmaster and schoolmistress address any remarks to them which may be suggested by the proceedings of the day.

" To accomplish the few and simple objects proposed in this scheme, a teacher of mild and persuasive manners, carefully trained in the best methods of instruction, ought to be selected.

" Certain sanatory precautions are necessary in all establishments in which many children are assembled. The liability of all children to contagious maladies, and the frequency with which pauper children are affected with certain other infectious diseases, render great care necessary in the cleansing of the children on their admission. They ought, also, in all cases to be minutely examined by the medical officer in the receiving wards before they are mingled with the rest of the children."

The following is an extract from the Report of Mr. Hall :—

" That I might be able to estimate the nature and extent of the instruction communicated, I have, since the commencement of the present quarter, visited all the workhouse schools, and have myself examined the children. The general impression resulting from my investigation is very unsatisfactory, both as regards the actual proficiency of the scholars, and the probability of their progressive improvement under the existing arrangement.

" I found that in most instances, though there were children in the upper classes who could read the Bible, yet it was evident that their reading was mere recitation of words, without a notion of their meaning. The teachers were themselves too destitute of information, and too inexperienced in the art of instruction, to be able to interrogate or cate-chise their pupils. I soon discovered in the course of my inquiry that to request a teacher to examine the scholars in my presence was to make him expose his own incompetency. I therefore desisted from that proceeding, as calculated to degrade him in the eyes of those who should feel confidence in his ability. Whenever I saw a child exhibit interest in my questions, and liveliness of manner, I was informed, on inquiry, that he had attended some National or British school before he became an inmate of the workhouse.

" A general and great defect in all the workhouse schools is an absence of system and regularity. In only one instance could I procure a list of the scholars. The teachers seemed frequently unable to specify the principle on which the classes were formed. In some schools the children were classed according to their age, in others according to their size, in some according to their proficiency, in others according to the duration of their residence in the workhouse. I nowhere saw any scheme, nor could I discover, except in a very few instances, any settled arrangement for the employment of school-hours; I mean for the succession of the various lessons the scholars were to learn. The industrial training of the children is imperfectly regulated. Those who can work, and are wanted in the house, are taken out of the schools at any hour, and remain absent for days or weeks together. If not wanted elsewhere, they are allowed to attend the schools constantly; and this seems to be done without the slightest reference to any advantage which the scholar is to gain, either in the one situation or the other, but solely as a matter of convenience : hence it happens that those who are active in body and dull in mind, that is, those who are useful in the house and troublesome in the school, are kept always at work; while those who are apt scholars, but bad workers, are detained constantly in the school.

" The same want of consideration exists with reference to the school-books used. In some schools elementary books are provided at the suggestion of the chaplain; in others they are purchased at the request of the teacher. Complaints have been frequently made to me by the teachers of a want of books. Sometimes I have found the children using their own books, or books belonging to the workhouse master. Those of the children who can read tolerably well are taught in the New Testament, and the 'ne plus ultra' of proficiency is to read in the Old Testament. It is true that a teacher who is thoroughly qualified for his task by possessing a competent stock of general information, and the art of imparting what he knows, so as to excite in his scholars a desire after knowledge, and to quicken their faculty of acquiring it, is in a great degree independent of books; but where, as in the majority of workhouse schools, the teacher is indifferently, or not at all, qualified for his office, the books become important as a medium of instruction. It is a common saying, that to enable the poor to read their Bible is the legitimate object of their education : but it is one thing to enable them, by suitable intellectual training, to read it with understanding; and quite another to degrade the Holy Scriptures into a mere lesson-book, the words of which are to be repeated mechanically, while the mind is left in so rude and uncultivated a state as to be unable to apprehend their general meaning, still less to imbibe the doctrines and precepts they contain.

"It is hardly possible to visit the workhouse schools without acquiring the conviction, that the education of the pauper children is made a matter of secondary importance in the economy of an Union. Many persons shrink from the ideal danger of over-educating the labouring classes. It is admitted generally that they ought to be taught something, *but* the limit within which it is thought profitable to enlighten them is very narrow. With some the mere art of reading is held to be quite as much as it is safe to communicate; others would comprehend writing in their system of instruction; a few would extend it to ciphering; but there seems to be a general persuasion that it is useless or inexpedient to attempt to *educate* the poor, that is, to develope the faculties of their minds, in the same way as necessity has led to the developement of their physical powers. Without stopping to reason against this persuasion, it is sufficient for me now to state that the result of my inspection of the workhouse schools and examination of the children is the opinion that, in no instance, is the education, whether industrial or intellectual, nearly so good as it ought to be.

"I find that it varies in quality almost in every instance, passing through the gradations between "very bad" and "tolerable;" and that this difference arises out of the different capacities of the teachers, the schools being similar in all other circumstances.

"Under the present system it is too much to reckon upon procuring a competent teacher for any workhouse school. Accident may have reduced a duly-qualified person to the necessity of accepting the situation, but there is no security that adequate services can in any one instance be obtained. The uncertainty is increased by the number of teachers that is required. In fact, there is not a sufficient supply. In the twenty-three Unions under my care there are thirty-eight teachers appointed for one thousand and ninety-seven pupils, being one teacher for about twenty-eight pupils. Nine teachers, or less than one-fourth of the actual number, would be enough were the scholars collected in three schools.

"It being thus difficult to procure the requisite number of competent teachers, this difficulty is heightened into impossibility by the amount of emoluments usually offered. The highest salary in this district is 30*l*.; the highest amount of emolument (including salary) is 33*l*. 18*s*.; the average rate of salary is 13*l*.; the average amount of emolument (by which term I mean salary, board, and lodging) is 17*l*. 11*s*. Again, the situation, subordinate to that of the workhouse master, in which the teacher is placed in a workhouse, is such as to repel a person of competent attainment and suitable character. The qualifications of a good schoolmaster are of a higher order than those of the master of a workhouse, must be acquired at greater expense, and in a different sphere of life. A person possessing them will not readily submit himself to one placed over his head in the same establishment, of whose intrinsic inferiority he cannot but be aware, yet who is empowered by virtue of his office to superintend the performance of his duties, and whose official superiority is recognised and attested by a salary three or four times as great as his.

"The whole being referable to the indifference or apprehension which unhappily prevails respecting the education (using the term in its comprehensive sense) of the lower orders, among those on whom devolves the care of friendless and destitute children.

" Upon arriving at these conclusions, the question naturally suggests itself, ' How can a change for the better be effected ?' Close upon which follows the consideration of expense ; for we must not depend upon being able to increase our pecuniary means far beyond the sum at present raised for this object. Our problem is, to devise a plan of amelioration which will not be more costly than the present system."

Mr. Hall then gives the detail of a plan for collecting the children from a number of Union workhouses into one similar in most respects to that of Dr. Kay; but differing in this, that he avoids building, by dispersing the adult paupers of one of the Unions among the workhouses of the adjoining Unions, and appropriating the workhouse which should thus be left vacant for the purposes of a district school.

Mr. Day also, in speaking of the difficulty of making fitting arrangements for the education of children where the numbers are so few as those in a Union workhouse, thus expresses himself :—

" To remedy this state of inefficiency, and to procure those advantages which must necessarily have resulted from a more enlarged management, the Atcham Union sent circulars to the neighbouring ones in the county, offering to take the boys upon such terms as would have justified unitedly the engagement of capable instructors. Had this plan succeeded, the Ellesmere guardians were equally prepared to have instituted a similar course with reference to the girls. I regret, however, to add, that, notwithstanding my earnest anxiety to effect this arrangement, in not a single instance was I successful. The reasons that were assigned were various. The principal ones, however, were, that the guardians had no security for the permanence of the system,—that they had no control over their children in a foreign workhouse,—and, I fear, in some instances, the apparent economy of their present course of *imperfect*, or rather of *no* instruction, may have operated in the minds of some of them, when compared with the increased expense which might have attended this new proposal.

" I can only add that, as far as my experience has led me to a conclusion, nothing short of a legislative enactment will ever effect this desirable object."

Such are the statements and conclusions of the assistant commissioners, and they appear not to have been lost upon the gentlemen who compose the Central Board in London. They, too, admit the intimate connexion between education and pauperism ; and, what is still more important, the obligation they consider themselves under to deal with the subject of education, as regards pauper children, as one of the most sacred duties which their office has imposed upon them.—The following is an extract from the Report which they have this year made to her Majesty's Government :—

" Mere considerations of economy would of themselves furnish adequate grounds for bestowing great attention on the education of the children whose only domicile is the workhouse.

" Children of this class, consisting for the most part of orphans, bastards, and deserted children, continued, under the former system of management, to remain inmates of the workhouse long after the period at which they might have earned their subsistence by their own exertions ; and those who obtained situations, or were apprenticed by means of the parish funds, turned out as might be expected of children whose education was utterly neglected, or at best confided to the superintendence of a pauper. They rarely remained long with their employer, but returned to the workhouse ; which, so far from being to them an object of dislike, they regarded as their home, and which they looked forward to as the ultimate asylum of their old age. In this manner, the workhouse instead of diminishing, increased pauperism, by keeping up a constant supply of that class of persons who most frequently, and for the longest periods, became its inmates.

" Pauperism, however, was only one of the evils which resulted from the neglect to provide proper means of instruction for their destitute children. Those who have ascertained the early history of persons who, in a greater or less degree, have offended against the laws, have found that a large proportion have passed their infancy and youth in the workhouse, and can trace the formation of the habits which have led them to the commission of crime to the entire want of moral training in those institutions.

" It must be admitted, however, that the separate parochial management presented difficulties almost insuperable to the establishment of a system of education for pauper children, except where the parishes were of large population and resources.

" The Poor Law Amendment Act, by authorising the formation of Unions, to a certain extent removed that difficulty, and gave us practically the power, and with that power expressly imposed on us the duty, of providing for the education of children in workhouses.

" In performance of that duty the attention of our assistant commissioners has been directed to the training of the children in the several workhouses ; and we authorised Dr. Kay (who, together with Mr. Tufnell, had employed a brief respite from their official duties in a tour of inquiry in Scotland, with reference to the education of the poorer classes) to examine into the state of workhouse education in the counties of Norfolk and Suffolk, and to suggest measures for its improvement. The results of that examination, and of a similar examination made by our assistant commissioner, Mr. Hall, in the counties of Berks and Oxford, have been laid before us by Dr. Kay and Mr. Hall respectively in their

Reports, in which the subject is so fully developed that we think it unnecessary to do more than to express our acquiescence in the views which are therein set forth.

" We especially concur in the remarks respecting the propriety of combining the pauper children of several Unions into one school, which would enable their education to be conducted on a more effective system, with a better class of teachers, and on more economical terms. *Our means of effecting this object under our present powers are circuitous and inefficient ; and, although we might occasionally find it possible to make arrangements of this nature, we could not introduce them generally, or place them on the best footing, without further assistance· from the Legislature.*

" In the mean time, however, we have found that the introduction into some of the workhouse schools of competent teachers, accustomed to the best modes of instruction and moral and industrial training, has already produced a most salutary result.

" We have taken measures for obtaining from our assistant commissioners an accurate account of all the pauper children throughout England and Wales who are likely to be permanently inmates of workhouses. Their number, as far as we can conjecture from our existing data, will exceed forty-five thousand.

" Looking at the ample means which the Legislature have placed at our disposal for improving this large portion of the community, and at the general effect on the social system which would be produced by training to habits of virtue and industry that particular class of the community who have hitherto been the most miserable and degraded portion,—adverting also to the general disposition which we find (with a few rare exceptions) in all classes to co-operate with us in this good work, and to the various other circumstances which, at the present time, are peculiarly favourable to measures of this nature,—we think ourselves called upon to apply ourselves without delay to this portion of our functions, and we do so with the most cheering anticipation of a successful result."

EDITOR.

ON THE STUDY OF COMPARATIVE GRAMMAR.

THE study of comparative language is of recent origin. Till the latter end of the last century, philologists were chiefly engaged in discussing the relative antiquity of languages, and in endeavouring to determine which of the various dialects ought to be considered the primæval language, which was originally spoken by all the inhabitants of the earth. The preference was usually given to the Hebrew; which was maintained by many writers to have been spoken in Paradise and to have been the original language, from which all others were derived. To support this opinion the most absurd and ridiculous arguments were brought forward; mere similarity of sound between words of different languages, in no wise related to each other, was supposed to be a sufficient proof of the connection of those languages; and the whole study was disgraced by such puerile trifling as to create in the minds of many scholars a rooted dislike to all inquiries which were presented to their notice under the suspicious name of Etymology. And indeed Etymology, as it used to be pursued, and as it is still taught generally in the academical institutions of this kingdom, merits all and more than the censures it has incurred, and scarcely deserves to be viewed in any other light than a species of punning. Nothing has more tended to correct the evils of which we have been complaining, and to diffuse more correct ideas respecting Etymology, and the study of language in general, than the comparison of several languages, which are related to each other and belong to the same family, instead of confining our observation to two or three tongues.

Our increased acquaintance with different languages within the last thirty or forty years has led to the notion of an affinity between languages; by which it is meant, that many languages resemble each other so closely in their grammatical forms, as well as in the words used in the expression of the most simple ideas, as to force upon us the conviction that they must originally have been one and the same language, or derived from some common language. The great improvements which have been made in linguistic study, may be dated from the discovery (for it may properly be called a discovery) of the Sanskrit, the antient language of the northern and central parts of Hindustan, by our own countrymen in the latter part of the last century. Mr. Halhed, in his Bengal grammar, published in 1778, was the first to remark the extraordinary similarity between the Sanskrit and the Latin and Greek languages; and his researches were diligently followed by Sir William Jones, Mr. Colebrooke, Sir Charles Wilkins, and Professor Wilson. But though the knowledge of the Sanskrit language was greatly promoted by the works of these scholars, they did nothing for the science of language in general; and it was left to the Germans to avail themselves of the labours of our countrymen, by showing how much use might be made of the Sanskrit in explaining the structure of the Latin and Greek languages.

In addition to the Sanskrit, the discovery of the Zend and Pehlvi languages by Anquetil Duperron, who brought some MSS. of the Zendavesta to Europe, must also be reckoned an important acquisition for the study of comparative language. The genuineness of these MSS., as well as of the languages themselves, have been doubted by many writers; but the researches of Burnouf and Bopp, who have devoted much time to the study of these MSS., leave little doubt respecting the genuineness of these languages, and disprove the assertion, which has been made by some writers, that they have been invented, that is, formed or compounded in the way of a forgery, from other dialects.

The Teutonic and Slavonic languages have also been studied with the greatest diligence of late years; and Grimm's great work on Teutonic grammar, together with the publication of some of the antient specimens of Teutonic and Slavonic poetry, have rendered these languages also available to the purpose of the comparative philologist. The results of these discoveries, as they may justly be called, have been embodied in Bopp's* " Com-

* " Vergleichende Grammatik des Sanskrit, Zend, Griechischen, Lateinischen, Litthauischen, Alt-Slavonischen, Gothischen und Deutschen."

parative Grammar of the Sanskrit, Zend, Greek, Latin, old Slavonic, Lithuanian, Gothic, and German," of which the first part appeared in 1833, which was followed by a second part in 1835, and a third in 1837; and also in Pott's* work on the same subject.

It is to be regretted that the scholars of this country have given so little attention to the study of comparative language ; since a knowledge of some of the other dialects, which belcng to the great family of the Indo-Germanic languages, particularly of the Sanskrit, would tend to correct many erroneous opinions, respecting the structure of the Latin and Greek languages, and would give a greater insight into the formation of these languages, than can possibly be obtained by any investigation, how-ever laborious and accurate, which is confined to the classical languages alone. It is not to be expected that a classical scholar should be able to devote so much time to Sanskrit as to enable him to read with ease any author in that language ; but we hope that the time is not far distant, when an elementary knowledge at the least of the Sanskrit language, will be considered necessary to form an accomplished scholar ; and sure we are, that no scho-lar, who would devote a few months to the study of this language (for a longer time is not necessary), would ever regret the attention he had bestowed upon the subject or consider the time mis-spent. Dr. Arnold, in his recent edition of Thucydides, has justly remarked,† "We seem now to have reached that point in our knowledge of the Greek language, at which other languages of the same family must be more largely studied, before we can make a fresh step in advance;" and if any proof of the correctness of this remark were needed, it might be furnished by Mr. Donaldson's recent treatise on the Greek language,‡ which is by far the most important work that has ap-peared in this country on comparative philology. §

* " Etymologische Forschungen aus dem Gebiete der Indo-Germani-schen Sprachen." Lemgo, Part I, 1833 ; Part II, 1836.

† Vol. iii. Preface. p. v.

‡ " The New Cratylus, or Contributions towards a more accurate Knowledge of the Greek Language," 1839.

§ The most useful books for beginners in Sanskrit are Bopp's " Kri-tische Grammatik der Sanscrita-Sprache," or " Grammatica critica Sans-

It has been justly remarked by Mr. Donaldson in the work already referred to, that the establishment of an English school of philology may be referred to the opening of the London University in 1828, and to the mode of teaching the classical languages adopted in that institution by the first Greek Professor and his colleague in the Latin chair. The former scholar has perhaps exercised a wider influence than any other individual of the present day in diffusing a knowledge of the principles on which philology ought to be studied; and the fruit of his exertions may be already seen, in the improved state of philological learning in this country, though it is to be wished that his example had been more generally followed in the other academical institutions of this kingdom.

It has been already remarked that cognate languages are those which, though spoken by different nations widely removed from each other, and at present mutually unintelligible to the people of each nation, exhibit such traces of similarity in their grammatical forms and in the words used to express the most common objects, actions, and relations, as to leave no doubt that they are closely related to each other, and are descended from one common origin. The languages with which we are best acquainted may be divided into two great families, the Semitic and Indo-Germanic; the former comprising the Hebrew, Arabic, Ethiopic, Phœnician, Syriac, Chaldee, &c., derives its name from the real or supposed descent of the people who speak these languages, from Shem the son of Noah; and the latter is so called, because the Sanskrit and Germanic languages form two of the most important branches of this family.

The family of the Indo-Germanic languages may be divided into six branches, two of which belong to Asia,

crita " (the former work is better adapted for beginners), and Lassen's " Anthologia Sanscrita," which also contains a Glossary. If however an individual has not the assistance of a master, he had better commence with Bopp's " Nalus," an episode of the Mahâ-Bhârata, and his " Glossarium Sanscritum;" since Lassen's "Anthologia" has no Latin version. The recent death of Dr. Rosen, who was Professor of Sanskrit in University College, London, has been a great loss to the study of Sanskrit and comparative philology; and it is much to be regretted that the council of that institution have not yet been able to fill the vacant chair.

and three to Europe, and through European colonies to other parts of the world.*

I. The *Indian* branch, in which the Sanskrit takes the lead and is followed by several derivate dialects, comprised under the name of the Prâkrit† languages, and deviating more or less in their structure from the Sanskrit. Among them the Pali deserves to be particularly mentioned, which is almost altogether Sanskrit, only softened in its pronunciation.

II. The *Medo-Persic,* or *Arian* branch, at the head of which stands the Zend, the language in which the antient sacred books of the Parsees are composed. The other antient languages of the country, the Pehlvi and the Deri, and also the modern Persian, belong to this division.

III. The *Teutonic* branch, with the Gothic at its head, and comprising the different German dialects, the Anglo-Saxon, the Icelandic, the Swedish, the Danish, &c.

IV. The *Græco-Latin* branch, comprising the two antient classical languages.

V. The *Slavonic* branch may be divided into three divisions; the first comprises the Lithuanian, with the antient Prussian and Lettic; the second, the Russian; the third, the Polish and Bohemian, and the languages of the Slowaks in Hungary, and of the Wends and Serbs in Lusatia and Saxony.

VI. The *Celtic* branch may be divided into two divisions: the first comprising the Erse in Ireland, the Gaelic in Scotland and the Manx in the Isle of Man; the second, the Welsh and Cornish in this kingdom, and the Bas Breton in France.

It has been commonly maintained by a certain class of philologists that the Latin language is derived from the Greek, forgetting or ignorant of the important fact, that the Latin possesses many more antient forms than the Greek; we might maintain with as much probability, that the Greek was derived from the Latin, as that the Latin comes from the Greek.

* This classification, chiefly founded upon Pott's " Etymologische Forschungen," is taken, with a few alterations, from a review of that work by the late Dr. Rosen in No. 18 of the " Journal of Education."

† The structure of the Prâkrit languages has been developed by Lassen in his " Institutiones Linguæ Pracriticæ." Bonn, 1837.

Many English words, which are said to be derived from the Latin and the Greek, are in reality as antient as the Latin and Greek words, from which they are said to be derived. Such words as *association, communicate, retrospective, extirpate, detriment,* are doubtless derived from the Latin, while others, such as *geology, astronomy, astrology,* have been borrowed directly from the Greek, or manufactured according to settled analogies; but such words as *know, lick, break, yoke, sit,* and numerous others are in fact the common property of many tongues, and belong equally to the Latin, Greek, Sanskrit, German, and Slavonic languages; and it might be said with as much truth that the Sanskrit *jnâ,* the Greek γι-γνώ-σκω, or the Latin *co-gno-sco,* was derived from the English *know,* as that the English word comes from the Latin.

It is now universally admitted by those who have written best on the comparative study of languages, that the affinity of languages should, above all things, be established by a comparison of their mode of forming and deriving words, and the system of their inflections. It has been well remarked by Dr. Rosen * that " detached words, especially names of natural productions and commodities, terms connected with certain offices and political institutions, &c., are frequently handed over like coin from one nation to another, and thus become the common property of languages utterly distinct from each other. The coincidence in sound and import of a number of isolated words in different languages, ought not therefore to be made the sole criterion of their affinity. There are other characteristics, more intimately connected with the intellectual constitution of the nation by which a language is spoken: we mean its system of grammatical inflections, those modifications in the form of words which convey an idea, not of things or acts, but of the relations of both. The names of things may always be considered as reflected images of the objects which they represent, and are, like these, liable to change from external causes; their grammatical forms seem to partake of the independent and enduring character of those intellectual powers the presence and action of which they manifest. Twelve

* " Journal of Education," No. 16, p. 339.

centuries of Mohammedan dominion have deluged the
language of Persia with numberless Arabian words and
phrases, but have not so far crushed its genius as to make
it submit to one single mode of semitic inflection."

In conformity with these remarks it is proposed in the
following pages to point out a few of the most striking
features in the comparative grammar of the Indo-Germanic languages, rather with a view of exciting attention to
a subject so replete with interest and information, than
with any idea of giving a complete outline, far less of attempting a systematic developement of the grammar of
the Indo-Germanic languages, which could not be accomplished within the limits of this Essay. In discussing
this subject a few remarks will be made on: 1. The
changes of Letters; 2. The Numerals; 3. The Pronouns;
4. The Nouns; and 5. The Verbs of the Indo-Germanic
languages.*

I. THE CHANGES OF LETTERS.

It is a striking proof of the great advances which philology has made in the present century, that the variable
and apparently capricious sounds of language have been
shown to be governed by laws, within limits as strict and
invariable as those to which matter in general is subject;
and that the changes of letters in the different branches
of the Indo-Germanic languages follow certain strict laws.
It may, however, be as well before we adduce any examples of these changes, to make a few remarks on the Sanskrit alphabet, which has been arranged in so systematic
a manner by the Hindu grammarians, as to make it an admirable basis for the comparison of the notation of sounds
in other branches of the Indo-Germanic languages.

The Sanskrit alphabet consists of forty-eight letters;
namely, fourteen vowels and thirty-four consonants.
The vowels, which are arranged first, are divided into

---

* The following tables have been principally taken from Bopp's
" Vergleichende Grammatik," Pott's " Etymologische Forschungen,"
and Grimm's great work on Teutonic Grammar. As many of the
preceding remarks may be found in the article " Language," in the
Penny Cyclopædia, it is right to state, that that article was written by
the author of these pages.

simple vowels, and diphthongs. The simple vowels, five in number, each of which may be short or long, are,—

*a, á ; i, í ; u, ú ; ri, rí ; lri, lrí.**

The four diphthongs are,—

ê, ai, ó, au.

The *ê* and the *ó* are formed by a short *a* being placed before the vowels *a, á,* and *i, í,* respectively; and the *ai,* and *au* are formed by a short *a* placed before the diphthongs *ê* and *ó* respectively.†

The corresponding vowels of the Greek language, which are expressed by separate characters, if arranged on the same plan, will stand thus :—

α, ε, o ; ι ; υ ; η ; ω.

The consonants in the Sanskrit alphabet are divided into three orders, mutes, semivowels, and sibilants. The mutes are subdivided into five orders, according to the organs of speech, by means of which they are pronounced; and each of these orders contains two hard (surd) and two soft (sonant) consonants, each being unaspirated or aspirated, as well as a nasal sound belonging to each order. The consonants in the Sanskrit alphabet are arranged in the following order :—

---

* *lri* is only found in the verb *klrip* and its derivates. Rosen remarks (Journal of Education, No. 16, p. 340), " We remember no instance of the long lrî in any Sanskrit word; Bhattoji, in Commentary on Pânini, I. 1, 9, says that it is not used."

† The former of these changes is called the *guna* or " corroboration," and the latter the *vriddhi* or " increment," of the respective simple vowels. The distinction of both is important in Sanskrit etymology. The *guna* is applied *generally* in forming primary, and the *vriddhi* in secondary derivates from verbal roots, as in the following examples :—

Root.	Form with *guna* (primary derivative).
Vid, to know.	*véda,* knowledge, the veda,
Budh, to know.	*bódha,* knowledge.

Form with *vriddhi* (secondary derivative).

Vaidika, relating to the veda.

Baudika, relating to knowledge.

—Rosen in " Journal of Education," No. 16, p. 341.

	Surd.		Sonant.		
	Not aspirated.	Aspirated.	Not aspirated.	Aspirated.	Nasal.
Gutturals,	k	kh	g	gh	n
Palatals,	ch	chh	j	jh	n
Linguals,	t	th	d	dh	n
Dentals,	ṭ	ṭh	ḍ	ḍh	ṇ
Labials,	p	ph	b	bh	m

Semivowels, *y, r, l, v.* Sibilants, *s, sh, ṣ ; h ; lr.*

The aspirate *h* is classed with the sibilants, and also *lr*; but the latter letter only occurs in the Vedas. The *ṣ*, marked with a dot, is called the palatal *s*, and is frequently represented by guttural letters in the other Indo-Germanic languages. Very few of the words which contain any of the *lingual* letters are etymologically connected with other words in the cognate languages. They are called *cerebrals* by some grammarians, and are said to be pronounced by applying the point of the tongue to the root of the teeth, or the upper part of the mouth.

The simple consonants of the Greek language, if arranged on the same plan, will stand thus ;—

	Surds.		Sonants.		
	Not aspirated.	Aspirated.	Not aspirated.	Aspirated.	Nasal.
Gutturals,	κ	χ	γ	—	γ *
Dentals,	τ	θ	δ	—	ν
Labials.	π	φ	β	—	μ

Semivowels, ρ, λ. Sibilant, s, and the aspirate.†

The mutes in the languages of the Indo-Germanic family, are changed according to a remarkable law, which was first pointed out and explained by J. Grimm, with reference to the Greek (including the Sanskrit and Latin), Gothic, and Old High German languages, and has since been extended to the Zend and Lithuanian by Bopp in his " Comparative Grammar." The changes of the mutes in these languages is shown by the following table :—

* γ is pronounced as a nasal, when it precedes any of the guttural lettres κ, γ, χ.

† The most complete arrangement of the consonants of the Greek alphabet would be as follows :—

	Surds.	Sonants.	Aspirates.	Nasals.	Compound Letters.	Aspirates or Sibilants.
Gutturals,	κ	γ	χ	γ	ξ	H afterwards *c*
Dentals,	τ	δ	θ	ν	ζ	σ
Labials	π	β	φ	μ	ψ	ϝ (digamma)

Semivowels, ρ, λ.

	Labials.	Dentals.	Gutturals.
Greek (Sanskrit, Latin)	p b f	t d th	k g ch
Gothic	f p b	th t d	— k g
Old High German	b(v) f p	d z t	g ch

The following exemplification of this law is taken from Bopp's Comparative Grammar :—

Sanskrit.	Greek.	Latin.	Gothic.	Old High German.
pâda-s	ποῦς, ποδ-ός	pes, ped-is	fotus	vuoz
panchan	πέμπε	quinque	fimf	vinf
pûrna	πλέος	plenus	fulls	vol
pitrĭ	πατήρ	pater	fadrein	vatar
upari	ὑπὲρ	super	ufar	ubar
bhang	ῥήγ-νυ-μι	frango	brikan	prëchan
bhratrĭ	φράτωρ	frater	brôthar	pruoder
bhrĭ	φέρ-ω	fer-o	baira	piru
kapâla	κεφαλή	caput	haubith	houpit
twam	τὺ	tu	thu	du
trĭ	τρεῖς, τρί-ων	tre-s, tri-um	threis	dri
antara	ἕτερος	alter	anthar	andar
danta-m	ὀ-δού-s, ὀ-δόντ-os	den-s, dent-is	thuntu-s	zand
dvan	δύο	duo	tvai	zuénê
dakshinâ	δεξία	dextra	taihsvô	zësawa
uda	ὕδωρ	unda	vatô	wazar
duhitrĭ	θυγάτηρ	—	dauhtar	tohtar
dwâr	θύρα	fores	daur	tor
swan	κύων	canis	hunths	hund
hrĭdaya	καρδία	cor, cord-is	hairtô	hërza
aksha	ὄκκος	oculus	augô	ouga
aṣru	δάκρυ	lacrima	tagr	zahar
paṣu	—	pecus	faihu	vihu
swaṣura	ἕκυρος	socer	svaihra	suehur
daṣan	δέκα	decem	taihun	zëhan
jnâ	γι-γνώ-σκω	co-gno-sco	kan	chan
jan	γέν-os	gen-us	kuni	chuni
jânu	γόνυ	genu	kniu	chniu
mahat	μέγας	magnus	mikils	mihil
hansa	χὴν	'anser	gans	kans
hyas	χθés	heri	gistra	këstar
lih	λείχ-ω	li(n)g-o	laigô	lêkôm

The following examples will show that the Lithuanian agrees with the Sanskrit, Greek, and Latin in the interchange of mutes :—

Lithuanian.		Sanskrit.	
rata-s	'a wheel'	ratha-s	'a chariot'
bûsu	'I shall be'	bhavishyâmi	
ka-s	'who'	ka-s	

	Lithuanian.		Sanskrit.
dumi	' I give '	da-dâ-mi	
pat-s	' a husband or master '	pati-s	
penki	' five '	panchan	
tri	' three '	tri	
keturi	' four '	chatur	
ketwirtas	' the fourth '	chaturthas	

It is absolutely necessary to acquire a knowledge of the regular changes of letters that occur between cognate languages; since the relation of many words, which at first sight would appear to have little in common, is fully established when we become acquainted with the regular changes of the letters. The connection between the Greek ἕπομαι and the Latin *sequor* is proved beyond all doubt, when it is known that π in Greek frequently corresponds to *qu* in Latin, as πέπ(τ)ω, *coquo*; λείπω, *li(n)quo*, &c.; and that an aspirate at the beginning of a Greek word is frequently changed into *s* in Latin, as the following examples will show:—

Greek.	Latin.	Greek.	Latin.
ἑπτά	septem	ὑπό	sub
ἕξ	sex	ὑπὲρ	super
ὕλη	silva	ὕπνος	somnus
ἕρπω	serpo	ἕκυρος	socer
ἁλ-ς	sal	ἥμι	semi
ὕδ-ωρ	sud-or	ὁμ-ὸς	sim-ul

In the same manner the German *herz* and the Latin *cor*, *cord-is* (crude form *cord)* are proved to be the same word, when it is known that *c* is generally *h* in the Teutonic languages, as *coll-um*, *hal-s*; *cel-a-re*, *hehl-en*; *cuti-s*, *haut*; *cornu*, *horn*; *cannabi-s*, *hanf*; *caput*, *haupt*, &c.; and that the Latin *d* frequently corresponds to the Teutonic *z*, as *den-s*, *dent-is* (crude form *dent)* *zahn*; *duc-ere*, *zieh-en*; *dec-em*, *zeh-en* or *zeh-n*, &c. Many similar examples might be produced from the cognate languages, of words which apparently have little in common but the meaning; but whose identity is fully established by a knowledge of the principal changes of the letters. The following table, taken from Pott's Etymologische Forschungen, (I., pp. 82, 83,) though far from complete, contains most of the principal transformations of letters in the most important branches of the Indo-Germanic languages.

	Sanskrit.	Greek.	Latin.
Gutturals.	k ·· ·· ··	κ, π, ·· ·· ·· ··	c (qu) ·· ··
	(ksh) ·· ··	ε, σσ, κτ, κ, (π) ·· ··	x (c-s), c, s··
	kh ·· ·· ··	χ, κ	
	g ·· ·· ··	γ, β, ·· ·· ·· ··	g, b ·· ··
	gh ·· ·· ··	χ	
	n (guttural) ··	γ (nasal) ·· ·· ··	n (guttural)··
Palatals.	ch ·· ·· ··	π, τ ·· ·· ·· ··	c (qu) ·· ··
	chh ·· ·· ··	σχ ·· ·· ·· ··	sc, c ·· ··
	j ·· ·· ··	γ (β, ζ?) ·· ·· ··	g ·· ·· ··
	jh	·· ·· ··	·· ··
	n (palatal) ··	Different nasal letters ··	n (guttural)
Dentals.	t ·· ·· ··	τ, σ ·· ·· ·· ··	t, s ·· ··
	th ·· ·· ··	τ ·· ·· ·· ·· ··	t ·· ·· ··
	d ·· ·· ··	δ, θ ·· ·· ·· ··	d, l ·· ··
	dh ·· ·· ··	θ, σ ·· ·· ·· ··	f, d ·· ··
	n ·· ·· ··	ν, λ ·· ·· ·· ··	n, l ·· ··
Labials.	p ·· ·· ··	π, φ ·· ·· ·· ··	p, c (qu) ··
	ph ·· ·· ··		
	b ·· ·· ··	β, π ·· ·· ·· ··	b
	bh ·· ·· ··	φ (β) ·· ·· ·· ··	f, b ·· ··
	m ·· ·· ··	μ, (β before liquids) ··	m ·· ·· ··
Semi-vowels.	y (palatal) ··	ι, ε, ζ, aspirate ·· ··	j, i ·· ··
	r (lingual) ··	ρ, λ ·· ·· ·· ··	r, l ·· ··
	l (dental) ··	λ ·· ·· ·· ·· ··	l ·· ·· ··
	w, v, (labial) ··	ϝ, υ, ε, β, φ, aspirate	v ·· ·· ··
Sibilants.	s (palatal) ··	κ, σ, aspirate ·· ··	c (qu) s ··
	sh (lingual) ··	σ, aspirate ·· ·· ··	s, r ·· ··
	s (dental) ··	σ, aspirate, ρ ·· ··	s, r ·· ··
	h (guttural) ··	χ, γ, κ ·· ·· ··	h, g, c ·· ··

Lithuanian.	Gothic.	Old High German.
k, *Lettic* k and z	h, g	h, g
kss, k, ss (pronounced sh)	hs, h, g ..	
Lettic z		
Lettic g	k	ch
cz (pronounced ch) k ; *Lettic*	f	v
chh, z, k		
.. ..	sk..	sk
g ; *Lettic* ds	k	ch
.. ..		
.. ..		
t	th..	d (t)
t	th (t)	..
d	t (d)	z (pronounced ss)
d	d	t
n (m)	n	n
p	f	v
b	b	p
m	m..	m
y	y	y
r, l	r, l	r, l
l	l	l
w	v	w
s, ss, sz, k	h, s	h, s
sz (pronounced sh)	s	s, r
s	s, z	s, r
z (pronounced as French j),	h, g	k
sz, g		

II. NUMERALS.

No.	Sanskrit.	Zend.	Persian.	Greek.	Latin.	Lithuanian.
1	êka ..	aêva ..	yik ..	εἶς .. .. ἕν-α	oinu-s ⎱ .. œnu-s ⎰ .. unu-s ⎰ ..	wena .. ..
2	dwi ..	dwa ..	du ..	δύο	duo	du .. ..
3	tri ..	thri ..	seh	τρεῖς .. .. τρι-ῶν	tres .. .. tri-um ..	tri .. ..
4	chatur ..	chatwar	chehaur	τέτταρ-ες τέσσαρ-ες ⎱ πέσσυρ-ες πέσυρ-ες πίσυρ-ες ⎰	quattuor .. quadra ..	keturi .. ..
5	panchan	panchan	penj ..	πέντε ⎱ .. πέμπε ⎰ ..	quinque ..	penki .. ..
6	shash ..	cswas ..	shesh ..	ἓξ	sex	szeszi .. ..
7	saptan ..	haptan..	heft ..	ἑπτὰ	septem ⎱ .. septua ⎰ ..	septyni.. ..
8	ashtan ..	astan ..	hesht ..	ὀκτὼ	octo	aztum .. ..
9	navan ..	navan ..	nuh ..	ἐννέϝα	novem ..	devyni .. ..
10	daṣan ..	dasan ..	deh ..	δέκα	decem ..	deszimt ..
20	vinṣati ..	vîṣaiti ..	bist ..	εἴκοσι ⎱ .. εἴκοντι .. ϝίκατι ⎰ ..	viginti ⎱ .. vinginti? ⎰	dwideszimpti
30	trinṣat ..	thriṣata	si	τριάκοντα ..	triginta ⎱ tringinta? ⎰	trisdeszimpti
100	ṣatam ..	ṣatem ..	sad ..	ἑκάτοντα .. ἑκατὸν	centum ..	szimta .. ..

II. NUMERALS.

Russian.	Gothic.	Old High German.	Modern German.	English.	Erse.	Welsh.
odin	am	ein ..	ein ..	one } .. an } .. a } ..	aen ..	un
dva } .. dvie } ..	twa	tue ..	zwei ..	two ..	da } .. do } ..	dau } dwy }
tri	thri	thri ..	drei ..	three ..	tri ..	tri } tain }
chetyre ..	fidwor	fiuuar ..	vier ..	four ..	keathair	pedwer } pedair }
pyat	fimf	finfe ..	fünf ..	five ..	kuig ..	pump
shest	saihs	sehs ..	sechs ..	six ..	se	chwech
sem	sibun	sibun ..	sieben .,	seven ..	secht ..	saith
osm } .. vosem } ..	ahtan	ohto ..	acht ..	eight ..	ocht ..	wyth
devyat ..	niun	niguni ..	neun ..	nine ..	noi ..	naw
desyat ..	taihun	zëhan ..	zehen } zehn }	ten ..	deich ..	dêg
dvatzat ..	twaimtigum ..	tuentig ..	zwanzig	twenty ..	fichid ..	ugain
tritzat ..	thrinstigum ..	thrittig ..	dreiszig	thirty ..	deichar fichid	dêg ar ugain
sto	hunta	hunt ..	hundert	hundred	kett ..	cant

The only numeral which appears to have more than one root to express the same number is " one." All the languages, with the exception of the Sanskrit, Zend, and Persian, express the notion of unity by the same word *en*, *un*, *ain*, *ein*, *&c.* with a *w* sound before it in some of the languages, as in the Lithuanian and English, and probably also in the Latin, judging from the antient forms of *oinus* and *œnus ;* in the Greek this sound probably appears under the form of an aspirate in εἶ-s=ἕν-s. There is considerable difficulty in accounting for the feminine of the Greek numeral, μία. Mr. Donaldson, in his " New Cratylus " (p. 186), maintains that it has no connection with εἷς : but though we would not expressly assert the connection, yet such a supposition is not altogether destitute of probability, when we consider that the word for *one* is preceded by a *w* sound in many of the cognate languages, and that the *w* might easily be changed into *m* in the Greek language. The Greek numeral may, therefore have once been Ϝεῖς, Ϝία, Ϝὲν, or μεῖς, μία, μὲν : the neuter μὲν is still preserved in the conjunction μὲν, which constantly means " the first thing," "in the first place ;" in the same manner as δὲ, which is connected with the second numeral, means " in the second place."

The Sanskrit *êka*, which is probably the same as the Persian *yik*, is also found in the cognate languages; as in the Greek ἕκα-s, ἑκά-τερος, and ἕκα-στος, and in the English *each ;* it is supposed by Bopp to be formed from the demonstrative root *ê*, and the relative or interrogative *kas*, with the signification of " that which." The Zend numeral for " one," *aêva* is probably connected with the Sanskrit pronominal-adverbs *êva* and *êvam*. Bopp has suggested that the difference in the words, which express the notion of unity in the Indo-Germanic languages, has arisen from this numeral being derived from the different pronouns of the third person.

The Ordinal Numerals require a few words of explanation ; they are given in the following table in the feminine gender of the Nominative singular ; since the resemblance is more striking in the feminine than in the masculine :—

No.	Sanskrit.	Zend.	Greek Doric.	Latin.	Gothic.	Lithuanian.
1st	prathamâ	frathĕma ..	πρώτα ..	prima ..	fruma ..	pirmà
2d	dwitîyâ ..	bitya ..	δευτέρα ..	altera ..	anthara ..	antrà
3rd	tritîyâ ..	thritya ..	τρίτα ..	tertia ..	thridjô' ..	tréchià
4th	chaturthâ..	tûirya ..	τετάρτα ..	quarta ..	(fidvôrdô')	ketwirtà
5th	panchamâ ..	pugdha ..	πέμπτα ..	quinta ..	fimftô'	penktà
6th	shashthâ ..	cstvâ ..	ἕκτα..	sexta ..	saihstô ..	szészta
7th	saptamâ ..	haptatha ..	ἑβδόμα ..	septima	(sibundô')	sékma
8th	ashth ..	astĕma ..	ὀγδόϝα ..	octava ..	ahtudô' ..	àszma
9th	navamâ ..	nâuma ...	ἐννάτα ..	nona ..	niundô' ..	dewintà
10th	daṣamâ ..	daṣĕma ..	δεκάτα ..	decima..	taihundô'..	deszimtà
11th	ékâdaṣâ ..	aêvandaṣa	ἐνδεκάτα ..	undecima	(ainliftô) ..	wienólikta
12th	vinṣatitamâ	vîṣaititema?	εἰκοστὰ ..	vicesima	—	dwideszimtà

The ordinal numerals are generally either comparatives or superlatives of the cardinal numbers; it is therefore necessary to make a few remarks on the mode of forming the comparatives and superlatives in the Sanskrit and cognate languages. The common Sanskrit termination for the comparative is *tara*, the same as the Greek τερο-ς, and the Latin *ter* in such words as *al-ter* "one of the two," *u-ter* "which of the two," *neu-ter* "neither of the two." The ordinal number for two, in Greek, Latin, Gothic, and Lithuanian, is thus formed by the comparative suffix, which is properly used to express the relation between two persons or things; and thus when more than two are spoken of, δεύ-τατος, which contains the superlative suffix, is used, and not δεύ-τερος. The most common form of the superlative in Greek is τατο-ς, which is supposed by some philologists to be a reduplication; and it is argued that the original termination of the superlative was τος, which occurs in πρώ-τος, τρί-τος, τέταρ-τος, πέμπ-τος, ἕκ-τος, ἔννα-τος, δέκα-τος, εἰκοσ-τὸς, &c., as well as in the Latin *quar-tus*, *quin-tus*, *sex-tus*, in the Sanskrit *chatur-thas* and *shash-tas*, and in most of the Gothic and Lithuanian numerals. Most of the other numerals end in μο-ς, *mu-s*, or *ma-s*; which is probably a shortened form of the common Sanskrit superlative *tama-s*, which answers to the Latin *timu-s*.

There is also a great similarity between the adverbs
formed from the numerals, as :—

	Sanskrit.	Zend.	Greek.	Latin.
twice,	dwis	bis	δίς	bis
thrice,	thris	thris	τρίς	ter
four times,	chatur for chaturs	chathrus	—	quater.

III. PRONOUNS.

Declension of the First Personal Pronoun.

		Sanskrit.	Zend.	Greek.	Latin.	Gothic.	Lithuanian.	Old Slavonic.	Old High German.	Russian.
Singular	Nom.	aham	azĕm	ἐγών ... 'γων, ἐγώ	egomet ego	ik	asz	az ...	ih	ya
	Acc.	mâm, mâ	manm mâ ..	μέ	mê ...	mik	manen	mja ...	mih	menya
	Gen.	mama, mê	mana mê, môi	μοῦ	mei, mis	meina	manens	mene	mîn	menya
	Dat.	mahyam mê ..	mê, môi	ἐμίν, μοί	mihi	mis	man	mnje, mi	mir	mne
Plural	Nom.	vayam asmê	vaêm	ἄμμες ἡμεῖς	nos	veis	mes	my	wîr	mi
	Acc.	asmân nas	nô ...	ἄμμε ἡμᾶς	nos	unsis	mus	ny	unsih	nas
	Gen.	asmâkam	ahmâkĕm	ὀμμέων ἡμῶν	nostri nostrum	unsara	musŭ	nas	unsar	nas
	Dat.	asmabhyam nas ..	nô ...	ἄμμι(ν) ἡμῖν	nobis	unsis	nam	nam	uns	nam

Declension of the Second Personal Pronoun.

		Sanskrit.	Zend.	Greek.	Latin.	Gothic.	Lithuanian.	Old Slavonic.	Old High German.	Russian.
Singular.	Nom.	twam	tûm	τ∂ν? τυ	tu	thu	tu	ty	dâ	tü
	Acc.	twâm, twâ	thwanm	τέ	tê	thuk	tawen	tja	dih	tebya
	Gen.	tava	thwâ; tava	τεῦ	tui, tis	theina	tawens	tebe	dîn	tebya
	Dat.	twê, tê; tubhyam; thwê, tê	thwôi, tê, tôi; thwôi, tê; tôi	τεῖν, τοί	tibi	thus	taw	tebje, ti	dir	tebe
Plural.	Nom.	yûyam	yûshêm	ὔμμες; ὑμεῖς	vos	yus	jûs	vy	îr	vü
	Acc.	yushmê; yushmân; vas	yûs; vô	ὔμμε; ὑμᾶς	vos	izvis	jus	vy	iwih	vas
	Gen.	yushmâkam; vas	yûsmâkêm; vô	ὑμμέων; ὑμῶν	vestri, vestrum	izvara	jusû	vas	iwar	vas
	Dat.	yushmabhyam; vas	yûsmaêibya	ὑμμι(ν); ὑμῖν	vobis	izvis	jumus	vam	tu	vam

Declension of the Demonstrative Pronoun.

	Sanskrit M.	F.	N.	Zend M.	F.	N.	Greek M.	F.	N.	Latin M.	F.	N.
Singular												
Nom.	sas	sâ	tat	hô	hâ	tat	ὁ	ἁ, ἡ	τό	hi-c	hæ-c	ho-c
Acc.	tam	tâm	tat	tem	tanm	tat	τόν	τάν, τήν	τό	hun-c	han-c	ho-c
Gen.	tasya	tasyâs	tasya	tahê	tanhâo	tahê	τοῖο	τᾶς, τῆς	τοῖο	hujus	hujus	hujus
Dat.	tasmai	tasyai	tasmai	tahmai	tanhai	tahmai	τῷ	τᾷ, τῇ	τῷ	hui-c	hui-c	hui-c
Plural												
Nom.	tê	tâs	tâni, tâ	tê	tâo	tâ	τοί, οἱ	ταί, αἱ	τά	hi	hæ	hæ.c
Acc.	tân	tâs	tâni, tâ	tan	tâo	tâ	τούς	τάς	τά	hôs	hâs	hæ.c
Gen.	têsham	tâshâm	têsham	taêshanm	tâonhanm	teêshanm	τῶν	τάων, τῶν	τῶν	hôrum	hârum	hôrum
Dat.	têbhyas	tâbhyas	têbhyas	taêibyô	tâbyô	taêibyô	τοῖσι	ταῖσι	τοῖσι	hîs	hîs	hîs

	Gothic M.	F.	N.	Lithuanian M.	F.	N.	Old Slavonic M.	F.	N.	Old High German M.	F.	N.
Singular												
Nom.	sa	so	thata	tas	ta	tai	t'	ta	to	der	diu	daz
Acc.	thana	tho	thata	tan	tan	tai	t'	tû	to	den	dia	daz
Gen.	this	thizôs	this	to	tôs	to	togo	toja	togo	des	dera	des
Dat.	thamma	thizai	thamma	tam	tai	tam	tomû	toi	tomû	demu	deru	demu
Plural												
Nom.	thai	thos	tho	tie	tos	:	ti	ty	ta	diê	dio	diu
Acc.	thans	thos	tho	tus	tas	:	ty	ty	ta	diê	dio	diu
Gen.	thizê	thizô	thizê	tû	tû	tû	tjech	tjech	tjech	dero	dero	dero
Dat.	thaim	thaim	thaim	tiem(u)s	tom(u)s	tiem(u)s	tjem	tjem	tjem	dêm	dêm	dêm

The primitive pronouns appear to have been very simple words, and were all monosyllables. It would require too much space to enter into an explanation of the formation of the various cases of the personal pronoun; but it is worthy of remark that while all the cases of the singular number of the second personal pronoun are formed from one root *tu*, the cases of the singular number of the first personal pronoun are formed apparently from two roots; one from which the nominative case is derived, and the other from which the oblique cases are formed. The Sanskrit nominative consists of two parts, *ah* and *am;* of which *am* is merely a termination occurring in the Zend *az-ĕm* and the Greek ἐγ-ὼν, and also in the nominative case of the second personal pronoun, in the Sanskrit *twam*, the Zend *tum*, and the Greek τὰν (vocative ὦ τάν). The root *ah* appears in ἐγ-ων, *az-em*, *eg-o*, *ik*, &c.; since it is well known that the letter *h* is interchangeable with the guttural letters *g*, *k*, *&c.*; but it is very unlikely, independent of other reasons, that the nominative case of the first personal pronoun should have been formed from two roots; it is more probable that the initial *m*, which appears in the oblique cases, was dropped in the nominative singular; and that the Sanskrit nominative *ah-am* was originally *mah-am;* whence the dative *mah-yam*. The final *h* has been dropped in most of the oblique cases; but it is still retained in the Gothic *mik* (the *k* is equivalent to an *h*), in the Old High German *mih*, the modern German *mich*, the Latin *mih-i*, &c. The same letter also occurred antiently in the accusative case in Latin according to Quintilian, who says (*Inst. Orat.* I. 5. § 21.), " *Mehe* quoque pro *me* apud antiquos, tragœdiarum præcipue scriptores, in veteribus libris invenimus."

The demonstrative pronoun, one declension of which is given in the preceding tables, appears to have been originally a personal pronoun. The termination of the third person of the verb was probably borrowed from this pronoun, of which the root is *sa* or *ta;* in the Greek article, which was originally a demonstrative pronoun, the *s* has been softened into an aspirate in the nominative singular; but the words σήμερον or τήμερον, " this day," and σῆτες, " this year," point to a primitive σὸς, σὴ, σὸ(τ), as in Sans-

krit and Gothic. The English article *the* contains the
same root, which also occurs without an aspirate in the
word *to-day*, answering to the Latin *ho-die*. In the Latin
hi-c, hæ-c, ho-c, the *c* is merely a shortened form of the
ordinary suffix *ce ;* thus in antient writers we find the
accusative *hun-ce*, and the genitive *hujus-ce, &c.* This *c*
is not confined to the cases of the singular, as some
writers have supposed ; we find in Plautus and Terence a
nominative plural *hi-ce* for *hi*, and *hæ-c* for *hæ, &c.* The
demonstrate *iste* in Latin also probably contains the same
root *sa* or *ta*.

The personal pronoun of the third person, answering to
the Greek $\overset{\varepsilon}{\epsilon}$ and the Latin *se*, is not found in the Sanskrit ; but it exists in many of the cognate languages, as
the following table will show :—

		Zend.	Greek.	Latin.	Gothic.	Lithu-anian.	Old Slavonic.
Singular.	Acc.	.. ..	σφὲ, ἔ	se ..	sik ..	sawen	sja
	Gen.	hê, hôi	οὗ ..	sui	seina..	sawens	sebe
	Dat.	hê, hôi	οἷ ..	sibi	sis ..	saw ..	sebje, si

The relative, indefinite, and interrogative pronouns
appear originally to have been the same in the Indo-Germanic languages. In Latin this is evidently the case; the
relative being *qui*, the indefinite *quis* or *qui*, and the interrogative also *quis* or *qui*. In Sanskrit, Zend, and Lithuanian, the crude form of the interrogative is *ka*, which
will scarcely be denied to contain the same root as the Latin interrogative, when we recollect how frequently the
guttural in the cognate languages is represented by *qu* in
Latin, and also bear in mind such Latin words as *ali-cubi,
ali-cunde, &c.*, where the guttural sound is retained. It
would seem probable, however, that the root of the interrogative was originially *ku* or *qu*, containing both a guttural
and labial sound, and that in some of the cognate languages the guttural sound only was retained, in others only
the labial, as in the instances which are next mentioned.

The Sanskrit has the root *ku* in the interrogative adverbs

ku-tas, "whence," and *ku-tra,* "where."—Both sounds
are preserved in the Gothic *hver* and *hva ;* in English the
guttural only is pronounced in *who, how,* and the labial
in *which, what; which* the same as *whilk* was formerly
written *quwhilk.* The indefinite pronoun in Sanskrit is
formed by adding *cha-na* and *chi-t* to the interrogative;
and this root is evidently only the softened form of *ka*
or *ki,* of which change we have examples in *church* and
kirk, chien from *canis, chambre* from *camera, cher* from
carus, &c.

The Sanskrit relative is *yas, yâ, yat,* the *y* standing for
the aspirate in the Greek relative ὅς, ἥ, ὅ. The *y* in
Sanskrit is often equivalent to the Greek aspirate; as *yaj*
ἅζω, *yakrit* ἧπαρ, *yudhma* ὑσμίνη, *yushme* ὑμεῖς (ὕσμες).

The relative, interrogative and indefinite pronouns
appear to contain the same root in Latin and Sanskrit;
it remains to be seen whether the same is the case in the
Greek. The Greek relative is ὅς, ἥ, ὅ, the interrogative
is τίς, and the indefinite τις without an accent. The
connection of the relative ὅς with the relative, interrogative, and indefinite pronouns, in the Sanskrit and Latin
has been already remarked; but it would appear at first
sight that τὶ-ς could have nothing in common with either
the guttural or labial elements of the root in Sanskrit
or Latin. It is, however, very probable that τὶ-ς is a
corrupted form of the interrogative and indefinite, and
that there was a more antient form, which contained the
labial and guttural root, as appears from the interchange
of κ and π in such words as κοῦ, ποῦ; κοῖ, ποῖ; κότε, πότε;
κῶς, πῶς; κόθεν, πόθεν; κόσος, πόσος; κοῖος, ποῖος; κότερον,
πότερον; κόσος, πόσος; κοῖος, ποῖος. The more antient form
would then have been κὶ-ς or πὶ-ς (*ki* is one form of the
interrogative in Sanskrit), which became changed in
course of time into τίς: there are examples of such a
change in τέτταρ-ες, *quattuor;* πέντε, Sanskrit *panchan,*
Latin *quinque.* In the same manner we have in Greek
the forms ὅκα and ὅτε, πόκα and πότε, τόκα and τότε: and
in English *nut,* Latin *nux, nuc-is;* and on the other hand
cork, Latin *cort-ex.*

The pronominal adverbs of the Indo-Germanic languages present many striking points of affinity. The

termination *dâ*, for instance, in Sanskrit, indicating time, occurs also in the Greek, Latin, Lithuanian, and old Slavonic tongues :—

Sanskrit.	Greek.	Latin.	Lithuanian.	Old Slavonic.
ka-dâ ..	κό-τε ..	qua-(n)do	ka-dà ..	ko-(g-)da
ta-dâ ..	τό-τε ..	ta-(n)dèm	ta-dà ..	to-(g)-da
ya-dâ ..	ὅ-τε ..	.. ..	.. ..	je-(g)da

IV. NOUNS.

The Latin and Greek grammarians usually divide the noun into different declensions; but there is abundant reason for believing that the case-endings were originally the same in all the declensions. It is proposed, therefore, to give tables of the terminations of each case, and to attempt to show, what was the original suffix of each case. As the number of cases differs at present in the different dialects of the Indo-Germanic languages, it will be advisable to select one language, as the basis of our inquiries; and we choose the Sanskrit in preference to the Latin and Greek, because it has retained a greater number of cases than these languages. In Sanskrit, there are three numbers, singular, dual, and plural; and, eight cases, nominative, accusative, instrumental or implementive, dative, ablative, genitive, locative, and vocative. Our limits must confine us to the singular and plural numbers. The examples in the following tables are classed according to the final letter of the Sanskrit crude forms, which are prefixed to the Sanskrit column of the Nominative Singular.

Nominative Singular of Nouns.

	Sanskrit.	Zend.	Greek.	Latin.	Lithuanian.	Gothic.
m.	(vríka) vríka-s (wolf)	vëhrkô (wolf)	λύκο-s	lupu-s	wilka-s (wolf)	vulf'-s* (wolf)
n.	(dâna) dâna-m (gift)	dâte-m (given)	δῶρο-ν	donu-m	géra (good)	daur' (door)
f.	(jihvâ) jihvâ (tongue)	hizva (tongue)	χώρα	terra	rankà (hand)	giba (gift)
m.	(pati) pati-s (master)	paiti-s (master)	πόσι-s	hosti-s	pati-s (master)	gast'-s (guest)
f.	(príti) príti-s (love)	âfríti-s (blessing)	πόρτι-s	siti-s	awi-s (sheep)	anst'-s (mercy)
n.	(vâri) vâri (water)	vairi (water)	ἴδρι	mare		
m.	(sûnu) sûnu-s (son)	pasu-s (beast)	ἴχθυ-s	portu-s	sunù-s (son)	sunu-s (son)
f.	(tanu) tanu-s (body)	tanu-s (body)	πίτυ-s	socru-s		handu-s (hand)
n.	(madhu) madhu (wine)	madhu (wine)	μέθυ	pecu	darkù (ugly)	faihu (beast)

	Sanskrit	Zend	Greek	Latin	Lithuanian	Gothic
m. f.	(gô) gau-s (cow, ox)	gâu-s (cow, ox)	βοῦ-s	bô-s	sukan-s (turning)	fijand-s (enemy)
f.	(nau) nau-s (ship)	..	ναῦ-s	nav(i)s	..	
f.	(vâch) vâk (speech)	vâk-s (speech)	Fόπ-s	voc-s	..	
m.	(bharat) bharan (bearing)	baran-s (bearing)	φέρον	feren-s	..	
m.	(âtman) âtmâ' (soul)	asma.. (heaven)	δαίμον	sermo'	akmu' (stone)	ahma (soul)
n.	(nâman) nâma. (name)	nâma' (name)	τάλαν	nomen	..	namô (name)
m.	(bhrâtri) bhrâtâ' (brother)	brâta' (brother)	πατήρ	frater	..	brôthar (brother)
f.	(duhitri) duhitâ' (daughter)	dughdha (daughter)	θυγάτηρ	mater	dukté' (daughter)	dauhtar (daughter)
m.	(dâtri) dâtâ' (giver)	dâta' (giver)	δοτήρ	dator	..	
n.	(vachas) vachas (word)	vachô (word)	Fέπος	opus	..	

* The apostrophe indicates that a letter has been dropped.

Nominative Plural of Nouns.

	Sanskrit.	Zend.	Greek.	Latin.	Lithuanian.	Gothic.
m.	vrĭkâ-s	..	λύκοι	lup'ī	wilkai	vulfô-s
n.	dânâ-n-i	dâta	δῶρα	dona	..	daura
f.	jihvâ-s	hizvâ-o	χῶραι	terrae	..	gibô-s
m.	patay-as	paity-ô	πόσι-ες	host'-ês	ranko-s	gastei-s
f.	prĭtay-as	âfrĭty-ô	πόρτι-ες..	mess-es	..	anstei-s
n.	vârĭ-n-i	var'-a	ĭδρι-α	mari-a	..	
m.	sûnav-as	pasv-ô	ἰχθύ-ες	portū-s..	sûnu-s	sunju-s
f.	tanav-as	tanvô-	πίτυ-ες	socru-s..	..	handju-s
n.	madhû-n-i	madhv-a	μέθυ-α	pecu-a		
m. f.	gâv-as	geu-s	βό(F)-ες	bov-es	..	
f.	nâv-as	..	ναῦ(F)-ες	nav'-es	..	
f.	vâch-as	vâch-ô	Fόπ-ες ..	voc-ês	..	
m.	bharant-as	barênt-ô	φέροντ-ες	ferent-ês	..	fijand-s
m.	âtmân-as	asman-ô	δαίμον-ες	sermon-ês	..	ahman-s
n.	nâmân-i	nâman-a	τδλαν-α	nomin-a	..	namôn-a
m.	bhrâtar-as	brâtar-ô	πατέρ-ες	fratr-ês..		
f.	duhitar-as	dughdhar-ô	θυγατέρ-ες	matr-ês	dughter-es	
m.	dâtâr-as	dâtâr-ô	δοτήρ-ες	datôr-ês		
n.	vacha(n)s-i	vachanh-a	Fέπε(σ)α	oper-a		

The proper sign of the nominative singular of masculine and feminine nouns is *s;* but in feminine nouns, whose crude form ends in *a*, this *s* is frequently dropped. Many nouns, whose crude forms end in a consonant, lose the *s* in the nominative singular for euphonic reasons. All neuter nouns, with the exception of those that add *m* to form the nominative singular, have no case-ending in the nominative singular, but keep the crude form in this case, as well as in the vocative and accusative singular, which are always the same in neuter nouns as the nominative. That the nominative singular is the same as the crude form will be evident by looking at those neuter nouns in the preceding table, whose crude forms end in *i, u,* and the consonant *n.* In the neuter nouns of the third declension in Latin and Greek, ending in *s*, as ἔπος, *opus, &c.,* it must not be supposed that the *s* even in those instances is the sign of the nominative case; since the *s* belongs to the crude form of the noun. That this is the case may be proved by a comparison of the Sanskrit *vachas* and similar nouns, which retain the *s* in all the other cases; as instrumental, *vachas-â;* dative, *vachas-ê;* genitive, *vachas-as, &c.;* and also by the declension of Latin neuters in *us*, as *corpus, corpor-is; opus, oper-is, &c.;* where the *r* represents the *s,* as it constantly does in Latin ; in fact, we might perhaps assert that all Latin words, which are now written with an *r*, had an *s* originally. We are told by Quintilian (I. iv. § 13.) that *Valerius, Furius, arbor, labor, vapor, clamor* and *lares* were originally written *Valesius, Fusius, arbos, labos, vapos, clamos* and *lases;* and many similar instances might be produced. The genitive singular of ἔπος and of similar nouns in Greek, must therefore have originally been ἔπε(σ)-*os*; and the σ was afterwards dropped as in the future of verbs whose crude forms end in a liquid, as μέν-εσω, μέν-εω, μεν-ῶ ; and in the second person singular of the present indicative passive, τύπτ-εσαι, τύπτ-εαι, τύπτ-ῃ.

The original termination of the nominative plural of masculine and feminine nouns was ᵃₑs. In the first and second declension in Greek we have αι and οι, and in Latin *æ* and *i;* but there can be but little doubt, that the nouns of these declensions also originally ended in *es* in the nominative plural, and that λύκοι, χῶραι, *lupi, terræ,* stand for λύκο-ες, χώρα-ες, *lupo-es, terra-es,* in the same way as we have *familiæ, familiai, familiâs=familia-is,* all as forms of the genitive singular.

The nominative, vocative, and accusative plural of neuter nouns end, in Zend, Greek, Latin, and Gothic, in short *a,* and in Sanskrit in short *i,* which is probably only a weakened form of the *a;* a euphonic *n* is sometimes inserted in Sanskrit between the crude form and the termination *i.*

Accusative Singular of Nouns.

	Sanskrit.	Zend.	Greek.	Latin.	Lithuanian.	Gothic.
m.	vrĭka-m	vĕhrkĕ-m	λύκο-ν	lupu-m	wilka-n	vulf'
n.	dâna-m	dâte-m	δῶρο-ν	donu-m	géra	daur'
f.	jihvâ-m	hizva-nm	χώρα-ν	terra-m	ranka-n	giba
m.	pati-m	paitî-m	πόστ-ν	hosti-m	páti-n	gast'
f.	prîti-m	âfrîtî-m	πόρτι-ν	siti-m	áwi-n	anst'
n.	vâri	vairi	ΐδρι	mare		
m.	sûnu-m	pasû-m	ἴχθυ-ν	portu-m	sunu-n	sunu
f.	tanu-m	tanû-m	πίτυ-ν	socru-n		handu
n.	madhu	madhu	μέθυ	pecu	darkù	faihu
m. f.	gâ-m	ga-nm	βοῦ-ν	bov-em		
f.	nâv-am		ναῦ-ν	nâv-em		
f.	vâch-am	vâch-em	Fóπ-α	voc-em		
m.	bharant-am	barĕnt-em	φέρουτ-α	ferent-em		fijand
m.	âtmân-am	asman-em	δαίμον-α	sermon-em		ahman
n.	nâma'	nâma'	τάλαυ	nomen		namô'
m.	bhrâtar-am	brâtar-ĕm	πατέρ-α	fratr-em		brôthar
f.	duhitar-am	dughdhar-ĕm	θυγατέρ-α	matr-em		dauhtar
m.	dâtâr-am	dâtâr-ĕm	δοτῆρ-α	datôr-em		
n.	vachas	vachô	Fέπος	opus		

Accusative Plural of Nouns.

	Sanskrit.	Zend.	Greek.	Latin.	Lithuanian.	Gothic.
m.	vrĭkâ-n	vêhrka-n	λύκου-s	lupō-s	wilkù-s	vulfan-s
n.	dânâ-n-i	dâta ..	δῶρα	dona ..		daura
f.	jihvâ-s	hizvâ-o	χώρᾱ-s	terrā-s	rankà-s	gibô-s
m.	pati-n	paity-ô	πόσι-ας	hosti-s		gasti-ns
f.	prîtî-s	âfrîtî-s	πόρτι-s	messi-s	ãwy-s	ansti-ns
n.	vârî-n-i	var'-a	ἴδρι-α	mari-a		
m.	sûnû-n	pasv-ô	ἰχθῦ-ας	portū-s	sûnu-s	sunu-ns
f.	tanû-s	tanû-s	πίτῡ-s	socru-s		handu-ns
n.	madhû-n-i	madhv-a	μέθυ-α	pecu-a		
m. f.	gâ-s	gâu-s	βό(ϝ)-ας	bov-ēs		
f.	nâv-as		νᾶ(ϝ)-ας	nav-ēs		
f.	vâch-as	vâch-ô	ϝόπ-ας	voc-ēs		
m.	bharat-as	barênt-ô	φέροντ-ας	ferent-ēs		
n.	âtman-as	asman-ô	δαίμον-ας	sermon-ēs		ahma-ns
m.	nâmân-i	nâman-a	τάλαν-α	nomin-a		namôn-a
f.	bhrâtrî-n	brâthr-eus?	πατέρ-ας	fratr-ēs		
m.	duhitrî-s	dughdhĕr-eus?	θυγατέρ-ας	matr-ēs	dughter-es	
n.	dâtri-n	dâthr-eus?	δοτῆρ-ας	dator-es		
	vachâ(ṅ)s-i	vachanh-a	ϝέπε(σ)α	oper-a		

The proper sign of the accusative singular of masculine and feminine nouns is *m*, with or without a short vowel *a* or *e* before it. In Greek the *m* is represented by *n ;* since no Greek word ends in *m*. Those Greek nouns, which end in *a* in the accusative, as πατέρ-α, &c., have probably dropped the final *a*, or have substituted the *a* for *n*. We have examples of this disuse of the *n* in such words as πρόσ-θε, πάλι, πέρα (πρόσ-θεν, πάλιν, πέραν being the original forms); and an *a* has been substituted for an *n* in the third person plural of some tenses of the verb, as τυπτοίατο for τύπτοιντο, ἐπειρώατο for ἐπειρῶντο, &c.

The accusative plural of masculine and feminine nouns appears to have been originally formed by adding *s* to the accusative singular. The Gothic has preserved the full form in *vulfa-ns, gasti-ns, ansti-ns, sunu-ns, &c.* If we compare these forms with the Sanskrit *vrĭkâ-n*, the Greek λύκου-ς, the Latin *lupō-s*, and the Lithuanian *wilkù-s*, it will be seen that the Sanskrit has lost the *s*, and the Greek, Latin, and Lithuanian the *n*, and that the loss is supplied by lengthening the final vowel of the crude form. In Greek the *o* in λύκο is lengthened into ου, just as in the dative plural λέο(ντ) σι becomes λέον-σι. When the crude form ends in a consonant in Sanskrit and Greek, it would appear that the final *m* or *n* of the accusative singular is dropped, as in the Greek πατέρ-α, and that the *s*, which marks plurality, is then added without having the effect of lengthening the vowel, as *vach-ăs*, ὄπ-ας, &c.; but in Latin the contrary is the case, *ēs* being always long, as *voc-ēs* for *voc-ens*, &c.

Instrumental Singular of Nouns.

	Sanskrit.	Zend.	Lithuanian.	Gothic.
m.	vrïkê-n-a ..	vĕhkra ..	wilkù	vulfa
f.	jihvay-â	hizvay-a ..	rankà	gibai
m.	paty-â ..	paithy-a ..	pati-mi	gast'-a
f.	prîty-à	âfrîthy-a ..	awi-mi ..	anstai
m.	sûnu-n-â	pasv-a ..	sunu-mi ..	sunau
f.	tanv-â	tanv-a ..	.. .. ..	handau
m. f.	gav-à	gav-a		
f.	vâch-â.. ..	vâch-a		
m.	bharat-â ..	barĕnt-a ..	.. .. ..	fijand
m.	âtman-â ..	asman-a ..	.. .. ..	ahmin
n.	nâmn-â ..	nâman-a ..	.. .. ..	namin
m.	bhrâtr-â ..	brâthr-a ..	.. .. ..	brôthr
f.	duhitr-â ..	dughdhĕr-a..	.. .. ..	dauhtr
m.	dâtr-â ..	dâthr-a		
n.	vachas-â	vacanh-a		

Dative Singular of Nouns.

	Sanskrit.	Zend.	Lithuanian.
m.	vrïkâya	vĕhrkâi	wilku-i
f.	jihvây-ai	hizvay-ai	ranka-i
m.	paty-ê	paite-ê ?	pách-ei
f.	prîtay-ê	âfrîte-ê	áwi-ei
m.	sunav-ê	pasv-ê	sunu-i
f.	tanâv-ê	tanu-y-ê	
m. f.	gav-ê	gav-ê	
f.	vach-ê	vach-ê	
m.	bharat-ê	barĕnt-ê	
m.	atman-ê	asmain-ê	
n.	nâmn-ê	nâmain-ê	

Locative Singular of Nouns.

	Sanskrit.	Zend.	Greek.	Latin.	Lithuanian.
m.	vrĭkê ..	vĕhrkê ..	λύκῳ	lup'-i ..	wilkè
f.	jihvây-âm	hizvaya ..	χώρᾳ	terra-i } ..	ranko-je
				terrae }	
m.	paty-au	.. ..	πόσι-ĭ	host'-i ..	páti-je
f.	prît-au ..	.. ..	πόρτι-ĭ	sit'-i ..	awi-je
m.	sûn'-au ..	.. ..	ἰχθύ-ι	portu-i ..	sunu-je
f.	tan'-au ..	tanv-i	πίτυ-ι	socru-i	
n.	madhu-n-i	.. ..	μέθυ-ι		
m. f.	gav-i ..	gav-i ..	ϐο(ϝ)-ì	bov-i	
m.	bharat-i ..	barĕnt-i ..	φέροντ-ι	ferent-i	
m.	âtman-i ..	asmain-i ..	δαίμον-ι	sermon-i	
n.	nâmn-i ..	nâmain-i ..	τάλαν-ι	nomin-i	
m.	bhrâtar-i..	brâthr-i? ..	πατρ-ι	fratr-ì	
f.	duhitar-i..	dughdhĕr-î ?	θυγατρ-ì	matr-i	
m.	dâtar-i ..	dâthr-i ?..	δοτῆρ-ι	dator-i	
n.	vachas-i ..	vacanh-i ..	ϝέπε(σ)-ι	oper-i	

Instrumental Plural of Nouns.

	Sanskrit.	Zend.	Greek.	Lithuanian.	Gothic.
m.	vrĭkê-bhis	.. ..	θεό-φιν ..	.. ..	vulfa-m
	vrĭkâ-is	vĕhrkâ-is	.. ..	wilka-is	
f.	jihvâ-bhis	hizva-bîs	.. ..	ranko-mis	gibô-m
m.	sûnu-bhis	pasu-bîs ..	...	sunu-mis	sunu-m
f.	nau-bhis	.. ..	ναῦ-φιν		
m.	âtma'-bhis	asma'-bîs	.. .	.. ..	ahma'-m
n.	nâma'-bhis	nâma'-bîs	.. ..	.. ..	nama'-m
n.	vachô-bhis	vachô-bîs	ὄχεσ-φιν		

Dative Plural of Nouns.

	Sanskrit.	Zend.	Latiṇ.	Lithuanian.
m.	vrĭkê-bhyas	vĕhrkaêi-byô	lupīs	wilka-m(u)s
f.	jihvâ-bhyas	hizvâ-byô ..	terris	ranko-m(u)s
m.	pati-bhyas ..	paiti-byô ..	hosti-bus	
f.	prîti-bhyas ..	âfrîti-byô ..	messi-bus ..	awi-m(u)s
m.	sûnu-bhyas	pasu-byô ..	portu-bus ..	sunu-m(u)s
f.	vâg-bhyas ..	vâch-e-byô	voc-i-bus	
m.	bharad-bhyas	barĕn-byô ..	ferenti-bus	
m.	âtma'-bhyas	asma'-byô ..	sermon-i-bus	
m.	bhrâtrĭ-bhyas	brâtar-ĕ-byö	fratr-i-bus	

Locative Plural of Nouns.

	Sanskrit.	Zend.	Greek.	Lithuanian.
m.	vrikê-shu ..	vĕhrkaê-shva	λύκοι-σι ..	wilku-se
f.	jihvâ-su ..	hisvâ-hvâ ..	χώραι-σι ..	ranko-sa
f.	prîti-shu ..	âfrîti-shva ..	πόρτι-σι ..	áwi-sa
m.	sûnu-shu ..	pasu-shva ..	ἰχθύ-σι ..	dangu-se
m. f.	gó-shu ..	.. .. ..	ϐου-σὶ	
f.	nau-shu ..	.. .. ..	ναυ-σὶ	
f.	vâk-shu ..	vâc-sva ? ..	ϝόπ-σὶ	
m. n.	bharat-su ..	brâtar-ĕ-shva	φέρου-σι	
m.	bhrâtri-shu..	.. .. ..	πατρά-σι	

In the preceding tables the three cases of the instrumental, dative, and locative are given together; since
there can be little doubt that they are closely related to
each other both in signification and form. The Greek
and Latin have neither instrumental nor locative case;
but it appears from the preceding examples that the
terminations of the dative case singular in the Latin and
Greek usually correspond to the locative singular of the
Sanskrit.

The common termination of the dative in Sanskrit is
$\hat{e}=ai$, and that of the locative i; so that the dative
would appear only to be a locative with a *guna* of the
termination. (See page 322, *note*.) In Greek the locative
case still appears in such words as Μαραθῶν-ι, Σαλαμῖν-ι,
οἶκο-ι, χαμα-ὶ, &c., and also in Latin in *dom'-i, hum'-i, Co-*
rinth'-i (at Corinth), &c.; which are incorrectly called
genitives by modern grammarians. But although the
case-ending of the dative singular in Latin and Greek is
usually *i*, there are strong reasons for believing that the
more antient termination was *bi, bhi* or *phi*. In Homer
we have frequent traces of φι as the case-ending of the
dative (see Thiersch's *Griechische Grammatik*, §. 177,
182, 186); and in Latin *bi*, is still preserved in the datives
ti-bi, si-bi, and also in *i-bi, u-bi*, &c., which are properly
datives; but in course of time the labial was dropped, and
the *i* was alone retained as the termination of the dative.
The case-ending of the instrumental singular in Sanskrit
is *â*, which Bopp considers to be the same as the prepo-
sition *â*; which is also synonymous with *abhi*. In Lithuanian this termination *bi, bhi*, or *phi* becomes *mi* as in
pati-mi, &c.

The case-endings of the instrumental and dative plural
are nearly the same in Sanskrit; the former being *bhis*
and the latter *bhyas*. The Latin has also the same termination *bus* in nouns of the third, fourth, and fifth declensions; but in the first and second declensions the *b*
has been dropped. There are, however, several examples
of the more antient termination even in the first and
second declensions, as *duo-bus, ambo-bus, dea-bus, nymfa-*
bus, hora-bus, dii-bus, amici-bus, &c. The *s* in this case-
ending *bu-s*, is the sign of the plural, and the *bu* is the
sign of the dative as in *ti-bi*, εὐνῆ-φι, &c.; so that the
words might be divided in the following manner:—

		Case-ending.	Plural sign.
Sanskrit.	vrĭkê	bhi	s
	vrikê	bhya	s
Zend.	pasu	bi	s
Latin.	navi	bu	s
Lithuanian.	sunu	mi	s

The common termination of the dative plural in Greek is σι, as ἰχθύ-σι, 'Αθήνη-σι, which is the same as *su*, the case-ending of the Sanskrit locative.

The Ablative Case. The ablative plural is the same as the dative plural in Sanskrit and Latin. The ablative singular in Sanskrit is always the same as the genitive, except in nouns whose crude forms end in *a*, which have *t* as the case-ending of the ablative: thus *siva* has an ablative *sivâ-t*, and almost all the pronouns form their ablative singular in the same manner, as *ma-t, tva-t,* &c. The same letter is the characteristic of the ablative singular in Zend; and also appears under the form of *d* to have been the original termination of the ablative in Latin. In the *columna rostrata* and the *senatus-consultum de bacchanalibus*, two of the oldest specimens of the Latin language which have come down to us, the ablatives end in *d* or *ed ;* thus we find *præsente-d, dictatore-d, navale-d, præda-d, alto-d, mari-d, senatu-d,* &c. This termination also appears in *me-t*, which occurs in *egomet* (that is, *I by myself*, or *I with myself), memet,* &c. Bopp imagines that the same termination may be traced in the adverbs in ως in Greek, which correspond to the Sanskrit suffix *ât ;* and that the ς in ως is a representative of the τ, because no Greek word ends in τ or δ. He therefore considers ὁμῶ-ς=ὁμῶ-τ, οὕτω-ς=οὕτω-τ, ὤ-ς=ὤ-τ, as old ablatives of ὁμὸς, οὗτος, &c. He also thinks that 'Αφροδίτη is compounded of ἄφροδ, an ablative of ἄφρος, and ιτη, " she who comes out of the foam," containing the root ι, " to go," and he compares it with the Sanskrit *abhrâd-itâ*, " she who comes out of a cloud."

Genitive Singular of Nouns.

	Sanskrit.	Zend.	Greek.	Latin.	Lithuanian.	Gothic.
m.	vrika-sya	vĕhrka-hê	λύκο-ιο	lup'-i	wilkō	vulf-s
m.	*ka-sya	ka-hê	..	cu-jus	kō	hvi-s
f.	jihvây-âs	hizvay-åo	χώρᾱ-s	(terra-is) terra-ï	rankô-s	gibô-s
m.	patê-s	patôi-s	πόσι-ος	hosti-s	..	gasti-s
f.	prîtê-s	âfrítôi-s	..	siti-s	..	anstai-s
	prîty-âs	..	φύσε-ως			
m.	sûnô-s	paseu-s pasv-ô	ἰχθύ-ος	portu-s	sunaû-s	sunau-s
m. f.	gô-s	geu-s	βο(F)-ός	bov-is	..	fijand-s
m.	bharat-as	bārent-ô	φέροντ-ος	ferenti-s	..	ahmin-s
m.	âtman-as	asman-ô	δαίμον-ος	sermon-is	ákmen-s	namin-s
n.	nâmn-as	nâman-ô	τάλαν-ος	nomin-is	..	brôthr-s
m.	bhrâtus	brâtar-s	πατρ-ός	fratr-is	..	dauhtr-s
f.	duhitu-s	dughdhar-s	θυγατρ-ός	matr-is	dugter-s	
n.	vachas-as	vachanh-ô	Fέπε(σ)-ος	oper-is	..	

* The interrogative pronoun.

Genitive Plural of Nouns.

	Sanskrit.	Zend.	Greek.	Latin.	Lithuanian.	Gothic.
m.	vrikâ-nâm	vĕhrka-naṇm	λύκ'-ων	lupō-rum	wilk'-û	vulf-ê
m. n.	* tê-shâm	taê-shaṇm	τ'-ῶν	hō-rum	t'-û	thi-zê
f.	jihvâ-nâm	hizva-naṇm	χωρά-ων	terrā-rum	rank'-û	kêpô-nô †
f.	* tâ-sâm	â-oṇham	τά-ων	hā-rum	t'-û	thi-zô
m. n.	trî-nâm	thray-aṇm	τρι-ῶν	tri-um	tri-û	thrij-ê
f.	pritî-nâm	âfrĭti-naṇm	πορτί-ων	messi-um	awi-û	anst'-e
m.	sûnû-nâm	pasv-aṇm	ἰχθύ-ων	pecu-um	sun'-û	suniv-ê
m. f.	gav-âm	gav-aṇm	βο(F)-ῶν	bov-um		
m. n.	bharat-âm	barĕnt-aṇm	φερόντ-ων	ferenti-um		fijand-ê
m.	âtman-âm	asman-aṇm	δαιμόν-ων	sermon-um	akmen-û	ahman-ê
n.	bhrâtrî-nâm	brâthr-aṇm	πατέρ-ων	fratr-um		

* The demonstrative pronoun.   † Old High German.

The original characteristic of the genitive singular appears to have been *s* with a vowel prefixed. Even those genitives, which do not end in *s*, as nouns of the first and second declensions in Latin, had an *s* in the older forms of the language. Thus in inscriptions we meet with the genitives *partis dimidia-es, Procula-es, Julia-es, Saturnia-es*, &c., and the words *paterfamiliâ-s* and *materfamaliâ-s* are contractions of *paterfamilia-is* and *materfamilia-is*.

The genitives *aura-i, picta-i*, &c. which we meet with in Virgil and Lucretius were originally *aura-is* and *picta-is ;* and in the same manner an *s* has been dropped in the genitive singular of nouns of the fifth declension, *die-i*= *die-is, re-i*=*re-is*. All Sanskrit nouns, whose crude forms end in short *a*, as well as the pronouns of the third person, make the genitive singular in *sya*, with which Bopp compares the antient Greek genitive in οιο, and maintains that the original form of τοῖο for instance was τό-σιο (*Sansk. ta-sya*), and that of λύκοιο, λυκό-σιο (*Sansk. vrika-sya*), the σ being dropped as in ἐδίδοσο, ἐδίδου, &c. (On the disappearance of the *s* in such cases, see *page* 343.)

The characteristic of the genitive plural in Sanskrit is *nâm* or *âm*, in Greek ων, and in Latin *rum* or *um*. It is commonly said that the sign of the genitive plural is *am* or *um* and that the *r* in Latin and the *n* in Sanskrit are merely euphonic letters ; but this is an arbitrary assumption, and is supported by no evidence. It is far more likely that the longer form should, as has constantly happened, have been shortened into the shorter form, *am* or *um*, than that an *n* or an *r* should have been united between the crude form and the case-ending. In many words of the first and second declensions, the *r* has been dropped, and the final *a* or *o* of the crude form contracted with *um*, as *cœlicolûm, deûm, virûm, Graiûm*, &c. instead of *cœlicola-rum, deo-rum, viro-rum, Graio-rum*, &c.; and Cicero in his *Orator* (*c.* 46) informs us that some persons used the forms *meûm factûm, exitiûm, consiliûm, auguriûm, prodigiûm, portentûm, armûm* ; which, however, he did not approve of, as they had not been sanctioned by custom.

It has been already remarked that *r* in Latin is usually the representative of an *s ;* and it appears probable that the *r* in the genitive plural of *terrā-r-um, diē-r-um*, &c.,

is the *s* of the genitive singular, and that the *um* merely
marks the plural; which accounts for the length of the
vowel before the *rum*, since *terrā-r-um* is, if the view we
have taken be correct, a contraction of *terra-is-um*, and
die-r-um of *die-is-um*. This opinion is confirmed by the
case-ending of the genitive plural of the third personal
pronouns in Sanskrit, which is *sâm;* and also by the Zend
taê-sh(n)m and the Lithuanian *thi-ze* and *thi-zo*. The *n*
in the genitive plural of the Sanskrit *vrĭkâ-nâm* and similar words, may therefore be considered as a representative
of the Latin *r*, or more properly of the *s* of the genitive
singular. That *n* is interchangeable both with *r* and *s*
may be proved by many examples. The termination *rum*
is even found in genitives of the third declension; thus
Varro (viii. 74) mentions *boverum* and *joverum*; and
Charisius, *lapiderum, regerum, nucerum.**

---

* See Allen's *Analysis of Latin verbs*. Introduction, pp. xv—xviii.;
in which an explanation is given of many of the terms, such as *crude
form, root,* &c., which have been employed in the preceding pages. Mr.
Allen's work, together with Mr. Donaldson's " New Cratylus," and
some very valuable articles in the Quarterly Journal of Education (such
as the review of Zampt's Latin Grammar, of Matthiä's Greek Grammar,
and Bopp's Comparative Grammar), are almost the only original works
published in this country (as far as the writer is aware), in which the
structure of the classical languages has been attempted to be developed
with the aid of comparative grammar.

Vocative Singular of Nouns.

	Sanskrit.	Zend.	Greek.	Latin.	Lithuanian.	Gothic.
m.	vrĭka	věhrka	λύκε	lupe	wilke	vulf'
n.	dāna	dâta	δῶρο-ν	donu-m	.	daur'
f.	jíhvĕ	hizvĕ?	χώρα	terra	ranka	giba?
m.	patĕ	paiti	πόσι	hosti-s	.	gast'
f.	prĭtĕ	âfrĭti	πόρτι	siti-s	.	.
n.	vāri	vairi	ἴδρι	mare	.	.
m.	sunô	pasu	ἴχθὺ	portu	sunaì	sunau
f.	tanô	tanu	πίτυ	socru-s	.	handau
			αἰδοῖ { Nom. αἰδώ-s / Gen. αἰδό-os } ἠχοῖ { Nom. ἠχὼ / Gen. ἠχό-os }			
n.	madhu	madhu	μέθυ	pecu	.	.
m. f.	gau-s	gau-s	βοῦ	bo-s	.	.
f.	vâk	vâc-s?	Ϝόπ-s	voc-s	.	.
m.	baran	baran-s	φέρον	feren-s	sukan-s	fijand
m.	âtman	asman	δαῖμον	sermo'	akmu'	ahma'
n.	nâman	nâman	τάλαν	nomen	.	namô'
m.	bhrâtar	brâtarě	πάτερ	frater	.	brôthar
f.	duhitar	dughdharě	θύγατερ	mater	.	dauhtar
m.	dâtar	dâtare	δοτήρ	dator	.	
n.	vaehas	vachô	Ϝέπος	opus	.	

In the plural the vocative is the same as the nominative.
In the singular the vocative appears to have been originally the same as the crude form; as, Sanskrit *atmân,*
Zend *asman,* Gr. δαῖμον, Goth. *fijand,* &c.   The final *e*
in vocatives of the second declension in Greek and Latin,
as λύκε, *lupe,* represents the final *o* of the crude form.   In
several nouns, however, the vocative is the same as the
nominative.   In Sanskrit, masculine and feminine nouns,
whose crude forms end in *i, u,* and *rĭ,* have a guna of the
final vowel; as *pati,* voc. *patê ; sunu,* voc. *sunô ; gô,* voc.
gau ; bhrâtrĭ, voc. *bhrâtar ;* with which we may compare
the vocatives αἰδοῖ and ἠχοῖ, of αἰδὼ-ς and ἠχὼ *(crude forms,*
αἴδο and *ἤχο);* and in Lithuanian the vocative *sunaù* (crude
form *sunu*) ; and in Gothic the vocatives *sunau* and *han-*
dau (crude forms, *sunu* and *handu).*

V. THE VERB.

The conjugation of the verb in the different branches
of the Indo-Germanic language presents so many and
such striking marks of agreement, that it will be necessary to confine our attention to only two or three points,
to avoid extending our remarks to an inconvenient
length.

It is admitted by all philologists, that the suffixes,
which are added to the different tenses of the verb in order to denote the persons, are the personal pronouns
more or less corrupted.   But before we proceed to an
examination of these suffixes, it may be advisable to give
a list of the present tenses of a few verbs, in order to show
the similarity of the person-endings in the different dialects of the Indo-Germanic language.

Present Tense of the Verb " To be."—Crude Form, *As or Es.*

		Sanskrit.	Greek.	Latin.	Lithuanian.	Old Slav.	Gothic.
Singular.	asmi	ἐμ-μὶ .. ἐ-μὶ ..	s-um ..	es-mi	jes-mj	ïs-m
	a-si	ἐσ-σὶ ..	es ..	es-si	je-si ..	ïs
	as-ti	ἐσ-τὶ ..	es-t ..	es-ti	jes-tj ..	ïs-t
Plural.	s-mas	ἔσ-μες	s-umus	es-me	jes-my	si-yum
	s-tha	ἔσ-τε ..	es-tis ..	es-te	jes-te ..	si-yuth
	s-anti	(σ)-έντι	s-unt ..	(same as sing.)	s-ùtj ..	s-ind

Present Tense of the Verb "To Place" (Stand).—Crude Form, Stha or Sta.

	Sanskrit.	Zend.	Greek.	Latin.	Old High German.	Lithuanian.	Old Slavonic.
Singular.	ti-sthâ-mi	hi-stâ-mi	ἱ-στᾱ-μι / ἱ-στη-μι	si-st-o	stâ-m	stow-mi	sto-jû
	ti-stha-si	hi-sta-hi	ἱ-στᾱ-s / ἱ-στη-s	si-st-is	stâ-s	stow-i	stô-ïsi
	ti-stha-ti	hi-sta-ti	ἱ-στᾱ-τι / ἱ-στη-τι	si-st-it	stâ-t	stow	stô-ïtj
Plural.	ti-sthâ-mas	hi-stâ-mahi	ἱ-στα-μες / ἱ-στα-μεν	si-st-imus	stâ-mês	stow-imè	sto-im
	ti-stha-tha	hi-sta-tha	ἱ-στα-τε	si-st-itis	stâ-t		sto-im
	ti-stha-nti	hi-stê-nti	ἱ-στα-ντι	si-st-unt	stâ-nt	(same as sing.)	sto-jatj

Present Tense of the Verb "To Give."—Crude Form, Da.

	Sanskrit.	Zend.	Greek.	Latin.	Lithuanian.	Old Slavonic.
Singular.	da-dâ-mi	da-dhâ-mi	δί-δω-μι	da-o, do	du-(d)-mi	da-(d)-mj
	da-dâ-si	da-dhâ-hi	δί-δω-s	da-s	du-d-i	da-(d)-si
	da-dâ-to	da-dhâi-ti	δί-δω-τι / δί-δω-σι	da-t	du-s-ti	da-s-tj
Plural.	da-d-mas	da-de-mahi	δί-δο-μες	da-mus	du-(d)-me	da-(d)-my
	da-t-tha	da-s-ta ?	δί-δο-τε	da-tis	du-s-te	da-s-te
	da-da-ti	da-dĕ-nti	δί-δό-ντι / δι-δό-ασι / δ-δοῦσι	da-nt	(same as sing.)	da-d-jatj

Present Tense of the Verb " To bear."—Crude Form, bhar or fer.

	Sanskrit.	Zend.	Greek.	Latin.	Gothic.
Singular.	bhar-â-mi	bar-â-mi	φέρ-ω	fer-o	bair-a
	bhar-a-si	bar-a-hi	φέρ-ε,ι-ς	fer-s	bair-is
	bhar-a-ti	bar-a,i-ti	φέρ-ε-(τ):	fer-t	bair-ith
Plural.	bhar-a-mas	bar-â-mahi	{ φέρ-ο-μες / φέρ-ο-μεν	fer-i-mus	bair-am
	bhar-a-tha	bar-a-tha	φέρ-ε-τε	fer-tis	bair-ith
	bhar-a-nti	bar-ĕ-nti	{ φέρ-ό-ντι / φέρ-ό-ασι / φέρ-ουσι	fer-u-nt	bair-and

Present Tense of the Verb " Vah," and the words connected with it in the cognate languages.

	Sanskrit.	Zend.	Greek.	Latin.	Gothic.	Lithuanian.	Old Slavonic.
Singular.	vah-â-mi	vaz-â-mi	ἔχ-ω	veh-o	vig-a	wez-û	vez-ì
	vah-a-si	vaz-a-hi	ἔχ-ε,ι-ς	veh-i-s	vig-is	wez-i	vez-eshi
	vahea-ti	vaz-a,i-ti	ἔχ-ε-(τ)ι	veh-i-t	vig-ith	wez-a	vez-etj
Plural.	vah-â-mas	vaz-â-mahi	{ ἔχ-ο-μες / ἔχ-ο-μεν	veh-i-mus	vig-am	wez-amè	vez-om
	vah-a-tha	vaz-a-tha	ἔχ-ε-τε	veh-i-tis	vigith	wez-ate	vez-ete
	vah-a-nti	vaz-ĕ-nti	{ ἔχ-ο-ντι / ἔχ-ό-ασι / ἔχ-οῦσι	veh-u-nt	vig-and	(same as sing.)	vez-ûtj

The characteristic of the first person singular is μι which contains the same root as the oblique cases of the first personal pronoun. To avoid, apparently, another syllable, the ι is dropped in many of the tenses, as in the Sanskrit preterites *akship-a-m* and *akshaips-a-m*, in the Latin *regeba-m*, *rega-m*, *rexera-m*, *regere-m*, &c., and in the Greek ἔλειπ-ο-ν, ἔλιπ-ο-ν, &c., where the final μ is changed into ν for euphonic reasons. In most Greek verbs, and in all Latin verbs, except *inquam* and *sum*, even the *m* disappears also in the present indicative active; as λείπω, *scribō*, instead of λείπο-μ, *scribo-m*, more antiently λείπο-μι, *scribo-mi*. The disappearance of μ at the end of words is not uncommon both in Greek and Latin; compare the accusatives φέροντ-α, δαίμον-α, &c., and the Latin words *posteā*, *anteā*, &c., which appear from the analogy of *postquam*, *antequam*, &c., to have originally ended in *m*. All the Latin adverbs ending in *o*, signifying *motion to*, also appear to have lost an *m*, as *quo*, *eo*, &c. The phrases *rēfert meā*, *rēfert Ciceronis*, *interest meā*, &c. are probably to be explained, as a writer in the "Penny Cyclopædia" remarks (Article M), by the full forms *rem fert meam*, *rem fert Ciceronis*, *inter rem est meam*. All trace of the *m* is also lost in the Greek tenses ἔτυπ-σα(μ), ἐλελοίπ-εα(μ), &c. In the English language the verb *am* still retains the suffix of the first person in its final *m*.

The characteristic of the second person singular is *si*, which represents the second personal pronoun *su*, *tu*, or *du*. As the final *i* of the first person-ending *mi* was dropped in many tenses, so we frequently find *s* as the sign of the second person without the *i;* as in Sanskrit, potent. *kshipê-s*, pret. *akshipa-s*, &c., λείπει-ς, ἔλειπε-ς, λέλοιπα-ς, ἔτυψα-ς, &c., and in Latin *scribi-s*, *scribeba-s*, *scribe-s*, *scripsera-s*, &c. In the second person singular of the Sanskrit perfect, the termination is *tha*, as *vet-tha ;* which termination is also another form of the second personal pronoun. This ending *tha* appears in the Greek perfects οἶσ-θα, ἦσ-θα, &c. in which θα, and not σθα, to be the termination of the perfect, since the crude form of οἶσ-θα=οἶδ-θα is Ϝιδ, and that of ἦσ-θα is ἐσ; and this supposition is confirmed by the imperatives ἴσ-θι, φά-θι, ἴ-θι,

κλῦ-θι, &c. The σ is inserted before the suffix θα in
τίθη-σ-θα, ἔφη-σ-θα, &c., in the same manner as in μνη-σ-
θείς, χρη-σ-θείς, &c. In Latin the termination of the second person of the perfect is *sti*, and not *ti ;* but the *st* is
probably a representative of the lost aspirate *th* of the
original termination, as it appears in the Sanskrit *vêt-tha.*

The characteristic of the third person singular is *ti*,
which is the same root, as appears in the Greek article
τό and the words connected with it in the cognate languages. This termination has been shortened in the same
manner as the first and second person-endings ; thus we
have the Sanskrit *kshipé-t, akshipa-t*, &c., and the Latin
scribi-t, scribeba-t, scribe-t, &c., without the *i ;* while in the
Greek tenses ἔλειπε(τ), λέλοιπε(τ), &c. the τ has entirely
disappeared in the same manner as the *m* was dropped in
the first person. In the present indicative of the Greek
verb the τ has been dropped and the two vowels contracted into ι; thus τύπτε-τι=τύπτε-ι=τύπτ-ει; in the same manner as the σ of the future has been dropped in the verbs
whose crude forms end in a liquid, and also in the second
person of the present indicative passive, as has been already remarked. Τύπτε-τι is not found; but the analogy
of ἐθελή-τι, and similar forms, shows that there must originally have been a form τύπτε-τι.

The terminations μαι, σαι, ται of the passive and middle
voices contain the same suffixes, with the final vowel
strengthened. The Sanskrit person-endings of the singular number of the present indicative middle are lengthened in the same manner ; they are *ê, sê, tê :* in the first
person the *m* has been dropped.

The first person plural appears to have been formed
by adding *s*, the suffix of plurality, to the termination of
the first person singular; as, Sanskrit *tisthâ-mi, tisthâ-
mas ;* Latin *sisto-(mi), sisti-mus ;* Old High German *stâ-m,
stâ-mês ;* in Greek the common termination is μεν, but there
was also an older form μες; in the Doric dialect μες is the
common form. The letter *n*, however, is a suffix of plurality, as well as *s*, in the Indo-Germanic languages ; thus
we have in English the plural *ox-en* as well as *dog-s.*

The second person plural is formed in the same manner,
namely, by adding *s* to the singular, as Latin *sisti-s=sisti-*

si, pl. *sisti-ti-s.* In the suffix *tis* the *t* represents the *s* of
the singular. In Sanskrit and Greek the final *s* has been
dropped, as *ti-stha-tha*, instead of *ti-stha-thas*, and λείπε-τε
instead of λείπε-τες.

The third person plural appears to have been formed
by inserting *n*, the suffix of plurality, before *ti*, the termination of the singular; as, Sanskrit, *tistha-n-ti*; Zend,
histe-n-ti; Latin, *sistu-n-t(i)*; Old High German, *stâ-n-
t(i)*, &c. In Greek the third person plural of the present
usually ends in ουσι; but there can be no doubt that this
is a corruption of an older form ο-ντι. The termination ντι
is still found in Doric, as in διδό-ντι, which became in
Attic Greek διδό-ασι, and afterwards διδοῦσι, the α representing the ν, which has been already shown to have been
frequently the case.

The formation of the various tenses of the Indo-Germanic languages could not be clearly explained without
entering into a long investigation. We can only therefore direct attention to two or three striking points of
similarity.

The past-imperfect and aorist tenses of the Greek verb
are formed in a manner very similar to the preterite
tenses of the Sanskrit. The Sanskrit preterite, which
corresponds to the past-imperfect of the Greek verb, is
formed by prefixing the augment *a*, and shortening the
personal terminations.

Example of Past-Imperfect.

	Sanskrit.	Greek.
Singular.	a-tud-am	ἔ-τυπτ-ον
	a-tud-as	ἔ-τυπτ-ες
	a-tud-at	ἔ-τυπτ-ε(τ)
Dual.	a-tud-âva	
	a-tud-atam	ἐ-τύπτ-ετον
	a-tud-atâm	ἐ-τυπτ-έτην
Plural.	a-tud-âma	ἐ-τύπτ-ομεν
	a-tud-ata	ἐ-τύπτ-ετε
	a-tud-an	ἔτυπτ-ον

The other Sanskrit preterite, which corresponds to the

two aorists of the Greek verb, has, according to Bopp's
division, seven forms ; of which the four first agree more
or less with the Greek first aorist; the fifth and sixth, with
the Greek second aorist; and the seventh, which, besides
the augment, has also a reduplication of the first syllable,
with the Greek past-perfect. The four first forms always
add the letter *s* in order to form the preterite ; thus from
the crude form *kship* is derived a preterite *a-kshaip-sam*,
corresponding to the Greek ἔ-τυπ-σα(μ). The fifth and
sixth forms have the same terminations as the past-
imperfect tense, and differ from that tense nearly in the
same manner as the second aorist in Greek differs from
the Greek imperfect; thus from the crude form *lip* is
derived a preterite *a-lip-am*, corresponding to the Greek
ἔ-τυπ-ον. In the same manner, from the crude form *dâ*,
the Sanskrit forms a past-imperfect *a-da-dâ-m*, and a
preterite *a-dâ-m*, analogous to the Greek ἐ-δί-δω-ν, and
ἔ-δω-ν.

The perfect tense seems originally to have been formed
on the same principles in the Sanskrit, Latin, Greek, and
Teutonic languages ; namely, by a complete or partial
reduplication of the crude form of the verb. Thus in
Sanskrit, from *bhrĭ* is formed the perfect *ba-bhār-a ;* from
tri, the perf. *ta-tār-a ;* from *tup*, the perf. *tu-tóp-a ;* from
kship, the perfect *chi-kshép-a*. In the same manner in
Greek, from λιπ is formed the perfect λέ-λοιπ-a; from θαλ,
the perf. τέθηλ-a ; from φαν, the perf. πέ-φην-a. In Latin
also we have the perfects *cucurr-i, spo-pond-i* for *spo-*
spond-i, ce-cĭd-i, ce-cīd-i, momord-i, and *po-posc-i*, from
the crude forms *curr, spond* or *sponde, căd, cæd, mord* or
morde, and *posc ;* and in Gothic we have the perfects *skái*
-skáid, mái-máit, hlái-hlaup, sáisalt, sái-slép, from the verbs
-káida, máita, hláupa, salta, and *slépa*. It is thought by
some philologists, that *did* in our own language is a re-
duplicated perfect of *do*. Those perfects in Latin which
are formed by a lengthening of the vowel of the crude
form, appear originally to have had a reduplication ; thus
vēn-i is probably a contraction of *vĕvĕn-i, mōv-i* of *mŏ-*
mŏv-i, &c.

The similarity of the person-endings of the perfect
tense will be best shown by the following table : —

	Sanskrit.	Greek.	Latin.	Gothic.
Singular.	vêda	οῖδ-α	vid-i	vait
	vêt-tha	οῖσ-θα	vid-isti	vais-t
	vêd-a	οῖδ ε	vid-it	vait
Plural.	vid-ima	ϝίδ-μεν	vid-imus	vit-um
	vid-a(tha)	ϝίσ-τε	vid-itis	vit-uth
	vid-as	ϝίσ-ασι	vid-erunt	vit-un

The Sanskrit verb is divided into ten conjugations, which are distinguished from each other by the various methods that have been employed to strengthen the crude form of the present tense, and those tenses, which are connected with the present. These conjugations may be separated into two divisions : —

I. VERBS, WHOSE PERSON-ENDINGS ARE JOINED IMMEDIATELY TO THE ROOT.

2nd *conjugation* ; as, *han-ti,* " he kills," from *han.*

3rd ——— as, *da-dá-ti,* " he gives," from *da* ; with the reduplication.

7th ——— as, *yu(n)k-ta,* " ye join," from *yuj* ; with a nasal letter inserted in the root.

II. VERBS, WHOSE PERSON-ENDINGS ARE NOT JOINED IMMEDIATELY TO THE ROOT.

6th *conjugation ;* as, *tud-a-ti,* " he worries," from *tud ; a* added between the root and the person-endings.

1st ——— as, *bódh-a-ti,* " he knows," from *bud ; a* added between the root and the person-endings, and the vowel of the root with guna.

4th ——— as, *nas-ya-ti,* " he perishes," from *nas ; ya* added between the root and the person-endings.

10th ——— as, *chór-aya-ti,* from *chur ; aya* added between the root and the person-endings, and the vowel of the root with guna. This conjugation consists mostly of derivative verbs, especially with a causal meaning.

5th ——— as, *áp-nu-mas,* " we obtain," from *áp ; nu* or *nó* added between the root and the person-endings.

8th ——— as, *tan-u-mus,* " we stretch out," from *tan ; u* added between the root and the person-endings.

9th ——— as, *yu-ni-mas,* " we join," from *yu ; ni* or *ná* added between the root and the person-endings.

In the Greek language, and in several of the other cognate tongues, the present tense, and the tenses derived from it, are frequently modified by the addition of the

same letters as in the Sanskrit conjugations. The verbs
in μι, as they are called, correspond to the first division
which we have made of the Sanskrit conjugations; since
they add the person-endings to the root without the medium of a connecting vowel. Thus such verbs as εἰ-μι,
φη-μὶ, εἰ-μὶ would answer to the second conjugation in
Sanskrit; and ῖ-στη-μι, δί-δω-μι, τί-θη μι, to the third.
Many verbs in Latin, as well as in Greek, insert a nasal
letter in the root, in the same manner as in the seventh
conjugation in Sanskrit; compare λα(ν)θ-άν-ω, μα(ν)θ-άν-ω,
λα(γ)χ-άν-ω, λα(μ)β-άν-ω, and fi(n)d-o, ta(n)g-o, li(n)qu-o,
fun(d)-o, tu(n)d-o, ru(m)p-o, cu(m)b-o.

In the Latin verb, and in the majority of Greek verbs,
the person-endings of the present tense are added to the
root by means of connecting vowels, as λύ-ο-μεν, λύ-ε-τε,
&c., scrib-i-mus, scrib-i-tis, &c., thus corresponding to the
sixth Sanskrit conjugation. Many Greek verbs have the
vowel of the root lengthened in the present tense, as in
the first Sanskrit conjugation; thus λιπ, λείπ-ω; σπερ,
σπείρ-ω; φαν, φαίν-ω, &c. Many other striking points of
similarity between the conjugations of the verb in the
Sanskrit and the cognate languages, might be mentioned
if our limits permitted. The following examples, for instance, will show that the Latin, Greek, and Slavonic
languages form the present tenses of many verbs in the
same manner as in the ninth Sanskrit conjugation: —

		Sanskrit.	Greek.	Latin.	Lithuanian.	Old Slavonic.
Sing.	1	strĭ-nâ-mi	δάκ-ν-ω	ster-n-o	gáu-nu	gyb-nú
	2	strĭ-nâ-si	δάκ-ν-ε῾ις	ster-n-i῾s	gáu-n'-i	gyb-ne-si
	3	strĭ-nâ-ti	δάκ-ν-ε(τ)ι	ster-n-i῾t	gáu-na'	gyb-ne-tj
Dual.	1	strĭ-nî-vas		.. ..	gáu-na-wa	gyb-ne-va
	2	strĭ-nî-thas	δάκ-ν-ε῾τον	.. ..	gáu-na-ta	gyb-ne-ta
	3	strĭ-nî-tas	δάκ-ν-ε῾τον	.. ..	same as sing.	gyb-ne-ta
Plural.	1	strĭ-nî-mas	δάκ-ν-ο῾μεν	ster-n-i῾mus	gáu-na-me	gyb-ne-m
	2	strĭ-nî-tha	δάκ-ν-ε῾τε	ster-n-i῾tis	gáu-na-te	gyb-ne-te
	3	strĭ-na-nti	{ δάκ-ν-ο῾ντι δάκ-ν--οῦσι	ster-n-u῾nt	same as sing.	gyb-nû-tj

The preceding remarks on the study of Comparative
Grammar do not lay claim to any originality; but are

merely intended to direct the attention of English scholars to an interesting branch of science, which has been cultivated with much success in Germany, and to exhibit a few of the most striking facts in this science, which have been elicited and explained by Bopp, Von Humboldt, Schlegel and many other eminent philologists of the present day.

WILLIAM SMITH.

RESULTS OF AN ENQUIRY INTO THE CON-DITION OF THE LABOURING CLASSES IN FIVE PARISHES IN THE COUNTY OF NOR-FOLK.

THE Central Society has continued, as far as its means and opportunities have allowed, its statistical enquiries into the social and intellectual condition of the working classes. Deeply impressed with the vast importance of these enquiries, and with the intimate connection that exists between the physical and moral condition of those classes and the solid and lasting prosperity of the whole community, the Committee would joyfully have extended its investigations to such an extent at least as would have afforded a correct idea of the condition of the most numerous class (the working class) in every division of the kingdom ; but its means are too limited to admit of its undertaking so extensive an operation. What the Society has already been instrumental in bringing to light upon this subject will, however, suffice to show the benefits which would result to our country,—and through it to the world at large,—if the whole social frame and organisation could be thus laid bare in every part, and brought within the observation of those who, by their knowledge, station, and power, might be able to suggest and to apply the necessary remedies for the evils that would thus be made apparent.

Such a minute acquaintance with the details of society as we have been in a small degree instrumental in procuring, would, among other beneficial effects, enable those who cannot feel satisfied to enjoy the luxuries of life themselves without striving to lessen its miseries to others, to carry out their benevolence of purpose with a better assurance than they now have that they are really benefiting the world through their cares and sacrifices. Ignorance upon this subject not only affords a pretext to the selfish to withhold what humanity demands from them, but proves a source of much disquietude to the benevolent, lest, by the direction they give to their liberality, they be not fostering indigence and holding forth a premium to vice. The least objectionable form which charity can put on, is when she offers an asylum to the sick and maimed, and seeks to restore them to health and usefulness. But who must not acknowledge that such plans of benevolence, if they could be formed, as should *preserve from sickness* and *shield from accident*, would be deserving of far higher praise? To which among the discoveries of our immortal Davy will he so much owe his immortality, as to that of the principle which he embodied and brought to practical use in his safety-lamp? The minds that would provide a safety-lamp against other and far more fatal explosions than were ever caused by firedamp, must, if they would work with an assurance of success, make themselves acquainted, as he did, with the sources of the evil they would conquer. It were very greatly to be desired that statistical enquiries, such as the Central Society has already made in certain localities, had been prosecuted in places which are the chief scenes of the disturbances that now contribute so much to the darkness that obscures our political horizon, that we might know how much of that darkness is attributable to avoidable, how much to unavoidable causes,— how much of it to misfortune, how much to mere groundless discontent, how much of the misfortune itself might be removed by the well-directed efforts of those who themselves are made to suffer under it, and in what respects the aid of the public and of the government is required and would avail to that end.

"The poor you have always with you" is a text that has been strangely perverted, and held to be a prophetic assertion of the necessity of pauperism. This is a reading which may square with the feelings of the prosperous sensualist, and may form his excuse for every degree of selfish indulgence. If nothing that he can do will suffice to remedy the evil, why need he trouble himself or sacrifice his ease in the vain endeavour? Those who look with a different eye upon human society, and, disregarding the accidents of birth and fortune and adverse circumstances, can see a brother in every child of humanity, will find in this diversity of lot an incentive to sympathy, means for the exercise of the best feelings of our nature, and will, above all things, desire so to direct their benevolence that it shall be really productive of the good which they desire to accomplish. To this end enquiry is necessary. It is not a case in which reasoning and reflection will suffice; still less is it one in which we may safely give the reins to our undirected feelings. Misfortune will overtake the evil and the good, sickness will break down the strength and the spirits equally of the prudent and the improvident, and it is not for us who witness calamity to be too strict in examining the character of such as claim our sympathy. But we have a higher duty to perform. We have to strive to *prevent* misfortune and vice, sickness and improvidence; and how shall we accomplish this, unless we examine in the spirit of kindness and humanity into the circumstances and habits, the wants and capabilities, of those whom we wish to befriend.

Such enquiries are an object of national, of universal concern—of universal duty. They can never be fully nor effectually made in this country but by the authority of the Legislature, since there is no machinery now at the disposal of government that would enable it to act successfully in the matter, and the task, to be properly executed, is too vast for any private efforts. Something may no doubt be done by very humble means towards its accomplishment, and our Society has not been deterred from attempting to lead the way in the good work. In this, however, it has been chiefly actuated by the hope of inducing others, with more power and influence than it possesses, to take up the task and to carry it forward; trusting that, by such means, the desirableness of the fullest information must be rendered so evident, that parliament may be induced to grant, and the government to employ, the necessary powers for obtaining the minutest returns from one end of the kingdom to the other. In the summer of 1841, a new census will be taken. Before then it will be necessary to make preparations for the satisfactory performance of that important work. Since

1831, when the last census was taken, public attention has been much directed to many subjects connected with social economy, the elucidation of which might be materially aided by an extension of the enquiries which were then thought sufficient. Such an extension cannot be effected without an organised machinery, which will occasion great additional labour and some increased expense; but, as regards this latter objection, it may be urged that it involves a present outlay only as the means for preventing future and greater, but far less satisfactory, expenditure. It is not, however, as a money question that this subject should be considered; but as a duty incumbent on the nation, and one which cannot be avoided nor long delayed if we would not see ourselves left behind by all the world in the race of moral and intellectual improvement.

The enquiries of which the result will be here given, were made in the parishes of Muttishall, East Tuddenham, Garveston, Hockering, and Elmham, forming part of the Misford and Launditch Unions, in the county of Norfolk. It embraced sixty-six families. There were among them—

    1 Carpenter,
    1 Smith,
    1 Shoemaker,
    1 Brickmaker,
    1 Chimney-sweeper, and
  61 Agricultural labourers.

These sixty-six families had among them three hundred and nine children, of whom one hundred and two were above, and two hundred and seven were under, fourteen years of age. There were but three of the families that, at the time the enquiry was made, were receiving parish relief. Of these, one had five children under fourteen years of age; one, seven children under fourteen; and in the third, that of a widow, there were two children under fourteen, and one above that age, who was insane. There were four other families, having among them twenty-one children, who appear at some other time to have had recourse to parish relief; but, as to fifty-nine of the families, it would appear that they had never been pauperized,—a most satisfactory state of things

Ten of the families are described as appearing in distress, five as being dirty, and one as idle, while thirty-seven are noticed as industrious. The remaining thirteen are passed over without any particular remark in this respect. As regards the condition of their dwellings, on which the comfort of the labouring man's family so much depends, fifty-three are said to inhabit good cottages, and thirteen indifferent or bad ones. Of the fathers of families only fourteen could use carpenters' tools, and fifty-one could not; in one family there was no father. There were sixty-two mothers of families who could sew, knit, wash, brew, and bake, and thirty-eight who could make butter; one was unable, from bad health, to perform any of those things. In every case except three, the families had gardens; their extent is given in the returns as follows :—

Rods	$\frac{1}{2}$	1	2	3	4	5	6	7	8	9	10	12	15	16	17	20	30	35
Gardens	1	3	2	3	16	2	5	1	7	2	6	1	1	1	1	8	1	2

In every case except one the garden is described as well cultivated; the badly kept garden was that of the chimney-sweeper. In twenty-two cases a pig was kept. In only one family, that of a labourer with six children, was there a cow kept, and that at the expense of the man's employer. Only six out of the whole number of families were wholly without books. In three of the remaining sixty there was only a Hymn-book; the rest were provided with Bible, Testament, and Prayer-Book, generally with two, and sometimes with all three; but there does not appear to have been any other description of book in any one of the cottages. Only two cases are noticed in the whole number of sixty-six families where any of the members could play on a musical instrument: in thirty-three families they are said to sing cheerful songs; and in the remaining thirty-one, or nearly one-half, this innocent and pleasing resource is not at their command. There were prints found in twenty-five of the cottages; in twenty-four they were on Scriptural subjects, and one was a picture of a slave. In forty-one of the dwellings there was not any picture to be seen. In regard to the very important subject of house accommodation, the following is the return:—Each family appears to have occupied a distinct dwelling; fifteen of them had each two rooms, thirty of them each three rooms, and the remaining twenty-one had each the ample accommodation of four rooms. The apartments in forty-nine of the houses were found to be all of them airy; in eleven houses only a part of the rooms were airy, and in six houses they are reported to be close. The whole of the windows in fifty houses were made to open and shut; in fifteen of the houses only a part were so made; and in one house with two rooms, for which a rent of 3*l.* per annum is charged, the windows do not open. In thirteen families the parents sleep in rooms apart from their children; in twenty-one families part of the children, and in twenty-four families the whole of them, occupy the same sleeping apartments with their parents; in eight of the houses there were no children. In thirty-six families the boys and girls are not placed in separate sleeping apartments, and in twenty-one families they are separated; in one family the children are all boys. There is a plentiful supply of water in forty-five cases, and in the remaining twenty-one cases the supply is deficient.

The state of intellectual cultivation in which the children were found is represented as follows :—

	Above 14 years.	Under 14 years.
Can read and write	8	5
Can read only	70	104
Can neither read nor write	24	98
Have employment	94	—
Have no employment	8	—
Attend school	—	116
Do not attend school	—	91

Of the one hundred and sixteen children that attend school forty-eight go only to Sunday schools, the remaining sixty-eight are instructed in day schools and a charity school. The teaching in the day schools is afforded at the rate of a penny a week for each scholar, which is paid by the parents. In the other schools the teaching is gratuitous.

The girls are for the most part taught sewing and knitting; but in only ten families are the boys taught gardening: in one they are taught carpentering, and in another are employed in chimney-sweeping,—following in both cases the occupation of the father.

The yearly rent paid for their cottages was stated as follows:—

£	s.							Cottages
£2	5	.	.	.	.	.	.	1 Cottage.
2	10	.	.	.	.	.	.	5
2	12	.	.	.	.	.	.	1
2	15	.	.	.	.	.	.	1
3	0	.	.	.	.	.	.	6
3	3	.	.	.	.	.	.	3
3	5	.	.	.	.	.	.	1
3	10	.	.	.	.	.	.	3
3	15	.	.	.	.	.	.	2
4	0	.	.	.	.	.	.	18
4	10	.	.	.	.	.	.	12
4	15	.	.	.	.	.	.	1
5	0	.	.	.	.	.	.	3
5	15	.	.	.	.	.	.	1
6	0	.	.	.	.	.	.	2
6	2	.	.	.	.	.	.	1
								61

For three of the cottages no rent was paid, by reason of the poverty of the tenants: one labourer was the owner of his cottage, and one refused to mention the rent that he covenanted to pay.

G. R. PORTER.

ON THE PRESENT STATE OF PRUSSIAN EDUCATION.

It is now some time since Cousin's Report on Prussian Education appeared in an English dress, in Mrs. Austin's excellent translation. It might have been expected that the information communicated in that instructive document would have gone far to remove many even of our most obstinate prejudices on the question of the utility and practicability of a national system of education. So far from such having been the case, even the Prussian system itself, (to display which in its true light, as to principles, applications, and results, was the great object of the Report,) continues to be misconceived and mis-stated amongst us. This, of itself, might be of little consequence, except to those immediately concerned ; but its influence on all educational questions, especially those affecting the policy of a general organization, is highly injurious. It thus becomes necessary to revert, not merely to the document itself, but to the sources from which it is derived ; and by a re-examination of many of the controverted points, and the facts upon which they rest, especially in their actual operation, to meet these mis-statements, whether intentional or otherwise. Prussian education since 1832 has not only made great progress in quantity and quality in all its branches, but this progress is directly traceable to the developement of the system to which M. Cousin's Report refers.

I spent a considerable portion of last autumn in the Rhenish provinces, of all others the most likely to put to proof the efficiency of the system. They are new acquisitions, of different religious communions, not very well disposed to their new masters, engaged at this moment and for some time back in a religious controversy, and, comparatively speaking, as yet undisciplined to the Prus-

sian code (principle and practice included) of instruction. I had many opportunities of enquiry into both;
not only into the system, but into its effects, physical, intellectual, moral, and religious, not upon one, but upon
all classes of the community. The result, I am bound to
say, was satisfactory. From personal observation and official authority, from the testimony of different professions,
ranks, and persuasions, I have reason to believe the Report below, and not above the reality.

The " New System," " the Prussian System," " the
Government System," these are the appellations with which
the system is honoured :—the object is clear : they are intended to mean " dangerous innovation," " foreign despotism," " ministerial interference with civil and religious
liberty." And yet it is none of all these things. The system
supposed to be so " new" began, as we shall see later, as
early as 1730. It is now the *old* law ; the *old* system ; the
" custom of the land," to which the whole of the past and
present generation have been born. The system supposed
to be so peculiarly " Prussian," is German ; and not only
German, but, with the exception of England, European ;
nay, portions of it are to be found at the other side of
the Atlantic. The system supposed to be so peculiarly
" Government," is quite as much " Communal ;" that is,
as much managed by the people as by the State,—as much
by the local as by the central power. It is to be met with
in various climates, under various governments, and amidst
various creeds : north and south, east and west ; in monarchies, in republics ; in countries solely inhabited by
Protestants, solely by Catholics ; and in countries inhabited by both. Prussia, so far from being the exception
to the general rule, *is* the general rule. So far from
" Prussian" being the proper designation, the proper designation is " Continental," as contradistinguished to English ; in other words, as *the system,* contradistinguished to
the *no-system* of this country.

Had this fact been kept in view, or rather had this
fact been known, we should probably not have heard
so much of its " despotism," " State interference," &c.
Had St. Marc Girardin's Report on Swiss Education
preceded Cousin's on Prussian, the case would very likely

have been the reverse. It would have been called the " Swiss System," and not " the Prussian." Guided as usual by names, we should at this hour have been complaining not of despotism, but of democracy.

In fact the system is neither despotic nor democratic,— any more than the judicial system, public force system, charity system, or any other system, taken by itself, is despotic or democratic : but it may be either, or between both, according to its application and exercise, according to the constitution under which it is in operation ; in other words, according to the moving and regulating powers by which it is applied. The mode in which it is applied in Prussia may not be consonant in some particulars to our habits and opinions, but it does not thence follow that the system itself is bad ; nay, it may be questioned whether even the mode is so objectionable as has been described. The objections taken against it, for the most part seem founded on inadequate examination, or on a gross if not wilful misconception or misrepresentation of facts.

The two prominent objections to the working of the education system of Prussia are, its compulsory character, and its State interference character. The first has been condemned in principle and practice ; it may be doubted whether, abstractedly considered, with justice. Each commune is required to provide a school, and every child not educated in its own family required to attend one. Is this a tyranny ? Let us see. The obligation to provide a school ought to be considered in a civilized community no greater grievance than to provide a Bridewell ; in a free country, not quite so great as to provide a standing military force. What is the practice elsewhere ?—nay, what was, and what is, our own practice at home ? Each township in the New England States, under pain of indictment before the grand jury, was required to establish a school. In Ireland, by the law of Henry VIII, each incumbent was obliged himself to teach, or to provide another to teach in his place ; the obligation it is presumed still exists, for the oath for its observance is taken. By the law of Elizabeth a free school was ordered to be erected in every diocese in the land ; and, by the statutes of Wil-

liam and the Georges, the duty of building them de-
volved on the counties through the means of the grand
juries. A statute still more compulsory was in force in
Scotland, so early as 1494. The principle of taxation for
school purposes, and of compelling attendance on school,
was recognized in that law. In 1615 an act of the Privy
Council, confirmed by an act of the Scotch parliament in
1633, gave it additional force. Even in England the
Factory Act obliges manufacturers to provide means for
the instruction of their work-children, and to see that
these duly avail themselves of such means when provided. Here there is much of Prussian legislation, and
worse than Prussian; for it is legislation merely nominal,
on paper, and inadequately enforced—or legislation partial,
i. e. confined to one class only of the community. If the regulation be bad, why call on clergymen to swear to its observance?—if good, why good for one class of the people,
and not for another? If it be right that the parish clergyman should provide a parish school and teacher, it is surely
right that the school should still be provided, though the
parish clergyman should neglect the duty; if it be of importance that the factory child should have the means of
education, is it not equally so that the child of the agriculturist should have as good, or better? England takes
precisely the worst of the three courses: she recognises
the advantage, she attempts to attain it; calls on the
clergy, who disobey; commands the manufacturer, who
complains; and, failing in both, turns round and consistently
calls out " tyranny " against the countries who, adopting
the same principle that she has done, have had more courage or skill than she has had, and not only see what is good,
but take care effectually and universally to carry it into
operation.

But this, after all, is not the gravamen of the charge. It
is an encroachment, doubtless, on the rights of the citizen
to require that each district should provide a school; but this
is not the worst; the great oppression is, to see that these
schools should be frequented. In this particular we and
the rest of Europe reason differently. The Continent holds
that the citizen should, by religious and moral training,
by exercise and improvement of his whole nature, by

knowledge and experience, be fitted to bear his part in the great family, not only to his own advantage but to that of his fellows. The Continent thinks that, for this end, means should be employed: she prepares, she offers, she gives, she enforces education. This enforcement is of various application — of various character. Sometimes it is limited to inducements only. In some States education is made a condition for admission, not only to honours and emoluments, but to rights and franchises. Some States proceed farther; and, leaving nothing to contingency, prescribe rather than invite; holding no one at liberty to remain irreligious, immoral, or ignorant. In other instances, again, the two processes are combined. Such is the case in most of the German communities.

Attendance is enforced—in the New England States formerly by fine; in Scotland, formerly by fine; in England (in the factories), by fine; in Bavaria, Wurtemberg, Switzerland, by fine; in Prussia also, by fine. These fines are recoverable from the parents by the same process as other fines. There is a great mistake, however, in supposing that they are inflicted for not frequenting the " Government" school. They are inflicted for not frequenting school — for not receiving education. The school of the commune is established by the commune, under the control of a committee of the commune, assisted occasionally by the government, but on occasions only when the commune is too poor to maintain it. The Prussian legislators have avoided the blunder committed by our own; they have not called upon the people to make bricks without straw, or to frequent schools where schools were not to be found. A law confining children exclusively to the government schools would, even in Germany, be resisted. In every town there exist several schools of different sizes, endowments, ranks, and communions; a great variety of choice, and perfect freedom of selection. Any parent may choose any one of them he prefers. True, indeed, teachers are not allowed to teach, unless qualified to teach;* but nei-

---

* This is the principle of the law, and active exertions have been made to carry it into effect. The teachers' seminaries, however, though numerous, have not as yet (as we shall see later) been enabled to supply all the schools.

ther are lawyers permitted to practise, nor physicians to prescribe, nor pastors to preach, without similar precautions. Nor do parents complain of this interference with their children; the children who have grown up into men consider the "obligation" a blessing. To the ignorant and rude populations to which it was first applied, it may possibly have appeared coercive; but with the present enlightened generation it has become a settled habit, a sacred duty. A parent of the present day no more thinks of keeping his child from school than from church. The injunction of the law is generally anticipated, its enforcement rendered almost unnecessary.

It is not intended, however, by these statements to recommend the adoption of a similar arrangement in this country. A system may be good, and yet not good for us; or good for us, and yet not good for us at the present moment. It would be highly unphilosophical, not to take all these circumstances into account. We are too much divided by sect and party, too suspicious of each other, too little impressed with the influence of education upon society, too insensible of the necessity of making it universal in order to make it really efficient, to suffer the introduction of a compulsory system on the German plan, however indirect or mitigated, amongst us. The object in view has simply been to remove many of the exaggerations so prevalent on this branch of the subject; to measure Germany by German habits and reasonings; in other words, to show that, though differing from us, the principles on which she acts are not quite so unreasonable, nor the application of those principles quite so tyrannical, as many friends to education believe.

Prussia directed her attention very early, though somewhat irregularly, to education, especially elementary. Already in 1736 she had declared it to be a duty imposed upon the State. The "*Principia Regulativa*" of the 30th of June of that year imposes the building and maintenance of school-houses on the patrons and communes (*Gemeinde*); applies the incomes of the church to the payment of teachers; determines their duties, rights, appointments, whether in garden, house, or salary; establishes the relations of patron, pastor, and commune, and appropriates a fund of 50,000 rixthalers for the extraordinary support of the schools.—(*Neigeb. sect.* 1.) By more recent ordinances these provisions are extended, especially by the General School Regulation for Country Schools, (*General Land-Schul-Reglement,*) 12th August 1763, and by the Regulation for the Catholic Schools of Silesia, (*Katholische Schul-Reglement für Schlesien,*) of the 3rd November 1765, two of the most beneficial laws of Frederick the Great. It is curious to find in these edicts a statement of the very same evils of which we complain. It is admitted in the preamble or introduction to the first, that the schools and education generally of the youth of the country had fallen into the most lamentable state of neglect, owing, principally, to the incompetency of the great majority of the parish clerks and schoolmasters; that the children in the villages had grown up in ignorance and barbarism, and that it had become of imperative necessity, for the well-being of the kingdom, that a good basis should be laid by means of sound intellectual instruction as well as Christian training of youth, for the diffusion of the true fear of God, and the acquisition of manual and other arts most useful in social life. The obligation of attending school, (*Schulpflichtigkeit,*) to which reference has been so often made, was then for the first time formally imposed on all children from five to fourteen years of age, in order that they might continue there, " until they had acquired not only the knowledge of the most necessary doctrines of Christianity, and could read and write with facility, but were also enabled to answer the questions proposed to them from the class or text-books ordered and approved by the Consistory." The same regulation fixes the school fee at a groschen or four kreutzers per week, for which were to be taught reading, writing, and accounts. The poorer children were not to be exempted from payment; it was contributed from the property of the Church, the commune, or some local charitable institution, " in order," as the law states, " that teachers should not be deprived of their means of support, and that thereby the poorer as well as richer children might be taught with equal fidelity and attention." In aid of these funds an annual " school sermon" was to be established, and at the close of service the parish minister was earnestly to recommend from the altar donations, especially for the purpose of providing the necessary books in village schools for the poorer children. Parents and guardians who impeded the attendance of their children or pupils at school were punishable by fine; and still further, to insure diligence in the pupil, and to maintain in rigour the assiduity of the teacher, it was required that a complete list should be made out from the parish registry, and sent to the proper authorities, of all children in the parish of an age to attend school. To the name of each child were attached the names and residence of the parents, the date of his reception in the school, the hours he had attended, &c. In another list were preserved the testimonials of diligence, progress, conduct, final examination, and period of departure.   These lists or rolls, properly ruled for every day of the month, after a uniform approved formula, were intended to give a general view of the proceeding of the school. They were open to the visiters, and ordered to be placed before the school inspector at his yearly visitation. The inspector, on his side, was required to report them, with remarks from his own observation, to the government of the circle. In the office of the government of the circle they were arranged and compared, and the collection of these tables formed the basis of the school statistics of the nation.

Great attention was required to be paid by this ordinance, not only to the competency, but still more to the conduct and character, to the morals and piety, of the teacher; and the consistories, superintendents, and ephors were charged to see that even in cases where the appointment was in the gift of private patrons, their choice should be regulated on these principles. Previous to admission, an examination (*Prüfung*) was to be held by the school inspectors; and in some of the provinces it was moreover required, that no one should be appointed to the place of schoolmaster who had not passed a certain period in the teacher's seminary of the province. In addition to these provisions there were many important regulations relative to the division of labour in schools, to the course and methods of instruction and training, to the sense and spirit in which the pupil should be educated, which, though they may appear in the present state of schools somewhat antiquated, are very characteristic of an age zealous, it is true, for education, but duly appreciating at the same time the sphere to which school instruction should be confined. To the clergyman of the place was confided the immediate inspection of schools. It was by this law his province and duty to visit the school twice a week, to hold conferences with the teacher, and to remind him, or to suggest to him, whatever improvement might be required. The superintendents, or superior clergy, (*Superintendenten, Oberpriester,*) had the inspection of the collective schools of their district, and were required to visit them once a year. Their reports were to be transferred to the superior consistory (*Oberconsistorium*) for examination, and approval. By a later regulation inspectors are not required to be superintendents, but they are still chosen, in many cases, from the body of the clergy.

Such is the "*Principia Regulativa,*" the oldest of the many edicts which collectively form the actual education-code of the country. The "Catholic School Regulation for the Province of Silesia" is in some measure its complement, and presents a number of similar arrangements for the Catholic schools of that province, and, by subsequent extension, of the whole Prussian monarchy. A number of eminent schools are raised by this ordinance to the rank of teachers' seminaries; the school of the cathedral of Breslau is placed at their head (*Hauptseminarium*) in this institution candidates (*Präparandi*) are to be educated. It is governed by a director, who superintends its progress and income, and reports on the capacity of the pupils at the time of their departure. All clergymen are obliged to learn in this seminary the duties of inspectors. For the erection of appropriate school-rooms, the maintenance of teachers from the funds furnished by endowments, land, &c. &c. every care is taken. In very small places the teacher, for the bettering of his condition, is permitted, in conjunction with his school duties, to exercise a trade, but not in the school-house, or at school hours. Those of innkeeper, of musicians at parties, marriages, &c. are forbidden. On the other hand, if he be of the clerical profession, he is exempted from clerical duty, and allowed to apply himself exclusively to the discharge of his functions as a teacher. In larger places, where there are three teachers in a school, the third is required to possess the rudiments of the Latin and French languages, as well as of general and special history, geography, &c. In order to furnish the pupils with some preliminary instruction in subjects, the knowledge of which is necessary for the social progress of every country, a short and simple text-book was proposed to be composed, comprising elementary notices relative to the leading facts in physics; in political, agricultural, and domestic economy; in trades, arts, manufactures, produce, &c. especially of the district where the school happened to be situated. The age for attending was determined, as in the case of Protestant children, from five to fourteen. Similar care was taken to provide for the payment of the poorer children, for school visits, for the proper keeping of the school-rolls. &c. Further regulations, modelled also on those of the Protestant schools, relative to religious instruction, the visitation of the priest and the inspector, the management and control of the school, the duties and functions of the vicar-general in its regard, were added; and the mode of carrying them into effect rendered intelligible by the publication and distribution of model tables. This school regulation for Catholic schools was confirmed, and considerably enlarged by a more recent one of the present king, in 1801. The improvements were numerous. The situation of the teacher was greatly raised; his maintenance better provided for, and more thoroughly secured; his salary regulated on a higher scale, and paid from more certain funds (the income of the suppressed Latin schools and gymnasia). The teachers' seminaries were rendered more effective. Amongst populations where the religious persuasions are intermingled; where, without too great a diminution of the emoluments of the teacher, a second cannot be appointed, the same teacher instructs all the children in all branches of knowledge which do not appertain to religion; but, during the time of religious instruction the children of the less numerous communions stay away, in order to receive from their own clergyman, or his curate, in the school-house, the necessary instruction in their own religious faith, for at least three hours every week. In order more effectually to secure the due performance of this duty, all candidates of the clerical order are not only obliged, as already prescribed in the first edict, to visit the teachers' seminary at Breslau, but also to receive from the director thereof theoretical and practical instruction in the art of teaching, and in all the sciences necessary for the exercise of the duty of an instructor of youth. The "cloister schools" were subjected to the same regulations. Ecclesiastical endowments, either wholly or in part, were appropriated in aid of the school-fees of the teachers: arrangements were made to better the inferior appointments ; but, on the other side, the permission to exercise particular trades (amongst which, curiously enough, that of tailor was included) was withdrawn : "inasmuch as the teacher ought to occupy himself solely with the teaching of his pupils, or with due preparation for the same " (§ 32). Nor was this attention to the interests of the teacher confined to salary : every care was evinced to raise him in his own and the public estimation. Kind treatment on the part of the nobility, commune, clergy, &c. was strictly enjoined. He held his situation as a right of which he could not be deprived, unless for incompetency or misconduct, on report of the school inspector, and after previous solemn trial. Repetition hours out of school hours were prescribed for the instruction of those children whose early education had been neglected, and at these the apprentices of artisans were required to attend. There were no specific provisions relative to class or text books (§ 42), on the ground that from year to year new books and better might be published, and any restriction in that particular might tend to impede rather than to advance improvement. The selection of the best suited, as to price and composition, was left to the school directors; they were at the same time cautioned against any unnecessary change. Instruction was to continue on full days for five hours, on half days for three. From Midsummer to Martinmas the afternoon school was dispensed with. When there was only one teacher the school was divided into three classes, and each in rotation was required to be kept employed. To constitute the local committee, besides the clergymen, two substantial householders were to be chosen by the commune; they were required to visit the school every fourteen days. The naming of the inspectors was left to the Prince Bishop of Breslau; they were to be selected from the clergy; but it was required they should be active intelligent men, experienced in the art of teaching, and be submitted to, and receive the approbation of the school directors upon entering on their office. This regulation, in the extension of the ordinance to other Catholic provinces, was so far changed that the school inspectors were allowed to be taken from the class of literary men with a reference, however, to the bishop, who had a vote on each appointment. Nor were other institutions passed by. Regulations were prescribed for the establishment and maintenance of industrial schools, in which the mechanical arts, for females as well as males, were to be taught, and funds appointed for their extension, (§ 58.) Teachers' seminaries, in a more especial manner, as may well be imagined, attracted the attention of government. Each province (such, at least, was the intention of the law) was to be provided with a sufficient number of seminaries, divided according to the respective religious communions, and for the instruction of such as should not have been brought up in such institutions, or whose education might otherwise have been neglected, provision was made by means of examinations, periodical school conferences, and public competitions of teachers.

These two fundamental laws form the groundwork, even at present, of the whole system of elementary education in Prussia, which through a number of more recent decisions, rescripts, and circulars on various details,* have been ren-

* They relate to almost every educational topic:—Duty of attendance on school; school discipline; control to be exercised by school visitation; instruction and inspection of children employed in manufactures; simultaneous instruction; public management of school funds; adaptation of instruction to objects and situation of pupil,— for which purpose the regulations (No. 8. § 171) appear especially well fitted; advancement of agricultural and mechanical knowledge; communication of instruction through means of well-chosen teachers, in industrial and manual occupations; superintendence and training; schools of Art; Reform schools for young criminals; guardianship of illegitimate children; protection against pleasures injurious to morals; instruction of deserted

dered every day more complete, and extended to the newly incorporated portions of the monarchy. It thus appears, that for now more than a century, but especially during the reigns of Frederick and his present majesty, elementary education in all its branches, necessities, and objects, has met with the most comprehensive and judicious attention. But the system does not yet form a compact and regular whole. The reducing to form and symmetry these various materials has long since more than once occupied the attention both of the country and the goverment. A "General School Law" was promised by the Government in the Instructions of 1817 (*Neigeb.* § 184), in these words: — " In order to lay a firm foundation for the edution of the youth of the nation, we have taken measures for the publication of a 'General School Regulation' (*Allgemeine Schul-Ordnung*), and grounded thereon especial rules for particular provinces, in which their respective peculiarities shall, as far as possible, be regarded." Eighteen years have now elapsed, and this royal assurance still remains unfulfilled. It may be that the results are not yet sufficiently ascertained in the newly arranged provinces, that ministers are deterred by the heaviness of the undertaking, or that sensible of the difference still existing on some material points in the management of the elementary as well as the learned schools, they do not wish by too premature an adoption of a general code, to preclude the still incomplete developement of educational opinions amongst the people.

The existing system, which may be thus considered as a series of decisions and instructions, rather than a single

children ; improvement of the condition of teachers ; school fees ; application of teaching to the advancement of manufactures ; pensioning and superannuation of teachers ; provision for their families after their decease by the establishment of teachers' savings' banks, &c. These injunctions frequently extend to the regulation of the spirit or nature of instruction. By the circular of 24th July, 1822, teachers are cautioned against encouraging half-knowledge, or excessive or inappropriate studies, " Dass nämlich es nicht auf viel und mancherlei sondern auf grundliches Wissen ankomme dass das Nothwendige und Unentbehrliche zunächst und recht gelehrt werden müsse, dass aber die Grundlage aller Bildung in der Erziehung zur Frömmigkeit, Gottesfurcht und christlichen Demuth bestehe."

organic law, is carried into effect throughout the monarchy by a machinery pretty nearly uniform.

By the ordinance of the 27th October 1810, immediately after the peace of Tilsit, a special government department was created for Public Worship, Public Instruction, and Medicine, presided over by a minister of State (for many years the Baron von Altenstein), with a director under him, and composed of a number of counsellors, selected from the higher departments of the administration. This council, or board, determines the estimate or budget, for the establishment or maintenance of all institutions belong-' ing to the higher branches of education, and is entrusted with the application of all funds destined to such purposes. Subordinate to this council, in each of the seven provinces of the kingdom is a Consistory (*Consistorium*), whose head is the president of the provincial government. Besides ecclesiastical matters, as far as they appertain to the State, this body has the management of middle and elementary education. The universities alone are placed under the immediate direction of the ministry. But as the provinces are again subdivided into governments, or government circles (*Regierungs Bezirke*), each circle, with the exception of that in which the capital is situated, has also its special board of Church and school commissioners, which, under the guidance and direction of the Provincial Consistory, administer those affairs which require a more immediate personal superintendence. The head of this board is a member of the council of the circle, and has the initiative in all school affairs which require the co-operation of that body. He appears once a-year, (with the right of voting in the Consistory,) at the seat of the government of the province, in order to present a report on the relations existing between them and the board of school commissioners of his circle. This will appear more intelligible from a comparison of the ordinances respecting the better regulation of the provincial authorities, from 30th April 1815. (*Neigeb.* § 178.)

In the management of all matters exclusively referring to the teaching and discipline of schools, both the Consistory of the province and the board of school commissioners of the circle are required to consult professional men, such as emeriti directors of gymnasia, &c. who are invited for this purpose to assist as members. In the management of financial and judicial concerns, those only are referred to who are officially connected with those departments. The Ordinance of the 30th April 1815, which forms the basis in a great measure of this organisation, was subsequently modified, and its provisions considerably enlarged and improved, by the regulations for the administration of the Provincial Consistories, of the 23d October 1817, and by Istructions to the provincial governments, bearing the same date. Conformably to these regulations, the Consistory, under its president, is confined in the management of elementary education to a general superintendence, including the training of teachers; but, on the other hand, it has the immediate direction and inspection of all the higher learned schools, with the exception of the Latin schools and universities, on the condition only that for the higher appointments, such as those of rectors, directors, and head masters, it should obtain the sanction of the ministry. Religious instruction is carefully provided for, and for this purpose reference is first required to be made by the president to the local school authorities, who, on the appearance of candidates for the situation of teacher, appoint commissioners, or examiners, to ascertain their competency to teach religion. The Consistory, on its side, in order to protect the office of teacher from the intrusion of candidates who have not acquired sufficient knowledge, or are likely to introduce injurious or improper methods, have also their commissioners, or examiners, composed chiefly of scientific men, selected from the professors of the universities, whose duty it is to pronounce on the qualifications of the young men who present themselves for appointment. Various other changes have been effected by more recent regulations. By the Instruction of 31st December 1823, the Provincial Consistory is divided into two sections or colleges:—1. "The Consistory," properly so called, to whose management is confided the administration of all matters exclusively relating to the Protestant religion. Under the president, the general superintendent of the province is appointed its director, by the Instruction of the 14th May

1829, with the obligation also of directing his attention to the elementary and lower Bürger schools, as preparatory schools for the Church, and to the religious tendency of the learned and higher Bürger schools of the province. 2. " The Provincial School College" (*Provinzial Schul-Collegium*), to administer all matters relating to public instruction. To the president, as common head of both colleges, is entrusted the office of placing the members in either or in both, regard being had to his qualifications for the discharge of their respective duties. At an earlier period, it was requisite to obtain for these arrangements, either of appointment or promotion, the previous authority of the ministry. They are, in addition, invested with the whole financial management of the educational establishments within their district. The school commissioners of the circle continue subject to their jurisdiction, and under the school commissioners are placed inspectors, to whom the local committees are subordinate.

It will be seen from this short sketch that there is much less centralisation in the system than is usually imagined. On the contrary, we find a minute division and subdivision of duties and powers, and due regard to all interests, local as well as general. In the first instance there is *a long series of authorities between the State and the school* :—1. The Council of Public Instruction, a department of the ministry, headed by a responsible officer of the Crown, representing directly the authority of the State. 2. The Provincial Consistory, an intermediate authority, representing the Church. 3. The School Commissioners, or Council of the Circle, a large local authority. 4. The School Commissioners, or Council of the Commune, or a small local authority, both representing in greater or lesser mass the people. II. *The same board does not execute all the functions of the department, nor the same section all the functions allocated to each board.* The religious functions are discharged by the ecclesiastical section ; the lay by the lay ; on matters strictly professional, professional men are called into consultation ; on affairs of teaching, teachers ; on matters financial, official financiers. III. *Each class shares in the powers and duties, lay and ecclesiastical, high and low, public and private.* Each sect, Catholic and Protestant, wherever the population is mixed members of the administrative department, &c. in the province and circle, substantial householders in the commune form the chief materials of the respective councils and committees; the pastors also of the respective communions are allowed their participation in the management, both general and local, and are specially called on to visit the schools, being, however, required to prepare themselves previously for the duty, by an appropriate course of study and practice in the Teachers' Seminary. IV. *Books used in the course of instruction are left in a great degree to the choice of the local bodies.* Those destined for religious instruction must have the sanction of the bishop or pastor of the communion by whom they are to be used. V. *The religious instructor must be examined by the commissioners of the local body, and approved of by the local body and local pastor.* VI. *The examiners of candidates for the situation of teacher are a distinct body from the ministerial, provincial, circle, or communal boards.* VII.* *United education is not a matter of compulsion:* it is left at the discretion of the commune. When adopted, it is required that religious instruction should be given to

---

* In the towns especially, such is the case, since the introduction of the new and revised municipal law. The principle that the people should have the power of managing their own local concerns, through bodies elected by themselves, is not only admitted, but acted on, to a much greater extent in those countries than even, in many particulars, in England and in Scotland. Amongst matters of local interest, none rank higher in the estimate of all branches of the German nation, whatever may be their several or political constitutions, than institutions which have reference to education, or, more generally speaking to intellectual and moral progress. Hence it is that, as a matter of course, the management of schools in each town forms, either directly or through committees, one of the principal objects of the municipal body. These bodies, as already mentioned, are elected by the people. Where none exist, the people choose respectable householders amongst their number to represent them in the school committee. To this local interference and control directly derived from a free municipal organisation, the Government is so far from being opposed, that in a late official report (*Beilage zur Allgemein. Prusse Staats-Zeitg, No.* 301,) it is admitted that to this cause, and to the appointment of intelligent and active school committees, by the several municipalities much of the present advanced state of elementary education is to be ascribed.

each sect in the school-house, but apart.* VIII. *Due provision is made for religious and moral instruction. (Religion und Sittenlehre), general and special, in every school without exception.* IX. *Education in the Government or Communal school is not enforced : the selection of the school is left to the parents or guardians of the child.* X. *No perfectly uniform system is yet established : modifications are permitted according to circumstances.*

Such, then, is the amount of government interference. The reader will scarcely discern in these arrangements any very glaring proofs of that deep-laid conspiracy against freedom and religion which has been ascribed to the founders of the Prussian system, who have been guided, we firmly believe, by the conviction that the happiness of a nation can only be secured by affording to all its members a sound intellectual and religious education. That such was their conviction, and that this conviction has been fully justified by results, ought, one would think, no longer to be questioned. We shall soon see, from the latest returns, that, through the judicious and energetic application of these laws, there is scarcely a child now in Prussia that is not in a course of education; that the course pursued is every day receiving new improvements both in matter and manner; and, that the consequences resulting from even its earlier and more imperfect operation have exceeded expectation, and led to the well-founded hope that, with the great amelioration which has since taken place, not only the next generation will vindicate

---

* The opinion entertained of the importance of this duty, and of the manner in which it is performed, is thus expressed in the official document. " The simple truths of positive religion are to every one of the utmost importance in life, and afford the poorest and humblest the best consolation, the best direction, the best support, under the burthens and afflictions of their existence. It is one of the fairest portions of the hallowed vocation of the country clergyman to gather around him young children, to inspect and visit schools ; and many most worthy ecclesiastics have devoted themselves to this occupation with especial love." It is elsewhere observed, that difference of religious opinion, even in the same neighbourhood, so far from injuriously influencing the exercise of this duty, has only stimulated to exertion,—to a more generous rivalry between the pastors of the several communions in doing good.

the system from these aspersions, but display to the fullest the forethought and benevolence of its authors. And first, as to numbers :—*There are few children now in Prussia not in a course of instruction.* This will appear from the last official report, which goes up to 1838. Taking the proportion of the number of children of the age fixed by law for attending school—*i. e.* from 6 to 14—as one-sixth of the whole population, we shall find that nearly the whole of that number are actually in attendance. In the public elementary schools in Prussia the number of children under education at the beginning of 1838 were 2,171,745. The population of the monarchy in the same year, exclusive of Neufchatel, was $14,098,125 - \frac{14,098,125}{2,171,745} =$ 6·49 ; so that in the Prussian states between the sixth and seventh child is actually at school. Yet, after all, this is scarcely an accurate answer to the inquiry — what is the number of attendants between the ages of six and fourteen ? It would approach more nearly to the truth if calculated at 6·15.* This is a strong contrast to what is

* The children in the Bürger and Middle schools are not all under fourteen, though they generally leave those institutions on the completion of that age. In the gymnasia those in prima and secunda, and a portion only of those in tertia, are above fourteen. In the gymnasia and pro-gymnasia there were in 1837, 25,267 pupils. Taking the average of attendance from the roll of several years, one-third of these classes may be considered as the proportion above fourteen. There will thus be two-thirds of pupils under that age, or 16,845

In the middle schools . . . 38,277

In girls' schools, not comprehended amongst the
    elementary schools, . . . 39,927

In the higher Bürger schools . . 11,807

                                      106,856

Given above 2,171,745

Total 2,278,601

That is $\frac{14098125}{227801} = 6·19$ of the population. But, if to these be still farther added all the children attending private schools, with the exception of the universities and higher schools, very probably amounting to something near 13,000, we shall have not 6·19 but 6·15, approximating closely to one-sixth of the entire population. Children between the ages of six and fourteen form one-sixth, so that it is not too much to say, relying on these tables, that the *whole* of the population of Prussia of an age to be educated is at this moment in a course of education.

observable in other countries. Both in England and France a far lower proportion is in course of education. To the condition of England in this respect it is scarcely necessary to advert. The late reports of the statistical societies, the publications of this society, and the evidence taken before the education committee (England) of the House of Commons in 1837, leave, unfortunately, little doubt as to our vast inferiority. The sixth of the population of France amounts to 6,512,187, equal to the number of children between six and fourteen. Of these there are actually under education only 3,309,656, so that there is now rising in France a generation of 3,202,531 altogether uneducated. Were the state of education the same in Prussia as it is in France — taking the ratio of the population of Prussia to that of France to be as 14 to $32\frac{1}{2}$ — there would be in Prussia 1,372,532 children without education. The tables lately published show that the difference between the number of children of an age to go to school and the number actually at school is only 540,601=2·55 ; nor must it be inferred that the whole even of this number remain altogether without education: 2,830,328 are the number of children between the ages of six and fourteen. When it is considered that very many children are employed in manufactures in various trades, and in agriculture, as early assistants to their parents, and thus often enter school at the age only of seven, and leave it at the age of thirteen, the deficiency of 540,601 will be more apparent than real, and be very easily accounted for. From the tables, indeed, it would follow that there were no children, generally speaking, without education in Prussia. *(See Table A.* p. 430.*)*

At the same time it is obvious that there are considerable differences at this moment observable between the different provinces. In those of Saxony, Pomerania, &c. education is universal. This is attributable to the exertions of the local authorities. The respective governments have taken great pains fully to remedy every defect. The clergy will not admit children to the instructions preparatory to confirmation until they can read and write. In the majority of the districts the deans and superintendents have been most assiduous and exemplary in visiting the schools; the same praise may be bestowed on the inspectors, to whom are confided in each district a certain number of the country schools. The periodical reports are exact and minute: the regulations respecting education punctually enforced; and, whenever necessary, strengthened by new instructions from the government. Much aid has also been derived in towns, according to the official report, from the salutary introduction of the municipal law, old and revised; the committees chosen by the town councils for the management of the town schools, have been of essential service. Even in the agricultural districts similar zeal for the improvement of education is every day becoming more conspicuous. Nor are many of the regulations lately introduced in other departments without their salutary influence. The universally-required military service in particular has had the most beneficial results. Every soldier must now be instructed. If, by any chance, he cannot read or write, both are immediately to be taught him whilst serving in the capacity of a soldier.

Notwithstanding these very favourable evidences, it must not, however, be asserted that nothing more remains to be done for elementary education in Prussia. In some of the other provinces, indications of neglect are here and there perceptible. This is more particularly the case in those where the peasant, not being originally of German race, has only of late years had the opportunity of enjoying the benefits of German civilization. Into the Duchy of Posen, for instance, and the government circles of Marienswerder and Danzig, of the province of antient West Prussia, generally inhabited by Poles, education has not yet universally penetrated. The tables represent only every seventh or ninth child as attending school. Similar deficiencies may be detected in places where there are numerous manufactures employing children — such as in the circles of Aix la Chapelle, Düsseldorf, &c. Government should take measures (though it be a matter of no small difficulty) to prevent children from working in those establishments so early as to interfere with their instruction.* The same

* Since the above was written, some salutary regulations have been promulgated by the government for the purpose of checking this evil.

inattention is still more conspicuous in the larger towns. Even in Berlin, the seat of Government, with all the recent exertions of the communes, the tenth of the population is not yet in attendance at school. From a recent official publication (*Preuss*. *Staats-zeitung*, *No.* 190, 1838) it appears that there are still in this city some thousand children who receive either none, or a very irregular and imperfect education. (*See Table B.* p. 429.)

The number of public elementary schools in Prussia amount to 22,910; a large proportion, considering the number of children under education. It allows, taking all matters into consideration, not more than one hundred pupils on an average to every public school.

The next interesting subject of inquiry which presents itself refers to expenditure. How are the expenses of these schools defrayed, and what is the proportion actually paid by the State? Taking the number of Elementary Schools at 22,910, as already stated, and supposing each school, according to official calculation, to require for payment of teachers, cost of school, outfit, apparatus, &c. a sum not exceeding 150 thalers yearly, the whole charge of all these schools would amount to an annual sum of 3,436,500 thalers = 515,475 pounds sterling. According to the estimates (*Haupt-Finanz-Etat*) for the year 1838, the whole amount appropriated to the service of the department of Public Instruction did not exceed 2,817,000 thalers; so that were the expenses of education to be exclusively defrayed by the State, and this sum were to be applied exclusively to elementary schools, it would be altogether insufficient even for that purpose.

It is not improbable that of this annual sum of 2,817,000 thalers, scarcely 100,000 are really allotted to the maintenance of elementary education. This is in full accord with the spirit of the law, and the principle at all times prevalent, and in practical operation in Prussia, that the establishment and support of elementary schools is a matter especially and almost exclusively belonging to the commune. In few instances indeed is this obligation eluded, much less resisted.* The poorer communes undoubtedly

---

* " Es ist," says one of the latest reports, in referring to this duty, " den gesetzlichen Bestimmungen gemäss, dass die Erhaltung der Ele-

labour under some difficulties, and it is important they should be provided with funds for the building, at least, of the school. Such funds, accordingly, are furnished in various ways, either from the special school fund of the province, or from endowments by proprietors, or the subscriptions of benevolent individuals, or, finally, from grants from the State. The King, too, on all such occasions, has uniformly shown every readiness to order extraordinary assistance from the treasury.

But, though the State does not consider itself bound, except on such special and extraordinary occasions, to assist in the support of elementary schools; yet, in reference generally to elementary education, it deems it a matter of the deepest obligation to maintain from the public funds the education of competent teachers. Notwithstanding the urgent recommendations of Basedow, many years elapsed, after the first efforts for the improvement of Prussian education, before any effective steps had been taken in this most essential of all reforms. Prussia. continued to suffer under the same evils with ourselves: superannuated invalids, tailors, tradesmen, and mechanics of various descriptions, who had received scarcely any education themselves, were often found in the situation of masters in the village-schools. Under such a system it was at length admitted, that all efforts for the improvement of education must be in vain ; and steps were at last taken, in order to check the evil, for the establishment of seminaries for teachers. One of the first of these on a good plan was established at Karalene, in the government circle of Gumbinnen, in the year 1809. From thence they soon spread to all other parts of the country. These institutions are generally under the management of a director, who has received a thoroughly scientific education ; and, in the larger ones, of such as had already distinguished themselves by their experience in the art of teaching. The age of admission is from eighteen to twenty. The course of study embraces,

mentarschule *Sache der Kommune sey* ;" and it adds, " This is quite reasonable. Every commune should consider that, as it is its duty to provide for its lighting and watering, so far more is it an obligation to attend to its churches and schools : it must be admitted that the desire to fulfil such obligation, is every day becoming more general amongst the communes."

besides the mother tongue — in which great facility, both as to speaking and writing, is considered essential,—a competent knowledge of mathematics; natural philosophy; those branches of botany which have immediate reference to the ordinary purposes of life, — such as relate, for instance, to poisonous plants, &c.; the elements of natural history, geography, history, music, comprehending playing on the organ, and singing by note; but, above all, the theory and practice of the art of teaching. With the view of presenting every facility for the acquirement of this latter branch, a school is generally attached to the seminary, where the seminarists give instruction daily under the direction of their teachers. A distinction exists between the rural seminaries educating teachers for the rural elementary school, and the town seminaries—such as exist at Berlin, Magdeburg, &c. — educating teachers for the town, or middle and Bürger schools. The plan of instruction is proportionately enlarged for the purposes of these latter.

The number of seminaries, or teachers' schools, in the Prussian states at the beginning of the year 1838 were forty-five; the number of pupils, or seminarists, 2,583. The number of teachers required for the service of all classes of schools were as follows :—

I. *Public Elementary Schools.*

Teachers	.	23,858
Assistants	.	2,468

II. *Middle Schools for Boys.*

Teachers	.	748
Assistants	.	191

III. *Schools for Girls, not comprehended under Elementary Schools.*

Teachers	.	479
Assistants	.	371

IV. *Higher Bürger Schools.*

Teachers	.	367
Assistants	.	200

Total . . 28,682

Calculating the period of the service of a teacher on an average at about thirty years, (a calculation justified by experience both in reference to the profession and the duration of human life,) there will be annually from 900 to 1000 teachers to replace in the four classes of schools just enumerated. The third of the seminarists under actual education generally leave their seminaries, after a three years' course, each year. This would give about 861; so that the present demand at first sight would appear to be tolerably well met by the supply. But, it must be remembered that, besides deductions for casualties and changes, many, destined under other circumstances for teachers in the elementary schools, are taken out for private instructors, inspectors, &c. It thus happens a considerable deficiency of well-educated masters still continues to exist, which is likely, however, to be supplied by the gradual extension of the seminaries. The rapidity with which those at present in existence have been established, (upwards of forty in the period of thirty years,) and the extraordinary impulse they have contributed to give to the diffusion of a really sound education, leave little doubt that what yet remains to be accomplished will be easily and cheerfully effected. In consequence of the intimate connection between elementary education and the religious persuasions of the people, the seminaries are divided into Catholic and Protestant, and are subject to the inspection of their respective ecclesiastical superiors. In the provinces of Posen, Silesia, Westphalia, and the Rhine, they are principally Catholic; in the others, principally Protestant.

The larger of these institutions are supported at the expense of the State. Many possess buildings and funds from bequests and endowments.

Such are the general provisions throughout the monarchy for elementary instruction; but, besides such as are common to all, there are others of a more special nature connected with elementary education. Some short notice of these latter may not prove uninteresting.

Schools for the Deaf and Dumb. — The deaf and dumb in the Prussian states amounted at the beginning of 1838 to 11,104. Taking the number of children from six to fourteen, as the proportion fit to go to school, we shall have 2,221 as the number of deaf and dumb requiring

instruction. They are in reality, however, more numerous; if we extend the period in which they continue
to attend school to the completion of the age of fifteen, they may be reckoned at 3,156. Deduction
must on the other side be made of all such as, in
consequence of extreme corporeal defect, are not susceptible of mental culture. There are establishments
for the education of the deaf and dumb, erected for
the greater part at the personal expense of the present
king, at Berlin, Königsberg, Breslau, Munster, and Cologne. As it is impossible in these establishments to educate all the deaf and dumb of the kingdom, it has been
thought advisable to prepare as large a number as possible
of teachers for the duty ; and, with this object, at the cost of
the province, there are attached two seminaries for teachers'
schools in which deaf and dumb children who may have
been given in charge to private families may be instructed ; and, in which the pupils in the teachers' seminaries
may have an opportunity of practically learning the art
of teaching this afflicted class of the community. This
suggestion has been already adopted with the happiest
results in the provinces of Saxony, Westphalia, Posen,
Prussia, and, it is to be hoped, will soon be imitated
with equal zeal by the other provinces.

Schools for the Blind.—The number of blind in the
Prussian states amounted, in the beginning of 1838, to
10,224. As many have been so visited at later periods of
life, we should not be justified, as in the case of the deaf and
dumb, in taking the fifth of 10,224, or 2,045, as the number of blind between six and fourteen capable of instruction. The true number is considerably smaller. Of the
total 10,224 there are not more than 915 blind under
fifteen. There are two large schools for the blind in
Prussia, the one at Berlin, the other at Breslau. The
first will receive in a short time, from the bequest of the
Rottenburg family, a very considerable accession to its present property.

Orphan Houses,—more properly belonging to the class
of charitable institutions,—such as the great Military Orphan House of Potsdam. They are to be found in all the
larger towns, for the most part erected and maintained at

the cost of private individuals or corporate bodies. They are noticed here for the admirable care taken in all of them of elementary education.

Infant Schools,—under various designations, and of various degrees,—*Warte-schulen, Kinder-bcwahrungs-Anstalten:*—like the *Ecoles d'Asyle* of France, principally intended for the reception of very young children, who otherwise would be left to wander about the house, or be given in care to other children, if left at home, during the absence of their parents, *Klein-kinder Schulen,*—preparatory schools for children, before they proceed to the elementary or *Volksschulen,* &c. &c. They owe their establishment in great measure to private benevolence, and have not as yet become very general. There are already, however, twenty-one at Berlin, educating 1,400 children.

Reform Schools,—more properly *Rescue Schools,*—*Rettungs-Anstalten,* for unprotected or convict children. This is a most important branch of elementary education, and many of the most eminent educationists in Prussia, Professor Julius, for instance, attribute to their establishment and extension the far more salutary influence exerted by elementary education in that country than in so many others. The object, and it may be added, result of these institutions, may be collected from the following observations of the official paper :—" The painful experience that crime, especially thieving, so often practised by children,—the farther experience, that the loss of parental protection, or neglect in attending school, often leads to these malpractices in early life,—the conviction that the young criminal may be restored to society corrected, provided that imprisonment (which, however, but too often draws the offender, by communication with adult criminals, still deeper into crime) be followed by a good course of education, combined with continued labour, under a rigorous restraint, have suggested to private benevolence the establishment of these institutions, now to be found, great and small, in many parts of the Prussian monarchy. And though, from a former very ample report, (16*th Nov.* 1837, *N.* 318,) it would appear that the number of young criminals in Prussia is by no means so great (not amounting to $\frac{1}{15346}$ of the entire population, or, in other words, to only one juvenile offender in 2,484, from the age of ten to sixteen,) still these institutions are of the highest benefit; and, from their efforts to bring back the lost sheep to the right fold, are deserving of the greatest gratitude of the country."— (*Preuss*^e. *Staats-Zeitz*^g, 1837.)

There are numerous other institutions, such as " Schools of Industry," " Horticultural Schools," &c. which might be classed in some respects under elementary education, but which appear more properly referrible to that degree, intermediate between it and collegiate or gymnasiac, indicated by the Bürger and middle schools already mentioned. The limits of this paper preclude the possibility of now entering into any discussion, however interesting, of the organisation or progress of these, or other higher branches which immediately succeed them. It must necessarily be deferred for the present, with the intention of resuming it on the earliest opportunity.

We have still to inquire somewhat more in detail into the operation of the system, and to see how far the favourable picture above noticed has been borne out by the reality. For this purpose, no part of Prussia, as I have already stated, seems better suited than the Rhenish provinces. They had under their former *régime* been neglected; their schools were few and indifferent; their other public institutions inferior; their commerce very partially protected. Here, then, the change and contrast were likely to be most conspicuous,—the true merits of the system most discernible. In addition, late religious divisions would serve to test especially that portion of education which referred to morals and religion. If these contests were still unable, however they might affect other arrangements of society, to disturb the course adopted in this, little doubt could exist of its soundness and impartiality. I congratulated myself, therefore, on being afforded, both at Bonn and other portions of the province, during a residence of some months, frequent opportunities of not only personally inspecting the various classes of schools, whilst in active operation, but of confirming by my own observation, the results already stated to have been produced on other portions of the community.

Bonn is a small town, of not more than 10,000 inhabitants, but the seat of the second university of the monarchy, educating 700 or 800 students, under the instruction of seventy professors, amongst whom are to be found names ranking amongst the highest in modern German science and philology. It thus forms, in a great degree, the intellectual capital, as Düsseldorf does the capital of the arts, of the whole of this interesting district, and presents peculiar facilities for all investigations of an educational character. In the neighbourhood is Brühl, Cologne, not far Neuwied, Kreuznach, &c. &c.

The province of the Rhine (*Rhein-Provinz*) is divided into five government circles :—

Aachen (Aix la Chapelle),	75 square miles	352,972 inhabitants	
Coblenz, . .	109 —	417,333	—
Köln (Cologne) .	82 —	392,315	—
Düsseldorf, . .	98 —	700,078	—
Trier (Trèves) . .	120 —	376,553	—
	484	2,239,251	

Two-thirds of this population is Catholic.

The seat of the provincial government is Coblentz. The constitution of its " Consistory " and " Provincial School-Commission," or board, will give a clear idea of the elements and powers of these bodies. There are six members: two ecclesiastical commissioners, or counsellors (*Kirchenräthen*), for Catholic and Protestant ecclesiastical affairs ; two school commissioners (*Schulräthen*), Bruchman, formerly director of the gymnasium of Düsseldorf, for the Catholics, and Euler, formerly director of the gymnasium at Kreuznach, for the Protestants ; two members from the government or administration of the province, whose duty it is to attend to the financial department, to the auditing of the accounts, the pecuniary administration of the schools, &c. &c. The four other circles of the province, excepting that of Cologne, have each for their Church and school commission or board, one ecclessiastical, and one school commissioner ; the latter of whom, besides superintendence over the elementary, middle, and Bürger schools, has also the management of the Learned schools, in which pupils for the lowest class of the gymnasium are usually

preferred. In each of these circles a number of inspectors,
adequate to the wants of the circle, are appointed, each of
whom has under his care from fifteen to twenty schools,
but not unfrequently double the number, and sometimes
even more. The salary of school-inspector is not fixed by
any certain rule. He is generally a clergyman of known
experience in matters of education. He is required to visit
annually, in company with the local school committee, every
school under his jurisdiction ; besides this more minute examination, he is every month obliged to hold a conference
with the entire body of teachers in the schools of his district. On these occasions, whatever relates to the profession, or affects the interests of the several schools, is
brought forward and freely discussed. These conferences
have been found much more conducive to the progress of
schools than formal official reports. The excellences or
defects of particular methods are practically exhibited:
the teacher has, by communication and comparison, an
ample opportunity of correcting errors, or adopting improvements, from the experience of his colleagues. Reports, on the contrary, usually run into generalities, suggest views merely theoretical, and fall at times into obscurity and trifling. The expenses of inspectors and
teachers on such occasions are defrayed by the Government
on a reasonable scale. There are 2,000 schools in the province, for the most part regulated by the church divisions,
and sometimes connected with the churches. Thus in
Cologne, where there are sixteen church jurisdictions,
there are sixteen male and sixteen female schools. Of
these 2,000 schools, 1,600 are Catholic.

Immediately subordinate to the officers just mentioned
are the local committees or boards (*Schulvorstände*). In
the Rhenish province, as elsewhere, their duties are defined
by law. Complaints have been made that there is considerable difficulty in enforcing the obligation of regularly
visiting the schools. The attendance, too, of the children
in some instances is said to be slack. There are parishes
where only one-third of the children have been got to attend. These cases, however, are very rare, and attributable to the relics of old habits. The payment of the monthly
school-fee, required without reference to attendance, is also

collected, too, not without some exertion, from families of limited means and with many children. Five or eight groschen (a groschen is somewhat more than a penny) for each child is, in poorer districts, too heavy. In some instances, force, or at least threats, have been found necessary. A better expedient to attract and increase the contributions and attendance, would be a better class of masters. Where children have been driven away by bad treatment, or inefficient teaching, all legal efforts have proved unavailing; the schools remain empty, but fill again the moment the true ground of desertion is removed, by the substitution of another teacher better qualified for the office, and more calculated to gain the confidence of the parents and the attachment of the children by his intelligence and good conduct. Much has been done, and more is still doing, in the Rhenish province, to obtain this most desirable of all results; but the country parishes are not yet fully supplied, as they have not yet had time to repair the errors or. neglect of the former system, nor to obtain all the benefits which the present is so well fitted to bestow.

During the French occupation, it was only necessary for any one who wished to teach to purchase a " patent," in order to qualify him for that duty, and teachers were attracted by no other than pecuniary considerations. On the annexation of the province to Prussia, an examination was substituted for the patent; and in 1829 the mode of payment to teachers was regulated by law. The school-fee was determined by the rules observed in the old provinces; it was raised like the other taxes, and paid over from the public treasury to the teachers, as might be required. When this payment was not sufficient, the communes were required to come in aid. In many places this additional assistance amounted to a considerable sum: in Cologne to about 8,000 thalers=1,200*l.* a-year. There is no general law, scale, or regulation, determining the minimum or maximum of such payments. The Aix la Chapelle board have lately raised it to 150 thalers=27*l.* 10*s.* a-year, not including house and garden, for each teacher, laying down at the same time as a fundamental rule, that communes not able to contribute this amount can have no pretension to a separate school. It has not,

however, been universally acted on: there are schools in
the circle with a salary annexed of not more than 80
thalers = 12*l.* In towns, it is easy to keep above this
minimum; the better description of schools go so high
as 500 or even 600 thalers=90*l.* The maximum number
of scholars which a single teacher is allowed to take has
been fixed by certain regulations at seventy-five; when
they exceed that number, an assistant (*Hülfslehrer*) is
required to be kept. This regulation, however, is not
observed in many parts of the province. It is difficult
enough to obtain a sufficient income for a teacher in the
more remote country districts, even where the teacher has
one hundred pupils and upwards. In such cases, no
surplus can remain for the payment of an assistant.

To ascertain the actual working of the system, both in
reference to elementary and teachers' schools, I visited the
more remarkable of each in the town and neighbourhood.
The limits of this paper will not allow me to notice all. I
have selected such as may serve for specimens.

The " Stadt Schule," or town school, of Bonn, gives a
tolerably favourable idea of a class of schools common to all
the considerable towns in Prussia. It is the great public
school of the place, supported by the municipality, and
frequented by the children of various ranks. It is divided
into a male and female school, and each school is again
subdivided into six classes. These classes are taught in
separate rooms, communicating with each other,—the girls
above, and the boys below. The course proceeds from the
simplest elements of reading, writing, and arithmetic, to
the rudiments of history, geography, natural history, together with singing and drawing, so as to prepare them
sufficiently, should they so wish on leaving it, for admission into the Learned school, or the Sext class of the gymnasium. The Fächer system is adopted. Each master
chooses some particular branch or branches of the course
(many being often united, such as natural history, &c.
&c.), and teaches them to the several classes in rotation.
There are advantages and disadvantages in this arrangement; the former, however, seem to predominate. I
was conducted first to the boys' school; the first class-
room I entered was crowded. The boys were, as in most

of our schools, seated at their desks in parallel lines across the room, ranged according to proficiency. This is by no means so good an arrangement as the theatre or gallery form usual in infant schools, &c. No reason can exist against its extension to schools of every description. It is adopted with benefit in the highest, such as the class-rooms of the university. The convenience to pupil and teacher is obvious; for the maintenance of order, inestimable. Where the theatre form cannot be implicitly followed, a perceptible inclination in the floor should be adopted. The teacher was young, both in years and experience; he had abundance of activity and earnestness, though not much discretion. By too much zeal, he often failed in preserving quiet or attention. During the short time I was present, two or three were consigned for disturbance to the corner. It must not, however, be imagined that there was anything like the tumult of our English schools; the comparison must be confined to Germany. One cause of this general tranquillity may very probably be the national phlegm; but a more immediate and obvious one is the mode of teaching. Mutual instruction is banished; the classes are small and separated; the teacher instructs *vivâ voce*, adopting the simultaneous and catechetical system, and sometimes (though not in as great a degree as in Scotland) the elliptical. Instead of confining himself to the desk or pulpit, he walks up and down at short intervals to every part of the school. Much, too, must be attributed to the skill of the teachers themselves, to the interest they throw into their instruction, to the just sense they have of the peculiarities of the youthful mind, and to the spirit and variety arising from change of class and teacher. The subject of the lesson was grammar; the questions were pressed with rapidity, and generally answered with ease. In some cases they appeared to be somewhat too refined for the pupils, and bordered a little on the pedantic and philological. This, however, must be taken with qualifications. —The attention which the Germans universally pay to their language in the course of elementary instruction may appear to us excessive and minute; but we must remember what that language is, and farther, the impression so general amongst German educationists, that the reasoning

powers can never be so well developed as by the thorough
study of language, and that no language is better fitted for
such logical discipline than their own. In the next class-
room we found the pupils engaged with arithmetic, both
mental (*Kopfrechnung*) and written. They showed more
accuracy than quickness — pronunciation and manner were
somewhat sluggish; but there was no guess-work—no error.
In a third room, the teacher was giving his lesson on natural
history. The school had not been many days assembled,
and he had one of the youngest classes under tuition. We
found him in the elements. By frequent and varied questions on the same points, returning to the same classifications in different shapes, and drawing out of the child, not
merely facts which he had learned, but reflections which
these facts suggested, he worked the subject of his hour
thoroughly into the minds of his young auditors, and they
must have left the room masters, not merely of the materials as far as they had been furnished, but well exercised
in the method of acquiring, without his assistance, a vast
deal more. Throughout, both here and elsewhere, " well "
seemed more the object than " much,"—non "multa," sed
" multum,"—" grundlich, grundlich," was the frequent injunction, — " festina lente," the text-word with every
teacher whom I approached. From the boys' school we
proceeded to the girls'. I heard with great pleasure a child
of eight years old go through the several questions applicable to household purposes, first orally, and then in writing on the black board. There was no attempt at display
or smartness; all was calm, clear, and correct. In the
adjoining class we found the mistress nearly at the close of
her reading lesson. I was permitted to take up the book,
and to select any subject I thought proper. I opened at a
beautiful moral tale called The Flowers (*Die Blumen*).
The reading was excellent; great precision, accurate em-
phasis, great purity of enunciation, great delicacy, great
sweetness of tone. I observed to the mistress, on closing
the book, that it was hardly necessary to ask the pupil any
questions, in order to ascertain how far the subject just
read had been comprehended: the just application of em-
phasis and accent I considered evidence enough. She was
anxious, however, to give some further proof, and imme-

diately required the child to narrate the whole of the tale in different language, which was accomplished with much readiness and skill. Industrial occupations, as far as the girls were concerned, were attended to as much as intellectual. Sewing, knitting, and other female work, were taught in an adjoining apartment.

The "Poor School" (*Armen Schule*) is superior to the *Stadt Schule*. The building is new, extensive, lofty, admirably distributed, and in the best possible situation, on the verge of the town, in the handsome new street, the Friederichstrasse. It was established, and continues to be supported, by the joint contributions of the municipality and of benevolent individuals. A certain number of the children are clothed. On entering the gate, we found on our left (detached) the infant, or rather little children's school (*Kleinkinder Schule*); and in the midst of the court or garden the school-buildings, the ground floor devoted to the boys, the first floor to the girls. The religious teacher was occupied with the children of the infant school when we entered. He was a young clergyman, kind in his manner, but very earnest and impressive. He was teaching a portion of the catechism: the children answered the questions in the order asked, and then gave simple but precise explanations of each. This was followed by brief instructions and applications to practical purposes on the part of the clergyman. In the boys' school, classed and divided in the same manner as the *Stadt Schule*, we found one of the classes engaged with geography and history. The teacher examined in turn several boys, up and down. The Rhenish province was the subject chosen in geography; Prussia generally, in history. The pupils answered with ease and discrimination. After giving an outline of the kingdom at large, they went into the geography of the selected province ; first describing it physically, then politically, finally statistically. The great natural features, the mountains and valleys, the course of the Rhine, the various streams flowing into it, and the several points at which they join, were all faithfully delineated ; the political divisions at different periods were then marked out ; and, at the close of the examination, a rapid sketch was given of the produce, manufactures, exports and imports, population, &c. &c. of each province, district, and town. When any of these particulars was demanded in another shape, —for instance the site of a particular mineral production, —the answer was equally prompt and accurate. After each answer, the teacher pointed out the places mentioned on a large map at the end of the room. The examination in history was equally minute. The several great epochs of the history of Prussia, from the time of Charlemagne to the present day; the gradual formation of the Margravate of Brandenburgh; the erection of that and other territories into a kingdom; the important reign of Frederic the Second; the conquest of Napoleon; the successful war of liberation; and the present position and organisation of the monarchy; were are all detailed by a number of different boys in great variety of language and manner, some adopting the dramatic, others the narrative, but all with fidelity, and perfect command of phraseology and subject. I did not perceive any exaggerated religious or political opinions in the whole of this, nor anything in phrase or thought, which might not have, with some little abatement for a natural preference for the virtues and glories of the father-land, been heard in the schools of our own free England. I wished to see the text-book from which these lessons had been taught: the teacher informed me there was none. He gave his lessons *vivâ voce;* and this accounted for the diversity, and perhaps spirit, just noticed. He added, that in general teachers were left pretty much to their own discretion, with the exception of books for religious instruction; they required the approbation—the " *mit Genehmigung* " — of the religious superior. Each school adopted its own, though the Government occasionally recommended; this statement I subsequently found confirmed by others. It is in accordance with the spirit of the early regulations; there are cases, however, in which books have been distinctly prescribed. In the girls' school, the first class we visited were occupied busily with their slates. They had nearly finished a composition: the subject was a short moral tale. In looking over two or three, the same diversity, both in thought and expression, and even in arrangement of subject, as what had just been observed in the boys' school, was perceptible. The mistress had given the subject *vivâ voce.* When finished, a short interval was allowed to elapse before the pupils were required to give an account of it on their slates. This was quite different from the old dictation system. It called out in every way the powers of the mind, and really deserved its German designation, " Thought exercise " (*Denkübung*). It was followed by reading:—the same excellencies already observed in the Stadt Schule attracted our attention. The book used was a collection of instructions, or practical applications of the words of our Redeemer to the duties and trials of every-day life, in reference especially to the position of the children of the poor. The chapter read was in illustration of the words, " Suffer little children to come unto me," parts of it were written with great simplicity and beauty. The next class was occupied with sewing, &c. Large tables, at which were seated about twenty girls, stretched across the room: each had her basket and music before her. The mistress walked up and down between the tables, ready to afford instruction or assistance when desired. The girls were neatly but simply dressed, their hair arranged in the best German fashion, and exhibiting every indication of cleanliness, cheerfulness, and good order. We inquired from the teacher if they were allowed to converse during this lesson, and were answered in the affirmative, but assured that they generally preferred singing. On professing a wish to hear them, one of the elder girls began at once a religious hymn, " Du Unbegreifliche! " " O thou Inconceivable!" and was soon followed by a second, third, fourth, &c. in parts. To this succeeded a more joyous air, " Willkommen! willkommen!" — " Welcome! welcome!" in which all joined. The ease and modesty, as much removed from all forwardness on one side as from awkwardness on the other—the propriety with which the whole was executed—spoke highly in commendation of the influence and example of their teachers. In a room nearly adjoining, a ruder description of work was taught; instruction also in domestic œconomics, in which the Germans of all classes excel, was not forgotten. In the boys' school we were shown their writing and drawing books. The writing was excellent. Nor was this

a holiday exhibition ; the slates, especially in the girls'
school, showed great attention and facility.   The drawing
was principally stereometrical, at least in the lower classes.
The higher had advanced to the delineation of flowers,
animals &c. as well as of articles of furniture and other
similar objects, and the more advanced pupils had added
shading to outline.   It was stiff, and hard, and somewhat
formal ; but, like the generality of German art, careful and
exact, and evincing considerable practice in the close observation and delineation of forms, &c.   Both singing and
drawing are considered not so much as arts as instruments
of developement, in a physical, intellectual, and moral
sense.   When I mentioned to a gentleman near, connected
with the school, the smile with which the proposition
to introduce both into our English schools had been received in a committee of the House of Commons, he asked
me gravely if we did not teach speaking, reading, and
writing — singing and drawing were only speaking and
writing of another kind.   Putting aside all consideration of
their ulterior use, there is little doubt that they add materially to the facility and perfection with which the elements of all instruction are taught in Germany.   Hence
the truth and delicacy of their reading, and the correctness, and often beauty, of their writing.   There were
600 children in the school ; but the greatest order, regularity, and quiet prevailed in every part—not the result of
fear, but of early habit, and the kindly influence of their
teachers.   " Die heilige Ruhe ! "—the beauty and sacred-
ness of tranquillity was ever in their mouths.   Greater
attention has been paid to their moral training than is,
I believe, usual in ordinary day-schools.   The teachers
attend and watch them during their hours of play in the
grounds near, as well as during their hours of class and
study.   The three hours of religious instruction are strictly
adhered to, even in the instance of the infant schools ;
and instruction in morals (*Sittenlehre*) accompany instruction in the articles of religious faith.   Throughout, great
regard has been shown to local arrangements ; the galleries, class-rooms, and teachers' rooms are all spacious
and lofty, with high windows, well ventilated, and well
warmed.   Some of the apartments, such as the girls' class-

rooms, we found ornamented with good engravings, religious and historical, well glazed and well framed. So far from thinking that these accessories are immaterial, they seemed to hold that nothing is to be despised which can give the pupil moral and mental pleasure, inspire pure taste, and assist in the developement and refinement of the spiritual being, and uphold its mastery over the corporeal. Bodily punishment, it may be imagined, to enforce all this, was extremely rare. The masters, and especially the mistresses, rely, and with reason, on the power of good temper and good example.

There are several other schools at Bonn, public and private, all more or less exhibiting the chief features noticed in the preceding. Amongst them I may mention with just praise the " Evangelische Schule," or Protestant school, not far from the cathedral; it is not large, but conducted remarkably well, and embraces all the objects of study cultivated in the Stadt Schule. I assisted at the lessons in history and religion with great pleasure. The whole aspect of the school, its order, attention to every particular, even to the comfort and neatness of the apartments, gave the idea more of a private than of a public establishment. The list of text-books received from the teacher I found extensive and good. Amongst the private schools which abound for the upper classes who do not often frequent the public schools, there are some excellent, amongst which may be noticed Mr. Emerich's.

Protestants and Catholics, it will thus be seen, have each their separate schools; but this arises from the circumstance of the population being in such large proportion Catholic, and the upper orders preferring in general their own schools. There is no indisposition, however, to joint education, wherever it becomes a matter of convenience. In the gymnasium, for instance, Catholics and Protestants are found constantly side by side. Their religious instruction is minute and ample, embracing not only religious dogma, but sacred and Church history, as appears from the school cursus; it is given regularly to each persuasion by their respective religious teachers, under the same roof, but apart. No evil seems to result from this arrangement; it leads neither to religious discord nor to religious indif-

ference.   Each adheres to his own faith, but respects that
of others.   Of thirteen "Abiturienten," or students, who,
after completing their course and final examination (*Abi-
turienten-Prüfung*) last year, were about to leave the gymnasium with their testimonial of maturity (*Reife Zeug-
niss*) for the university, eight were Protestants and five
Catholics. The administration of the gymnasium is chiefly
Catholic, and two-thirds of the population, as already remarked, are of the same communion. A similar spirit appears to reign in many other institutions. It was a remark
more than once made, in answer to queries on this head,
that whatever religious differences did exist in schools, they
were rather to be found between members of the same persuasion, than between the persuasions themselves.

The progress of elementary schools depending so materially as it does on the state of the seminaries, from
which their instructors are supplied, it becomes an object of interest to examine such as are established for
this purpose in the Rhenish province.   There are two
for the supply of Protestant, and two for that of Catholic
schools:— the Protestant, at Neuwied and Meurs, both
small, educating each from thirty to thirty-six pupils;
the Catholic at Brühl, near Cologne, educating about 100,
and the one just commenced at Trèves.   The Catholic establishment is naturally the largest, the Catholics possessing 1,600 out of the 2,000 schools of the province.   We
preferred, therefore, visiting Brühl.

We left Bonn on a fine clear morning in October; and,
after keeping the road to Cologne for a short way, turned
to the left, and over a very indifferent by-way, at length
reached the small village of Brühl.   The imposing pa-
lace of the Electors of Cologne stretched out before us;
and near to the right, and opening on the village, what was
formerly a convent of Franciscans, the present seminary.
It is large,—more so, perhaps, than is required for the
number of its present inmates,—gloomy, and, to judge from
the neglected appearance of the court-yard, the dingy
walls, and somewhat injured roof, not very carefully kept.
It lies in a flat, and has the reputation of being unhealthy.*

* Near are some stagnant pools. Brühl has been of late frequently
affected by ophthalmia; it has been ascribed to this cause. Every effort

On entering, we were led along the old corridor (it still retains much of its former cloistral character); and, after some delay, introduced to the director. He received us in a very simple chamber; and gave us, though apparently with some reluctance, the information we required. The course of study, from his account, appeared limited, especially in history, sacred and profane; in geometry and the elements of useful knowledge, by no means extensive. The religious instruction was in great degree doctrinal. Here, as elsewhere, all books used in this department were required to be sanctioned with the approbation of the archbishop. Somewhat more attention seemed to be paid to language, composition, drawing, singing (especially choral), and to playing on the organ. We proceeded from the director's room to the class-rooms. They were ranged on the ground-floor, opening into the corridors or cloisters. The students had only just returned from vacation, and had scarcely yet resumed their ordinary studies. In one of the classes the singing lesson was going on. The students, to the number of about forty, were ranged standing on each side of the table; the teacher used the violin, and, after practising the Solfege for some time, gave out two or three hymns (sacred), which were sung in parts, and by note. Most of the students were well dressed and cleanly; no uniform; their demeanour grave, orderly, and collected. During the lesson, the utmost attention seemed to be paid by pupils and teacher; the latter showing in his tuition great gentleness and the most conscientious care. We next visited the dormitories. They form a series of rooms, some larger some smaller, the beds ranged side by side, each with the trunks, books, &c. of their occupiers, tolerably clean; but with not much appearance of comfort—none of luxury. Musical instruments seemed almost as common as books. We saw no ground devoted to industrial purposes, agricultural or technical; nor do gymnastic exercises appear to be as much cultivated as we might have expected. There seemed to hang over the whole a certain air of asceticism or melan-

has been made to remove it by washing, applying chlorate of lime, airing, fumigating, and even exchanging the furniture, to little purpose. The house is roomy; the evil appears to be in the air; yet of late only have such visitations been felt.

choly,—whether to be ascribed to discipline, situation, the
small number of the pupils, or want of health, it is difficult
to say.

The seminary of Brühl has been in existence since 1833.
The funds are by no means great. In 1833 and 1834, they
amounted to 6,571 thalers; in 1835 and 1836, to not more
than 6,682=1,002*l.* thus distributed:

Director,	. .	800 thalers
First Teacher,	. .	700
Second do.	. .	400
Assistant,	. .	220
Administrator,	. .	100
Reserved Fund,	.	200
Infirmary,	. .	60
		2,480

The remainder is applied to lighting, firing, school-appa-
ratus, and especially to stipends for the students.

It is understood by the regulations that the student is to
provide his clothing and maintenance himself, the institution taking charge only of his instruction, and preparation
for his future functions. At the same time it lightens
these burthens by granting stipends and other means, on
specified conditions. He is allowed his lodgings in the
house free, together with fire, lighting, &c. He contracts
with the housekeeper (*Hausmeister*) for his table, under
the inspection of the authorities, at the rate of 4 gr. 4 pfen.
about 6*d.* a-day. The seminary also takes charge of the
cleaning of the house, but does not furnish attendance:
this service is performed in rotation by the seminarists
themselves. A seminarist requires for his yearly subsistence on an average about 80 thalers=12*l.* a portion of
which demand is met by the stipend. The stipends, to
the defraying of which not more than 2,000 thalers are
annually paid, though stated in the estimate at 2,400, were
formerly given on the admission of the pupil. They are
now distributed quarterly; but not till evidence be first
furnished by the quarterly testimonial (*Quartel Censur*)
of sufficient exertion and proficiency in that interval.
The wants also and conduct of the applicant are taken into
consideration. Nor are they any longer given to the pupil

in specie, but paid over to meet charges for living, so as in general to cover it. There are at present three classes of stipends, answering to one-fourth, one-half, and three-fourths of the annual subsistence of the pupil. These are distributed according to the claims of each seminarist.

The admission to the seminary takes place on the decision of the government, founded on a previous examination. The examination is conducted at the seat of the government of the circle, under the guidance of the school commission or board of the circle, aided by certain experienced teachers, who are called in for the occasion. The minutes of these proceedings are sent to the school commission or board of the province, who, on the proposition of the examiners, usually grant the desired admission. The subjects proposed for examination are as follows :—

1. History of the Bible and Catechism.

2. Arithmetic, Four Rules, Fractions, Rule of Three.

3. Mother Tongue ; simpler rules of Orthography, Composition.

4. Music ; Pianoforte, and some acquaintance also with the Violin. This is not indispensable ; evidence of a disposition to music is considered sufficient.

5. Singing, so that a simple church melody can be sung by note. This is not always insisted on : it is sufficient to give proof of a good voice.

The candidate is required to be eighteen years of age (formerly they were admitted at sixteen), and of good frame, healthy constitution, and unimpeachable character. No precise period is fixed for the departure of the students ; those who are beyond their thirtieth year, are allowed to pass ; not, however, without great precaution.

The following is the result of the admission examination of 1837 :—

> Circle of Düsseldorf, of 56 examined, 10 admitted
> Do. of Aix la Chapelle, 32   —   16 —
> Do. Cologne,   .   32   —   16 —

In Coblenz fifty appeared ; but none were admitted. In Trèves, those who passed were attached to the local institution of the district. The disproportion between those appearing and admitted is accounted for from the anxiety to obtain a place in the seminary, and subsequently in a public school; but, considering the slender advantages offered by either, in comparison to many other positions, this would hardly be intelligible except upon other grounds. Those admitted are placed in that class of young men who are permitted, in quality of volunteers, to complete the period of their military service in one year; and even that period is, under particular circumstances, abridged. Should the young pupil give proof of dispositions for the profession of teacher, he is permitted to return after a short inteval : six months are deemed sufficient for duty with his company. Applicants who are not admitted are bound with others to the usual term of three years.*

The objects held in view, and inculcated throughout the whole of the course, by the director and teachers of the seminary are,

1. Accurate training.

2. The introduction to a proper method in the teaching and managing of children.

3. The acquisition and strengthening of a pious and virtuous disposition.

The subjects of instruction, in order to attain these ends, are,

1. *Religion*,—sufficiently extensive information to enable the pupils to give a just account of the nature and best

---

* Every one of the legal age, prince and peasant, is obliged to serve as a soldier. This duty (*Dienstpflicht*), with the *Schulpflicht* and *Steuerpflicht*, constitute the three great obligations of the citizen. Three years are the usual term ; abridgement of that period, viz. reduction to one year, is allowed to volunteers, and others, on such grounds as those above mentioned, always purely intellectual, *i. e.* proficiency in knowledge proveable on examination. No substitution, no exemption is permitted, either by grant or purchase. Every one enters in the ranks, and from thence rises by intelligence and conduct. I have seen relatives to sovereign princes, some destined to be princes themselves, on guard before the Town-hall, in their regimentals as privates, and a few hours afterwards in the halls of the university, or in the drawing-rooms of the nobility of the place. " All countries," said an officer of high rank to me one day, " have their habits and laws, good possibly for each, though not good for all. The French wish to make an army of conquerors,—they use the stimulant of glory,—promote from the lowest to the highest for an ex-

mode of religious instruction, besides the principles and practice of religion.

2. *German Language,*—comprising accurate exposition of the meaning of words and phrases, correct orthography, facility in composition, fair hand. Some knowledge also of the nature of style, distinguishing poetical from prose, is required.

3. *Arithmetic,*—exercises in practical accounts; geometry, theoretical and practical, &c.

4. *Geography.—Elements of History.*

5. *"Pædagogik"* and *"Didaktik,"* or the principles and practice of teaching.

6. *Plain and Ornamental Writing.—Drawing.*

7. *Singing—Music.*

8. *Introduction to the culture of fruit-trees.*

Of these, religion, or religious instruction, arithmetic, writing, and singing are considered indispensable; the others, though important, of minor necessity. The hours of study are so divided, that the pupils have daily from three to four hours in the morning, and three in the afternoon. The director has from sixteen to eighteen hours of teaching, the other masters from twenty-four to twenty-six, in the course of the week. The necessities of the elementary schools of the province, and the limited pecuniary

ploit, and have succeeded in what they aimed at. The English look to discipline and subordination; they introduce into the army the same aristocracy that exists in the state; they allow purchase and political influence;—wealth and family draw the barrier between the officer and private. We have other views, and take another course. We wish, to a certain degree, to provide for the same objects as the French and English, but not to the exclusion of either. We wish to call into exercise military disposition and capacity, like the first; like the second, we wish to maintain order. Our course is, therefore, different from theirs. We stimulate, by encouraging not only courage, but intelligence, assiduity, and conduct; we graduate and separate inferior from superior, by the best of all tests, *superior education.* No private, noble or bourgeois, can become an officer who is not *instructed.* The situation is not fitted to him,—he is fitted to the situation." The result is what might be expected. The Prussian officer of 1839, whatever he might have been at an earlier period, is an excellent soldier, an accomplished scholar, a true gentleman; and, from the influence of other regulations, requiring more explanation than can be given here, a good citizen.

means of the majority of the seminarists, render it necessary to restrict the course for the present to two years.
This is too short a period. The addition of another year,
for the advantage both of the pupil and the public school,
would be highly desirable. The seminarists are daily examined in the art of teaching in an elementary school
connected with the seminary, but under the management of its own teacher.

Brühl has sent out, from 1828 to 1834, the following
number of qualified teachers each year:—

1828	.	.	.	43
1829	.	.	.	37
1830	.	.	.	31
1831	.	.	.	42
1832	.	.	.	44
1833	.	.	.	36
1834	.	.	.	52

285

In seven years, a total of 285. If 1,600 be taken as the
number of Catholic schools in the Rhenish province, as
already shown, there will remain 1,315 schools without
teachers regularly prepared for their duties on the new
plan. Even this calculation is considerably below the
number. It presupposes that every school requires only
one teacher, and no allowance is made for casualties
occurring by death, retirement, &c.

The supply thus continuing so inadequate to the actual
demand, the government has directed its attention to the
alleviation of the evil, by doing whatever is in its power
to improve the present race of teachers. In order to
awaken amongst those who have not had the advantage of
being educated in a seminary the sense and desire of educational improvement, they have appointed periodical examinations to be held, by means of which opportunity is
furnished them to prove their capacity, and a prospect
opened of promotion and profit in their professional career.
This plan has been of great use, in conjunction with others
which we shall notice later. At these examinations the
following number of candidates appeared, and obtained

the testimonial of competency *(Fähigkeitszeugnisse)*, from 1827 to 1834, each year :—

In the year 1827, of	37 teachers,	45
1828, —	118 —	34
1829, —	89 —	38
1830, —	66 —	31
1831, —	84 —	47
1832, —	95 —	56
1833, —	82 —	39
1834, —	85 —	38
		328

That is in eight years, of a total of 706 teachers who presented themselves for examination, 328 passed, and were declared competent. But, though this is no small addition to the number of tolerably qualified teachers, there will yet appear, deducting the amount from the number already given (1315), that there are not less than 987 elementary schools in the Rhenish province whose teachers are recognised as incompetent, or who, at least, have given no authentic proof of their competency. Nor must it be forgotten that the number of teachers presenting themselves is apparently greater than what was really the case, not a few who were at first rejected having returned to the examination a second and a third time. Death also every year thins the ranks of those who have passed ; so that it will appear that 987 is below, and not above, the fact, and that it is no exaggeration to say that upwards of 1,000, or about two-thirds of these schools, are to this moment unprovided with regularly approved teachers.—(*See Table C.* p. 432.)

Besides this expedient of periodical examinations, which it is highly desirable should be rendered still more extended and permanent, the Government has endeavoured to raise the position and character of the actual teacher, and to improve the methods in use in schools, by means of a methodical course of lectures. These are held annually in the seminary a month before the return of the seminarists from vacation, and intended for the teachers actually in employment. It is not propoosd to render, by this arrangement, inferior teachers competent, but to improve

those who are already sufficiently well prepared, and who
have evinced special talent in any one branch of teaching.
Each school inspector points out the best teachers in his
district to the board of his circle, which, on its part, returns
the list to the director of the seminary ; the director calls
together those who are so approved for a month.   The following is the number of those who have attended this
methodical course :—

In the year 1828	.	.	.	35
1829	.	.	.	48
1830	.	.	.	54
1831	.	.	.	35
1832	.	.	.	36
1833	.	.	.	25
1834	.	.	.	22
Total in seven years,				265

The number, in proportion to circumstances, is not inconsiderable.   A much greater body would no doubt have
attended, had they been insured the expenses incurred by
travelling and absence from four to six weeks from home.
Such was formerly the case ; but this indulgence has lately
been withdrawn, owing, it is said, to deficiency of funds.
This course is of a high character : it developes the principles of the art, and proposes various practical improvements
in elementary instruction, drawn from experience and fact.
Their introduction into practical teaching is rendered especially easy, from the circumstance of the lectures being
addressed not to young pupils, but to men already of some
standing in the profession, and who have already evinced,
by their conduct, zeal, assiduity, and perseverance in discharging its important duties.   If it has yet but only partially been extended, it is a circumstance to be ascribed, not
to any impression of its inadequacy as an instrument of
improvement, but rather to the limited means applied to
the execution of so important and comprehensive a plan.
This observation is not less applicable to the number and
extent of the seminaries themselves ; they are obviously
inferior to the exigencies of the country and the times.
Were the estimate to be raised to the yearly sum of 30,000
thalers=2,500l. it would, it is conceived, be fully adequate

not only to establish the requisite number of seminaries for
the five circles, but also to render far more general, effective,
and beneficial, these after-examinations and teachers' conferences and courses, which, even in their limited action,
have already done so much good. It is to be hoped that
funds will yet be found for this purpose. To no one object
could they be applied with greater probability of advantage
and success.

The Protestant seminary at Neuwied is much more
limited than that of Brühl; a considerable advantage, as
it has thus been enabled to establish a better system, and a
greater degree of order. Through the exertions of the director, Braün, and the first teacher, Bauman, now director
of the seminary at Cassel, it has acquired a high reputation.
Neuwied had formerly a gymnasium, for the support of
which the town paid 500 thalers, the prince 500, and the
king a similar sum; the remainder of the expenses were
defrayed by school fees. The gymnasium was suppressed,
and in its place a higher Bürgher school and the present
seminary established.

The estimate limits the number of pupils to thirty (less
than half of those at Brühl,) and fixes the cost at 3,000
thalers=450*l*. As at Brühl, this sum is divided; a portion applied to payment of the salaries of the teachers and
the expenses of the house, and the other to the stipends of
the pupils, from which their living is in part or in whole
defrayed. Neuwied is distinguished for the greatest
regularity. The domestic management is excellent; the
cleanliness, neatness of the rooms, passages, &c. perfect. It
is kept by the seminarists themselves, under an inspector
of their own choice, who is responsible for any injury done
to the furniture, musical instruments, &c. The inspector
has immediately under his orders a certain number of over-
seers, to whom all complaints are made before they are
laid before the intendant, and who acts as mediator and
peace-maker between him and the students. They are
much more restricted for room than at Brühl; the same
hall answers as a lecture, study, and dining room, to
which it is successively converted with ease and quickness
by the pupils themselves. The table is provided, as at
Brühl, by contract; but the wife of the director acts as

housekeeper (*Hausmutter,*) settles the expenses, and inspects all the details of provisions, &c. served up in the house, &c. &c.　The conduct of the director is reported as kind and respectable; the superintendence and inspection as sound and vigilant; the demeanour and appearance of the seminarists themselves as evincing diligence and contentment; the whole establishment, in its economy and administration, exhibits more the characteristics of a well-conducted family than of a public school.

The subjects of examination on entrance are much the same as at Brühl.　They have lately been somewhat restricted, in consequence of a representation from the government inspector. It was believed that in the elementary schools too little attention had been given to the essentials, such as reading and arithmetic, and even to religious instruction, and perhaps too much to less important matters, to geography, history, natural history, &c.　This evil was intended to be met by calling back elementary education to a more limited circle, and applying a similar restriction to the education of teachers.　The instruction at Neuwied is good, and has a special reference to the practical.　The singing in parts (four voices) and choral are more fitted to church purposes; its character is more precise and grave than seems to be the case in other seminaries, such as Kaiserslautern.　The methodical course already described is also pursued here, and with the best effect. On a recent occasion, during the four weeks it lasted, a general view was given of the whole art of teaching, the most approved methods communicated, and, when required, exemplified by a reference to practice at full.

One of the difficulties with which the present system for the education of teachers has to contend, is how to occupy the period elapsing between the pupil's departure from the elementary school and his admission into the seminary, that is, from the age of fourteen or fifteen to that of eighteen, or still later.　If left to himself, he is liable not only to forget much of what he had already learned, but is exposed to the danger, from distraction and other causes, of becoming useless in his intended profession. This is endeavoured to be obviated by placing the young candidates under the direction of teachers in actual employment, in quality of assistant. Many teachers, without any special permission, are in the habit of employing several of these assistants, who pay them for being allowed thus to aid them in their school duties a larger or smaller yearly fee. This, probably, is the best course ; but then the State or the school boards should take its management directly under their direction. They should point out the best teachers to such pupils as are willing to serve, and should furnish the pupils with such means for meeting the expenses of the fees, &c. as the inspector, in conjunction with the teacher, shall judge fit. The young candidates would thus go to the seminary after some practical experience in the management of a school, and now that they understand its meaning, would be much better prepared to appreciate and retain whatever instruction they receive. It is a matter of some moment that practice should precede theory. When theory precedes practice, it is liable to produce showy and super-ficial instead of sound and useful knowledge, vanity in-stead of dexterity, confusion instead of clearness. The candidate may turn out a clever scholar, but is not very likely to become a good practical country schoolmaster.

There is one consideration more, with which we shall close. What is the real social result of all this? How has it affected the population—for good or ill? How is it likely to affect them in future? It would be a hazardous attempt to decide this question in any one sense peremp-torily. It must be recollected that there is no more com-mon fallacy either in morals or statistics than " post hoc, propter hoc." The existence of particular social pheno-mena with diffused and improved education may be insuf-ficient to prove that to this circumstance any of them owe their origin. The present system, or rather the present improvements of the old system, have scarcely been long enough in action very widely or materially to affect the larger or more influential portion of the present generation. In all reasoning, therefore, on this subject, we should be on our guard, not giving greater weight or extension to facts, or their relations, than is strictly warranted. Every day must necessarily furnish new data, and show more distinctly the connection of the old with the new, or of the new with each other. At the same time, this caution does not pre-

clude reference either to results acknowledged to be produced, though in a limited sphere, by the operation of the
system, or to a state of knowledge and morals not only co-
existing, but improving and extending, in a direct ratio with
its improvement and extension. The narratives given by
Pestalozzi, De Fellenberg, Oberlin, and the Père Girard, of
the singular revolution, mental and moral, I may also add
physical, effected by the application of their system of teaching on a hitherto ignorant and vicious population, though
admitted to be isolated experiments, ought not the less to
be considered evidences of the intrinsic force of the instrument itself, and of its power to produce similar results,
wherever and whenever fairly tried, without reference to
country or numbers,—that is, whenever applied with the
same earnestness, honesty, and skill in other instances as
in theirs. And of this portion of Prussia—of the Rhenish
province—it may be surely averred, that it has now been
for some time under the influence of this system, and that
during that period, whether resulting from such influence
or not, its progress in intelligence, industry, and morality,
in the chief elements of virtue and happiness, has been
steadily and strikingly progressive. In few parts of civilised Europe is there more marked exemption from all
crimes of violence than in this happy land, not only from
those graver delinquencies which stain the calendars of the
more luxurious states of Europe, but even from those
minor offences against the person, such as riot, assault, &c.
from which none scarcely are wholly to be excepted. A
witness before the late commission " appointed to inquire as to the best means of establishing an efficient
Constabulary Force " * has given a most favourable testimony to the honesty of the Prussian population.
The safety of the public roads, contrasted with their noto-
rious insecurity in many parts of England, is supported by
unequivocal facts. The same abstinence from offences
against property is conspicuous in towns. I have already
had occasion to refer to the comparative rarity of thieving
amongst the lower classes, especially to the diminution of
the offence in that very class and age most subject to it in

* Evidence of Mr. T. Burt, 1 Rep. p. 90.

England, and most likely to be influenced by the want or supply, the badness or goodness, of education. There is not only little amount of crime, and few juvenile offenders, but this amount and number are progressively diminishing. Doubtless much of this most gratifying result may be ascribed to comfort and employment. But this again must be ascribed to some still higher cause There is comfort, because there is frugality. " I Tedeschi sono ricchi," says Machiavelli, " perchè sanno vivere da poveri " — there is employment, because there is the desire and search and love of it. There is industry, incessant, universal, in every class, from high to low; because there are the early habits of useful occupation, and there are these habits, because these is sound and general education. In all those relations of life where truth, honour, confidence, and mutual kindness are most required, where fraud is most easy, but most injurious,—where reciprocal good faith is of such import, but so easily disturbed,—in all pecuniary, especially in all commercial transactions, the " Deutsche Treue " is more than ever proverbial. A promise is a bond,—a word an oath. " Ein Mann, ein Wort," is the maxim,—a maxim in deed, as well as phrase, of noble and peasant, of young and old. A deeper, and more earnest, and more operative conviction of their several creeds is nowhere to be found ; but a conviction which is not bigotry, a faith which does not shut out charity ; they believe but as intelligent heads, and as honest hearts, and as pure lives as themselves. In all the observances of religion they are punctual and exemplary ; their churches are well filled, and those who fill them pray ; their congregations are as reverent as they are crowded ; their pastors are poor, zealous, and beloved. If there be scepticism, not in the great masses of the community is it to be found. Let any one who thinks so assist at their Sunday service, —let him enter any church, Lutheran, Calvinist, or Catholic,—let him take any rank, any age, any sex, from the grey father of fourscore to the young girl at his side,—let him watch in their cemeteries,—let him read their books,— let him sit by their hearths,—and there, and not in newspaper paragraphs, or pulpit invectives, or platform declamations, will he find a reply. To this evidence in favour of education many are the witnesses; from all classes I heard but one voice. The clergyman admitted that his flock had not become worse Christians for becoming more intelligent men; the officer, that his men had grown more obedient as they had grown more instructed,—a word now led, where a cane formerly was insufficient; the farmer, for the increased profits of his farm, as the manufacturer for those of his factory, thanked the school. Skill had increased and conduct had improved with knowledge, profits with both. Even household management had reaped its advantage, when the first vanity and presumption arising out of the partial nature of instruction had worn off, when it had become general, sound, and appropriate,— the, servant, especially the female servant, was not less faithful, and had become far more useful than before. As long, then, as such is the social state,—as long as those who are best entitled to speak are so found to speak,— one thing is certain, that Prussian education cannot have done much ill. If, on the other hand, it can be shown that to Prussian education any one of these benefits can legitimately be attributed, there is no one surely so rash or so unjust as not to admit that it has done some good.

So much for Elementary Education. A future opportunity will present itself to continue the inquiry through the other branches, Academical, Collegiate, &c. &c. which still remain.

THOMAS WYSE.

(B)

General View of the State of Elementary Education, in Ten of the Principal Cities and Towns of Prussia at the beginning of the Year 1838.

CITIES AND TOWNS.	Number of Inhabitants, including the Military, at the close of 1837.	Number of Public Schools.	Number of Teachers, Male and Female.	Number of Scholars, Male and Female.			Number of Scholars in other Public Schools, viz. Middle Schools, Burger, Gymnasia, &c.	Total Number of Scholars.	Number of Children of an age to go to School, viz. from beginning of 6th to end of 14th year.	Number of Children who are not at Public Schools.	Centesimal proportion of Children at Public Schools to Population.	Proportion of total number of Children at School to total Population.	Centesimal proportion of Children at Public Schools to Children of an age to go to School.
				Boys.	Girls.	Total.							
1. Berlin,	283,722	115	480	8,820	7,920	16,740	10,492	27,232	44,860	17,628	9·6	1-10	60·7
2. Breslau,	94,540	37	102	3,846	4,040	7,886	2,396	10,282	13,061	2,779	10·9	1-9	78·7
3. Cologne, with Deuz,	75,962	74	139	4,225	3,970	8,195	1,376	9,571	12,228	2,717	12·6	1-8	77·9
4. Konigsberg in Pr.,	69,600	46	77	2,875	2,519	5,394	2,283	7,677	11,290	3,613	11·	1-9	68·
5. Danzig,	62,766	41	98	2,499	2,102	4,601	1,380	5,981	10,545	4,564	9·5	1-11	56·7
6. Madgeburg, with sub.	57,965	24	85	2,837	2,245	5,082	2,003	7,085	9,176	2,091	12·2	1-8	77·2
7. Elberfeld with Barmen,	55,745	26	61	3,767	3,140	6,907	818	7,725	9,747	2,022	13·8	1-7	79·3
8. Aix-la-Chapelle,	39,852	28	52	1,437	1,005	2,442	572	3,016	8,034	5,018	7·6	1-13	37·5
9. Posen,	36,829	25	41	1,120	537	1,657	1,108	2,765	5,555	2,790	7·6	1-13	49·8
10. Stettin,	35,594	13	42	1,373	1,010	2,383	1,217	3,600	5,352	1,732	10·1	1-10	67·

(A)

General View of the State of Elementary Education in

PROVINCIAL CIRCLES AND PROVINCES.	Number of Inhabitants, including theMilitary, at the close of 1837.	Number of Public Schools.	Number of Teachers, Male and Female.	Number of Scholars, Male and Female.		
				Boys.	Girls.	Total.
1. Königsberg, .	746,462	1,542	1,762	56,417	55,246	111,663
2. Gumbinnen, .	558,192	1,051	1,184	44,533	43,031	87,564
3. Danzig, . .	349,218	613	732	24,795	22,285	47,080
4. Marienwerder, .	499,001	994	1,051	35,953	32,560	68,513
I. PRUSSIA, . .	2,152,873	4,200	4,729	161,698	153,122	314,820
5. Posen, . .	788,578	1,041	1,349	51,684	50,103	101,787
6. Bromberg, . .	381,128	594	656	22,998	20,529	43,527
II. POSEN, . .	11,69,706	1,635	2,005	74,682	70,632	145,314
7. Potsdam, with Berlin,	1,005,322	1,640	2,340	69,561	68,259	137,820
8. Frankfort, . .	736,089	1,245	1,522	58,658	57,773	116,431
III. BRANDENBURG,	1,741,411	2,885	3,862	128,219	126,032	254,251
9. Stettin, . .	464,440	1,069	1,204	36,646	34,843	71,489
10. Köslin, . .	365,417	962	1,055	27,415	26,050	53,465
11. Stralsund, . .	160,428	357	388	10,235	8,280	18,515
IV. POMERANIA, .	990,285	2,388	2,647	74,296	143,469	143,469
12. Breslau, . .	1,027,799	1,454	1,798	81,474	80,962	162,436
13. Oppeln, . .	307,393	867	1,192	75,642	72,983	148,625
14. Liegnitz, . .	844,281	1,315	1,411	63,627	64,773	128,400
V. SILESIA, . .	2,679,473	3,636	4,401	220,743	218,718	439,461
15. Magdeburg, .	598,981	1,066	1,389	51,747	50,089	101,836
16. Merseburg, .	652,591	1,244	1,467	57,596	57,373	115,169
17. Erfurt, . .	312,615	493	601	26,718	26,205	52,923
VI. SAXONY, . .	1,564,187	2,803	3,457	136,061	133,867	269,928
18. Munster, . .	405,275	509	563	31,880	30,762	62,642
19. Minden, . .	417,276	529	662	37,775	35,748	73,523
20. Arnsberg, . .	503,916	811	908	44,597	40,836	85,433
VII. WESTPHALIA,	1,326,467	1,849	2,133	114,252	107,346	221,598
21. Cologne, . .	426,694	518	690	33,145	30,358	63,503
22. Dusseldorf, .	766,837	715	1,001	58,117	51,891	110,008
23. Coblentz, . .	461,907	934	1,042	41,877	39,564	81,441
24. Trèves, . .	446,796	847	1,009	38,214	36,464	74,678
25. Aix la Chapelle,	371,489	500	599	28,049	25,225	53,274
VIII.—RHENISH PROVINCE.	2,473,723	3,514	4,341	199,402	183,502	382,904
Total, .	14,098,125	22,910	27,575	1,109,353	1,062,392	2,171,745

(A)

Prussia at the beginning of the Year 1838.

Number of Scholars in other Public Schools, Middle Schools, Burger Schools, Gymnasia.	Total Number of Scholars.	Number of Children of an age to go to School, viz. from beginning of 6th to end of 14th year.	Number of Children not at Public Schools.	Centesimal proportion of Children at Public Schools to Population.	Proportion of total number of Children at School to total Population.	Centesimal proportion of Children at Public Schools to Children of an age to go to School.
5,597	117,260	154,053	36,793	15·7	1·6	76·3
2,543	90,107	115,331	25,224	16·1	1·6	78·1
3,215	50,295	72,140	21,845	14·4	1·7	69·9
2,271	70,784	102,857	32,073	14·2	1·7	69·
13,626	328,446	444,381	115.935	15 3	1·7	74·
4,136	105,923	161,284	55,361	13 4	1·7	65·7
500	44,027	81,794	37,767	11·6	1·9	53·8
4,636	149,950	243,078	93,128	12·8	1·8	61·7
23,577	161,397	194,148	32,751	16·1	1·6	83·1
7,196	123,627	144,213	20,586	16·7	1·6	85·7
30,773	285,024	338,361	53,337	16·4	1·6	84·2
7,619	79,108	94,095	14,987	17·1	1·6	84·3
4,748	58,213	78,861	20,648	15.9	1·6	73·8
1,616	20,131	32,480	12,349	12·5	1·8	62·
13,983	157,452	205,436	47,984	15·9	1·6	7(·8
9,703	172,139	193,438	21,299	16·8	1·6	89
2,200	150,825	181,333	30,508	18·7	1·5	83·2
6,554	134,954	154,090	19,136	16·	1·6	87·6
18,457	457,918	528,861	70,943	17·1	1·6	86 6
10,242	112,078	120,110	8,032	18·7	1·5	93·3
9,621	124,790	132,232	7,442	19·1	1·5	94·4
4,177	57,100	61,323	4,223	18·3	1·5	93·1
24,040	293,968	313,665	19,697	18·8	1·5	93·7
1,546	64,188	75,803	11,615	15·3	1·6	84·7
1,792	75,315	92,443	17,128	18·	1·6	81·5
1,298	86,731	102,324	15,593	17·2	1·6	84·8
4,636	226,234	270,570	44,336	17·1	1·6	83 6
1,742	65,245	83,985	18,740	15·3	1·7	77·7
2,932	112,940	147,228	34,288	14·7	1·7	76·7
1,138	82,579	90,348	7,769	17·9	1·6	91·4
954	75,632	93,030	17,398	16·9	1·6	81·ß
1,065	54,339	71,385	17,046	14·6	1·7	76·1
7,831	390,735	485,976	95,241	15·8	1·6	80·4
117,982	2,289,727	2,830,328	540,601	16·2	1·6	80·9

(C)

Statement of the Number of Teachers, Teachers' Seminaries; and Pupils educated and supplied by them annually.

GOVERNMENT CIRCLES AND PROVINCES.	Seminaries for the Training of Teachers for Elementary Schools.		Number of *all* Teachers in the total number of Elementary, Middle, and Higher Bürger Schools.	Of these retire (after service, on an average of 30 years) annually, about 1-26th.	Their place supplied by about one-third of the Pupils who leave annually, after a course of 3 years.
	Number of Institutions.	Number of Pupils therein.			
1. Königsberg,	2	140	1,831	61	47
2. Gumbinnen,	2	96	1,220	41	32
3. Dantzig,	2	79	697	23	26
4. Marienwerder,	2	101	1,104	37	34
I. PRUSSIA	8	416	4,852	162	139
5. Posen,	6	217	1,197	40	72
6. Bromberg,	3	98	648	22	33
II. POSEN,	9	315	1,845	62	103
7. City of Berlin,	1	46	845	28	16
8. Potsdam,	1	110	1,978	66	37
9. Frankfort,	1	100	1,615	54	33
III. BRANDENBURG,	3	256	4,438	148	86

10. Breslau,	2	275	1,870	62	92
11. Oppeln,	1	150	1,232	41	50
12. Liegnitz,	1	141	1,532	51	47
IV. SILESIA,	4	566	4,634	154	189
13. Stettin,	2	73	1,316	44	24
14. Köslin,	1	50	1,094	37	17
15. Stralsund,	1	16	400	13	5
V. POMERANIA,	4	139	2,810	94	46
16. Magdeburg,	3	145	1,534	51	48
17. Merseburg,	3	136	1,599	53	45
18. Erfwrh,	3	136	653	22	45
VI. SAXONY,	9	417	3,786	126	138
19. Münster,	1	37	484	16	12
20. Minden,	2	160	635	21	53
21. Arnsberg,	1	75	895	30	25
VII. WESTPHALIA,	4	272	2,014	67	90
22. COLOGNE,	1	102	613	20	34
23. Düsseldorf,	1	38	1,095	37	13
24. Koblenz,	1	33	1,045	35	11
25. TREVES,	1	29	976	32	10
26. AIX-LA-CHAPELLE,	—	—	574	19	—
VIII. RHENISH PROVINCES,	4	202	4,303	143	68
Total,	45	2583	28,682	956	861

INDEX.

436   INDEX.

ERRATUM.

Page 266, l. 35, *for* " In 79 academies subject to the visitation of
the regents ;" *read*, " In 106 academies which are subject to the visitation of the regents, and which have made reports."—See *Report of*
the Regents for 1838, just received.